D0966237

# Japanese
# Management Accounting

# Japanese Management Accounting

## A World Class Approach to Profit Management

Yasuhiro Monden
University of Tsukuba

Michiharu Sakurai
Senshu University

Editors

Forewords by Ronald V. Hartley
American Accounting Association

and Robert A. Howell
Professor of Management and Accounting
New York University, and President
Howell Management Corporation

**Productivity Press**
Cambridge, Massachusetts     Norwalk, Connecticut

Productivity Press
P.O. Box 3007
Cambridge, Massachusetts 02140
U.S.A.
telephone: (617) 497-5146
telefax: (617) 868-3524

Library of Congress Catalog Card Number: 88-43575
ISBN: 0-915299-50-X

Cover design by Joyce C. Weston
Typeset by Rudra Press
Printed and bound by Maple-Vail Book Manufacturing Group
Printed in the United States of America

**Library of Congress Cataloging-in-Publication Data**

Japanese management accounting: a world class approach to profit management/Yasuhiro Monden, Michiharu Sakurai, editors.
   Articles translated from the Japanese.
   Includes bibliographies and index.
   ISBN 0-915299-50-X
   1. Managerial accounting — Japan.  2. Corporations — Japan-Accounting.
3. Business enterprises — Japan — Accounting.  I. Monden, Yasuhiro,
1940-  .  II. Sakurai, Michiharu.
HF5657.4.J37  1989         88-43575
658.15'11'0952 — dc20       CIP

92      10  9  8  7  6  5  4  3

# Contents

# Acknowledgements

Grateful acknowledgement is made to the following for permission to reprint previously published material:

Swets & Zeitlinger B.V.: For "Principles of QC Circle Activities and Their Effects on Productivity in Japan" by Akira Ishikawa. Copyright © *Management International Review* (Vol. 25, 1985/3).

*Journal of Business Administration* (University of British Columbia): For "Full Cost-based Transfer Pricing in the Japanese Auto Industry: Risk-sharing and Risk-spreading Behavior" by Yasuhiro Monden and Teruya Nagao (Vol. 17, No. 1 & 2, 1987-88, pp. 117-136).

Association for Computing Machinery: For "A Generalized Approach to Decision Support System Based on Structural Matrix" by Kyosuke Sakate and Takayuki Toyama. Copyright © APL 1988 Conference Proceedings, Quote Quad, Vol. 18, No. 2, December 1987.

Institute of Industrial Engineering: For "Toyota Cost Management System in Japanese Automobile Corporations," "Framework of the Just-In-Time System," and "Management Control Systems in Japan" by Yasuhiro Monden. Full credit listed in text.

# A Note
# from the Publisher

To keep up with the new state of today's manufacturing environment, traditional management accounting functions must change. I travel worldwide studying the state of manufacturing and know this is already happening in Japan. For this reason we have published *Japanese Management Accounting: A World Class Approach to Profit Management* compiled by Professors Monden and Sakurai, two of Japan's leading accounting experts.

These chapters present a cross section of what is going on in the management accounting area in Japanese companies of various sizes and types. The underlying premise, however, is that — to strengthen a corporation — accounting information and input must be distributed among, and come from, all people in an organization. Over the years, we have created a division of labor and job specialization that, in today's environment, limits people's need to know and, in turn, limits people's growth. Today, as in just-in-time, we must look at the total process.

A hundred years ago, a carpenter made a chair from scratch. He would measure you and then produce a chair built to those specifications. He would deliver it to you with the pride of a skilled craftsman. In creating a division of labor, we have narrowed job skills and eliminated growth opportunities. Today we have quality assurance managers, industrial engineering managers, design managers, mechanical engineer managers, distribution managers, and so forth. We have built up skills and made people responsible for specific job areas. For example, a QA manager is responsible for quality. But isn't anyone else? Everyone should be responsible for quality.

Through QC circles we teach statistical quality control, quality function deployment, total quality control, and other techniques. We are moving away from specialization and giving people greater learning opportunities. Initially, we thought automation would create an environment in which people needed to know less; in reality, automation has taught us that people must know more than ever. Organizations depend on every employee for improvement ideas.

One fundamentally neglected area in this changing time has been accounting. Many people now recognize that as production methods change, so should accounting methods. Is this just-in- time accounting? Maybe. In Japan anyway, this means involving more of an organization's people in management accounting. The function is not limited to the accounting department.

Under the large lot system, job skill was limited because the same product was being made in large quantities. With small lots, the opportunity for acquiring additional skills arises because we need flexible, skilled, and knowledgeable workers. New measures exist to enhance our productivity where previous measures encumbered our success. Historically — and by design — traditional accounting is out of date because it always analyzes old data. This is a wrong approach. Today's managers need data today to make decisions for tomorrow. Analyzing yesterday rarely matters.

Some of today's new measures include productivity, long-term success, market share, employee involvement (inviting improvement ideas from the workforce), investment in training, job rotation/job growth, time lines/lead times, eliminating waste (value-added versus non-value-added time), process (toward one-piece flow), customer satisfaction, corporate goals/targets, profit.

In Japan, management accounting is visible in every department and becomes part of every worker's mentality. Accounting is part of the work environment. The role of today's accountants must change to include directing the company toward becoming world class. Accountants must know where the company is going — not simply where it has been.

There is a new way to manage, and responsible financial managers must understand this. We must rethink measures that cause managers to make wrong decisions. For instance, emphasizing the number of hours a machine is running to absorb overhead makes a manager feel it must run as much as possible. The result is excess inventory and wasted resources. We understand today that quality is free. And although the pursuit of quality can account for 30 percent of some company's resources, accountants have not looked at quality as a cost. The accounting function must become active.

We gratefully acknowledge the assistance of Tom Jackson, Associate Professor, School of Business Administration, University of Vermont; Joel M. Marver, Chief Fixed Income Analyst, Technical Data Global Markets Group; Regina Paolillo, Controller, Productivity, Inc.; George Smith, a Japanese scholar and translator; freelance editors Marianne L'Abbate and Carla Reissman; cover designer Joyce Weston; Esmé McTighe and David Lennon, Productivity Press' production team; and the entire staff of Rudra Press, first-class compositors and artists.

Norman Bodek
Publisher

Cheryl Rosen
Editor

# Forewords

Worldwide attention is now focused on the advancements in Japanese manufacturing technology and management style. A natural derivative of these new technologies and styles is the possibility for additional ways in which the accounting system can be of service to management. This book provides keen insights about how Japanese companies respond to the need for accounting changes.

It has always been true that each management style requires a custom accounting system. The Japanese success stories are attracting renewed attention to the limitations of traditional systems and to the fact that one system cannot meet all needs. We hope this book will provide another strike against the worldwide practice of compelling all parties to live with a single accounting system. It is my personal viewpoint that the support of the management functions of planning, decision making, and control should be at the *core* of accounting. At the least, a management accounting system must be equal to financial accounting. Forcing executives to manage solely on the basis of how their actions affect financial statements carries many negative consequences.

If accountants do not give adequate support to management activities, there will ultimately be no need for financial accounting because the firm will not survive. While reading this book, discard your conventional ideas about accounting and think about the new roles for the field. The book will provide ideas not only about what accounting is becoming, or can become, in the Japanese commercial world, but also what it can become in the United States. Read with care, thoughtful concern, an innovative mind, and a desire to act. Knowledge and ideas without action result in the same outcome as ignorance.

The theme of the American Accounting Association for 1987-1988 was "What We Have in Common." It is appropriate that this book is published now — it is certainly in keeping with the AAA theme. The book represents a cooperative venture and suggests what Japanese, U.S., and other accountants have in common. As the 1987-1988 chair of the AAA Management Accounting Section, it is my honor and pleasure to recommend this book for your thoughtful consideration. Read and react!

RONALD V. HARTLEY

*Japanese Management Accounting: A World Class Approach to Profit Management* demonstrates once again how Japanese manufacturers — and in this case, their management accountants — have taken concepts and practices developed in the United States, modified them, and used them to beat us in the international marketplace. A number of U.S. academics and consultants have suggested for several years that management accounting changes are needed, and a few U.S. companies have begun to implement some of them. But my study of this material, combined with my own experience, shows me that Japanese management accounting practices are further developed and more appropriate for today's competitive environment than U.S academics and executives realize.

For example:

- When General Motors was the dominant power in the U.S. automotive oligopoly, it used target pricing, and by inference, target costing, to achieve its long-term return on investment objectives. Currently, Japanese companies use target pricing to achieve and assure market share and target costing to achieve cost reduction and sufficiently high profits.
- American companies have used DuPont's system of return on investment (ROI) since the early 1900s. Some thoughtful academics (e.g., Hayes and Abernathy, just to name two) and practitioners have argued that its emphasis prompts a short-term orientation and causes dysfunctional behavior, such as the failure to make strategic new product development expenditures and capital investments. Yet, a significant majority of U.S. companies still use ROI. Japanese companies instead focus on ROS, return on sales, in combination with their manufacturing improvement (Just-In-Time) efforts. Separating the return component from the investment component allows for the benefits of ROI — but with less adverse consequences.
- Standard cost accounting systems and variance analysis are fundamental cost control tools in American industry. Japanese manufacturers put much more emphasis on target costing, value engineering during the product design stage, and actual cost tracking.
- Most U.S. companies utilize budgets for measurement and control; the Japanese emphasize rolling budgets and their use in planning.
- U.S. companies view cost accounting as a mechanistic, bookkeeping activity, the cost of which should be minimized. Japanese companies view cost management as a critical vehicle for success and, like quality and productivity, the responsibility of all employees. This is especially true during business and product planning periods, when product designs and manufacturing processes are not yet cast in concrete.

These are just some of the topics covered in *Japanese Management Accounting: A World Class Approach to Profit Management*.

W. Edwards Deming first visited Japan in 1950; the Deming Prize for Quality was established in 1951. By the 1960s and 1970s, the American public began to appreciate the quality products put out by Honda, Nissan, and Sony. Yet it wasn't until the late 1970s and 1980s — 30 years later! — that many U.S. manufacturers undertook their own efforts to achieve what we call Total Quality.

Similarly, at Toyota in the 1960s, Taiichi Ohno introduced Kanban (the "pull system" of production) — the foundation of just-in-time manufacturing. It was not until the late 1970s, at the earliest, that the central ideas of JIT — speed, flexibility, the elimination of waste, and the optimal utilization of assets — took hold in U.S. companies. Some others only began to appreciate and apply JIT in the 1980s. Others still, have not yet implemented JIT.

Now, with cost management, will the U.S. again find itself ten, fifteen, or twenty years behind? Or will academics and practitioners alike thoroughly study the competition, reflect, make modifications and improvements, and reestablish the U.S.'s leadership in management accounting theory and practice?

The authors of these articles know Japan well. The examples they use are all Japanese. If you want to get an excellent sense of the state of the art of Japanese management accounting practices, and be able to relate how U.S. practices, generally, and your firm's practices, specifically, compare, this book is an excellent place to start.

ROBERT A. HOWELL

# Preface

Management accounting in modern Japanese corporations has been developed by importing Western systems. In other words, the United States and Europe have taught Japan about the many concepts and techniques of modern management accounting such as standard cost systems, budgeting, performance evaluation systems, and capital budgeting.

With the recent, remarkable technological developments in major Japanese industries, however, a number of new management accounting concepts and techniques have been developed specifically for Japanese businesses. These include both technically "hard" systems and "soft" methods of application.

Examples of "hard" systems are accounting departments, management control systems for factory automation (FA), internal capital systems for divisional organization, cost planning systems, and cost accounting for computer software. "Soft" systems apply traditional management accounting systems, such as budgeting and standard cost systems, in unique ways to environments where, for instance, Total Employee Involvement (TEI), small group systems with Management By Objectives (MBO), Total Quality Control (TQC), Total Productive Maintenance (TPM), companywide cost management, and Just-In-Time (JIT) production systems exist. In effect, innovative Japanese companies are managing employees, as well as profit. This could profoundly affect U.S. management accountants, especially those trained to think only in financial terms such as return on investment (ROI).

While Japanese corporations are busy "exporting" many goods and services to foreign countries, we researchers still find ourselves involved mostly in "importing" foreign research. We believe, however, that Japanese researchers should at the same time do their utmost to contribute to the economic prosperity of Western and newly industrializing economies (NIEs). If these Japanese systems are of some service to other countries — and we believe they can be — we would be very happy.

Some researchers are now trying to implement these new Japanese systems in other countries. This makes it more difficult for us to describe these unique systems systematically. This book should be viewed, therefore, as a first step in theorizing and systematizing new breeds of management accounting for the world.

While the chapters reflect various approaches — including case studies, surveys, and theoretical research incorporating uniquely Japanese features — every author's goal is practicality. Our aim is to create a text that shares what we have learned. The chapters in this book can be read in any order, a reader's approach to the information being dependent on need.

The chapters were written by Japan's foremost researchers in managerial cost accounting. The editors express our heartfelt appreciation to these authors. We are also very grateful for the cooperation extended on all levels of management by the Japanese corporations whose management accounting practices were being investigated.

We are deeply grateful to Jeffrey W. Brown of Wiley & Sons for motivating us to initiate this project. Alfred M. King, managing director of professional services for the National Association of Accountants, made valuable comments during our revision and restructuring process. Also, we wish to thank Irvin Otis of Chrysler Motor Company and Norman Bodek, president of Productivity, Inc., for their long-time friendship and kind treatment of this book. Lastly, thanks is due to Steven Ott, general manager of Productivity Press, and Cheryl Rosen, managing editor, for their efforts to make the book readable and understandable.

The Editors

# Japanese
# Management Accounting

# PART I

## Cost Management Systems in the Japanese Manufacturing Environment

# 1

# Recent Trends in Japan's Cost Management Practices[1]

*Takao Makido, School of Economics, Nagoya University*

This chapter presents some recent trends in the cost accounting and cost management practices of some typical, large Japanese companies. At the time this chapter was prepared, only one-third of the research work had been completed. The trends discussed here are:

1. Cost reduction tends to be emphasized at the planning or design stage.[2]
2. Firms that produce a variety of goods, as well as those producing a single product, tend to adopt estimated cost accounting in their financial accounting system.
3. There are two systems of cost management for each product. One system incorporates both cost reduction and cost control functions, while the other consists only of the cost reduction function. The latter system is more prevalent in today's manufacturing environment.

***Trend #1: Emphasis on Cost Reduction, Especially at the New Product Planning Stage.*** Cost management is understood in two ways. Some people think of it in terms of cost reduction and cost control activities; others think of it solely as cost control. Those who insist on the second interpretation will lose ground in a period of low economic growth. Thus, we will define cost management as the first interpretation. Cost management's first step is to reduce the cost level itself by improving design and production techniques while still at the design stage of products and production processes. This activity is called *cost reduction*. The next step is to control production activities by applying the standards established in the first step. This activity is called *cost control*.[3]

The essence of cost reduction is to cut the present cost standards themselves. The essence of cost control is to maintain the reduced cost standards. We could also call the former "cost cutting" and the latter "cost maintenance." Cost reduction is, therefore, a product of cost maintenance, but cost maintenance does not produce profits without reducing the cost level to be maintained. Considering the present low economic growth, we cannot rely on increasing profits by enlarging the proceeds. Consequently, cost reduction is becoming more important than cost maintenance.

Cost reduction has little effect once production starts. This, in particular, applies to companies engaged in mass production using automation because almost all production conditions (such as production organization, equipment, and method) are fixed at the product planning level. These production conditions govern a large part of cost components. Consequently, there is little room for cost reduction at the production stage in which production conditions have been pre-established. It is possible to plan a large cost reduction by changing production conditions, however, the investment in changing production conditions would probably exceed the projected cost savings. Furthermore, changed production conditions may cause other problems.

Therefore, reducing cost at the production level is limited to:

1. Costs that could not be addressed at the planning level due to time constraints.
2. Instances when changes in the external or internal environment create opportunities for cost reduction.

Even in the production stage, a budgeted reduction in a cost category, like material or labor costs,[4] could produce effects not obtainable in the product planning stage, since costs common to some product types are dealt with as a group.[5]

As stated before, there is little chance of effectively reducing costs of each product at the production stage and, consequently, it is common to plan a large cost reduction at the product planning stage.

In practice, however, the number of companies that have successfully cut costs at the planning stage is small. To succeed, they have to overcome the following obstacles, even when the system for cutting costs is instituted at the planning stage.

First, the target cost must be determined at the planning stage in a rational manner. It is necessary to control the designing activity to cut costs dramatically at this stage. If it is not determined rationally, the designing activities cannot be controlled, and standards will be ineffective.

An effective way to determine the target cost rationally is to link cost reduction activity to profit planning, and to approach the target cost based on long-range profit planning. By this method, (1) a product's profitability is estimated based on the target profitability index,[6] determined in the long-range profit plan,[7] and then (2) the product price and cost is determined to arrive at the target profit. This is what we call the allowable cost method, as shown in Figure 1.1.

**Figure 1.1 Allowable Cost Method**

The advantage of linking cost reduction to profit planning does not exclude developing products whose sales prices greatly exceed their high costs because of their high quality. This method is based on the understanding that a company's ultimate goal is not cost reduction but higher profits. This makes it difficult to estimate demand correctly and set a rational target profitability index. In these uncertain times, it is extremely difficult to estimate future demand for products with no sales history. Failure to estimate accurately can create significant loss for companies that overinvested in capital assets.

The target profitability index of a product tends to be based on that of similar products. This method is appropriate, however, only when reducing the cost of new products that are slightly modified versions of existing ones.

Second, cost reduction activity at the product planning stage involves two basic processes:

1. Extracting the target cost from the profit goal.
2. Evaluating the design activity with the intention of achieving the target cost.

It is necessary to establish an individual target cost for each design department in the second process. The costs set for each department communicate the expected result; that is, each department tries to maintain a certain level of quality within the costs set forth. Finally, each department's ability to maintain the quality demanded within the established costs is monitored. To ensure the success of the second process, it is important to identify the entire cost established for each department and to obtain everyone's understanding.

A third area is the quality of cost estimates. The success of what we call value engineering (VE) during the second process greatly depends on the correctness of estimated costs. In VE activities, product specifications are examined from various angles, with the aim of reducing the difference between the target and estimated costs. This is possible only with a timely flow of correctly estimated costs. In addition, it is expensive to improve the quality and quantity of engineers and provide them with the tools to estimate costs more accurately.

A fourth area relates to subcontractors. Cost reduction activities in these companies are difficult to achieve because product specifications are controlled by the customer. This problem is unavoidable, and must be addressed before costs can be reduced. Although it may be difficult, it is necessary to plan according to customer needs.

Many problems in cost reduction originate at the product planning stage. As a result, many firms cannot execute cost reduction effectively. Nonetheless, current trends indicate a continued emphasis on cost management through cost reduction activities at the product planning stage.

***Trend #2: Adopting an Estimated Cost Accounting System.*** In terms of timing, we can think of costs as being divided into predetermined[8] (*ex anate*) costs and actual (*ex post*) costs. Predetermined costs are expected measures of cost *before* production. Actual costs are measures calculated *after* production. Predetermined costs are divided further into standard costs and estimated costs. Standard costs depend on statistical data, and are utilized as an index for cost management. Estimated costs depend on management's past experience or intuition.

Estimated cost accounting is used in the financial accounting systems of companies producing a variety of goods continuously because it is almost impossible or too costly to calculate the actual cost of each product.

The procedure of estimated cost accounting can be explained as follows. Current manufacturing costs consisting of material costs, labor costs, and other direct expenses are arrived at as a whole through predetermined measures, as indicated in Figure 1.1. The most remarkable feature of estimated cost accounting is that individual product costs are not calculated. The cost of finished products, in turn, is calculated by multiplying quantities times unit estimated costs. At the end of the period, work in process is determined by multiplying the physical inventories (strictly speaking, the finished goods inventory) times the unit estimated cost of each product. Consequently, there can be a difference between the actual manufacturing costs debited to the finished goods inventory and the estimated costs of the finished goods inventory credited to work in process.

The difference should be distributed rationally. When the difference results in a debit to a variance account, estimated costs are lower than actual costs. In this case, costs distributed to finished goods and work in process are lower than the entire actual manufacturing costs (see Figure 1.2) and the difference must be distributed to final inventories of work in process (A) and finished goods (B), and costs of goods sold (C).

Accordingly, adopting estimated cost accounting as the institutional cost accounting system does not require a company to calculate the actual cost of each product separately. This system is simpler and less expensive when compared with the actual cost accounting system. It is used in practice not only for financial accounting, but also for management accounting, such as pricing, improving product mix, budgeting, cost management of nonprofitable or principal products, and cost reduction activities. Some companies calculate estimated cost only for management accounting purposes, not financial accounting.

The second point is that companies producing a single line of products also tend to adopt estimated cost accounting instead of the actual cost accounting system. This tendency depends on the following business understandings:

- No matter how elaborate the cost accounting system, its usefulness as a tool of management accounting is limited due to social restrictions related to financial accounting.

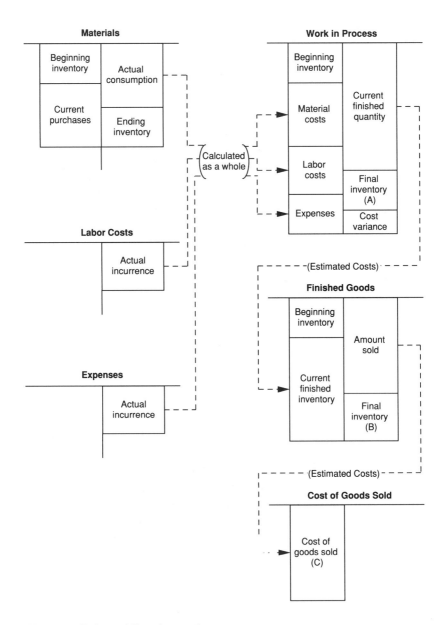

**Figure 1.2  Estimated Cost Accounting**

- Accordingly, a cost accounting system for management accounting purposes must be separate from the companywide financial accounting system. To provide management with useful information, it must be run independently.
- In this case, it is unnecessary to practice the complicated and costly actual cost accounting system because estimated cost accounting itself is enough. It has to meet only the needs of financial accounting companywide.

Because of intrinsic differences, financial accounting and management accounting must be dealt with separately. Financial accounting provides information to external users, such as investors, creditors, and the government, who are interested in the company. As a social system, it ensures a company's economic rights in terms of its assets, profits, and equity. Consequently, financial accounting must provide impartial information, making social restrictions unavoidable. Management accounting, on the other hand, provides for management the information necessary for the planning and controlling of company activities. There are no rules applied to information provided by management accounting.[9]

Modifying information provided by the financial accounting system to satisfy the needs of managers is limited by the intrinsic differences between financial and management accounting. The motivation behind the current tendency to separate the management and financial accounting systems instead of modifying the existing information, can be explained by comparing the value of the information provided in a new accounting system rather than focusing on the expense of its creation.

It was once believed that the value of two separate accounting systems was not worth the investment. Over time, however, operating activities have become more complex, and market share has become increasingly competitive. To face these challenges, today's top management needs precise information. The value of the information provided by management accounting, therefore, has become increasingly important. In addition, advances in computer technology have been accompanied by improved application methods that, in turn, have decreased the cost of processing information.

The savings realized by adopting the simple estimated cost accounting system for financial accounting purposes can be used to develop a new system. In Japan today, there is a growing tendency to revise current cost accounting standards. Management should take these conditions already discussed into account when revising the standards.

***Trend #3: To Use a Cost Management System Only as a Cost Reduction Function.*** Firms doing actual cost accounting can adopt a product cost management system to handle both the functions of cost reduction and cost control, as indicated in Figure 1.3. Beginning at the planning stage, a product cost management system analyzes the difference between the target costs and standard or estimated costs to determine the level of technology required to reach the target costs. Improving technology reduces the standard or estimated cost level, thus reducing costs. In this case, standard or estimated costs show the performance of costs resulting from technological improvements. The resulting differences between the estimated and actual costs are analyzed in turn, and immediate actions are taken on the production floor to eliminate the causes of the difference. The result of this process is that standard or estimated costs are maintained. Cost performance means actual costs.

Companies that produce a variety of products and practice estimated cost accounting do not calculate actual costs. Thus, they do not

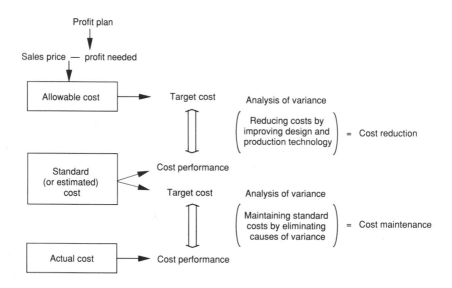

**Figure 1.3 Product Cost Management System**

show cost performance corresponding to the cost target, and they adopt a cost management system without a cost maintenance function, as indicated in Figure 1.4.

In this case, cost maintenance activities based on real cost elements, such as a production department's cost control activities in a budget, can be utilized. In some cases, a company's cost management success depends on the results of these cost maintenance activities.

Some companies adopt estimated cost accounting systems and calculate actual costs for different product groups. They are forced to adopt systems without cost maintenance functions for individual products because they practice estimated cost accounting without calculating actual costs. For each product group in which actual costs are calculated, however, they can adopt a cost management system that has both cost reduction and cost maintenance functions.

Regarding this third trend, I can say that more companies are adopting a system with a cost reduction function only. This relates closely to the second trend, in which more companies are adopting estimated cost accounting systems, because this second trend necessarily leads to adopting a system with a cost reduction function only. This, in turn, relates to the first trend, in which the cost reduction function is gaining greater emphasis. Companies tend to emphasize the cost reduction function while applying cost maintenance activities as simply as possible, even when they have the opportunity to adopt a system having both cost reduction and cost maintenance functions. This tendency is acceptable given the effectiveness of cost maintenance activities outside the estimated cost accounting system. These include financial analysis of individual cost elements, technical analysis of individual cost items, and utilization of departmental budgets. It is at this level that cost maintenance activities are practiced.

These are the current trends of cost management practices in Japan. More research is needed to prove these trends statistically.

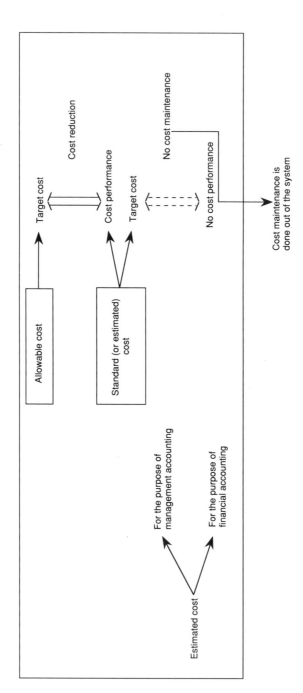

**Figure 1.4 Cost Maintenance Activities**

## Notes

1. From *Kigyokaikei*, Vol.31, No.3 (March 1979), pp. 126-132. Translated into English from Japanese.
2. At Toyota Motors and its affiliated companies, this activity is called "cost planning."
3. The author considers cost management as a broader function and will elaborate this point in a future paper.
4. Costs are subdivided further. For example, material costs are divided into main material cost, purchased parts cost, indirect material cost, consumable tools, and furniture cost.
5. When different kinds of materials are used for each product, costs must be reduced for each product. When common materials are used for some products, however, it is possible to reduce the cost of the shared materials. In such a case, effective ideas for cost reduction may arise.
6. Profit ratio to net sales or profit ratio to capital. The former seems to be used more frequently.
7. In fact, the target profitability index of each product group — for example, particular car models — is determined. And the target profitability index of the group to which the new product belongs is applied in many cases.
8. There is some confusion in the treatment of the term "predetermined cost." Some people regard it as estimated or standard cost in the narrowest sense, others regard it as both estimated and standard cost. The author uses this term in the latter — and wider — sense.
9. A detailed description of differences between financial and management accounting can be found in Chapter 1 of the author's book, *Theory of Managerial Cost Accounting* (Dobun-kan Publishing Co., 1975).

# 2

## Total Cost Management System in Japanese Automobile Corporations*

*Yasuhiro Monden, Institute of Socio-Economic Planning,
University of Tsukuba*

The Japanese auto industry has expanded and earned large profits consistent with Japan's high economic growth. Due to the lower economic growth and import restrictions of the United States and other nations, however, the auto industry is now in a position — even in Japan — where it cannot avoid a decrease in its growth rate. Companies experiencing the greatest difficulty with growth need to implement cost reduction measures to increase profits. These measures include eliminating waste and producing high quality goods at the lowest possible price. Cost reduction methods have a natural association with total cost management, which is largely concerned with product planning and design activities.

To follow the steps of total cost management, a corporation must:

1. Plan a product that meets the customer's demand for quality.
2. Determine a target cost under which the customer's demand for

* Reprinted with permission from *Applying Just-In-Time: The American/Japanese Experience*, Y. Monden, ed. (Atlanta: Institute of Industrial Engineers, 1986). This chapter is a revised version of an article co-authored with Yoshiteru Noboru.

quality is attainable by using a blueprint based on value engineering (cost reduction in a narrower sense).
3. Determine which processes achieve the target cost in production performance (cost control).[1]

Nearly every company in the Toyota Group has completed its implementation of the total cost management system under the guidance of Toyota Motors. Toyota considers the system capable of horizontally governing the cost management of multiple departments. The total cost management system is of great significance in what Toyota calls "functional management."[2]

The total cost management system discussed in this chapter takes a similar approach. A characteristic of the system is that accounting takes on a more subservient role when compared to management science. Many Japanese manufacturers have implemented this approach and broken down their cost management departments as follows:

- *Cost control section*:  Profit planning, budget control, cost accounting for financial accounting
- *Cost planning section*:  General advocate of cost planning, cost estimation by blueprints, cost reduction by value engineering (VE)
- *Cost improvement section*:  General promotion of cost improvement activities at the factory

The cost management department supervises the general progress of the total cost management processes mentioned above. Many other departments, however, also play a definitive role in the process. These include the corporate planning, product planning, exporting, technology planning, design, purchasing, and production technology departments. As a result, the relative significance of conventional accounting or cost control decreases. From a profit standpoint, a focus on cost as an economic measure of value unites the entire corporation under the coordination of cost management in creating innovative approaches to cost reduction and cost control.

A cost management system is generally divided into these three stages:

1. Corporate planning
2. Cost planning
3. Cost improvement

First, an outline of the three stages is explained. At the corporate planning stage, a long-term corporate profit plan is established. The target profit of each product, and the required capital outlay and human resources are presented in a structural project plan. A target profit is identified for each new product development planning project. Eventually, the target profit will be one of the objectives to be accomplished through cost planning activities.

The cost planning stage is the point when cost management is divided into cost reduction and cost control. Broadly speaking, the corporate management planning of stage 1 is included in the cost planning of stage 2. A simple interpretation of cost planning would be two processes roughly classified as: (a) the process of planning a specific product that satisfies customer needs and takes on a target cost inferred from the target profit of the new product, and (b) the design department's process for monitoring the accomplishment of the target cost using VE and a comparison to established cost estimates.

Finally, to be more accurate, the final cost improvement stage can be restated as the cost maintenance and cost improvement stage. This step controls the target cost for the blueprint. The blueprint identifies the actual production processes determined at the cost planning stage. Cost improvement activities continue to be conducted throughout a car model's life.

These processes are shown in Figure 2.1. The following discussion will refer to this figure.

***Corporate Planning.*** For Japanese companies, the corporate planning stage is when a medium-term (three- or four-year period) profit plan for the whole corporation is established. The medium-term profit plan is established anticipating both variable and period costs. Its purpose is to (1) establish a target profit for each period and (2) lower the company's breakeven point. It is well known that the breakeven sales point is obtained by dividing fixed costs by the contribution margin ratio. Therefore, to improve the contribution margin three years down the line, the question becomes: What new approach will be taken for the new product development plan and the sales plan of each automobile model during project planning? Reducing fixed costs is addressed in the medium-term profit plan. Fixed costs can be adjusted through project planning to include equipment investment, personnel, and funds procurement. Through this planning process, the target profit of each new product is determined.

The medium-term corporate plan is determined at top management's corporate planning meeting, and is drafted by the corporate

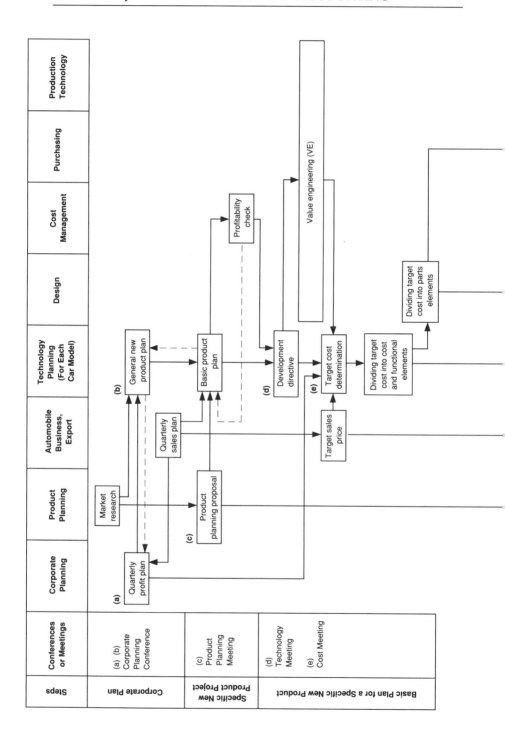

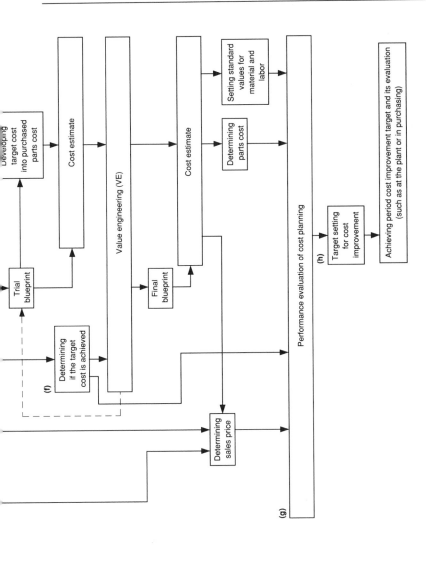

**Figure 2.1 System for Cost Planning**

planning department responsible for the company's overall planning activities. Among the project plans that comprise management's corporate plan are new product development plans. These plans are drafted by the technology planning department, and are revised in the process of establishing a corporate new product plan. In the corporate new product plan, the chairpeople (or departmental managers supervising each automobile model) identify the life cycle of each model by year, draft any model changes or modifications, and integrate them into new product groups. When a corporate new product plan is authorized at a corporate planning meeting, it is presented in the form shown in Figure 2.2.

*Cost Planning.* We now proceed to the four-step cost planning stage:

1. Specific new product project
2. Basic plan for a specific new product
3. Product design
4. Production transfer plan

Step 1 occurs when management formulates its recommendations for new products, with new car development, model changes,

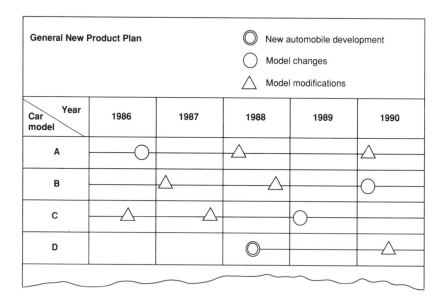

Figure 2.2 General New Product Plan

and modifications. The basic plan for a specific new product will establish the target cost necessary to achieve the required target profit for new products. During product design, cost is estimated based on a design blueprint and VE discussions. Processes are redesigned where there is a gap between target cost and the estimate. Finally, the production transfer plan, which sets the target cost for the production stage, is prepared. Production equipment requirements, the cost of parts, raw material standards, labor hours, and sales price are all determined at this stage.

**Specific new product project.** At the first stage of a specific new product project, product planning asks technology planning to determine the type of new product to be developed based on market research. After observing the marketplace, the technology planning department determines the objective and content of the model changes required to meet user trends. The product planning proposal is usually presented at a top management product planning meeting. Figure 2.3 illustrates a draft for a specific product project.

| **Product Planning Proposal** | Preparation date |
|---|---|
| | Product planning department |
| 1   Background | 2   Aim |
| 3   Contents | 4   Full grades of this car model |
| 5   Sales price &<br>     expected sales quantity | 6   Sales starting date |

**Figure 2.3  Product Planning Proposal**

Under the supervision of the technology planning product manager, the project progresses to the planning stage to establish the basic product plan. The basic structure consisting of those items critical to cost behavior are determined during this step. For example, engine type, drive type (front engine, front drive or front engine, rear drive), body size, setting of performance targets, components for new development, and the determination whether or not existing parts will be improved are established in the planning stage.

It can be said that the approximate cost of a new product such as a car model is largely determined by the basic product plan. Therefore, the cost management department examines whether or not the plan can provide the target profit. They collect information on the product manager's recommendations about the product structure, and estimate the cost of the planned car based on existing products. In addition, the payback period of invested capital is reviewed in conjunction with sales projections. As a result of this profitability check, the cost management department may request modifications to the basic plan when the project does not appear profitable.

**The basic plan for a specific new product.** After reviewing feedback several times and following the profitability check, a top management technology team determines whether or not to continue project development. Information for each department involved in the development is disseminated in the form of a directive that generally includes:

- Development target
- Basic development plan
- Basic policies
- Structural outline
- Quality target
- Conditions for production
- Cost planning
- Weight target
- Development schedule

This is the beginning of the basic plan for a specific new product. The purpose of the basic plan is to determine the major cost factors, such as design and structure. It is also the step when target costs are assigned to the appropriate departments. It is appropriate to say that the success of cost planning depends on the extent to which cost reduction is achieved in this stage, the main activities of which are explained in the following discussion:

1. *Cost reduction through VE activities.* In the technology planning department, the product manager of the car model in question holds a meeting to explain the basic plan communicated in the development directive, and to elicit each department's cooperation. At this point, a thorough VE analysis is required to identify innovative yet cost effective product features that will fulfill customer demands. The focus should be on material requirements and the details of the manufacturing process.

Each section of the design department develops a detailed structural plan, after dividing the product's basic plan into the component parts for which they have responsibility. At the same time, they identify cost reduction strategies, such as a new processing system or a new material. The production technology department is responsible for generating a VE proposal that addresses improvement at the factory level. This includes manufacturing productivity equipment. In the factory, the cost reduction activities of existing products are reviewed, and improvement proposals related to new or altered products are generated. To provide adequate communication of the various VE proposals, several discussion meetings are held by the departments supervising the various aspects of product development. Discussions may be held, for example, about the clay model of the planned car, or an analysis of competitors' disassembled automobiles. Each proposal is subjected to a technological and profitability screening. As a result, problems worthy of further consideration are separately identified.

2. *Establishing the target cost.* Using the basic plan communicated through the development directives, target sales prices are gathered from the appropriate business divisions, in this example, the domestic and export auto divisions. The target cost is approximated by subtracting the target or required profit, established in the medium term corporate plan, from the sales price. The result is the *allowable cost*.

Simultaneously, the cumulative cost estimate of the product's basic plan, after adjusting for the financial effect of VE proposals, or the *potential cost*, is calculated. There is usually a gap between the allowable and potential costs, which is closed after allocation of fixed costs. As a result of this allocation process, a formal target cost of a representative automobile is determined and subsequently authorized at a top management cost meeting. At this point, the probability of achieving the target gross profit of the product in question is estimated by examining the target contribution margin per unit, the target sales units, and the target equipment investment. From management's viewpoint, it is best to plan for the greatest possible target profit because the initial allowable cost is likely to be high. The potential cost accumulated from a financial interpretation of present conditions, however, is not an appropriate cost objective. It is necessary to establish a target cost that represents an attainable objective, and is both economical and motivational.

3. *Developing the cost and functional elements of the target cost.* The technology planning department first develops the total target cost, for example, of a single car by identifying cost and functional elements with the help of the cost management department. Identifying the cost elements requires separating the target cost into material, parts, direct labor, special equipment (stamping die, welding machines, etc.), depreciation, overhead, direct sales, administration, and so forth. The cost elements of the existing products are used as a basis for this breakdown. When planning a product, the basic structure (including internal and external manufacturing) is considered, although not yet finalized.

Developing the functional elements classifies the target cost into structural categories, similar to the way in which sections in the design department are classified, such as the engine, transmission system, and chassis. In this process, the product manager's recommendations for the product plan are presented according to each function's cost. Comparing these costs to the current product's itemized costs should determine the relative emphasis for each function (see Figure 2.4). This information is passed on to the design department.

4. *Developing part elements of the target cost.* The design department develops the target cost for each part as directed by the technology planning department. Each section of the design department separates its functions into major units (such as front accelerator and front and rear brakes), and then further subdivides them, since a car's target cost includes a number of purchased and internally produced parts. At this stage, the design department elaborates on the product manager's recommendations for the function and structure of the automobile relative to parts. At the same time, the VE proposals prepared in step 1 are considered, and the design department begins to focus on the cost reduction objective. This situation is summarized in Figure 2.5.

| Cost Elements / Functions | Material Costs | Purchased Parts Costs | Direct Labor Costs | . . . . . | Total |
|---|---|---|---|---|---|
| Engine | ¥ | ¥ | ¥ | | ¥ |
| Transmission System | | | | | |
| Chassis | | | | | |
| ⋮ | | | | | |
| Total | | | | | |

* The amount should be presented either in the form of the total cost of a single car (in the case of new model or model change) or as a deviation from the existing car (in the case of model modifications).

**Figure 2.4  Target Cost Broken into Cost Elements and Functions**

**Product design.** Next, the design department drafts a trial blueprint that must show the given target cost of each part while meeting quality standards. This provides for the incorporation of cost into the blueprint. Needless to say, experienced designers are required for this task, and each department involved in product development must cooperate by supplying information and assistance.

The target cost and the trial blueprint are presented to vendors, which account for 60 to 70 percent of the cost. The vendors present VE proposals using their own specialized techniques and expertise.

Based on this first trial blueprint, a trial product is manufactured. At the same time, a cost estimate is prepared. The production technology department supplies information about the cost of external parts to the cost management department, which incorporates this information with figures on internally produced parts. The possibility of achieving the target cost is examined based on the accumulation of this information. Each department cooperates in performing additional VE activities if target cost expectations are not met. The results of these additional activities are returned to the design department

| Function | | Assembly Number | | | | | | | Name | | | |
|---|---|---|---|---|---|---|---|---|---|---|---|---|
| | | | | | Car Model | | | | | Direct Labor Cost | | |
| Major Units | Parts Number | Parts Name | Quantity | Process | A | B | C | Materials Cost | Purchased Parts Cost | Department | Worker Hours (Minimum) | Amount |
| | | | | | | | | | ¥ | ¥ | | ¥ |

**Figure 2.5 Target Cost Broken into Parts Elements**

and the appropriate adjustments are made to the trial blueprint. After repeating this process several times, the final blueprint is drafted. This step accomplishes two goals: it (1) ensures that sections in charge of certain parts have accomplished the target cost based on the trial blueprint cost estimate, and (2) promotes VE activities.

**Production transfer plan.** The production transfer plan is the last step in cost planning. After repeating the circular process (trial blueprint, cost estimate, VE activities, adjustments to the trial blueprint), the final blueprint is drawn. Internal capital equipment requirements are finalized, and external production equipment is prepared with the appropriate vendors. Based on the final blueprint and completion of production equipment installation, a final cost estimate is prepared. It is now six or seven months prior to the start of production. The cost management department reviews the final cost estimate, and presents it to the business department as a reference for establishing the sales price for domestic and foreign markets. Based on the final estimate and testing results, the production technology department establishes standard values for the material required for each part's coating requirements, labor hours, and so forth. These standard values are immediately presented to the factory. Using the final estimated sales price, the purchasing department starts negotiating with vendors for parts prices. In principle, the sales price is determined by the time production begins.

After accomplishing these final tasks, the planning stage of cost planning is complete. The planning stage continues in the production and sales departments, where performance is measured and evaluated. In this case, the performance in question occurs three months after production has started because a greater number of labor hours and abnormalities are inflated as a result of the learning curve during the first three months of production. Normal production values are commonly achieved by the end of the fourth month.

To compare the target and actual costs of purchased parts requires a comparison of the target price of a part and the actual purchase price. The direct labor cost, however, is not compared from a dollar perspective. Since the target was determined by the number of labor hours, target and actual labor hours are compared.

There are two purposes for evaluating cost planning's performance. One reason is to ascertain whether or not the target cost established in the basic new product plan is being achieved. If not, it clarifies who is responsible — the blueprint (design) or the production process (purchasing/factory). The second reason is to judge whether or not the cost planning activities were effective. The following questions are addressed: Did activities proceed according to the development schedule? Were production methods satisfactory? Were cost planning activities useful? The results of this evaluation are used in subsequent product planning cycles.

The performance evaluation just mentioned is based on a comparison between target and actual costs. Japanese companies regard this comparison strictly as a control over cost planning and as the final step of the cost planning process. In this respect, as will be mentioned later, it is necessary to differentiate daily cost control activities between target and actual costs in attempting to achieve the target cost.

**Cost Improvement Activities.** As previously mentioned, a final evaluation of cost planning is made following the third month of production. If the target cost is missed by a large margin, an improvement team is organized to conduct a thorough *value analysis* (VA). To distinguish our terms, *value engineering* (VE) refers to cost improvements that address basic functional changes in the new product development stage. Cost improvements requiring design changes are VA.

The target cost should be firmly established during the planning stage. Any increases subsequent to cost reduction losses after production must be minimized. There are instances, however, when production commences prior to completion of the target cost, as a result of delays in the development schedule or planning changes.

**Cost improvement committee.** When failure to achieve the target cost occurs, a special project team called "the X- model cost improvement committee" is organized. In most cases, the committee is comprised of the person in charge of cost control as the chairperson, the product manager as co-chairperson, and the cost control department as staff members. With managers in charge, the committee then breaks into two subcommittees — one focusing on purchased parts, and one focusing on the individual processing costs of each department involved with the product in question. These subcommittees, through which intense VE activity is conducted, usually last for six months.

VA activities always include the following processes: drafting the blueprint, trial production, experiment, and evaluation. Extreme effort from each participating department is necessary for the success of these activities. The establishment of a cost improvement committee implies that a car model's improvement is a top priority. Keeping the process — from drafting the blueprint to evaluation — as short as possible minimizes any lost opportunities.

**Periodic cost improvement.** Periodic cost improvement means reaching a cost reduction target established for every field as a result of a short-term profit plan. Cost items are divided into two groups: (1) variable cost items (such as purchased parts and factory variable overhead) and (2) fixed cost items (such as indirect labor costs and overhead expenses).

*1. Variable overhead.* Reducing purchased parts cost is achieved through VA and price negotiation. Periodically, VA sets forth the total amount and target total amount of cost reduction expected from each product. VA proposals are received from all departments and vendors. Every process from subsequent investigation to part changes is managed within the system. Proposals from vendors are encouraged; they are pushed through the resolution system and rewarded based on the results. The purchasing department begins price negotiations with vendors to reduce costs during the periodic price reform stages. To avoid an exclusive focus on price reductions, guidance for parts improvement is given to the factories involved.

The variable costs of a factory (such as material, coating, indirect material, energy, and direct labor costs) are managed by setting a cost reduction target for each product type. The purchasing department supervises the purchased cost management from outside suppliers, such as material and coating costs. The factories primarily work on reducing consumption through VA and savings. Direct labor costs are quantified in labor hours. At the beginning of each period, the target for reduced direct labor cost is determined for each factory and automobile type. Monthly targets are set for each work area and given to supervisors.

Management of the variable cost items already mentioned can be called variable (or flexible) budget management when the target cost per unit is previously determined.

*2. Fixed costs.* Fixed costs are also analyzed by applying the total cost reduction target. Once the labor costs of general management and related departments are identified, a target incorporating the number of personnel, overtime hours, and an appropriation of expenses is established. These are under management's budgetary control. The total amount of these cost items is compiled from each individual structural plan in the overall management plan. The individual structural plan includes sales, personnel, and equipment investment plans. Fixed costs are allocated by cost category and by factory within the total budget plan.

**Management by objectives and the cost accounting system.** In comparing the target and actual costs during cost maintenance improvement activities, accountants are likely to recall the traditional cost control system. As discussed earlier, cost control activities are not based on the conventional standard costing system. They are based either on quantity units (such as labor-hour management or management by *kanban*) outside the standard costing system, or they are conducted departmentally by subjecting each cost item to the budgetary management process. Some Japanese automobile companies use the standard cost system. At present, however, the main purpose of a standard cost system is considered to be budget accounting.

The reason cost control (or cost improvement) is conducted outside the standard cost system is not because of a lack of importance, but rather a degree of importance warranting an independent system.[3] Since standard costs have constraints from a financial accounting perspective, they are inappropriate measures for management. A typical constraint is the infrequency in which quantity standards, such as processing time per product unit or material requirements, are revised. Normally, these standards are maintained at the same level throughout the year.

The Japanese auto industry, therefore, differentiates between standard cost and target cost, controlling production by the target cost. In the current standard costing system of a certain Japanese company, for example, the standard processing hours per part or per product for each cost division are first determined. By multiplying the standard hours by the processing cost allocation rate, the standard processing cost per part or per product is determined. The standard processing hours by division is the expected numerical value, and is averaged as the yearly mean. Therefore, the same value is used throughout the year. The target value of a given month varies, however, and is derived by multiplying cycle time by the number of labor hours. The value decreases a little every month because of what the Toyota production system calls "manufacturing process improvement." Cycle time in this context is the required production time per part or per product (for one process), and usually is quite short (maybe one or two minutes). Multiplying the labor hours by the cycle time becomes the standard production time per product unit. The target labor time is derived from the target reduction rate anticipated in the profit plan. Labor time calculated this way is the evaluation measure. The monthly reduction target is fixed during a given period.

In a month when large quantities of products are expected, measures must be taken to increase overtime or shorten cycle time to provide the necessary increases in direct labor time. Increasing direct labor time, however, is generally discouraged. Instead, each work area is encouraged to improve the manufacturing process. Allocating individual worker targets, in accordance with scheduled production levels, should emphasize process improvement in attempting to achieve the target production. This is what the Toyota production system calls "worker savings."[4] In contrast, it must be made clear that the standard accounting time should be the same throughout the year — not changed to accommodate monthly targets.

**Conclusion.** Cost reduction activities have been conducted with primary emphasis on cost maintenance and improvement. It has long been recognized that the application of management by objectives at the product development stage is important in achieving increased profit margins. Under this method, target profits are achieved by establishing a new product's target profit in accordance with the company's long-term profit plan. This requires calculating the target cost, based on the target profit and VE activities applied at the developmental and planning stages. Accordingly, each company in Japan integrates a product's characteristics, its method of development, and the skills of its supervisory employees in creating production systems.

Nevertheless, several problems exist at present. For example, the new product development department has too much work. The cost planning steps as presented here assume a three-year lead in scheduling new product development, with heavy emphasis on the first year. To meet the demands of new users, and increased diversification, competition, and technological advancement, the development department is forced to work simultaneously on several models and shorten development periods. As a result, business efficiency becomes increasingly important to cost planning activities that are supposed to receive appropriate labor resources.

Recently developed computer-aided design (CAD) and computer-aided manufacturing (CAM) systems are becoming indispensable for automobile makers. CAD computerizes the requisite data for design, enabling design work to be done on a graphic display. The computer — not the worker — quickly and precisely carries out data processing and complicated curved lines or three-dimensional designs. CAM produces tapes for numerical control (NC) production machines that produce parts according to the data in the CAD-drawn blueprint. Although futuristic, there is an attempt being made to combine CAD/CAM into a robot or flexible manufacturing system (FMS).

To solve the problem just mentioned, cost estimation requires improvement. The ability to estimate the product manager's recommendation from an outline before the blueprint is drawn, and the ability to promptly estimate the cost during and after blueprint completion are two key factors in accomplishing the ultimate target.

In conventional cost estimating, the engineering department designs the process plan based on a blueprint, and estimates the value of factors such as material consumption and processing time. The cost management department multiplies the unit cost of material and the processing cost rate by the material consumption and processing time, respectively. Although an estimate of the cost planning activity for each part is often documented on the blueprint, not all cost estimating systems, for example, conventional cost systems, work that way. Cost estimating during blueprint preparation requires instant judgment, and the data for estimating does not need to be sent to a supervising department. The designers themselves must (1) be able to judge whether or not a certain kind of material will raise the cost, and (2) know how a certain automobile design will affect the cost.

Subjects for future consideration include (1) the ability to identify the cost effect of new or changed materials and/or designs, and (2) determining cost data required from supervisory departments to increase the accuracy of evaluations.

## Notes

1. Refer to the following articles for recent investigations of cost control in the planning and design processes of new products:

    Koura, K., "Product quality and economic efficiency," in *Operations Research*, August 1981, pp. 437-442.

    Makito, T., "Current trends in Japan's cost control practice," in *Enterprise Accounting*, March 1979, pp. 126-132.

    Nakamori, K., "Cost control of the design department (1) (2)" in *Industrial Engineering*, November 1981, pp. 65-70, and December, pp. 58-64.

    Tanaka, M., "Development of cost control — Cost control in technological decision-making processes," in *Costing*, Vol. 255, December 1981, pp. 3-32.
2. Aoki, S., "Functional management as top management: Examples of management concepts at Toyota," in *Quality Control*, Vol. 32, No. 2, (pp. 92-98), No. 3, (pp. 66-71), No. 4, (pp. 65-69).
3. Makito, T., *op.cit.*, p. 132.
4. Refer to the following for the framework of the Toyota production system: Monden, Y., "What makes the Toyota production system really tick?" in *Industrial Engineering*, January 1981. Monden, Y., *Toyota Production System*, American Institute of Industrial Engineers, 1983.

# 3

## Cost Accounting and Control in the Just-In-Time Production System: The Daihatsu Kogyo Experience*

*Yasuhiro Monden, Institute of Socio-Economic Planning, University of Tsukuba*

The topic of this chapter is the relationship between the just-in-time (JIT) system and cost accounting/control, a relationship that has been the topic of a number of case studies published in the United States. Despite interest in Japan, however, there has been almost no empirical research done there on the topic. Given the fact that Japan gave birth to the JIT production system, it would appear that case studies, questionnaires, and the like, directed at Japanese firms would serve a useful purpose. Thus, while it may only scratch the surface, this chapter will present a case study of Daihatsu Kogyo, Ltd., and some observations on its cost accounting/control systems as they have developed under the JIT production system. The information presented has been gathered with the cooperation of Daihatsu Kogyo.

In an effort to become acquainted with the main problems in this field, we will consider first the evidence available from the United

* Translated with permission from *Kigyō Kaikei* (Business Accounting Journal), 40, No. 5 (1988).

States concerning cost accounting/control under the JIT production system. We will then look at the Japanese situation as revealed in a question-and-answer format with Daihatsu Kogyo. Finally, we will present a short summary of the information collected.

***The U.S. Situation.*** In a study of Hewlett-Packard, Hunt and Merz[1] list three ways in which the company's JIT system has affected its cost accounting system:

1. The elimination of the direct labor cost category, and its incorporation as indirect manufacturing costs.
2. The treatment of indirect manufacturing costs, including direct labor costs (processing costs) as a period expense, and directly figuring them as a part of sales costs.
3. The reduction of cost accounting for failed and redone jobs.

These three points are summarized in Figure 3.1. As is evident, their new "simplified system" is none other than a system, commonly used in Japan, of "integrated cost accounting by machine cost and process."

**Hewlett-Packard's Simplified System**

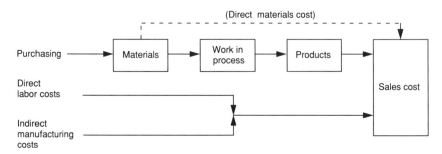

**Traditional Product Cost Accounting System**

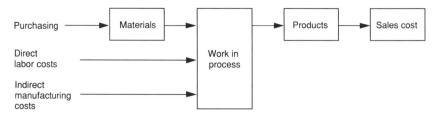

Figure 3.1  Cost Control Comparisons: Hewlett-Packard's Simplified System and the Traditional System

Further, Boer describes a joint conference held with the National Association of Accountants (NAA) on "Cost Accounting Robotics and the New Manufacturing Environment."[2] The conference's 170 participants had just visited a Nissan plant. Boer summarized the papers presented at this conference, particularly those dealing with the JIT production system's influence on cost accounting and cost control:

1. Labor costs have become an increasingly minor portion of overall manufacturing costs, and there is no particular need to apportion time directly for specific orders, products, or the like. (This suggests that there is no need to independently figure direct labor costs and directly calculate them as part of product costs.)
2. The traditional distinctions between manufacturing and support sections are becoming increasingly blurred because there is an increased tendency for service functions to be considered as part of the manufacturing process. For example, direct labor by itself is a part of machine maintenance.
3. A simplified accounting system is a prerequisite for a simplified factory.
4. When workers are considered part of the management team, reform activities tend to be conducted autonomously. Detailed accounting control procedures are thus not only impractical, but a waste of time.
5. Inventories perform the undesirable role of hiding a variety of management control problems.
6. It is necessary to recognize the numerous factors that can influence cost standards and to control them. (It is important to note that we are not speaking here of monetary, dollar-figure costs, but rather of target management control of the various factors influencing costs after they have been broken down.)

Points 4 and 6 of Boer's summary deserve special attention. The reasoning here is that there is an increasing tendency to believe that applying accounting controls is impractical or even redundant. What is important, however, is to control the physical elements of production that can influence cost standards. Cost control in this sense implies workplace reforms. It is now believed that the JIT production system is crucial to this type of workplace reform.

***Daihatsu Kogyo's Cost Accounting and Cost Reform System.*** The information in this section was provided during the course of an interview conducted July 13, 1987, at the Daihatsu corporate headquarters with Mr. Shigeaki Fukamori, head of the cost accounting department, and Mr. Kagahiko Yoshioka, head of the company's cost planning section. The results of the interview are reported in a question-and-answer format. Additional information is drawn from an earlier article written by the author in conjunction with a member of Daihatsu's board of directors and head of the purchasing department.[3]

*Question 1:* According to a recent issue of the U.S. journal *Management Accounting*, Hewlett- Packard's use of the just-in-time kanban system has resulted in changes in its cost accounting practices. Using the JIT system has shrunk the company's inventory levels considerably, reducing the time required from the beginning of production to shipment of the finished product. This means that indirect manufacturing costs — including direct labor costs, or what we might call processing costs — can now be included in the monthly sales costs. In other words, processing costs are now treated as quarterly expenses charged directly to sales costs. But processing costs, including those for finished goods or work in process inventoried at the end of the quarter, are then adjusted at the end of the quarter. Since Daihatsu Kogyo has adopted the Toyota production system in all facets of its organization, I want to know if you have really seen changes like this in your cost accounting practices.

*Answer:* Even before we adopted the Toyota system, we were using a system similar to the just-in-time format. It's true, however, that our inventory levels went down when we introduced the kanban system. Our year's inventory levels do not fluctuate much, but even so, this has not caused any basic changes in our cost accounting system.

Like Hewlett-Packard, Daihatsu uses direct costing as part of its management accounting, which allows us to carry fixed costs as direct quarterly expenses. But we don't calculate direct labor costs as quarterly expenses. Direct labor costs are variable expenses when factors such as overtime and part-time labor are calculated.

*Question 2:* The trend toward automated factories has grown lately. At companies such as Hewlett-Packard, it has become the practice to eliminate direct labor costs as an expense item, calculating them as part of the indirect manufacturing costs. This allows them to reduce direct labor costs to between 3 and 5 percent of manufacturing costs. Do you follow this practice at Daihatsu Kogyo?

*Answer:* We combine direct labor costs with indirect manufacturing costs and treat them as processing costs.

*Question 3:* If you eliminate the direct labor costs by combining them with indirect costs to be treated as processing costs, then it seems only natural to assume that direct labor costs themselves would not be calculated on individual products. They would be treated differently than direct materials costs. Is that the case? How do you calculate the processing costs of individual products?

*Answer:* Direct labor costs are calculated with indirect costs and are shifted to individual product cost accounts through departmental cost accounts. In other words, we establish a rate for distributing processing costs among the individual departments. At the same time, each department establishes standard times for the manufacture of each of its products and for each model vehicle. We use these to figure standard processing costs for individual products or vehicle models, costs that are calculated as a part of each individual product's cost accounting. We do not calculate direct labor costs independently and treat them the way we treat direct materials costs — we do not factor direct labor costs immediately into individual product costs the same way we factor in direct materials costs. Instead, we combine them with indirect costs and first calculate them as part of the costs for the individual departments. We have used this type of system for some time at Daihatsu. Direct labor costs, as always, carry considerable weight within processing costs.

*Question 4:* Another trend in this period of increased automation is that the amount of direct machining or processing is dropping, while the time spent on indirect machining is rising. I suppose this is true in Japan as well. One influence of this on cost accounting systems is that emphasis is shifted from worker rates to machine rates. This gives us a more accurate picture of costs. What can you tell us about this trend at Daihatsu Kogyo?

*Answer:* We have seen the same trends here. Automation has proceeded apace at the engine unit plant at our Takio manufacturing facility, for example, and parts are made in one-minute cycles. Nearly all machining there is unmanned now, so we have started using a machine rate. Also, because a considerable amount of press work is automated, we have established a machine rate for each punch. Automation is now progressing in the machining divisions, shifting us to machine rates there.

But in other areas, such as automotive assembly, painting, and mounting engines and other parts, we still determine standard times for each model vehicle or each part based on our old formula of cycle time multiplied by number of workers. The cycle time for these divisions is the same as the cycle time for the conveyor. And even in our machining divisions, we have established standard times for individual automobiles based on the formula of machining cycle time multiplied by number of workers. So you can see that, in the automotive industry, the worker rate still carries considerable weight. *Cycle time* is calculated from demand during the month in question, and is the amount of time needed to manufacture one model vehicle or one part. It is calculated for each individual process. At automotive plants, we are normally dealing with short time spans of one or two minutes.

*Question 5:* A legacy of the just-in-time system at companies such as Hewlett-Packard is that many cost reforms are now being implemented. This means that accounting control measures, such as variance analysis based on standard cost accounting procedures, are not only no longer practical, they are even a waste of time. Workers are now organized into small groups, such as quality control circles, and autonomously carry out continuous incremental improvements, which then become the cost controls for the workplace. Have you seen this at Daihatsu Kogyo?

*Answer:* An accountant hearing the words *continuous incremental cost improvements* tends to think of cost control systems based on standard cost accounting. Cost control activities undertaken at Daihatsu, however, have not been based on standard cost accounting systems. Working outside these systems, as part of our overall budget control system, we have seen (1) reforms based on material resource levels (labor hour controls and controls affected by kanban) and (2) reforms at the departmental and expense item level.

We started using the standard cost accounting system at Daihatsu in 1957. At the end of each month, we would calculate items, such as variations between budgeted funds and funds actually spent in each division, variations between ideal and actual productivity rates, operational variations, and so on. But now we have given up balancing these accounts and are using the standard cost accounting system primarily for financial accounting. The reason we conduct cost reforms outside the standard cost accounting system is not because we take these reforms less seriously — rather, it is because they are very important to us. The standard cost is limited by financial accounting restrictions, which means it is sometimes inappropriate for us to explain physical differences as part of the management system. This is reflected by the fact that material level standards, such as processing time for each product, and materials costs tend to balance out over the course of a year.

So at Daihatsu, we distinguish between standard cost and target cost. In fact, we control our manufacturing activities on the basis of target cost. For example, even with the standard cost accounting system currently used at Daihatsu, we determine the standard time for parts or individual vehicle models in terms of each department's costs. We then multiply this by the processing cost distribution rate assumed by the department in question to determine standard processing costs for each part and model vehicle. These standard times are done annually for each department. In the assembly department, we average out the number of workers and the conveyor time over a year and use this figure in our calculations, the same figure over the entire year.

We have a similar practice for purchased parts. We use the actual price for the parts paid at the end of the previous quarter to determine standard costs. For parts we make in-house, we calculate a standard cost based on the plant's average capacity, taking into consideration factors such as the degree of skilled labor or level of automation. These standard cost figures are maintained over the course of an entire year, which enables us to estimate yearly averages. We also have a rule of rounding off the basic unit.

Concerning the standard times for each department, it should be noted that the target value for the month to come is derived by multiplying the cycle time by the number of workers for the current month, which means the target figures will differ monthly. Because of what the Toyota production system calls process job reforms, the number generally decreases slightly each month. The basic unit for labor hours is derived by multiplying the cycle time by the number of workers working directly on the job in question. The targeted number of labor hours is calculated by applying an evaluative measure to the number of labor hours determined as already explained, then figuring in the targeted reduction rate from the profitability plan. A reduction target line is then plotted for each month from the first to last quarter.

In months when the predicted production level is high, either overtime is increased or the cycle time is shortened and direct labor increased as is necessary to cover the work to be done. These are the only ways we have of dealing with busy months. We do attempt, however, to pool all the knowledge and experience present in the plant to institute job reforms to keep increases in direct labor to a minimum. Conversely, we can allocate people within the range established by the formula of targeted worker hours times the estimated production quantity, then perform as many job reforms as necessary to reach the targeted production level for the month. At Toyota, this is called "worker saving."

*Question 6:* Are you saying that the use of accounting controls is decreasing at Daihatsu Kogyo?

*Answer:* We unquestionably use quantity-based controls in our plants, but fundamentally we use financial-type monetary controls. To begin with, we formulate quarterly profitability plans, expressed in cash terms. These are used to determine the target costs for the coming year (cost = target cost for the quarter *divided by* anticipated production volume). The targeted cost for the direct cost of products is broken down for each shop in the plant as a cost target figure.

Our budget period is for one year, but only the first six months are really set up with precision. The second half of the year is comparatively loose. We use the rolling method to correct the six-month periods. In fact, you can think of our targeted reduction rates as applied in six-month cycles.

The base figures multiplied by the targeted reduction rate are the targeted costs from the cost plan as applied to new products. These levels are expected to be attained within three months from the time production is started on new products. After that, these figures are also subject to reductions, and are multiplied by the targeted reduction rate from the profitability plan to determine the new target costs for the coming year. From the second year on, the figures from the end of the previous year are used as the base that is multiplied by the targeted reduction rate.

Materials, paint, indirect materials, energy, direct labor, and other fluctuating costs at the factory are controlled by setting reduction target figures for each vehicle model. The purchasing department supervises pricing controls for materials, paints, and other items purchased from outside. The primary activities conducted at the plant include adding value to purchased items and using conservation measures to reduce their consumption. Control measures taken for direct labor costs include quantitative controls and control of labor hours.

The target values for each month are called "rationalization targets," or "reduction targets." The target values for in-house items such as labor hours and the like are set each month. Our general rule, however, is to attain departmental expenses, such as expenditure budgets, over a three-month period or to evaluate them in terms of average figures taken over a six-month period. Items from the fixed costs line are subjected to target controls based on overall cash reduction targets and not to these "per vehicle reduction target controls." This, in itself, is a budgetary restriction.

Monthly targets for direct labor costs in the profitability plan are converted at the factory level to labor hour controls; the act of reaching these goals is known as "target control." Certain aspects of the concept of efficiency variance set out in standard cost accounting are somewhat difficult for workers in the factory to understand. Even in a classification such as labor hours control, if you simply take the difference between targeted labor hours and actual labor hours and multiply this by the labor hour rate, you can immediately see what is meant by efficiency variance. In any event, you can say that variance analysis as found in standard cost accounting has been pushed to the background in this process — the target control system now predominates because it comes in the form of labor hour controls, which are easy for the supervisors and factory workers to understand. This increases efficiency in our attempts to lower costs.

*Question 7:* Hewlett-Packard and other U.S. firms have found that measures such as the JIT system or total quality control have cut their defectives rate, which in turn has reduced the amount of rework required. This results in less need for cost accounting regarding losses or rework. Is this true at Daihatsu?

*Answer:* The thoroughness of our quality control program has led to considerably fewer job-related defects than before. When we do have failed job problems, they are more likely caused by defective materials. The role that failed jobs play in costs has also been reduced. Even so, however, it would not be true to say that this has brought about changes in our cost accounting system.

*Question 8:* The competition in product development among home appliance manufacturers — particularly makers of electronics products — is quite fierce and, consequently, product life cycles are now extremely short. Companies are forced to come out yearly with new models for each of their products. Of course, companies want to recover their development costs as early as possible. To do this, they calculate development costs as part of product costs when pricing the product. In financial accounting, this is dropped into quarterly expenses. Does Daihatsu follow this practice?

*Answer:* Research and development costs are inevitably treated as fixed costs in terms of financial accounting, but when we set our target costs, they are treated as plan-related costs and calculated into the product cost. By "plan-related costs," we mean that they will be objects of control during cost planning. Common fixed costs, such as amortization of general use equipment, are not plan-related costs. The costs for the development of prototypes were usually treated as common fixed costs. They are now calculated into the target costs as special fixed costs for each model.

The significance of considering design and development costs as plan-related costs, and hence a part of the target costs, is that we can calculate the total design and development labor hours (estimated labor hours × rate) to make them part of the target costs. This allows us to treat design and development costs in a way that can be controlled by the product manager.

The Daihatsu Kogyo cost accounting system is outlined in Figures 3.2 and 3.3.

**Conclusion.** Based on this study, it can safely be said that the JIT production system has had little impact on standard cost accounting procedures as they pertain to financial accounting, or on actual cost accounting systems, at least insofar as this system is practiced at Daihatsu Kogyo. As one of the most powerful members of the Toyota group, Daihatsu is one of the primary practitioners of the Toyota production system.

Even so, the standard cost control system no longer has the importance it once had in cost control because, under the JIT production system, more emphasis is placed in physically-oriented target control systems implemented in the workplace. Although it does not represent a retreat of financially-oriented or management accounting

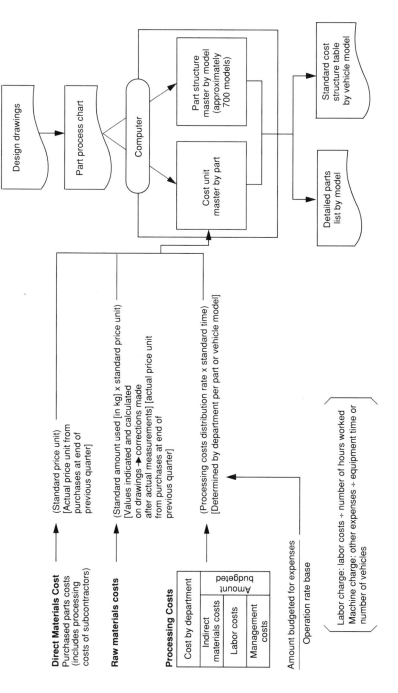

**Figure 3.2  Standard Procedures for Setting Cost (Automotive)**

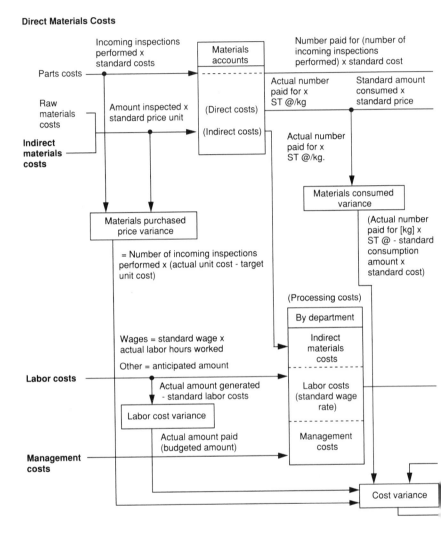

**Figure 3.3 Administration of Standard Cost Accounting System (Automotive)**

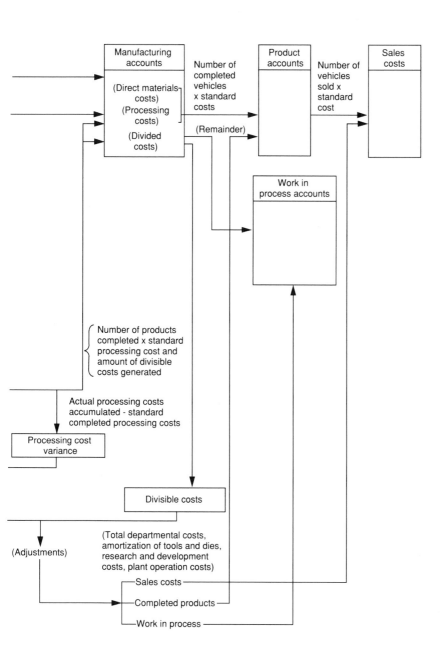

types of management control systems, it must be perceived as part of the proliferation of financial control directives and the target control system.

## Notes

1. Hunt, R., Garrett, L., and Merz, C.M., "Direct Labor Cost Not Always Relevant at HP," *Management Accounting*, (1985): 58-62.
2. Boer, Germain B. *Management Accounting: News and Views*, 5, No. 1 (1987): 1.
3. Monden, Yasuhiro, and Noboru, Yoshiteru. "Integrated Cost Control Systems in the Japanese Automotive Industry." *Kigyō Kaikei* ("Business Accounting") 35, No. 2 (1983). [A revised version of this article appears in *"High Tech Accounting,"* by Okamoto, Miyamoto, and Sakurai, eds. (Doyukan, 1988).]

# 4

## Cost Planning and Control Systems in the Design Phase of a New Product*

*Masayasu Tanaka, Department of Industrial Administration, Science University of Tokyo*

Traditionally, new product designers have been concerned with scheduling and performance at the development and design phase, and not with cost. This lack of concern about a new product's cost often results in high quality but reduced profitability. To solve this problem, as well as establish performance targets and schedule the development and design of new products, a target cost adhered to by the new product designers should be established. A cost control system is developed from the target cost in the design phase.

The life cycle cost of a new product is 80 to 90 percent committed at the design phase. Therefore, cost control in this phase is sorely needed. We will describe in this chapter how targeted cost control systems are developed based on a survey of large Japanese manufacturing industries. A case study will show how the proposed method works.

***Outline of Cost Planning and Control System.*** The development of a cost control system has five stages: planning, concept design, basic

* This chapter is a revision of an earlier paper published in the *International Journal of Production Research*, 1985, Vol. 23, No. 24, pp. 626-637. Original material and artwork are reprinted with kind permission of the publisher, Taylor & Francis Ltd.

design, detailed design, and, finally, manufacturing preparation. The necessary steps in each stage are outlined below.

*Step 1. Planning.* A new product plan is summarized in a document or table that defines and clarifies the design requirements. Usually, the following categories are included:

1. Outline of the product's concept and mission.
2. Primary specifications for the product's performance and design.
3. Schedule of the product's design, manufacturing and marketing activities.
4. The product's target cost, selling price, and volume.

*Step 2. Concept design.* In this stage, we formulate the basic concept of the new product based on the design requirements mentioned in step 1. Usually, it is composed of:

1. Formulating the main functional areas.
2. Assigning the target cost to the functional area of the new product.
3. Designing the basic product concept under the target cost.
4. Using a rough cost estimate to ascertain whether the basic product concept is designed to fit the target cost.

*Step 3. Basic design.* A general drawing of the product is made based on the basic concept and the target cost. In many cases, it is composed of:

1. Assigning target cost to the top and middle functions of each function area or main component of the new product.
2. Framing a general drawing under the target cost.
3. Using a rough cost estimate to ascertain whether the general drawing of the product is designed to fit the target cost.

*Step 4. Detail design.* A product's manufacturing specifications are written based on:

1. The detailed manufacturing specifications under the target cost.
2. A detailed cost estimate to ascertain whether a product's manufacturing specifications are designed to fit the target cost.

*Step 5. Manufacturing preparation.* A new product's manufacturing system is designed with its methods and processes determined under the target cost. Usually, the following steps are included:

1. Designing the manufacturing process, type, and jig under the target cost.

2. Using a detailed cost estimate to ascertain whether manufacturing preparations for the product are accomplished within the target cost.

**Practical Cost Planning and Control System.** Based on the five steps, the company's practical cost planning and control system is developed. The significance of cost targets and the procedure in establishing cost targets will be discussed.

In a new product's design phase, the target cost as well as performance and schedule targets should be established. Design activities must be carried out accordingly; they are complete only when it is possible to design the new product within the established target cost.

Of course, we must establish the target cost so that new product profitability is ensured. In addition, it is necessary to establish a target cost that can be achieved through the designer's efforts. The target cost level of big Japanese corporations is generally so low that it cannot be achieved without extra effort. Further, the target cost should be established for all activities of a new product's life cycle. According to our survey of 209 companies, the target cost is established in the design stage of a new product's life cycle as shown in Table 4.1.

| | |
|---|---|
| Target cost for design activity (developmental cost) | 41.0% |
| Target cost for manufacturing activity (manufacturing cost) | 100.0 |
| Target cost for distribution activity (distribution cost) | 37.1 |
| Target cost for user activity (user's cost) | 12.7 |

(Based on multiple responses)

**Table 4.1  Establishing Conditions of Target Cost**

The target cost:

• Is generally established as a current cost.
• Must motivate the design team.
• Is expressed as a range, which allows a trade-off among the performance, schedule, and cost of the new product.
• Is assigned to the functional areas or blocks of the product.
• Is used as a measure of alternatives.
• Differs from a standard cost.

Typically, manufacturing target costs are established by two methods: the subtraction method and the addition method.

*1. Subtraction method.* The target cost is reached using: manufacturing target cost = selling price − gross margin. The subtraction method is used when the selling price and gross margin are much the same for a group of similar products. In this case, the target cost of the product in the group is established by applying the subtraction method formula. If the correlation between them is not adequate, we recalculate the target cost by using a reasonable gross margin rate for the selling price of similar products shown for the quarter or project plan.

*2. Addition method.* In the addition method, there are three ways to determine the target cost on the basis of the normal current cost of the product or subassembly:

1. A normal current cost graph.
2. A single primary design parameter.
3. Multiple primary design parameters.

**Assigning the Target Cost.** There are two methods used to allocate the target cost to components of a new product. The first is to allocate the target cost to component blocks, composed of subassemblies of the new products, as shown in Figure 4.1. The second method is to allocate the target cost according to the product's functional area, as shown in Figure 4.2.

The component method is usually applied to new products that are similar in design to other, previously manufactured products. Generally, such products allow no room for adoption of new technology, or else they are subject to a tight design schedule. This method is

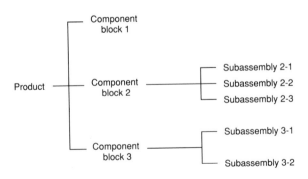

**Figure 4.1  Composition of the New Product**

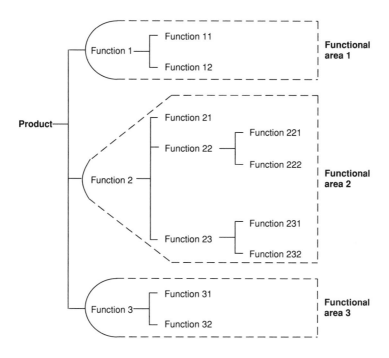

**Figure 4.2 Functional Block Diagram**

not recommended for innovative products. If target costs are allocated to component blocks, designers tend to be materials-oriented rather than function-oriented. To create a function-allocated design that can satisfy consumer needs, target costs should not be allocated to component blocks, but instead to functional areas of the new product. Therefore, in the case of complex, new, large-scale products, the functional area method is usually applied. Tables 4.2 and 4.3 show results from a survey of target costing by large Japanese corporations. These tables show the importance of design from the standpoint of function. Large companies in Japan tend to assign target cost according to the degree of importance of the functional areas regardless of the historical cost.

***Estimating Cost.*** Designers create the concept and basic designs of the new product based on the target cost assigned to the functions. First, they make trial products to satisfy the given target cost. A cost estimate is then carried out for the trial products to evaluate the new product's profitability.

| Functional areas | 76.0% |
|---|---|
| Component blocks | 25.9 |
| Strategy | 31.7 |
| Other | 34.7 |

(Based on multiple responses)

**Table 4.2 Assigning Target Cost**

| Degree of importance for each functional area | 59.9% |
|---|---|
| Estimated cost ratio for each functional area or component block | 25.9 |
| Strategy | 30.8 |
| Other | 34.6 |

(Based on multiple responses)

**Table 4.3 Assignment Criteria of Target Cost**

To confirm whether or not the cost of general drawings and manufacturing specifications are within the target cost, several methods of estimating costs are adopted at the design stage. Unless the cost of general drawings and manufacturing specifications are achieved within the target cost, the designers may have to alter the designs to achieve the target cost. This same procedure must be followed at each of the stages of concept, basic, and detailed design. The designers should not proceed with a design without achieving the target cost at each of these stages.

To evaluate cost performance for design alternatives, it is necessary to prepare multiple cost estimating systems that suit the purpose. According to our survey, estimating cost for design alternatives is carried out at both the detailed design and manufacturing preparation stages. This type of cost estimating is called a detailed cost estimate. Although it takes hours to estimate the cost of manufacturing specifications, it ensures accuracy. Large Japanese companies emphasize the accuracy of estimated costs. Degrees of accuracy are shown in the survey results of Table 4.4. From this table, it appears that estimating costs at the stages of concept design and basic design is insufficient. About 25 percent of large Japanese companies have adopted cost estimating at the function or performance level instead of physical components or parts in the design phase. This method is suitable for both the stages of concept and basic design. Because designers determine the function level of a new product in their design activities, estimating cost at the design phase is necessary to estimate the cost of a specific function or performance level.

| | Rough Cost Estimate | Detailed Cost Estimate |
|---|---|---|
| Over 97% | 2.0% | 27.4% |
| 97-95 | 14.9 | 30.8 |
| 95-90 | 33.9 | 25.4 |
| 90-85 | 16.9 | 3.5 |
| 85-80 | 14.4 | 4.5 |
| Under 80 | 4.1 | 0.5 |
| Others | 13.8 | 7.9 |
| **Total** | 100.0% | 100.0% |

Table 4.4 Degrees of Accuracy

*Cost Improvement.* Designers must make design changes if the cost of general drawings and manufacturing specifications is not within the target cost. This is the general concept of design to cost (DTC), and the main principle of cost planning and control at the new product's design phase. In large Japanese companies, value engineering (VE) techniques are applied to cost control activities to achieve the target cost. And while VE is conducted in three stages (before, during, and after the design phase), according to our survey, 50 percent of VE activity hours are spent in the design phase. Although the product designers try hard to achieve cost and value improvements, there are cases in which the target cost cannot be achieved. What then? In principle, product designers will be asked to make design changes; however, this is not always best. In some cases, there will be a compromise among cost, schedule, and performance; use of a cost reserve for the product; and so forth.

***A Practical Example.*** In this section, we show how the functional area method works in establishing a target cost for a marking pen. Because marking pens have a large competitive market, the target cost is determined with the subtraction method. To assign a target cost to the new product, we must (1) define and classify its functions, (2) evaluate the importance of its functions, and (3) assign target costs to each functional area of the product.

**Defining and classifying functions.** First we define the user functions of the new product and classify them by use and value. We further classify the use function into mechanical and convenience functions. Mechanical functions are called "hard." Convenience and value functions are called "soft." (See Figure 4.3.) We then define the functions, classifying them into hard and soft, as shown in Figures 4.4 and 4.5.

The functional block diagram shows the interrelationship of each function. In this case, we construct the functional block diagram for the hard function in terms of "why" or "how to." The functional block diagram for the soft function compares functions by "degree of importance." Function matrices are shown in Figures 4.6 and 4.7.

**Evaluating hard and soft functions.** We evaluate each function in pairs by degrees of importance. We generally evaluate each top-level function, followed by middle-level then low-level functions. The results of evaluating these hard and soft functions are shown in Tables 4.5 and 4.6 (see pages 57, 58).

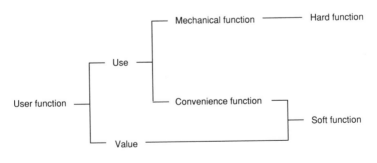

**Figure 4.3 Defining Functions**

$R_1$: *Writing Feel*
$h_{11}$: Nib's writing smoothness
$h_{12}$: Nib scratchiness
$h_{13}$: Adequate ink supply
$h_{14}$: Nib balance

$R_2$: *Design*
Shape and design

$R_3$: *Presentation*
$h_{31}$: Presentation of manufacturer's name
$h_{32}$: Presentation of product name
$h_{33}$: Presentation of ink color

$R_4$: *Writing Appearance*
$h_{41}$: Color quality
$h_{42}$: Uniformity of line width
$h_{43}$: Color consistency
$h_{44}$: Ink blotches
$h_{45}$: Color evenness

$R_5$: *User Convenience*
$h_{51}$: Cap and penholder fit
$h_{52}$: Convenient size
$h_{53}$: Attachment ease
$h_{54}$: Staining fingers
$h_{55}$: Ease of handling

**Figure 4.5  Defining Soft Functions**

$S_1$ = to mark
$S_2$ = to maintain ink
$S_3$ = to guide ink
$S_4$ = to fix the nib
$S_5$ = to store ink
$S_6$ = to mark air space in the penholder
$S_7$ = to ventilate the penholder
$S_8$ = to prevent ink leakage
$S_9$ = to protect inside parts
$S_{10}$ = to maintain internal parts
$S_{11}$ = to affix the pen ring
$S_{12}$ = to affix the tail cap
$S_{13}$ = to prevent ink evaporation
$S_{14}$ = to connect the material soaking ink with the pen ring
$S_{15}$ = to protect the nib

**Figure 4.4  Defining Hard Functions**

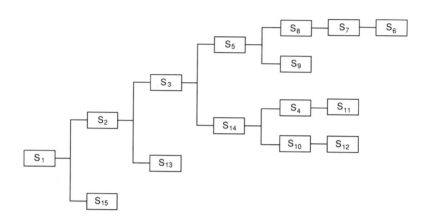

**Figure 4.6  Block Diagram for Hard Functions**

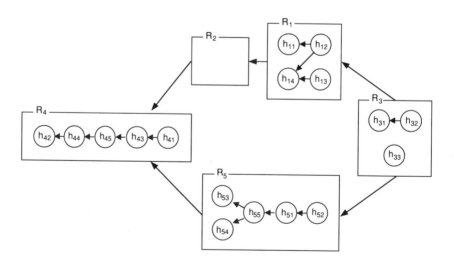

**Figure 4.7  Block Diagram for Soft Functions**

| Hard Functions | $S_1$ | $S_2$ | $S_3$ | $S_4$ | $S_5$ | $S_6$ | $S_7$ | $S_8$ | $S_9$ | $S_{10}$ | $S_{11}$ | $S_{12}$ | $S_{13}$ | $S_{14}$ | $S_{15}$ | Total |
|---|---|---|---|---|---|---|---|---|---|---|---|---|---|---|---|---|
| Degrees of Importance ($k_h$) | 16.2 | 13.6 | 12.5 | 5.3 | 8.3 | 4.1 | 5.3 | 6.7 | 3.9 | 3.9 | 3.3 | 3.0 | 4.6 | 6.0 | 3.3 | 100.0% |

Table 4.5  Degrees of Importance for Hard Functions

| Soft Functions | $R_1$ | | | | $R_2$ | $R_3$ | | | $R_4$ | | | | | $R_5$ | | | | Total |
|---|---|---|---|---|---|---|---|---|---|---|---|---|---|---|---|---|---|---|
| | $h_{11}$ | $h_{12}$ | $h_{13}$ | $h_{14}$ | | $h_{31}$ | $h_{32}$ | $h_{33}$ | $h_{41}$ | $h_{42}$ | $h_{43}$ | $h_{44}$ | $h_{45}$ | $h_{51}$ | $h_{52}$ | $h_{53}$ | $h_{54}$ | $h_{55}$ | |
| Degrees of Importance ($K_s$) | 5.5 | 6.6 | 5.9 | 5.8 | 17.4 | 3.7 | 3.6 | 6.1 | 3.8 | 4.9 | 4.6 | 5.5 | 5.0 | 3.7 | 3.9 | 3.5 | 5.8 | 4.7 | 100.0% |

Table 4.6  Degrees of Importance for Soft Functions

**Assigning the target cost to functions.** The target cost is generally allocated to each function according to the value ratios. In this case, we have adopted the degrees of importance for functions as the criteria for assigning the target cost. The procedures of this stage follow.

1. *Determining the degrees of importance between the hard and soft function groups.* We sent a questionnaire to 1,200 users to discover how they distinguish degrees of importance between the hard and soft function groups. As shown in Figure 4.8, 35 percent of the target cost was assigned to the hard function group and 65 percent to the soft function group.
2. *Assigning the target cost to each function.* The target cost, allocated to the hard and soft function groups, was re-allocated to each function in the function group according to its degree of importance in Tables 4.5 and 4.6. In this way, the target cost of the new product was allocated to each specific function.

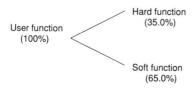

User function
(100%)

Hard function
(35.0%)

Soft function
(65.0%)

**Figure 4.8  Degrees of Importance Between Hard and Soft Function Groups**

*Concept Design, Basic Design, Trial Product, and Cost Estimate.* The designers create a concept design of the basic new product based on the target cost allocated to the hard and soft functions. They then produce trial products based on the design that satisfies the target cost. A cost estimate is done on the trial product to evaluate its profitability. The trial product chosen is the one that best achieves the required performance within the allowable range of the target cost. (See Figure 4.9.)

**Calculating degrees of importance for each component.** The target cost allocated to each function is re-allocated in turn to each component part to determine its target cost. In this stage, the degrees of importance of each component part to each function are used. Our results are shown in Tables 4.7, 4.8, and 4.9 (see pages 58, 61).

**Calculating the value index for component parts.** Our value index (VI) is shown in Equation 1.

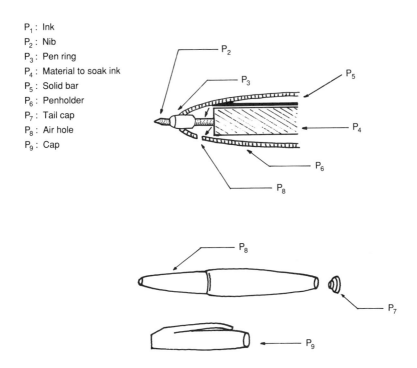

$P_1$ : Ink
$P_2$ : Nib
$P_3$ : Pen ring
$P_4$ : Material to soak ink
$P_5$ : Solid bar
$P_6$ : Penholder
$P_7$ : Tail cap
$P_8$ : Air hole
$P_9$ : Cap

**Figure 4.9 Components of a Marking Pen**

$$VI = \frac{function\ value}{cost}$$

The VI for each component part can also be calculated using the degrees of importance and percentage of component part cost shown in Equation 2.

$$VI = \frac{degrees\ of\ importance}{percentage\ of\ cost}$$

The results in Table 4.10 show the value index of component parts from the viewpoint of hard and soft functions. For component parts, the value index should approach 1.0. This is the optimal value of VI. Let $x$ equal the degrees of importance of a functional area,

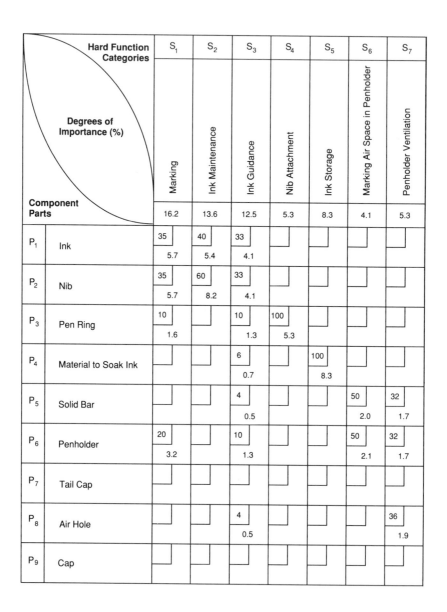

| Component Parts | Hard Function Categories | $S_1$ Marking | $S_2$ Ink Maintenance | $S_3$ Ink Guidance | $S_4$ Nib Attachment | $S_5$ Ink Storage | $S_6$ Marking Air Space in Penholder | $S_7$ Penholder Ventilation |
|---|---|---|---|---|---|---|---|---|
| | Degrees of Importance (%) | 16.2 | 13.6 | 12.5 | 5.3 | 8.3 | 4.1 | 5.3 |
| $P_1$ | Ink | 35 / 5.7 | 40 / 5.4 | 33 / 4.1 | | | | |
| $P_2$ | Nib | 35 / 5.7 | 60 / 8.2 | 33 / 4.1 | | | | |
| $P_3$ | Pen Ring | 10 / 1.6 | | 10 / 1.3 | 100 / 5.3 | | | |
| $P_4$ | Material to Soak Ink | | | 6 / 0.7 | | 100 / 8.3 | | |
| $P_5$ | Solid Bar | | | 4 / 0.5 | | | 50 / 2.0 | 32 / 1.7 |
| $P_6$ | Penholder | 20 / 3.2 | | 10 / 1.3 | | | 50 / 2.1 | 32 / 1.7 |
| $P_7$ | Tail Cap | | | | | | | |
| $P_8$ | Air Hole | | | 4 / 0.5 | | | | 36 / 1.9 |
| $P_9$ | Cap | | | | | | | |

Table 4-7. Degrees of Importance: Component Parts for Hard Functions

| S8 Leak Prevention | S9 Protecting Inside Parts | S10 Maintaining Inside Parts | S11 Pen Ring Attachment | S12 Cap Attachment | S13 Preventing Ink Evaporation | S14 Connection Between Material Soaking Ink and the Pen Ring | S15 Nib Protection | Total |
|---|---|---|---|---|---|---|---|---|
| 6.7 | 3.9 | 3.9 | 3.3 | 3.0 | 4.6 | 6.0 | 3.3 | 100% |
| 15 / 1.0 | | | | | 20 / 0.9 | | 5 / 0.2 | 17.3 |
| | | | | | 6 / 0.3 | | | 18.3 |
| 10 / 0.7 | | | | | 4 / 0.2 | 30 / 1.8 | | 10.9 |
| 10 / 0.7 | | | | | | | | 9.7 |
| 10 / 0.7 | | | | | | | | 4.9 |
| 30 / 2.0 | 90 / 3.5 | 90 / 3.5 | 100 / 3.3 | 100 / 3.0 | 50 / 2.2 | 50 / 3.0 | | 28.8 |
| 5 / 0.3 | 10 / 0.4 | 10 / 0.4 | | | 10 / 0.5 | 20 / 1.2 | | 2.8 |
| 15 / 1.0 | | | | | | | | 3.4 |
| 5 / 0.3 | | | | | 10 / 0.5 | | 95 / 3.1 | 3.9 |

| Soft Function Categories / Component Parts | | Writing Feel (R₁) | | | | Design | Presentation | | |
|---|---|---|---|---|---|---|---|---|---|
| | | $h_{11}$ | $h_{12}$ | $h_{13}$ | $h_{14}$ | $(R_2)$ | $h_{31}$ | $h_{32}$ | $h_{33}$ |
| Degrees of Importance (%) | | Smoothness of Nib in Writing | Nib Scratchiness | Adequate Ink Supply | Nib Balance | Shape and Design | Presentation of Manufacturer Name | Presentation of Product Name | Presentation of Ink Color |
| | | 5.9 | 6.2 | 5.9 | 5.8 | 17.4 | 3.7 | 3.6 | 6.1 |
| $P_1$ | Ink | 40 / 2.4 | 15 / 0.9 | 15 / 0.9 | 10 / 0.6 | | | | |
| $P_2$ | Nib | 60 / 3.5 | 25 / 1.6 | 15 / 0.9 | 50 / 2.9 | 11 / 1.9 | | | |
| $P_3$ | Pen Ring | | 8 / 0.5 | 10 / 0.6 | 30 / 1.7 | 11 / 1.9 | | | |
| $P_4$ | Material to Soak Ink | | 10 / 0.6 | 10 / 0.6 | | | | | |
| $P_5$ | Solid Bar | | 14 / 0.9 | 18 / 1.1 | | | | | |
| $P_6$ | Penholder | | 10 / 0.6 | 10 / 0.6 | 10 / 0.6 | 37 / 6.4 | 100 / 3.7 | 100 / 3.6 | 50 / 3.0 |
| $P_7$ | Tail Cap | | 4 / 0.2 | 4 / 0.2 | | 4 / 0.8 | | | |
| $P_8$ | Air Hole | | 14 / 0.9 | 18 / 1.0 | | | | | |
| $P_9$ | Cap | | | | | 37 / 6.4 | | | 50 / 3.1 |

Table 4.8  Degrees of Importance: Component Parts for Soft Functions

| Writing Appearance (R₄) | | | | | User Convenience (R₅) | | | | | |
|---|---|---|---|---|---|---|---|---|---|---|
| $h_{41}$ | $h_{42}$ | $h_{43}$ | $h_{44}$ | $h_{45}$ | $h_{51}$ | $h_{52}$ | $h_{53}$ | $h_{54}$ | $h_{55}$ | |
| Color Quality | Uniformity of Line Width | Color Consistency | Ink Blotches | Color Evenness | Cap and Penholder Fit | Convenient Size | Attachment Ease | Staining Fingers | Feel of Holding | Total |
| 3.8 | 4.9 | 4.6 | 5.5 | 5.0 | 3.7 | 3.9 | 3.5 | 5.8 | 4.7 | 100% |
| 95 | 10 | 95 | 95 | 70 | | | | | | 22.0 |
| 3.6 | 0.5 | 4.4 | 5.2 | 3.5 | | | | | | |
| 5 | 80 | 5 | 5 | 30 | | | | | | 16.9 |
| 0.2 | 3.9 | 0.2 | 0.3 | 1.5 | | | | | | |
| | 10 | | | | | | | | | 5.2 |
| | 0.5 | | | | | | | | | |
| | | | | | | | | | | 1.2 |
| | | | | | | | | | | 2.0 |
| | | | | | 50 | 50 | 50 | 53 | 80 | 31.0 |
| | | | | | 1.8 | 2.0 | 1.8 | 3.1 | 3.8 | |
| | | | | | | | | 8 | | 1.7 |
| | | | | | | | | 0.5 | | |
| | | | | | | | | 5 | | 2.2 |
| | | | | | | | | 0.3 | | |
| | | | | | 50 | 50 | 50 | 34 | 20 | 17.8 |
| | | | | | 1.9 | 1.9 | 1.7 | 1.9 | 0.9 | |

| Component Parts | | Ink | Nib | Pen Ring | Material to Soak Ink | Solid Bar | Penholder | Tail Cap | Air Hole | Cap | Total |
|---|---|---|---|---|---|---|---|---|---|---|---|
| Degrees of Importance | Hard | 17.3 | 18.3 | 10.9 | 9.7 | 4.9 | 28.8 | 2.8 | 3.4 | 3.9 | 100.0% |
| | Soft | 22.0 | 16.9 | 5.2 | 1.2 | 2.0 | 31.0 | 1.7 | 2.2 | 17.8 | 100.0% |

**Table 4.9  Degrees of Importance for Component Parts**

expressed as a percentage. Let $y$ equal the percentage of target cost assigned to the same functional area. The value index (Equation 2) may be expressed as $x/y$. If $x/y = 1$, then it will be true that $x = y$. In other words, target cost should be allocated exactly in accordance with the degrees of importance of a product's functional areas.

Such a standard is too strict, however, in practice. So it is useful to express the optimal value of the value index as an optimal range or zone or value. This can be done in a number of ways. In Figure 4.10, we have suggested one possible optimal value zone by representing

| | Percentage of Cost $(CP_i)$ | Hard Function | | Soft Function | |
|---|---|---|---|---|---|
| | | Degrees of Importance $(K_h)$ | Value Index $(V_h)$ | Degrees of Importance $(K_s)$ | Value Index $(V_s)$ |
| $P_1$: Ink | 6.9 | 17.3 | 2.51 | 22.0 | 3.19 |
| $P_2$: Nib | 18.5 | 18.3 | 0.99 | 16.9 | 0.91 |
| $P_3$: Pen Ring | 6.5 | 10.9 | 1.68 | 5.2 | 0.80 |
| $P_4$: Material to Soak Ink | 11.6 | 9.7 | 0.84 | 1.2 | 0.10 |
| $P_5$: Solid Bar | 1.2 | 4.9 | 4.08 | 2.0 | 1.67 |
| $P_6$: Penholder | 36.3 | 28.8 | 0.79 | 31.0 | 1.67 |
| $P_7$: Tail Cap | 3.9 | 2.8 | 0.72 | 1.7 | 0.44 |
| $P_8$: Air Hole | 1.1 | 3.4 | 3.09 | 2.2 | 2.00 |
| $P_9$: Cap | 14.0 | 3.9 | 0.28 | 17.8 | 1.26 |
| **Total** | 100.0% | 100.0% | | 100.0% | |

**Table 4.10  Value Index for Component Parts**

target cost as a range of allowable values based on deviations from the degrees of importance of the functional area of the product. Figure 4.10 is referred to as a value control chart. The optimal value zone in the chart is represented by the area between the two curves defined by Equations 3 and 4:

$$Y_1 : y = (x^2 - q_1^2)^{\frac{1}{2}}$$

$$Y_2 : y = (x^2 + q_2^2)^{\frac{1}{2}}$$

where Y1 and Y2 represent the lower and upper boundary target cost values, respectively, and $q_i$ (i = 1, 2) stands for allowable deviations from $x$, the degrees of importance of the functional area. The $q_i$ values are decision parameters set by management. Empirical studies usually reveal that $q_i < 20$. In the present example, we have let $q_i = 16$.

Value control charts have important applications. For example, if the value index of a functional area falls to the northwest of the optimal value zone, then cost reductions should be made to bring the value index within the zone. If the value index falls to the southeast of the zone, cost increases may be necessary to ensure that the product performs its functions satisfactorily.

**Evaluating the value of component parts.** To judge the value of each component part in this section, we proceed functional area by functional area. In the next section, we will integrate our analysis of functional areas. Value index points, or value points, have been calculated and plotted for hard and soft functions of the new marking pen. Value points for the hard functions have been plotted in the value chart in Figure 4.11. Value points for the soft functions have been plotted in the value chart in Figure 4.12. The results from these two figures show that the value point for $P_6$ (penholder) does not fall within the optimal value zone for either its hard or soft functions. This tells us that $P_6$ must be improved.

**Value point integration for each part.** To make cost improvements, we must make adjustments to the cost of components that will affect all functions of the product simultaneously. Because each component part of a new product will usually have more than one function, we cannot assign target costs on the basis of only one value point. We need to integrate value points simultaneously into the optimal value zone. In the present example, we have adopted a simple

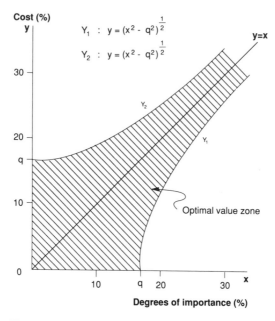

**Figure 4.10  Optimal Value Zone**

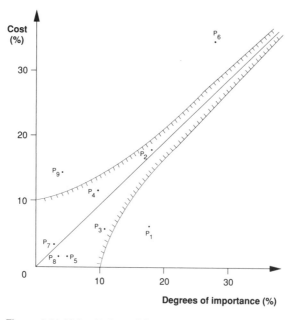

**Figure 4.11  Value Points of Component Parts for Hard Functions**

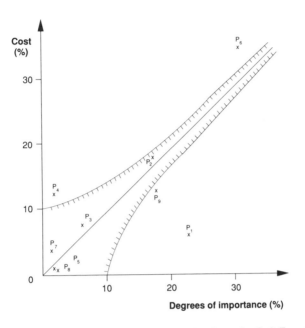

**Figure 4.12  Value Points of Component Parts for Soft Functions**

approach that assumes we may trade off proportionally between the functional areas of the product. Let $VP_i$ stand for a synthetic value point for component $i$. A synthetic value point results when target costs are reassigned to components and functional areas in an integrated fashion. To calculate the synthetic value point of each component $i$ of our marking pen, the following equation has been used:

$$VP_i = r\,VP_{hi} + (1 - r)\,VP_{si} \qquad (0 \leq r \leq 1)$$

where   $VP_i$   = artificial value point for part $i$
        $r$    = weight
        $VP_{hi}$ = hard function value point for part $i$
        $VP_{si}$ = soft function value point for part $i$

Once again, the equation assumes that we may trade off proportionally between the hard and soft functions. In Figure 4.13, we have recalculated target costs by letting $r = 3.35$, which suggests intuitively that the soft functions of the pen should be given more importance to bring the target cost of the pen within the optimal range.

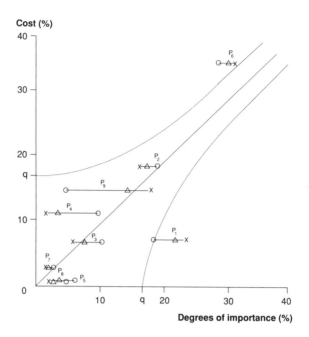

**Figure 4.13 Value Point Integration**

**Cost improvement.** In Figure 4.14, we see the results of a trial and error reassignment of target costs for all components of the marking pen. Usually in such exercises, VE techniques are used to redesign the product so that the target cost falls within the optimal zone. Here we found that the cost of the penholder (P6) should be improved between 36.3 and 34.2 percent to fall within the optimal zone. Ultimately, we found that this could be accomplished by transforming the functions of other marking pen components.

***Conclusion.*** In the cost planning and control system of the design phase, it is necessary to specify a reasonable target cost before designing a new product. We assign the target cost to the principal functional areas and component blocks. The designers control the design activities of the new product by using the target cost as an economic guideline. We evaluate achievement of the target cost by means of the cost estimate. Both rough and detailed cost estimating systems will be necessary to realize the process described in this chapter. If the

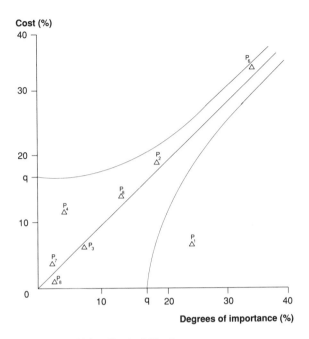

**Figure 4.14 Value Control Chart**

cost of general drawings and manufacturing specifications are within a product's given target cost, we usually adopt techniques such as VE, the tradeoff method, and cost reserve method.

## References

1. Amagasa, M. "On systems approach for structural modeling of large scale and complex systems." *Economic Journal of Daito-Bunka University*, 1981, No. 32, pp. 35-58 (in Japanese).
2. Tanaka, M. "Evaluation of function and value improvement by rating approach." Proceedings of the Society of American Value Engineers (SAVE), 1973, pp. 69-77.
3. Tanaka, M. "New approach to the function evaluation system in value engineering." *International Journal of Production Research*, 1985, Vol. 23, No. 4, pp. 625-637.

# 5

## Principles of QC Circle Activities and Their Effects on Productivity in Japan: A Corporate Analysis*

*Akira Ishikawa, School of International Politics and Economics, Aoyama Gakuin University*

A QC is a small group that is voluntarily organized within a series of companywide, participatory, quality control (QC) activities. Three objectives of organizing QC circles are:

1. To foster study groups in which foremen or workers study *QC for Foremen* (FQC) together.
2. To apply the results of their studies to their work areas, thereby creating more effective management and an improved work environment.
3. To expand and enrich the personalities of foremen and workers.

Being voluntary in nature and without a top-down approach, it took a long time to effectively implement QC circles nationwide. Success seems due to well-organized communication, as well as to participation and leadership on the part of workers. By the end of the 1970s, over 100,000 QC circles were registered. In addition, the number of unregistered circles was estimated at more than 1 million.[1]

* This chapter first appeared in *Management International Review*, Vol. 25, 1985/3 and is reprinted with kind permission of Swets & Zeitlinger BV.

QC circle activities contain many features unique to Japan. Table 5.1 lists the top 20 principles, or key words, of these activities[2] under which QC circles should be operated. I have added ten additional principles:

1. Providing a forum for educating and cultivating individuals in an effort to establish relations with others.
2. Discovering a new aspect of self and developing one's potential.
3. Finding pleasure and meaning in life in one's work.
4. Maintaining voluntary and pleasant activities within an organization's framework.

---

1. QC circles should be initiated in the workplace on a voluntary basis.
2. As a means of communication, QC circle activities are guided by a monthly magazine.
3. It is a group activity that accommodates everyone — even those who tend to be indifferent. It is not an activity for a chosen few.
4. QC circle activities occur during working hours — not before or after.
5. Specific — not abstract — problems are studied, beginning with immediate yet small, concrete issues. The ability to solve more difficult problems is acquired gradually, and members will begin to have fun.
6. Establish a stable, controlled operating environment. Take steps to stop recurring problems and to anticipate new ones.
7. Improving work standards is within the capability of the workplace.
8. All workers should be involved. QC circles should not be monopolized by either supervisors or management.
9. There should be total — but voluntary — participation. QC circles are not just for the most capable, outgoing, or prominent workers.
10. Discussions should be entered into freely and frankly and seen as an opportunity for all members to listen with open minds.
11. Sharing problems should be encouraged with participation according to individual capability.
12. Members should get ample practice in idea generation and application.
13. Solving problems should give members a feeling of confidence and accomplishment.
14. Problem-solving techniques are not easy to learn. They require the application of QC and IE methods, among others.
15. Members study to improve themselves.
16. Participation is voluntary — not coerced.
17. A QC leader should see that members cooperate with each other and share jobs equitably according to ability.
18. QC circles should not confine members to a specific work area but encourage participation in exchange meetings within and outside the company. QC's goal is to broaden each member's understanding.
19. A work area is not simply a place for physical labor, but a place where one's creativity can be utilized. Workers are encouraged to think.
20. QC circle activities should bring harmony to the workplace.

**Table 5.1  Principles of QC Circle Activities**

5. Increasing the manager's understanding — QC circles can grow only if managers are committed to giving guidance, training, and support, and to showing respect for humanity. Managers must reject their traditional distrust of shop workers.
6. Developing in harmony with nationwide QC circle activities.
7. Possessing a spirit of give and take. QC circles can help transcend corporate boundaries while still developing friendly rivalry.
8. Helping one another. QC circles are expected to be dedicated to service.
9. Recognizing the integral part of companywide quality control, in cooperation with top management, managers, supervisors, and staff.
10. Cultivating and strengthening personality.

To summarize, these principles or ideas are the nucleus that justify the existence of QC circle activities.

- To contribute to the improvement and development of the enterprise.
- To build respect for humanity and a bright and happy workshop with meaningful work.
- To reveal the infinite possibilities and capabilities of all workers.

I will now explore how these principles have become forces that increase productivity. To highlight the point, QC circle activities in the United States and Japan will be compared from three dimensions.

*Comparing QC Circle Activities in the United States and Japan.* In Table 5.2, we compare QC circle activities in these two countries on the basis of organization, activities, and issues and difficulties.

**QC organization.** One of the most notable differences is its formality. While in the United States a QC circle is often initiated as a *formal* staff organization, in Japan a QC circle is an *informal* group among workers. As a result, a manager in Japan serves as an advisor or consultant, whereas the U.S. counterpart serves as a QC manager with a staff of QC facilitators, instructors, and circle leaders. This means that the U.S. leadership style is straightforward and evident, while Japan has adopted an indirect and supportive role for the manager.

The next characteristic is the degree of participation. Although in principle it is voluntary in Japan, there is generally full participation by all workers due to group pressure. Although it is also voluntary in the United States, managers need to be more forceful in persuading workers to join QC activities because group pressure in U.S. companies is not necessarily as strong as that fostered by their Japanese counterparts.[3]

**United States**

*I. Organization*

1. QC circles are formally established in the company. Ordinarily, under a QC manager (from an upper management position), there are QC facilitators, instructors, and circle leaders. Often a supervisor becomes an instructor or a circle leader.
2. Although participation is voluntary in principle, management tries to persuade the worker to join the activities (same in Japan).
3. Middle management takes the lead in developing QC activities.

*II. Activities*

1. Often the meeting guidelines and theme are initiated by upper management.
2. Meetings are held during working hours. If not, overtime compensation is paid.
3. The individual worker — not the group — is evaluated for his or her performance.
4. Incentives are usually offered to individual workers.
5. Because circle activities take time, ad hoc methods have been adopted.

*III. Issues and Difficulties*

1. In companies where management and labor are in conflict, considerable time is required to introduce QC activities. (Labor unions tend to use the activities as a way to strengthen worker unity and union influence.)
2. Due to layoffs and high turnover, members rarely belong to the same circle for long.
3. There is no commitment to long-term QC education and training.
4. Even though QC benefits take time, top management tends to expect excessive short-term effects and benefits.
5. An emphasis on individual effort defeats the fostering of teamwork and group activities.
6. It is difficult for participants to understand the importance of organizing QC circles.
7. Gaining the support of lower management and QC engineers in an advisory and consulting capacity is difficult.

**Table 5.2  Comparing QC Circle Activities in the United States and Japan**

A third characteristic is the range of support by management. The Japanese company as a whole — regardless of top, middle, or lower management — supports QC circle activities and, in fact, involves workers (nonmanagers) as leaders of the activities. Only middle management in U.S. companies tends to lead evolving QC circle activities. Top and lower management appear more or less indifferent.

**QC activities.** The first difference is the selection of an agenda for meetings. Because of the different leadership style in the United

**Japan**

*I. Organization*

1. QC circles are organized as informal groups among workers, with managers acting in an advisory capacity. They parallel the company's formal organization.
2. Although participation is voluntary in principle, there is peer pressure among workers to participate.
3. The company, at top, middle, or lower management levels, supports circle activities. Note, however, that QC leaders come from worker ranks — not management.

*II. Activities*

1. Worker members decide on the theme and meeting guidelines.
2. Meetings are held both during and outside working hours. When held before or after hours, overtime compensation is seldom paid.
3. Proposals to the company combine individual and group efforts.
4. Rewards to an individual or circle for company-adopted proposals are minimal. Rather, the benefits accrued are distributed to all employees as bonuses.
5. Circle activities take time because of their voluntary nature.

*III. Issues and Difficulties*

1. It's difficult to achieve full worker participation even when confrontation between management and labor union doesn't exist.
2. Active participation tends to focus on the leaders. Other members are often indifferent.
3. Members move from place to place and seldom remain in the same QC circle.
4. Middle management needs to play a more active role.
5. QC education and training are inadequate.
6. The power of the promoting body is weak.
7. The number of ideas is not a product of the number of meetings. Participation and role flexibility are the important ingredients.

States, the agenda, project selection, and how to proceed with meetings fall under the manager's direction. In Japan, the workers decide.

A second difference is the timing of meetings. While held during work hours in the United States, meetings are scheduled during and after hours in Japan. This results in a difference in compensation. U.S. workers receive overtime compensation if they meet before or after work. In Japan, there is no compensation for meetings before and after hours.

Evaluation methods are a third difference. If a new idea comes from a worker in the United States, he or she is evaluated solely on his or her performance. On the other hand, many Japanese companies adopt a system in which either an individual or a group is evaluated, depending on the idea's source. Generally, group evaluations are more prevalent.

A fourth difference is in the reward system. While most incentive schemes in the United States focus on individual workers, benefits, usually in the form of modest bonuses, are distributed to all employees involved in a proposal in Japan. Recognition of group achievement therefore supersedes its monetary benefit in Japan.

**QC issues and difficulties.** Initially, full worker participation is achieved with difficulty in both the United States and Japan, even in work environments where labor/management confrontation is nonexistent. It takes a lot of time to introduce QC circle activities in U.S. companies, particularly in those companies with labor/management confrontations. Labor leaders, in addition, tend to use QC circle activities as a new way to strengthen worker unity, or as a platform from which to promote the union's influence.

A second difficulty lies in maintaining QC activities throughout U.S. periods of layoff and turnover. In Japan, a worker may be a long-time member of a QC circle, but, in reality, active participation is likely to be concentrated in a leader and only a few members. The remaining members tend to be indifferent or avoid any responsibility.

A third difficulty arises out of the second one. Because members rarely belong to the same circle for long, there is no long-term QC training and education in the United States. In Japan, the same problem exists because members move from place to place within the same company. Japanese workers, however, seem to have relatively greater opportunities for consistent education on a long-term basis.

A fourth area of difficulty is key management's expectations and participation. For example, upper management and even QC circle leaders in the United States tend to expect excessive short-term effects and benefits. On the other hand, middle management's active participation in Japan is not as influential as its role as initiator and activator.

Finally, a fifth difference lies with motivation. U.S. companies find it difficult to convince workers of the importance of organizing a QC circle. Even when this question is resolved without difficulty in Japan, the activating body's power is often not strong and/or influential enough to achieve new ideas in the resulting meetings. In the United States, QC supervisors and QC engineers in an advisory and consulting position have a difficult time achieving the willingness and motivation needed for the truly challenging QC circle activities.

***Suggestions to Enhance Productivity.*** Reasons why productivity has been curtailed in most of the well-developed nations are multifaceted. Suggestions to enhance productivity, therefore, must also be multifaceted, if they are to be realistic and workable. The factors to be described here are: (1) macroscopic, including economic policy and social and cultural factors; (2) semimacroscopic, including both domestic and foreign market conditions; and (3) microscopic, including internal research and development (R&D), marketing, production, finance, and personnel.

Macroscopic factors are:

*1. Economic policy factors*

- Coping with recession, stagflation, and deflation.
- Reducing the size of excessively large governments while still maintaining effectiveness and efficiency.
- Reforming to encourage saving (particularly in the United States) and investment and domestic consumption (in Japan).
- Reducing the excessive number of government regulations.
- Changing from confrontation to cooperation between government and industry.
- Avoiding excessive and undue protectionism.
- Establishing solid, long-term, cooperative economic policy without excessive transition (particularly among advanced countries).

*2. Social and cultural factors*

- Alleviating excessive individualism or "me-ism."
- Readjusting society from unequal to equal. (The rich should not get richer at the poor's expense.)
- Lowering the unemployment rate.
- Providing greater retraining opportunities to the unemployed.
- Reducing the social trend of exorbitant legal settlements.
- Redirecting these positive judgments toward social revitalization.
- Rebuilding traditional standards and codes of ethics that collapsed after the Vietnam war.
- Reappraising the social security system in the direction of social revitalization.

Semimacroscopic factors emphasize the following marketing conditions:

*1. Domestic market factors*

- Surmounting saturated growth, for instance, cultivating new markets for different client groups in different geographical areas with current and new products.

- Creating a strong and enduring customer demand structure that allows consumption, while encouraging increased savings and investment.
- Building up more competitive tertiary and quaternary industries, represented by high technology education, communications, and biotech areas.

### 2. Foreign market factors

- Fostering and developing export markets sufficiently and effectively.
- Removing legislation, regulation, and trading policies that prevent active and creative exporting.
- Creating unique, high quality products to help expand foreign markets.
- Recognizing the different kinds of products and services that developed, developing, and less-developed countries can provide. If all countries, regardless of their level of development, compete in the same product and service areas, the results will be mutually destructive.

The microscopic factors of capital investment and use, technological breakthrough, management, labor, and natural resources are:

### 1. Capital investment and use

- Saturating capital investment, as compared with the deteriorating quality of assets and facilities.
- Increasing investment in nonproductive and intangible assets and facilities.
- Limiting investment efficiency.
- Ineffective investing by venture capitalists.

### 2. Technological breakthrough

- Decreasing levels of innovation, creativity, and technological breakthroughs.
- Insufficient R&D expenditures.
- Insufficient investment in R&D research, especially at the graduate school level.
- Lack of long-term R&D policy.

### 3. Management

- Inflexible management policy regarding short-term ROI and/or RI pursuits.
- Lack of dynamic, competitive strategy.
- Bureaucratic characteristics exhibited in older, larger organizations.
- Confrontation between management and labor unions.

### 4. Labor

- A growing but underqualified work force.
- Workers' lack of discipline.
- Inadequate on-the-job training.
- Lack of worker incentive.

### 5. Natural resources

- Deteriorating quality of domestic resources.
- Increasing cost of imported resources.
- Insufficient export of abundant natural resources.

Some of these factors are interdependent, supplementary, or at odds. With more creative investment, for example, we may be more likely to produce — and thereby export — more unique products. This would invite additional investment based on rising profits and employment. Economics in general, therefore, will be activated and the gross national product (GNP) increased. It would be natural for a company to provide better worker incentives, training and education, thereby increasing productivity. Since this is only one of many assumptions, we can conceivably create numerous realistic scenarios on the basis of truly achievable productivity increases. I do not intend to explore it further here, but I would like to point out that:

1. These three classes of factors (macroscopic, semimacroscopic, and microscopic) are inseparably intertwined, and we cannot resolve productivity issues by focusing on microscopic factors alone.
2. Productivity issues should be the concern of not just management, but of government, labor unions, and the public.
3. Productivity issues must be resolved by each individual. In other words, the approach should be based on the willingness and participation of the individuals involved. The aspiration levels of management, labor unions, and employees toward higher productivity will become equally high.

**Conclusion.** Mutual trust and respect bolstered by confidence and shared profits are the keys to increased productivity. It is by no means procedural or standards-oriented. In the Japanese examples examined in this chapter, informality, incentives, and worker initiatives were especially important. It is conceivable that this approach could be adopted in both U.S. and European environments. It is most important that individuals understand these multifaceted factors and continually seek the most effective solution in our present and foreseeable environments.

## Notes

1. Union of Japanese Scientists and Engineers. *QC Circle Koryo: General Principles of the QC Circle*, JUSE, Tokyo, 1978, pp. iii-iv.
2. *Ibid.*, pp. 36-39.
3. In fact, some critics are apprehensive of a recent trend in some Japanese companies where there is excessive pressure on top management's part to win the Deming Award. They warn that this will result in an undesirable disparity between managers and the established, voluntary nature of QC circle participation. See Masaru Kamada, *A Proposal of Human-Based TQC (Korede Iinoka TQC)*. (Tokyo: Nihon Jitsugyo Shuppansha, 1985), pp. 36-46.

# 6

## Framework of the
## Just-In-Time Production System*

*Yasuhiro Monden, Institute of Socio-Economic Planning,
University of Tsukuba*

The Toyota production system was developed and promoted by
Toyota Motors, and is being adopted by many Japanese companies in
the aftermath of the 1973 oil crisis. Although the main purpose of the
system is to reduce costs, it also helps increase the turnover ratio of
capital (total sales/total assets) and improve the total productivity of a
company.

Even during periods of slow growth, the Toyota production system could make a profit by decreasing costs in a unique manner —
that is, by completely eliminating excessive inventory or workforce.
We would probably not overstate our case by saying that this is
another revolutionary production management system. It follows
the Taylor system (scientific management) and the Ford system
(mass-assembly line). This chapter examines the basic idea behind
this production system, how it makes products, and the specific
areas in which Japanese innovation can be seen. The framework of
this production system is examined as a unit by connecting its basic

* Reprinted with permission from Yasuhiro Monden, *Toyota Production System*,
(Atlanta: Institute of Industrial Engineers, 1983).

ideas or goals with the various tools and methods used for achieving these goals.

*Basic Idea and Framework.* The Toyota production system is a reasonable method of making products because it completely eliminates unnecessary production elements to reduce costs. The basic idea in such a production system is to produce the kind of units needed, at the time needed, in the quantities needed. The realization of this concept would eliminate unnecessary intermediate and finished product inventories.

Even though the system's most important goal is cost reduction, three subgoals must be achieved before its primary objective is achieved. They are:

1. *Quantity control*, which enables the system to adapt to daily and monthly demand fluctuations in quantity and variety.
2. *Quality assurance*, which ensures that each process will supply only defect-free units to subsequent processes.
3. *Respect for the worker*, which must be cultivated to allow full use of the human resources necessary for attaining the system's cost objectives.

It should be emphasized here that these three goals cannot exist or be achieved independently. They influence each other and the primary goal of cost reduction. A special feature of the Toyota production system is that the primary goal cannot be achieved without realizing these subgoals, and vice versa. All goals are outputs of the same system. With productivity as the ultimate purpose and guiding concept, the Toyota production system strives to realize each of the goals for which it was designed.

Before discussing the Toyota production system in detail, an overview, which is shown in Figure 6.1 is in order. The outputs or results side (costs, quality, and labor) as well as the inputs or constituents side of the Toyota production system are depicted.

A continuous flow of production, or adapting to demand changes in quantity and variety, is created by achieving two key concepts: just-in-time (JIT) and autonomation, the two pillars of the Toyota production system. *Just-in-time* means producing the needed units in the needed quantities at the needed time. *Autonomation* (*jidoka*) may be loosely interpreted as autonomous defect control. It supports JIT by never allowing defective units from a preceding process to flow into and disrupt a subsequent process. Two concepts also important to the Toyota production system include *flexible workforce* (*shojinka*), which means varying the number of workers based on demand changes, and *creative thinking or inventive ideas* (*soikufu*), capitalizing on worker suggestions.

To implement these four concepts, Toyota has established the following systems and methods:

1. The *kanban* system to maintain JIT production.
2. A production-leveling method to allow adaptation to demand changes.
3. Shortened setup times that reduce production lead times.
4. Standardizing operations to attain line balancing.
5. Machine layouts that promote multi-skilled workers and the flexible workforce concept.
6. Small-group improvement activities and a worker suggestion system to reduce the workforce and increase morale, respectively.
7. A visual control system to achieve autonomation.
8. A "functional management" system that promotes companywide quality control, and so forth.

***Just-In-Time Production.*** The idea of producing what is needed in the needed quantities, at the needed time, is described by the words "just-in-time." Just-in-time means, for example, that in the process of assembling the parts needed to build a car, the subassemblies needed by the subsequent processes should arrive at the production line exactly when needed and in the quantity needed. To realize JIT companywide, unnecessary inventories as well as storage areas and warehouses in the factory will be completely eliminated. Inventory-carrying costs will be diminished, and the ratio of capital turnover will increase.

To rely solely on the central planning approach (informing all processes simultaneously of the production schedules) makes it difficult to achieve just-in-time in all processes for a product like an automobile, which consists of thousands of parts. In the Toyota system, therefore, it is necessary to look at the production flow conversely; in other words, a subsequent process goes to the preceding process to withdraw the needed units in the needed quantities when needed. The preceding process then only produces the number of units withdrawn.

In this system, the type and quantity of units needed are written on a tag card called a *kanban*. Kanban are sent to a preceding process from the subsequent process. This results in better communication between processes, as well as better quantity control. Toyota's kanban system is supported by the following:

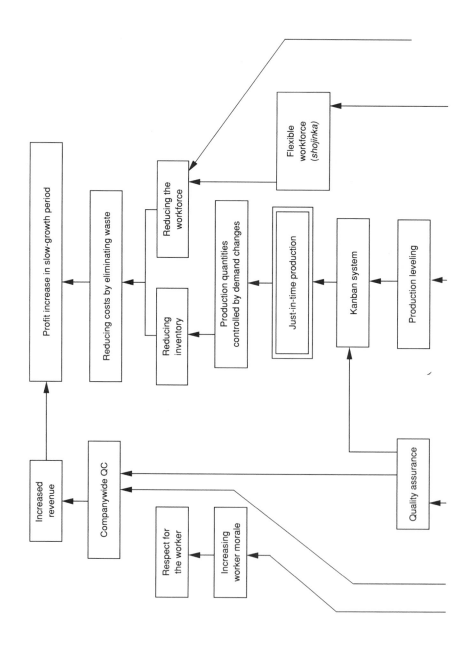

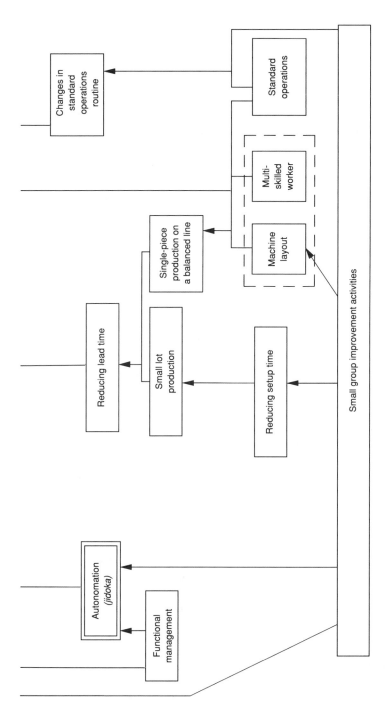

**Figure 6.1 How Costs, Quantity, Quality, and Humanity Are Improved by the Toyota Production System**

- Production leveling
- Job standardization
- Reduction of setup time
- Improvement activities
- Design of machine layout
- Autonomation

***Kanban System.*** Many people call the Toyota production system a kanban system. This is incorrect. The Toyota production system is a way to make products, whereas the kanban system is a way to manage JIT production methods. In short, the kanban system is an information system to control the production quantities in and between processes. Unless the various prerequisites of this system are implemented perfectly (process design, standardized operations, production leveling, and so on), just-in-time will be achieved with difficulty, even with the introduction of the kanban system.

A kanban is usually a card put in a rectangular vinyl envelope. The two principle kinds used are withdrawal and production-ordering kanban. A *withdrawal kanban* tells the subsequent process to withdraw a certain quantity, while a *production-ordering kanban* tells the preceding process what quantity to produce. These cards circulate within Toyota factories, between Toyota and its many cooperative companies, and within the factories of cooperative companies. In this way, kanban contribute information on withdrawal and production quantities to achieve JIT production.

Suppose we are making product *A*, *B*, and *C* on an assembly line. The parts necessary to produce these products are *a* and *b*, which are produced by the preceding machining line (see Figure 6.2). Parts *a* and *b* produced by the machining line are stored behind it, and the line's production-ordering kanban are attached to these parts. The transporter from the assembly line making product *A* will go to the machining line to withdraw the needed parts *a* with its withdrawal kanban. Then, at storage *a*, he picks up as many boxes of this part as his withdrawal kanban dictates, and detaches the production-ordering kanban attached to these boxes. He returns again to the assembly line, with both the boxes and the withdrawal kanban.

At this time, the production-ordering kanban showing the number of units withdrawn are left at the machining line's storage *a*. These kanban will be the dispatch information to the machining line. Part *a* is then produced in the quantity directed by that number of

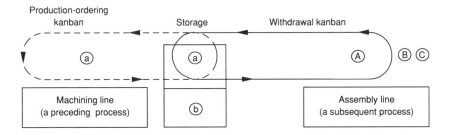

**Figure 6.2 The Flow of Two Types of Kanban**

kanban. In this machining line, parts *a* and *b* are both withdrawn, but these parts are produced according to the detached order of the production-ordering kanban.

***Fine-Tuning Production.*** Let's consider fine-tuning production by using a kanban. Assume that an engine manufacturing process must produce 100 engines a day. The subsequent process requests five engines per one-time lot via a withdrawal kanban. These lots are then picked up 20 times a day, which amounts to a daily production of exactly 100 engines.

If we need to decrease all processes by 10 percent to fine-tune our production planning, this example's final process will have to withdraw engines 18 times a day. Then, since the engine process produces only 90 units a day, working hours will be reduced by the time needed to produce the now 10 unneeded units. On the other hand, if we need to increase production quantities by 10 percent, the final process must withdraw engines 22 times a day with the kanban. The preceding process then has to produce 110 units, these additional 10 units being covered by overtime.

Although the Toyota production system is based on the assumption that units can be produced without any slack or unnecessary stock by regarding all human resources, machines, and materials as perfect, the risk of variations in production needs still exists. This risk is countered by paying overtime and encouraging improvement activities at each process.

***Production Leveling.*** Production leveling is the most important condition of kanban-inspired production for minimizing slack time in terms of workforce, equipment, and work in process. It is the cornerstone of the Toyota production system.

As described previously, the subsequent process goes to the preceding processes to withdraw goods needed, when needed, and in the quantities needed. If the subsequent process fluctuates its withdrawal of parts in terms of time or quantity, then the preceding process should prepare the inventory, equipment, and workforce that will be necessary to adapt to the highest variance of quantities demanded. Where there are many sequential processes, the variance of quantities withdrawn by each subsequent process may increase as we move further back along the preceding processes. To prevent such large variances in all production lines, including those of a company's subcontractors, an effort must be made to minimize production fluctuation in the final assembly line. Therefore, as Toyota's final process, the finished car assembly line will convey each type of automobile in the smallest possible lot size to achieve the ideal of one-piece production and flow. The line, in turn, will receive needed parts in their small lot sizes from the preceding processes.

In short, production leveling minimizes the variation in the withdrawal quantities of parts produced at each subassembly, thereby allowing the subassemblies to produce each part at a constant speed, or at a fixed quantity per hour. Such a production leveling is illustrated by the following example.

Suppose a production line is required to produce 10,000 Toyota Coronas in 20 eight-hour operating days. The 10,000 Coronas consist of 5,000 sedans, 2,500 hardtops, and 2,500 wagons. Dividing these numbers by 20 operating days results in 250 sedans, 125 hardtops, and 125 wagons per day; this levels the average daily production of each car type. During an eight-hour operating shift (480 minutes), all 500 units must be produced. Therefore, the *unit cycle time*, or average time required to produce one vehicle of any type, is 0.96 minutes (480 ÷ 500), or approximately 57.5 seconds.

The proper mix, or *production sequence*, can be determined by comparing the cycle time needed to produce one vehicle of any type with the maximum time permitted to produce a specific Corona model. For example, the maximum time needed to produce one Corona sedan is determined by dividing the shift time (480 minutes) by the number of sedans to be produced in the shift (250); in this case, the maximum time is 1 minute, 55 seconds. This means a sedan must and will be generated every 1 minute, 55 seconds. Comparing this time interval with the cycle time of 57.5 seconds, it is obvious that another car type could be produced between the time one sedan is completed and another must be produced. So, the basic sequence is sedan, other, sedan, other, and so forth.

The maximum time needed to produce a wagon or hardtop is 3 minutes, 50 seconds (480 ÷ 125). Comparing this figure with the cycle time of 57.5 seconds, it is obvious that three cars of any type can be produced between each wagon or hardtop. If a wagon follows the first sedan in production, then the production sequence would be sedan, wagon, sedan, hardtop, sedan, wagon, sedan, hardtop, and so on. This is an example of leveling the production of a variety of products.

When considering manufacturing equipment, a conflict arises between product variety and production leveling. When producing a smaller variety of products, specialized equipment for mass production can be a powerful weapon for reducing costs. Toyota, however, has numerous car types in various combinations of model, tires, options, color, and so forth. For example, 3,000 or 4,000 kinds of Coronas are being produced. To promote leveled production in such a variety of products, it is necessary to have general purpose or flexible machines. By using a minimal number of instruments and tools on these machines, Toyota's specialized production processes accommodate the efficiency of these machines.

An advantage of leveled production's response to product variety is that the system can adapt smoothly to fluctuating customer demands by gradually changing the frequency of lots without altering the lot size in each process. This is fine-tuning production using kanban. To achieve leveled production, reducing production lead time will be necessary to produce various product types promptly. Minimizing lot sizes, in turn, will require reducing lead times for setup.

**Setup Problems.** The most difficult point in promoting smooth production is setup. In a pressing process, for example, common sense dictates that costs can be reduced by continuously using one type of die, thereby producing large lot sizes and reducing setup costs. However, when the final process has averaged its production and reduced the stocks between the punchpress and its subsequent body line, the pressing department as a preceding process must make frequent and rapid setups. This means frequently altering the die types corresponding to the greater variety of products being withdrawn by the subsequent process.

At Toyota, from 1945 to 1954, the pressing department's setup time had been 2 or 3 hours. It was reduced to a quarter hour in the years 1955 to 1964, and to only 3 minutes after 1970.

To shorten setup times, it is important to prepare neatly in advance the necessary jigs, tools, the next die, and materials, and remove the detached die and jigs after the new die is set and the machine begins to operate. This phase of setup actions is called the *external* setup. The worker should concentrate on actions needed while the machine is stopping. This phase of setup actions is called the *internal* setup. It is crucial to convert as much internal setup as possible to external setup.

**Process Design.** Consider the design or layout of processes in a plant. Each of five stands of lathes, milling machines, and drilling machines are laid out side by side, with one worker assigned to each machine so that a turner handles only a lathe. In the Toyota production system, the layout of machines is rearranged to smooth the production flow. One worker, therefore, might handle three types of machines; for example, a lathe, milling machine, and drilling machine, at the same time. This system is called *multiprocess holding*. In other words, the single-skilled worker, a concept which previously prevailed in Toyota factories, has become a *multiskilled worker*.

In a multiprocess holding line, a worker handles several machines of various processes one by one. Work at each process will proceed only when the worker completes his or her given jobs within a cycle time. As a result, the introduction of each unit to the line is balanced by the completion of another unit of finished product, as ordered by the operations of a cycle time. Such production is called *one-piece production and conveyance*. This rearrangement produces the following benefits:

- The elimination of unnecessary inventory between each process.
- A decrease in the number of workers required, and a resulting increase in productivity.
- As workers become multiskilled, they can participate in the total system of a factory and feel greater job satisfaction.
- By becoming multiskilled, workers can work in teams and help each other.

The concept of multiskilled workers is Japanese. In U.S. and European companies, many different labor unions co-exist in a single plant. A turner, for example, handles only a lathe, and usually will not work on any other kind of machine. In Japan, on the other hand, only one companywide union exists in each company, which facilitates worker mobility. Obviously, this difference may pose a major obstacle for U.S. and European companies wishing to adopt the Toyota production system.

***Job Standardization.*** Toyota's standard operations differ from the usual operations in that they mainly show the sequential routine of various operations overseen by a multifunctional worker handling multiple kinds of machines. Two kinds of sheets show standard operations: (1) the *standard operations routine sheet*, which looks like the usual worker-machine chart, and (2) the *standard operations sheet*, which is displayed in the factory for all workers to see. The latter sheet specifies the cycle time, standard operations routine, and standard quantity of the work in process.

*Cycle time*, or tact time, is the standard specified number of minutes and seconds in which each line must produce one product or part. This is computed using the following formulas (the necessary output per month is predetermined from the demand side):

$$\text{Required daily output} = \frac{\text{required monthly output}}{\text{operating days per month}}$$

$$\text{Cycle Time} = \frac{\text{daily operating hours}}{\text{required daily output}}$$

Once a month, the central planning office will inform each production department of this required daily quantity and the cycle time. In turn, each process manager will determine the number of workers required to produce one unit of output in a cycle time for this process. The factory's entire workforce must then be repositioned to reduce the operation rate of each process to a minimum number of workers.

Kanban are not the only sources of information given to each process. A kanban is a type of production dispatching information during the month in question, whereas the daily quantity and cycle time information are given in advance to prepare the factorywide master production schedule.

The standard operations routine indicates the operations sequence that should be followed by a worker handling multiple processes. This is the work order to pick up the material, put it on the machine, and remove it after processing. This operations order continues for the various machines handled. Line balancing can be achieved among workers in this department because they will finish all their operations within the cycle time.

The standard quantity of work in process is the minimum quantity of work in process within a production line, which includes the work attached to machines. Without this quantity of work, the predetermined sequence of various kinds of machines in the whole line cannot operate simultaneously. Theoretically, however, if the invisible conveyor belt is achieved in this line, there is no need to have any between-process inventory.

**Autonomation.** As noted previously, the two pillars that support the Toyota production system are just-in-time and autonomation. To achieve perfect JIT, all the units flowing to the subsequent process must be defect-free, and this flow must be rhythmic and without interruption. Therefore, quality control must co-exist with the JIT operation throughout the kanban system. Autonomation means building into a mechanism the means to prevent mass-producing defects in machines or production lines. The word "autonomation" (*jidoka*) is not automation, but the ability to respond to any abnormalities that occur in a process.

The autonomous machine is a machine to which an automatic stopping device is attached. Almost all Toyota machines are autonomous, preventing the mass-production of defects and automatically checking machine breakdowns. This so-called "mistake-proofing" (*baka-yoke* or *poka-yoke*) system is one mechanism that prevents defects by putting checking devices on the tools and machines.

Autonomation also extends to manual production lines. If something abnormal occurs in a production line, the worker pushes a stop button, thereby stopping the entire line. At Toyota, the *andon* system is important in performing this autonomous check, and it is an example of Toyota's visual control system (VCS). For the purpose of troubleshooting in each process, an electric light board, or *andon*, indicating a line stop is hung high enough in a factory to be seen easily by everyone. When a worker needs help adjusting to a job delay, he or she turns on the yellow light. If he or she needs the line stopped to make a machine adjustment, the red light is turned on. In summary, autonomation is a mechanism that autonomously checks anything unusual in a process.

*Improvement Activities.* The Toyota production system integrates and attains different goals, such as quantity control, quality assurance, and respect for the worker, while pursuing its ultimate goal of reducing costs. The process by which all these goals are realized is *improvement activities*, a fundamental element of the Toyota system. Each worker has the opportunity to make suggestions and propose improvements via small groups called *QC circles*. This suggestion-making process encourages improvements in quantity control, by adapting standard operations routines to changes in cycle time; in quality assurance, by preventing recurrence of defective works and machines; and, lastly, in respect for the worker, by allowing each worker to participate in the production process.

*Conclusion.* The basic purpose of the Toyota production system is to increase profits by reducing costs — that is, by completely eliminating waste such as excessive inventory or workforce. The concept of costs in this context is broad. It is essentially the past, present, or future cash outlay deducted from sales revenue to attain a profit. Therefore, costs include not only manufacturing costs (reduced by cutting the workforce), but also administrative, capital (reduced by inventory cuts), and sales costs. To achieve cost reduction, production must promptly and flexibly adapt to changes in market demand without having wasteful slacks. This ideal is accomplished through just-in-time, producing the necessary items in the necessary quantities, at the necessary time. At Toyota, the kanban system has been developed to facilitate production during a month and manage JIT. To implement the kanban system, production must be smoothed to level both quantities and variety in the withdrawal of parts by the final assembly line. Such leveling will require reducing the production lead time because various parts must be produced promptly each day. This can be attained by small-lot or one-piece production and conveyance. Small-lot production can be achieved through short-ened setup times, and one-piece production achieved by the multi-skilled workers of the multiprocess holding line. Standard operations routines will ensure the completion of all jobs necessary to process one unit of a product in a cycle time. The JIT production of 100-percent defect-free products will be ensured by autonomation (autonomous defect control systems). Finally, improvement activities will contribute to the overall process by modifying standard operations, eliminating defects, and, finally, by raising worker morale.

Where have these basic ideas come from? What need evoked them? They are believed to have come from the market constraints that characterized the Japanese automobile industry in postwar days: great variety within small production quantities. After 1950, Toyota thought it would be dangerous to blindly imitate the Ford system, which minimized the average unit cost by producing large quantities. U.S. techniques of mass production were effective in the high-growth period, which lasted until 1973. In the low-growth period that followed the oil crisis, however, the Toyota production system attracted more attention and was adopted by many industries in Japan to increase profit by decreasing costs and waste.

The Toyota production system is a unique, revolutionary system. The only problems foreign companies may have adopting it are labor unions and the multiskilled worker concept. U.S. and European companies could adopt this system, but might encounter difficulties if they apply it partially. Many Japanese companies are already using it in its imperfect, as well as its perfect form. The kanban system and production leveling could be particularly important to U.S. and European companies. To implement fully the Toyota system, upper management must proceed through the bargaining process with unions, a process often experienced by many Japanese companies as well.

# 7

## Planning and Control of Maintenance Costs for Total Productive Maintenance

*Kiyoshi Okamoto, Professor of Accounting,*
*Hitotsubashi University*

When operators played the primary role in producing goods, the secret to a manufacturing company's success was to increase operator efficiency. Efficiency engineers, therefore, conducted time and motion studies to determine physical standards that ultimately developed into the standard costs system used in the United States.

In Japan today, highly automated manufacturing facilities are used in industrial plants. Japan, in fact, has the largest number of robots in the world. Under these circumstances, machines as well as operators play an essential part in production. As a result, the secret to a manufacturer's success is to maximize the effectiveness of machines and equipment. The total productive maintenance (TPM) concept was developed by Japanese manufacturing companies to meet such needs. Because this managerial technique is remarkably useful not only for making full use of manufacturing facilities, but for improving the business constitution of a company as a whole, TPM is accepted as a profitable technique throughout leading manufacturing companies. Thus, a cost system is urgently required to supply relevant information for TPM activities.

*The Irrelevance of U.S. Productive Maintenance (PM) for Japan.* First, a brief explanation of TPM is necessary. Its origin, productive maintenance (PM), can be found in many U.S. industries. It was first introduced in Japan in the early 1950s, when a PM study group was organized by 20 Japanese companies. This study group later became the Japan Institute of Plant Maintenance (JIPM).

It should be noted that maintenance costs have gradually replaced repair costs in the field of cost accounting. This phenomenon is undoubtedly due to the development of PM, which consists of:

1. *Maintenance prevention*: In the first step, a design department's goal is to design maintenance-free equipment.
2. *Preventive maintenance*: After introducing equipment into manufacturing departments, periodic as well as predictive maintenance should be made by the maintenance department. It will prevent breakdown of machines by monitoring the oscillation and heat of equipment.
3. *Breakdown maintenance*: These are *ex post facto* repairs that include unexpected as well as expected failures. It should be noted that, for economic reasons, some repairs should be made after failure.
4. *Corrective maintenance*: This means the redesigning of equipment to prevent or reduce failures, and to facilitate easy maintenance.

Although the concept of PM was attractive, it did not work in Japanese factories. The reason was that, in the United States, PM was carried out by the maintenance department — not the operators. When a machine stopped, the operator would simply ask the maintenance person to repair it. The operator felt the repair was not his or her job. Because of this functional division, operators knew little about their machines, and improper use resulted in damage and stoppages. The rate of operator injuries was high, and the quality of manufactured goods was low. Much of the work in process was defective. And while the maintenance workers repaired the machines, the operators were idle. The long and short of PM based on function was that, while it encouraged individual responsibility, it diminished the goal orientation of employees.

*TPM's Essential Nature.* In 1969, Nippondenso Co., Ltd., part of the Toyota group and one of the largest manufacturers of automobile electrical parts, developed TPM — or "PM with all employees participating through small-group activities." Continuing its implementation of the TPM program until 1971, the company was awarded the 1971 Distinguished Plant Prize, or PM prize, for its results by the PM

Prize Committee of the Japan Institute of Plant Engineers, predecessor of the JIPM. The committee understood the value of Nippondenso's PM methods, and decided to encourage TPM concepts and procedures throughout Japan's manufacturing companies.

"Total" has three meanings in TPM. First, it means the total system of PM; that is, establishing a production maintenance system that covers the entire life of the equipment, from initial investment to disinvestment. Second, it means realizing total or overall equipment effectiveness at minimum life-cycle costs. To maximize equipment effectiveness, TPM makes every effort to eliminate the six major losses that interfere with effective equipment operation. These are downtime losses caused by (1) equipment failure, (2) setup and adjustment, (3) idling and minor stoppages, (4) reduced speed of equipment, (5) defects and rework, and (6) reduced yield due to the discrepancy between startup and stable production. The overall equipment effectiveness can be calculated as follows:

$$\text{Overall equipment effectiveness} = \begin{array}{l} \text{Availability} \times \\ \text{Performance efficiency} \times \\ \text{Rate of quality products} \end{array}$$

$$(\text{Availability} = \frac{\text{loading time} - \text{downtime}}{\text{loading time} \times 100})$$

$$\begin{array}{l}(\text{Performance} \\ \text{efficiency}\end{array} = \frac{\text{theoretical cycle time} \times \text{processed amount}}{}$$

$$\begin{array}{l}(\text{Rate of quality} \\ \text{products}\end{array} = \frac{\text{processed amount} - \text{amount of defects}}{}$$

Third, "total" means the total participation of all company people, from the president to workers on the plant floor, in TPM activities. When top management decides to adopt TPM projects, it officially declares the importance of implementing TPM and winning the PM Prize as a company goal for the next three or four years. TPM groups are established from top to bottom, according to the company's organizational structure. A specific line or plant is designated as a model, and PM activities are thoroughly implemented under the guidance of a special consultant sent by JIPM. The information and expertise gathered at the model site is diffused throughout the system.

TPM's unique feature is its motivational management through small-group activities. At the bottom of the TPM organization are small groups of floor workers. A group consists of several operators and one leader. They all choose a name for their group, such as a flower or comic-book hero. Their first step in implementing TPM is to clean up the dust and dirt on their equipment and floor. They decide among themselves who will clean what part and how. They discuss how to improve and alleviate problems, such as places that are difficult to clean and lubricate. Maintenance specialists teach the group leader how the machines work and how to inspect them. The leaders, in turn, teach the operators. Say, for instance, that a machine is out of order every five minutes or so. Operators record the details of these stoppages, such as what part of the machine stops and for how long, on a piece of paper taped to the piece of equipment. They learn from analyzing the data, and propose improvement methods to the company, such as changing the shape or material of the machine part. The consciousness of operators is gradually changed. They begin to think, "This equipment is mine. I'll take care of it." It should be emphasized that TPM is supported and promoted through independent operator maintenance, in cooperation with the maintenance department.

*Some Outstanding TPM Results.* I recently observed a company that had successfully decreased the number of unexpected equipment failures, from 298 cases to 20 cases a month, about a 97-percent decrease, over four years of TPM activities. This enabled the company to integrate lot production previously manufactured in separate processes into a single, continuous-flow production process. From this one production change, the total distance between processes decreased 60 percent, labor hours for a main product decreased 35 percent, and total amount of work in process decreased 45 percent. Such results are not unusual for PM prize winners. Visiting customers are surprised now by the factory's cleanliness and are more willing to place orders with the company. They trust that product quality must be high because the equipment is well maintained and the factory floor is spotless. As the number of improvement proposals by employees increases, most major equipment is constructed from designs developed within the company, rather than being purchased from outside. No doubt the high employee morale and the ability to develop and design equipment have produced an immeasurable earning power for the future.[1]

*Establishing a Maintenance Cost Concept.* Because its goal is to maximize equipment effectiveness at minimum life-cycle costs, TPM needs relevant cost information for its implementation. The life-cycle costs consist of (1) the initial investment, including research and development costs; (2) running costs, including maintenance costs; (3) logistic costs, including training costs; and (4) divestment. Because the information for capital expenditure decisions is significant for TPM, we will limit this chapter to the important area of maintenance costs. These are all costs incurred for equipment maintenance, which consist of:

1. *Maintenance expense:* This expense is comprised of (a) maintenance material, (b) maintenance labor, and (c) maintenance expense disbursed to other companies. These costs are outlay costs used for costing products and determining income. Although this natural classification of maintenance expense is important for external reporting, more significant classifications that should be adopted for internal TPM reporting will be described later.

2. *Downtime losses from equipment stoppages:* These losses are classified into downtime losses from (a) planned PM maintenance, and (b) unexpected equipment failure. Both are evaluated by opportunity costs. Companies without TPM rarely calculate downtime losses, even though the information is important for judging the effectiveness of maintenance activities.

3. *Other losses due to equipment failure:* These losses include (a) spoilage loss, (b) the cost of rework, and (c) loss due to accidents directly caused by unexpected equipment failure.

Next, we will discuss planning and controlling maintenance costs.

*Changing the Emphasis from Breakdown Maintenance to Preventive Maintenance.* In companies without TPM, maintenance costs usually are planned and controlled by the budget department. Maintenance materials, labor, and expenses paid to outside repair shops are compared with a department's budget, item by item. Some companies use a variable or flexible budget instead of a static one for planning and controlling maintenance costs. This method, however, has two significant limitations.

First, a variable budget lacks information on maintenance objectives. When the total system of productive maintenance is introduced in a company, top management should emphasize a shift from breakdown maintenance to preventive maintenance. In other words, the budgeted cost of preventive maintenance should be increased and that of breakdown maintenance decreased. Such a policy should be confirmed in the control process. To confirm the preventive maintenance policy, some companies measure the following indexes in maintenance hours:

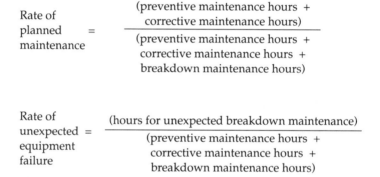

$$\text{Rate of planned maintenance} = \frac{\text{(preventive maintenance hours + corrective maintenance hours)}}{\text{(preventive maintenance hours + corrective maintenance hours + breakdown maintenance hours)}}$$

$$\text{Rate of unexpected equipment failure} = \frac{\text{(hours for unexpected breakdown maintenance)}}{\text{(preventive maintenance hours + corrective maintenance hours + breakdown maintenance hours)}}$$

Although these indexes are useful, the physical data should be evaluated in dollars as well. Thus, the budget for maintenance costs should be classified and planned in terms of productive maintenance objectives: MP (maintenance prevention), PM (preventive maintenance), CM (corrective maintenance), and BM (breakdown maintenance).

Second, a variable budget lacks information for maintenance costs by equipment unit. The departmental comparison of materials, labor, and expenses of maintenance with their budget is not accurate enough for practical use. The comparison of actual costs with the budget allowance should be made for an equipment unit, as well as for the objectives of productive maintenance. Without this information, it is impossible for management to judge the effectiveness of maintenance costs, which should be realized by a decrease in unexpected equipment failures.

*Rating the Importance of Equipment by PM Standards.* It is difficult and troublesome for a cost center to record maintenance costs both by equipment unit and by maintenance objectives. Most TPM factories rate equipment importance by PM standards.

I once observed an electrical appliances factory producing refrigerators ranking their equipment into *A*, *B*, and *C* categories according to production, quality, safety, and maintenance standards. For example, equipment *A* are those machines that:

- Have a potential for producing a large decrease in production.
- Have a potential for producing significant defects in product quality.
- Produce dangerous situations for operators during equipment failure.
- Might fail more often than once every three months.

If a machine falls into one of the above categories, it is classified as an *A* and the letter "A" is attached to it. Internally developed equipment is usually ranked *A*.

As an aside, the operators in this factory gave *A* equipment a pet name. A photograph of the leader was pasted on it and its "birthday" (the day the machine was installed) was indicated on a neighboring bulletin board.

Each group of operators had its own microcomputer, into which they input data such as development costs; installation costs; monthly operation rate; numbers and causes of failure; mean time between failures (MTBF); and maintenance costs for PM, CM, BM, and others. Using these data, they investigated failure causes and planned when parts would be replaced and by whom. Through their small-group activities, they kept the company informed about how the equipment could be improved. Accordingly, we should compare the actual maintenance costs of *A* equipment with the proposed budget by each equipment unit and also by the maintenance objectives. On the other hand, we need only compare the actual costs for *B* and *C* equipment with their proposed budgets in the departmental gross amounts.

*Planning Maintenance Costs.* Most non-TPM companies base their maintenance costs budget for a coming period on past experience. They divide the maintenance costs by sales, production volume, manufacturing costs, or the amount of fixed assets. This type of developed budget is, however, only a rough estimate. The TPM companies, on the other hand, base their budget on the following procedures:

1. With the maintenance department's support, top management determines the maintenance cost policy for the coming period. The following points are considered:

   - The budget for maintenance costs should be planned to include adjustments of variable factors, such as additional investments or disinvestments, the planned production volume for the next period, and any changes of maintenance standards or other considerations. To do this, maintenance costs should be classified into long-term and short-term costs. Some equipment has a long-term (or more than a year) maintenance cycle. Additionally, some maintenance costs will be incurred in the next year only. Such long-term cycle costs and extraordinary costs should be estimated specifically, while the short-term cycle costs should be classified into variable and fixed components.
   - The special priority given to allocating more money for maintenance costs should go to preventive maintenance (PM) and corrective maintenance (CM). Equipment with an A ranking, which experiences frequent unexpected failures in this period, deserves additional allocations.
   - The main themes for improving maintenance costs for the next period should be established. A special project team, for example, can be organized to reduce the inventory of spare parts. In-house maintenance workers are encouraged to decrease the repair costs incurred by using outside repair companies. This requires classifying the maintenance costs into internal and external maintenance.

2. Based on a profit plan, the cost center determines a gross limit for the next period's maintenance costs.
3. Considering the maintenance costs policy as well as past experience, each department that requires maintenance work prepares a maintenance budget. As already described, small groups of operators in each manufacturing department implement self-maintenance, although the highly technical repairs are implemented by the maintenance department.
4. In the maintenance department, the total departmental budget requirements for maintenance is reconciled with the gross limits recommended by the cost center.
5. Top management's executive committee determines a formal maintenance budget.

***Downtime Loss Evaluated by Opportunity Costs.*** The object of using downtime loss information is not only to evaluate the performance of TPM activities, but also to make decisions, such as whether or not specific maintenance should come from within or outside the company. A film manufacturer calculated the downtime loss by departmental fixed cost rate in the following way:

$$\text{A process's hourly fixed cost rate} = \frac{\text{(the process costs — variable costs + applied fixed costs of service departments)}}{\text{(a process's total monthly operating hours}}$$

$$\text{Downtime loss} = \text{a process's hourly fixed cost rate} \times \text{unexpected failure hours of stoppage}$$

This is the traditional method of computing idle capacity variance. While it might be useful for performance evaluation, it is not useful for decision making.

For companies using TPM, we recommend the following method. The cost factor should be an opportunity cost because downtime represents lost opportunities in equipment use. The kind of opportunity cost used, however, depends on the situation. If the equipment loss simply cannot be recovered and results in lost sales, the lost hours should be viewed in light of the product's contribution margin. If the cost opportunity is recoverable through overtime or by using an outside repair company, the lost hours should be equated to overtime labor costs or as disbursed maintenance expense. It should be noted that lost hours have no value when broken equipment is idle.

*Evaluating the Effectiveness of Maintenance Costs.* It is difficult to measure the effectiveness of incurred maintenance costs. A decrease in maintenance costs simply may reflect a poor level of maintenance. Engineers, on the other hand, are apt to overemphasize equipment maintenance without considering economics. Because the relationship between cause and effect in maintenance is ambiguous and difficult to trace, most TPM companies adopt multiple measures for evaluation.

1. *Observing incurred maintenance costs:*

   • First, total incurred maintenance costs, with their constituent elements of variable costs, fixed costs, and downtime losses, should be reported and compared with past data to reach an overview on the situation. (See Figure 7.1.)

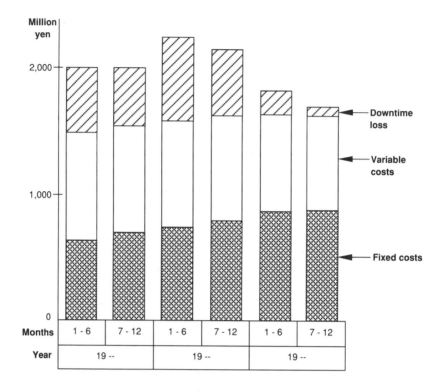

Figure 7.1 Hypothetical Overview of Maintenance Costs

• Next, the increase or decrease of maintenance costs must be related to production volume and the number of machines because increased maintenance costs might be expected with increases in production and fixed assets. The two rates, therefore, should be computed and compared with the past (see Figure 7.2).

$$(1) \text{ Variable cost rate } = \frac{\text{variable maintenance costs}}{\text{current production volume}}$$

$$(2) \text{ Fixed cost rate } = \frac{\text{fixed maintenance costs}}{\text{average number of machines}}$$

It is favorable to have a decrease in both rates when there is also a decrease in unexpected equipment failure.

• Another measure is the comparison of disbursed maintenance expenses with those budgeted. A top management policy for the

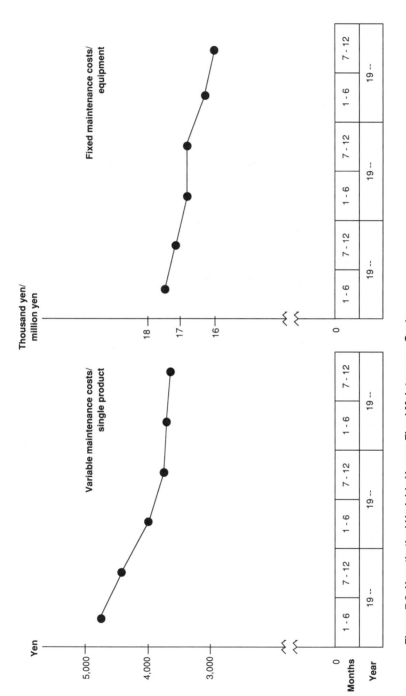

**Figure 7.2 Hypothetical Variable Versus Fixed Maintenance Costs**

period already described is to encourage internal maintenance to reduce outside maintenance expenses. It should be determined whether or not each department's maintenance expenses stay within the budget. If the payments are more than the budget allows, there should be an investigation. (See Figure 7.3.)

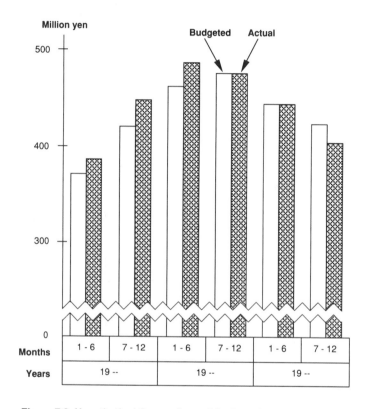

Figure 7.3 Hypothetical Comparison of Budgeted Versus Actual Maintenance Costs

2. *Reviewing the performance of maintenance objectives.* It is important for TPM companies to confirm increases in the rate of planned maintenance

(PM + CM/PM + CM + BM)

which signifies a change of company attitude from defensive to aggressive maintenance. Actual maintenance costs incurred, classified by preventive (PM), corrective (CM), and breakdown (BM), should be reported and compared with the past. (See Figure 7.4.)

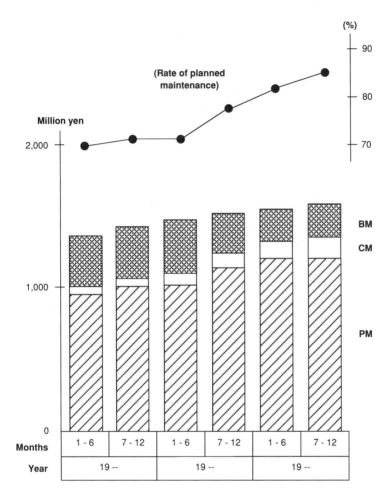

Figure 7.4 Hypothetical Comparison of Preventive Maintenance (PM), Corrective Maintenance (CM), and Breakdown Maintenance (BM)

Corrective maintenance investment and its effect on opportunity costs should be compared. (See Figure 7.5.)

3. *Evaluating progress toward the maintenance goal.* The goal of incurring maintenance costs is to improve equipment effectiveness. We

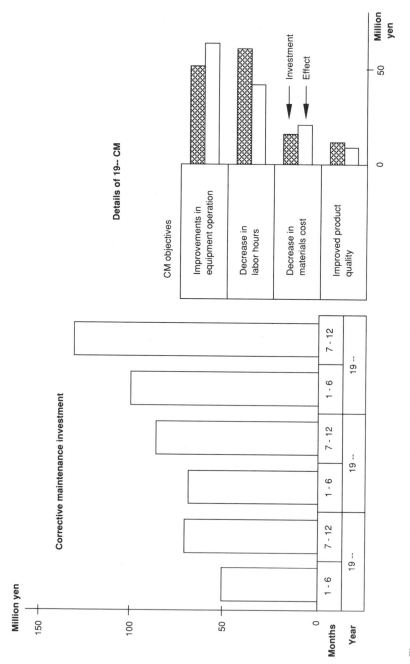

**Figure 7.5 Hypothetical Comparison of Corrective Maintenance Investment**

can measure this achievement by a variety of indexes. The following are typical examples:

- The number of unexpected equipment failures per month (see Figure 7.6).

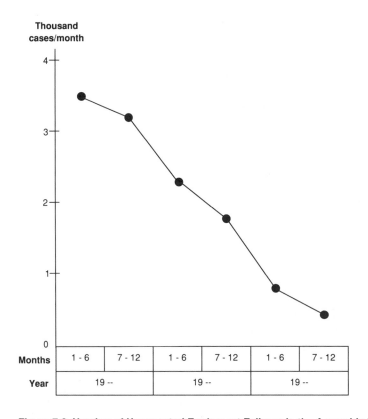

**Figure 7.6 Number of Unexpected Equipment Failures in the Assembly Department**

$$\text{The rate of unexpected equipment failure hours} = \frac{\text{stoppage hours due to unexpected equipment failures}}{\text{planned operating hours}}$$

The above equation is computed by workers in the manufacturing cells in each process, and evaluated with the maintenance costs incurred in those cells. (See Figure 7.7.)

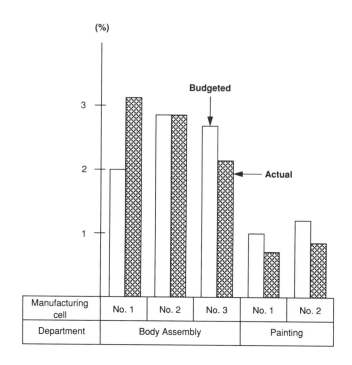

**Figure 7.7 Rate of Unexpected Equipment Failure Hours**

***The Future's Unsolved Problems.*** We have thus far considered TPM's maintenance costs. Can we now determine the optimal amount for equipment? Since maintenance costs are one of the constituent elements of a machine's life-cycle cost, they should be considered in connection with costs for research and development, construction, installation, operation, logistics, and disinvestment of the equipment. The study of life-cycle costing, however, has its limits. On the one hand, this costing can be applied to equipment with a life of four or five years and can be reinvested. Automotive companies have paid close attention to this costing, and have accumulated the necessary data in their maintenance departments. On the other hand, it cannot be applied to equipment with a life-span of, say, 20 years. Flour milling companies, for example, are not particularly interested in life-cycle costing.

There are additional problems. A leading company announced that it has earned ¥400 million from a four-year TPM project at a cost of ¥100 million. Although this was an accumulated result of four years, a periodic income determination for a TPM project would be necessary because of the time lag between input and output of TPM activities. The largest output might be achieved the year following TPM activities. It is necessary for management to know whether or not the output or effect of TPM can be maintained in the future. The earnings from a TPM project include cost savings that would have been lost had the TPM project not been introduced. A manufacturing cell, for example, may use TPM to successfully decrease lot processing by 5 hours. The cost of labor saved might be computed by multiplying the 5 hours saved by the cell's average labor rate. If these 5 hours are not spent in some productive use, however, a labor savings is not achieved. Saving labor hours does not always result in decreasing the number of workers. Thus, finding the method for computing the effects of a TPM project is one of the largest and most urgent problems for Japanese TPM companies.

### Notes

1. For more details about TPM, please refer to Plant Engineering, File 5543 (March 13, 1986). For more details about the Japanese Institute of Plant Engineers (JIPE), refer to *Plant Engineering*, File 5501 (June 12, 1986).

# 8

## Using a Structured Matrix as a Decision Support System in Materials Flow and Cost Planning

*Hiroshi Sugiura, Systems Planning Section,*
*Fukuyama Ironworks, NKK Steel*
*Yasuhiro Monden, Institute of Socio-Economic Planning,*
*University of Tsukuba*

Cost calculation systems have evolved from simple financial accounting and cost control to those having a role in administrative planning. Until now, however, they lacked a multipurpose function capable of responding to any decision-making problems. Also, they have functioned apart from consolidated systems capable of simultaneously achieving materials flow control and cost control.

This chapter will explain a new cost calculation system: a decision-making support system that applies and develops the "structured matrix" theory. This new system, called "SMART," can aid managers in such areas as equipment investment, operations planning, technical development, and budget formulation, helping them predict the effects changes in the make-up of products, or alterations in the flow of goods, might exert upon cost. It will now be possible to evaluate the record of operations in terms of individual cost factors, uncovering the items pertinent to rationalization. This system can also provide the information necessary for making prompt, clear decisions.

*Problems of the Previous Cost Reduction System.* The case study introduced in this chapter describes Fukuyama Ironworks of Nippon Steel, or Nippon Kokan (NKK). Since 1966, we had been developing cost reduction systems aimed at operations effectiveness and meeting successive demands. Our improvement goal was to reduce the number of calculations, which were rapidly increasing with the development and expansion of the foundries. With the variety of our needs increasing, the system's inflexibility became more manifest.

The purpose of cost reduction at Nippon Steel is to analyze quickly and accurately all the information needed for profit accounting in the corporate profit management system. When the previous cost reduction systems were viewed with that in mind, all batch processing formulae lacked flexibility. Even small recalculations were impossible to handle. The new, complicated, and diversified management demands were even more impossible to incorporate. Information needed for sales forecasts was received from the head office. The costs and logistics needed to calculate the product quantities and necessary work hours for each mill and the cost accounting of finished products by ton were carried out on separate processing systems.

The ease and rapidity of carrying out cost analysis that copes with cost pressure factors caused by unreliability of raw materials, changing energy prices, increasing labor costs, and sluggish operating rates are important functional conditions in cost reduction systems. At the same time, a system was needed that could quickly adapt to the constantly changing business environment of high quality, value-adding products being demanded in greater variety and smaller lot sizes — not to speak of developing technology and new production processes. It became apparent that we needed to upgrade our cost reduction systems from being centered around financial accounting to control accounting through a cost control concept and, then, on to planning accounting. This is the background for NKK's development of SMART described here.

*Contributions of the New System.* To allow flexible and prompt response to changes in multiple management viewpoints, the Decision Support System (DSS) requirement should first and foremost be incorporated into the new cost-price management system is. With this, managers themselves can autonomously drive the system. In other words, the system should possess an on-line interactive processing function in which the flow of system processing itself is in a form the user can readily understand. The most important requirement for this is the system's ability to immediately reflect the user's intentions. With this in mind, research was initiated to explore how to construct a mechanism capable of accomplishing the following:

- Accommodating the fact that for materials flow, which is the basic process in cost accounting, accumulation and calculation occur in a downstream process (the finished product manufacturing process).
- Accommodating cost, which flows in an upstream process (the raw material processes).
- Easily grasping changes in calculation methods, changes in the materials flow, or fluctuations in cost.

In the course of this research, the "structured matrix" was encountered. This means the materialization of the "datafication" of program logic, always a problem for the systems division. For the cost control division, it embodies a visual and commutable system. It is, moreover, a system friendly to users.

In developing the new system, it became clear that if the "structured matrix" was not adopted, the desired system was impossible. In the midst of development there appeared "SMART," an on-line, interactive, all-purpose package that uses a structured matrix. SMART will be described later, but its position in the cost control system is shown in Figure 8.1.

The system's special feature, in terms of calculation structure, is its consolidation of materials flow and cost calculation operations. Moreover, rather than representing the entire materials flow (see Figure 8.2) in a single structured matrix, there is a subdivision into nine plant structures and one supporting division structure, in accordance with actual business. When it comes to single- and multi-structure processing linked into chained-structure processing, it is possible for the user to freely make the selection.

The new system fulfills two special requirements: (1) the fulfillment of the on-line interactive function, and (2) improved maintenance. We might add that these are indispensable requirements for a decision-making support system. The on-line interactive functioning puts all information needed for management purposes is put in data bases; it can be freely retrieved, altered, or erased at any time due to general purpose data references and maintenance tools.

In addition, there is often a demand for a dynamic response to sudden and rapidly changing control needs. Conventional report processing, until now used for range analysis and special cost accounting figuring in cost reduction management tasks, is by itself no

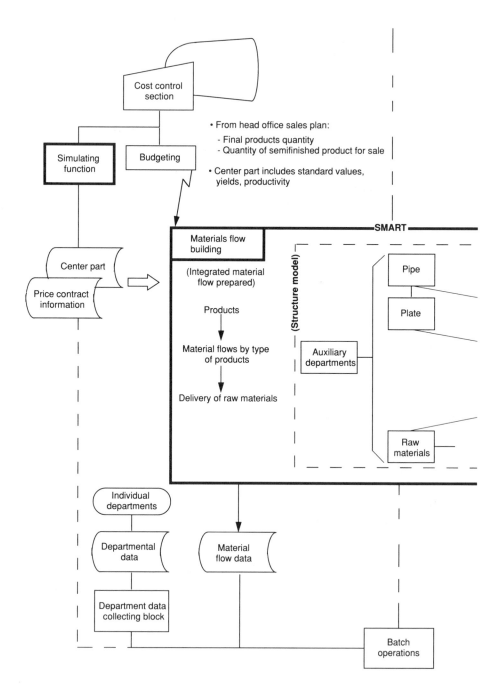

**Figure 8.1  SMART's Position in the New System**

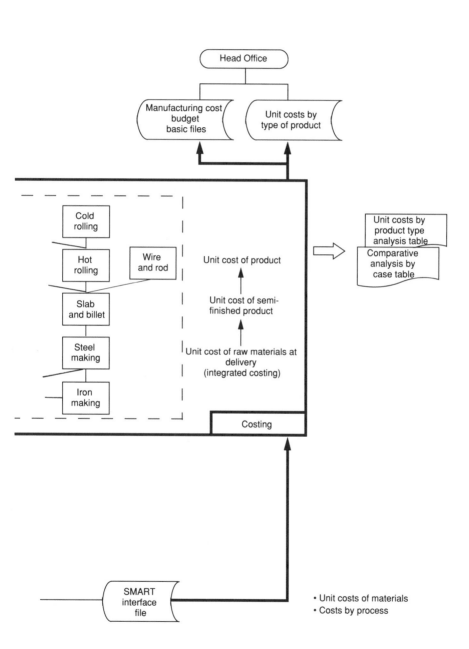

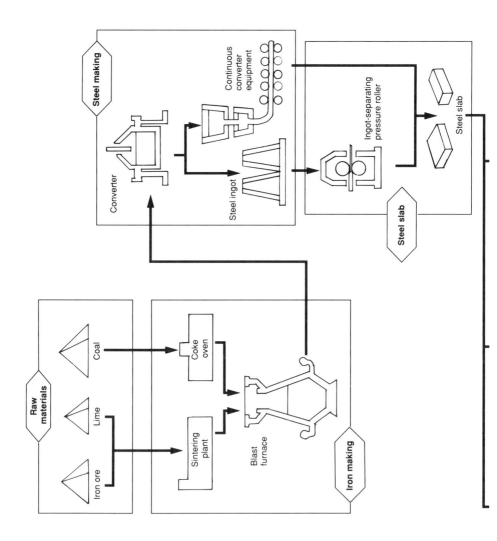

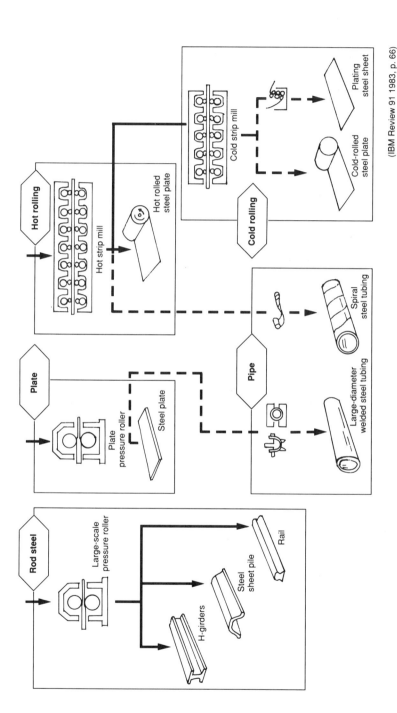

(IBM Review 91 1983, p. 66)

**Figure 8.2  How Materials Flow and Cost Calculation Operations Are Consolidated**

longer adequate to deal with the demands of today. General purpose packages for drawing up simple reports are available on computer terminals, and ways are being devised to allow what-if calculations to be carried out in interactive form through the utilization of SMART.

Another special feature of the new system is batch processing. Portions to be trial-and-error processed can take place on-line. For example, when a large quantity of calculations must be executed simultaneously, batch processing can accomplish this task. Functional allotment through batch processing can be planned with the aim of increasing the system's operating efficiency.

The next feature discussed is improved maintenance. In previous systems, changes in processing tasks were always directly linked with programming modifications. It is now possible to build a maintenance-free system that easily makes changes in materials flow, additions to the process, and control index changes. These changes can all be carried out easily and directly by the user.

The structured matrix also promotes mastery of accounting logic previously inexpressible with a structured matrix. When calculating cost allocations, for example, by making shifts in the control point, it is possible to flexibly modify the method or coefficient of the allocation process. For the user, this is the mark of a very effective new system. In addition, conventional calculation features such as materials flow and cost, once processed separately, can now be built into a simple system structure unified by a single common structural expression. This contributes greatly to improved ease of maintenance.

The new system, in any case, has at its nucleus the interactive general purpose, structured matrix handler SMART. It enjoys all the advantages of the structured matrix principle and can be said to represent a decision-making support tool. From the user's point of view, an important advantage of the new system is that the materials flow and cost calculation procedures, which were previously incorporated as program logic, are now expressed as structures. This makes them easy to understand. In light of the back-and-forth nature of the monitoring activity that takes place between management and manufacturing divisions, this transparency and impartiality of systems processing is significant.

With earlier systems, the person in charge was required to spend many hours learning the system's arrangement. With the structured matrix application, however, merely comprehending the structure makes both the task and the system understandable; the process of facing the screen, looking up the present structure, and executing it, becomes part of the basic training for managers.

There are other advantages. With the adoption of interactive-style processing, the calculation cycle becomes short, and managing becomes easy. As managers, themselves, carry out system mainte-nance such as process modifications, their abilities improve, and more scrupulous management becomes possible. With various simu-lations easily achievable, particularly by altering standard values in cost calculation, it becomes possible to carry out precise information processing in the midst of a wide variety of choices.

*The Structure of the New System.* As previously described, the new cost control system exploits the structured matrix principle, and is structured around the general purpose package SMART.

SMART (which stands for Structured Matrices Advancing Ra-tional Technology) is an on-line interactive general purpose system package that we developed based on the theory and principles of structured matrices. Without an understanding of SMART it is not possible to explain the new system's structure. The special features and functions of SMART, accordingly, will be introduced here by way of explaining the structure of the new system.

SMART is a general purpose tool which, through the medium of all the screen functions, in interactive fashion, carries out tasks such as structural matrix construction, modification, and execution. Before introducing SMART, we will briefly explain the structured matrix upon which it is based.

**Structure and principle of structured matrices.** The structure of a structured matrix, as Figure 8.3 illustrates, is a table of multi-level structure in which single matrix elements in turn form matrices (a table of progressively detailed development). In the upper and left-hand margins of the table are the data and list of constituent ele-ments, or "komponent list" (KOL), that describe the items. The upper and left-hand margins arrange the same content. KOLs that bear no quantitative relationship whatsoever to other KOLs can be omitted.

As far as the structured matrix calculation principle is con-cerned, as Figure 8.4 illustrates there is a vertical multiplication and horizontal summing-up theoretical relationship among the various data of the upper, middle, and left margins. These are expressed in

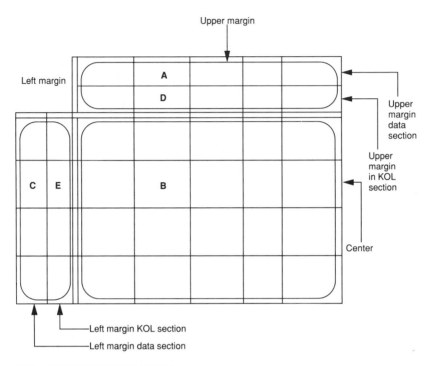

A, C = Vectors (data arranged in a row)

B = Matrix (data arrayed)

D = Description of individual data in A

E = Description of individual data in C

Individual data in B are explained by both D and E

**Figure 8.3  The Structure of a Structured Matrix**

formulas, $B = M1 \times A$, $C = M2 \times B$, and $D = M3 \times B + M4 \times C$. Along with these vertical multiplication and horizontal summing-up relationships, depending on the structure, there are cases in which horizontal-multiplication and vertical summing-up relationships arise. In the cost system, the materials flow calculations and cost calculations are both carried out with a single structural expression. This is referred to as a bi-linear relationship.

The structure and principle of the structured matrix is a matter of these simple rules. For a deeper understanding, however, additional explanations are required of procedures for system development using the structured matrix.

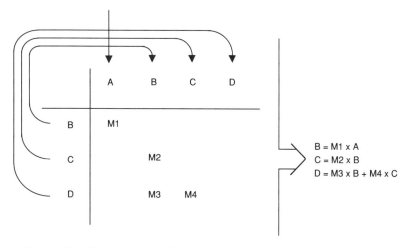

(Left margin: B, C, D; upper margin: A, B, C, D where A is predetermined variable)

**Figure 8.4 The Structured Matrix Calculation Principle**

First, the business application is analyzed, and its theory is expressed as a structured matrix. In other words, the cause-effect relationships among the relevant items are expressed in the vertical-horizontal format. This differs from previous network representations because it carries out clearly and simply the delineation of the relationships. Next, the structures' detailed data (matrix and vectors) is recorded. At this point, the preliminaries have been completed. The upper margin's departure point and predetermined variables are decided. The vertical-multiplication, horizontal summing-up principle is carried out, so that the left-hand and upper data margins are completed in gradual succession. It is also possible, when necessary, to alter the central and upper margins' data (predetermined variables) and execute a case-study simulation.

Figure 8.5 depicts the interrelationships of materials flow from plant A to plant E in terms of materials allocations and yield rates. This is, it shows that 75 percent of plant A's production output is disbursed to plant B, and 25 percent to plant D, respectively. It also shows that plant B's yield rate is 98 percent, and plant D's yield rate is 95 percent (Other process explanations are ignored for the sake of the example.). If, at present, the total volume disbursed from plant A is 100 tons, what will be the final product volume at plant E? Following

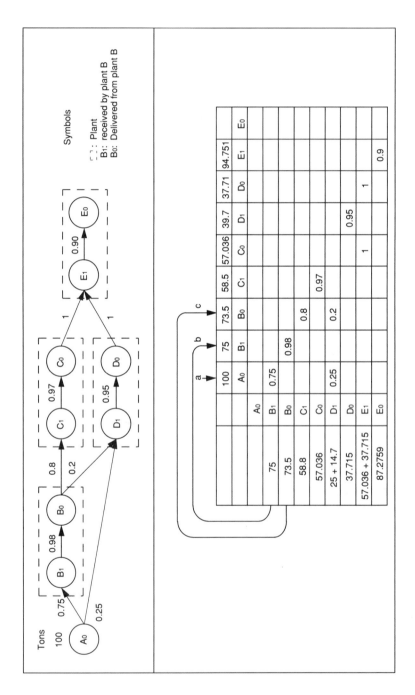

**Figure 8.5  One Example of a Structured Matrix**

the actual calculation procedures of the structured matrix, with (a) as the given amount, it is revealed that as the vertical multiplication and horizontal summing-up is repeatedly performed in a clockwise direction, (b) and (c) can be gradually determined, and the final product amount is 87.3 tons.

Compared to Figure 8.4, Figure 8.6 adds in even more in terms of product variety. It is difficult enough to visually illustrate complex and intricate processes with conventional network formats. Here, with more product varieties added, the structured matrix format is even more convenient. Moreover, even with the addition of a new process, it is not necessary to rewrite the elements, paying attention to order, as in the network format. The structured matrix is simple enough that additional entries can be made in the right margin, making sure to determine their relationships with the others. This capacity is based upon the structured matrix principle. It states that merely by structurally expressing multilevel cause-effect relationships or business processing procedures in a matrix at the start of calculations, the necessary variable items as well as the calculating system will automatically take shape.

In short, the fundamental idea of the structured matrix is to make possible a wider scope of matrix calculations of linear relationships, based upon quantitative information expressing cause-effect relationships. By applying this method, it is possible to realize in data form the calculation processing and procedures that were previously incorporated into program logic. It is also possible to easily carry out multi-faceted case study simulations. Accordingly, with qualities such as transparency of calculation processes, and the ability to respond to multi-purpose demands, the system has application effects that are both in-depth and wide-ranging.

**Materials flow calculation and cost calculation with the structured matrix.** Finally, a model example of utilizing SMART with the new cost system will be shown with Figures 8.7, 8.8, and 8.9. By following along and checking the actual calculation procedures, the reader should find it possible to imagine the new system's structure and realize SMART's effectiveness.

The left side of Figure 8.7 is the structure's macro-definition, a compressed image of the structured matrix that is displayed on the screen. On the right side, the structure's micro-definition has been appended. With these structure definitions alone, both materials flow calculations and cost calculations become possible.

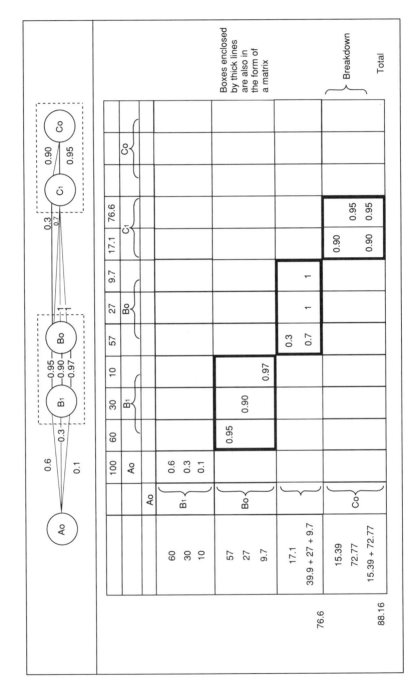

**Figure 8.6 Another Example of a Structured Matrix**

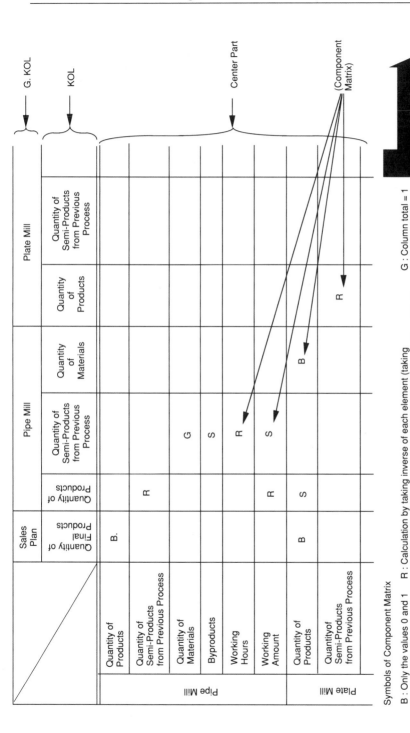

**Figure 8.7A Structure of SMART (Structured Matrix)**

Symbols of Component Matrix

B : Only the values 0 and 1   R : Calculation by taking inverse of each element (taking inverse of element in R gives working hours because element in R is tons per hour)

G : Column total = 1   S : Miscellaneous

| | | | | Sales Plan | | | | Pipe Mill | | |
|---|---|---|---|---|---|---|---|---|---|---|
| | | | | Quantity of Final Product | | | | Quantity of Products | | |
| | | | | Pipe A | Pipe B | Pipe C | Plate | Pipe A | Pipe B | Pipe C |
| | | | | $100^T$ | $200^T$ | $300^T$ | $400^T$ | 100 | 200 | 300 |
| Pipe Mill | Quantity of Products | Pipe A | 100 | 1 | 0 | 0 | 0 | | | |
| | | Pipe B | 200 | 0 | 1 | 0 | 0 | | | |
| | | Pipe C | 300 | 0 | 0 | 1 | 0 | | | |
| | Quantity of Semi-Products from Previous Process | Pipe A | 102 | | | | | .98 | 0 | 0 |
| | | Pipe B | 208 | | | | | 0 | .96 | 0 |
| | | Pipe C | 333 | | | | | 0 | 0 | .90 |
| | Quantity of Materials | Plate D | 144 | | | | | | | |
| | | Plate E | 499 | | | | | | | |
| | Byproducts | Byproducts F | -10 | | | | | | | |
| | | Byproducts G | -35 | | | | | | | |
| | Working Hours | Pipe Forming | $7.^5$ | | | | | 0 | 0 | 0 |
| | | Finishing | $8.^5$ | | | | | 100 | 80 | 60 |
| | Working Amounts | Usual | 643 | | | | | 0 | 0 | 0 |
| | | Inspection | 440 | | | | | .2 | .6 | 1 |
| | | Packing | 600 | | | | | 1 | 1 | 1 |
| Plate Mill | Quantity of Products | Plate | 400 | 0 | 0 | 0 | 1 | | | |
| | | Plate D | 144 | 0 | 0 | 0 | 0 | | | |
| | | Plate E | 499 | 0 | 0 | 0 | 0 | | | |

**Figure 8.7B**

| Pipe Mill | | | | | ◄─ G. KOL |
|---|---|---|---|---|---|
| Quantity of Semi-Products from Previous Process | | | Quantity of Materials | | ◄─ KOL |
| Pipe A | Pipe B | Pipe C | Plate D | Plate E | ◄─ KOL Item |
| 102 | 208 | 333 | 144 | 499 | ◄─ STRAND Value |
| 1 | .2 | 0 | | | |
| 0 | .8 | 1 | | | |
| -.01 | -.01 | -.02 | | | |
| -.02 | -.03 | -.08 | | | |
| 100 | 90 | 80 | | | |
| 0 | 0 | 0 | | | |
| 1 | 1 | 1 | | | |
| 0 | 0 | 0 | | | |
| 0 | 0 | 0 | | | |
| | | | 0 | 0 | |
| | | | 1 | 0 | |
| | | | 0 | 1 | |

With materials flow calculations, final product amount is calculated by going back upstream to previous processes. Thus the calculation must make rebates for the field rate, which is the in-plant management target. It must also determine the quantities of semi-products from previous processes. With the structured matrix principle alone, the inverse of the yield will have to be input into the central portion. By exploiting the matrix explained beneath Figure 8.7A (called "R"), the value of the management target itself can be input. This, too, is part of SMART's workmanship.

Figures 8.8 and 8.9 show materials flow calculations and cost calculations appearing simultaneously. By actually checking the calculation mechanism, it should be possible to see, with the same structural matrix, how materials flow calculations as well as cost calculations take place. In essence, the structure's definitions in themselves express the cost calculation mechanism.

It would be possible to represent the materials flow structure for an entire ironworks plant with a single matrix. In actual cost management systems, however, as illustrated in Figure 8.10 (see page 139), nine separate structures are defined. By linking these, processing takes place.

Among other things, this structural partitioning also makes possible narrow-field simulations with each structural unit. It facilitates management that conforms with the actual applications of the organizational entity.

The application areas of the structured matrix are not limited to the cost calculations of the present chapter. It can be applied to all planning areas, including: calculating required part quantities based on demand fluctuations (procurement planning); transport cost simulations for individual distribution channels in the sales distribution net (materials distribution planning); materials flow simulations and manufacturing cost analyses in manufacturing processes (production planning); sales terms and investment amount simulations in sales strategies (investment planning); and comprehensive planning simulations in time-series deployment (corporate administrative planning).

The MATPLAN-2 recently announced by Nihon IBM Inc. is an offshoot of the SMART program, and already nearly 30 Japanese companies are implementing it. Furthermore, its uses are not limited to industries such as iron and steel manufacturers. The structured matrix concept can be useful in building decision-making support systems in a wide range of fields.

**(1)** Initial input values (predetermined variables)
Quantity of final products = ($100^T$, $200^T$, $300^T$, $400^T$)

**(2)** Order of calculations
$1 \rightarrow 2 \rightarrow 3 \rightarrow 4 \rightarrow 5 \rightarrow 6 \rightarrow 7 \rightarrow 8 \rightarrow 9 \rightarrow 10$

**(3)** Mechanism of calculations
"Vertical multiplication and horizontal summing-up"

| | | | | |
|---|---|---|---|---|
| **Pipe Mill** | Quantity of Products | Pipe A | $100^T$ | $= 100^T \times 1 + 200^T \times 0 + 300^T \times 0 + 400^T \times 0$ |
| | | Pipe B | $200^T$ | $= 100^T \times 0 + 200^T \times 1 + 300^T \times 0 + 400^T \times 0$ |
| | | Pipe C | $300^T$ | $= 100^T \times 0 + 200^T \times 0 + 300^T \times 1 + 400^T \times 0$ |
| | Quantity of Semi-Products from Previous Process | Pipe A | $102^T$ | $= 100^T \times \frac{1}{0.98} + 200^T \times 0 + 300^T \times 0$ |
| | | Pipe B | $208^T$ | $= 100^T \times 0 + 200^T \times \frac{1}{0.96} + 300^T \times 0$ |
| | | Pipe C | $333^T$ | $= 100^T \times 0 + 200^T \times 0 + 300^T \times \frac{1}{0.90}$ |
| | Quantity of Materials | Plate D | $144^T$ | $= 102^T \times 1 + 208^T \times 0.2 + 333^T \times 0$ |
| | | Plate E | $499^T$ | $= 102^T \times 0 + 208^T \times 0.8 + 333^T \times 1$ |
| | Byproducts | Byproducts F | $-10^T$ | $= 102^T \times (-0.01) + 208^T \times (-0.01) + 333^T \times (-0.02)$ |
| | | Byproducts G | $-35^T$ | $= 102^T \times (-0.02) + 208^T \times (-0.03) + 333^T \times (-0.08)$ |
| | Working Hours | Pipe Forming | $7.5^H$ | $= 100^T \times 0 + 200^T \times 0 + 300^T \times 0 + 102^T \times \frac{1}{100\ T/H}$ $+ 208^T \times \frac{1}{90\ T/H} \times 333^T \times \frac{1}{800\ T/H}$ |
| | | Finishing | $8.5^H$ | $= 100^T \times \frac{1}{100\ T/H} + 200^T \times \frac{1}{80\ T/H} + 300^T \times \frac{1}{60\ T/H}$ $+ 102^T \times 0 + 208^T \times 0 + 333^T \times 0$ |
| | Working Amounts | Usual | $643^T$ | $= 100^T \times 0 + 200^T \times 0 + 300^T \times 0 + 102^T\ 1 + 208^T \times 1 + 333^T \times 1$ |
| | | Inspection | $440^T$ | $= 100^T \times 0.2 + 200^T \times 0.6 + 300^T \times 1 + 102^T \times 0 + 208^T \times 0 + 333^T \times 0$ |
| | | Packing | $600^T$ | $= 100^T \times 1 + 200^T \times 1 + 300^T \times 1 + 102^T \times 0 + 208^T \times 0 + 333^T \times 0$ |
| **Plate Mill** | Quantity of Products | Plate | $400^T$ | $= 100^T \times 0 + 200^T \times 0 + 300^T \times 0 + 400^T \times 1 + 144^T \times 0 + 499^T \times 0$ |
| | | Plate D | $144^T$ | $= 100^T \times 0 + 200^T \times 0 + 300^T \times 0 + 400^T \times 1 + 144^T \times 1 + 499^T \times 0$ |
| | | Plate E | $499^T$ | $= 100^T \times 0 + 200^T \times 0 + 300^T \times 0 + 400^T \times 0 + 144^T \times 0 + 499^T \times 1$ |

**Figure 8.8A. Physical Distribution Calculations (Clockwise): Flow**

| | | | Sales Plan | | | | Pipe Mill | | |
|---|---|---|---|---|---|---|---|---|---|
| | | | Quantity of Final Product | | | | Quantity of Products | | |
| | | | Pipe A | Pipe B | Pipe C | Plate | Pipe A | Pipe B | Pipe C |
| | | | $100^T$ | $200^T$ | $300^T$ | $400^T$ | 100 | 200 | 300 |
| **Pipe Mill** | Quantity of Products | Pipe A | 100 | 1 | 0 | 0 | 0 | (1) | | |
| | | Pipe B | 200 | 0 | 1 | 0 | 0 | | | |
| | | Pipe C | 300 | 0 | 0 | 1 | 0 | | | |
| | Quantity of Semi-Products from Previous Process | Pipe A | 102 | | | | | .98 | 0 | 0 |
| | | Pipe B | 208 | | | | | 0 | .96 | 0 |
| | | Pipe C | 333 | | | | | 0 | 0 | .90 |
| | Quantity of Materials | Plate D | 144 | | | | | | | |
| | | Plate E | 499 | | | | | | | |
| | Byproducts | Byproducts F | -10 | | | | | | | |
| | | Byproducts G | -35 | | | | | | | |
| | Working Hours | Pipe Forming | $7.^5$ | | | | | (5) 0 | 0 | 0 |
| | | Finishing | $8.^5$ | | | | | 100 | 80 | 60 |
| | Working Amounts | Usual | 643 | | | | | (7) 0 | 0 | 0 |
| | | Inspection | 440 | | | | | .2 | .6 | 1 |
| | | Packing | 600 | | | | | 1 | 1 | 1 |
| **Plate Mill** | Quantity of Products | Plate | 400 | 0 | 0 | 0 | 1 | (9) | | |
| | | Plate D | 144 | 0 | 0 | 0 | 0 | | | |
| | | Plate E | 499 | 0 | 0 | 0 | 0 | | | |

Figure 8.8B

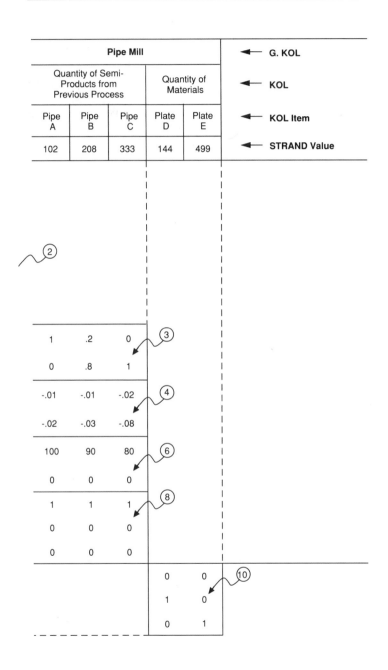

| Pipe Mill | | | | | ◄── G. KOL |
| Quantity of Semi-Products from Previous Process | | | Quantity of Materials | | ◄── KOL |
| Pipe A | Pipe B | Pipe C | Plate D | Plate E | ◄── KOL Item |
| 102 | 208 | 333 | 144 | 499 | ◄── STRAND Value |

②

| 1 | .2 | 0 | ③ |
| 0 | .8 | 1 | |
| -.01 | -.01 | -.02 | ④ |
| -.02 | -.03 | -.08 | |
| 100 | 90 | 80 | ⑥ |
| 0 | 0 | 0 | |
| 1 | 1 | 1 | ⑧ |
| 0 | 0 | 0 | |
| 0 | 0 | 0 | |

| 0 | 0 | ⑩ |
| 1 | 0 | |
| 0 | 1 | |

| | | | Sales Plan | | | | Pipe Mill | | |
| --- | --- | --- | --- | --- | --- | --- | --- | --- | --- |
| | | | Quantity of Final Product | | | | Quantity of Products | | |
| | | | Pipe A | Pipe B | Pipe C | Plate | Pipe A | Pipe B | Pipe C |
| | | | 52604 | 46054 | 46825 | 60000 | 52604 | 46054 | 46825 |
| Pipe Mill | Quantity of Products | Pipe A | 52604 | 1 | 0 | 0 | 0 | (10) | | |
| | | Pipe B | 46054 | 0 | 1 | 0 | 0 | | | |
| | | Pipe C | 46825 | 0 | 0 | 1 | 0 | | | |
| | Quantity of Semi-Products from Previous Process | Pipe A | 50650 | | | | | .98 | 0 | 0 |
| | | Pipe B | 42556 | | | | (8) | 0 | .96 | 0 |
| | | Pipe C | 39863 | | | | | 0 | 0 | .90 |
| | Quantity of Materials | Plate D | 50000 | | | | | | | |
| | | Plate E | 40000 | | | | | | | |
| | Byproducts | Byproducts F | 20000 /T | | | | | | | |
| | | Byproducts G | 10000 / T | | | | | | | |
| | Working Hours | Pipe Forming | 5000 / H | | | | (7) | 0 | 0 | 0 |
| | | Finishing | 2000 / H | | | | | 100 | 80 | 60 |
| | Working Amounts | Usual | 1000 / T | | | | (6) | 0 | 0 | 0 |
| | | Inspection | 2000 / T | | | | | .2 | .6 | 1 |
| | | Packing | 500 / T | | | | | 1 | 1 | 1 |
| Plate Mill | Quantity of Products | Plate | 60000 / T | 0 | 0 | 0 | 1 | (9) | | |
| | | Plate D | 50000 / T | 0 | 0 | 0 | 0 | | | |
| | | Plate E | 40000 / T | 0 | 0 | 0 | 0 | | | |

Figure 8.9A   Cost Calculations (Counterclockwise)

| Pipe Mill | | | | | ← G. KOL |
|---|---|---|---|---|---|
| Quantity of Semi-Products from Previous Process | | Quantity of Materials | | | ← KOL |
| Pipe A | Pipe B | Pipe C | Plate D | Plate E | ← KOL Item |
| 50650 | 42556 | 39863 | 50000 | 40000 | ← STRAND Value |

| | | | |
|---|---|---|---|
| 1 | .2 | 0 | ⑤ |
| 0 | .8 | 1 | |
| -.01 | -.01 | -.02 | ④ |
| -.02 | -.03 | -.08 | |
| 100 | 90 | 80 | ③ |
| 0 | 0 | 0 | |
| 1 | 1 | 1 | ② |
| 0 | 0 | 0 | |
| 0 | 0 | 0 | |

| | | |
|---|---|---|
| 0 | 0 | ① |
| 1 | 0 | |
| 0 | 1 | |

(1) Initial input values (predetermined variables)

Plate mill: costs per ton of products = 60,000 ¥/T, 50,000 ¥/T, 40,000 ¥/T

Pipe mill: operating costs per ton = 1,000 ¥/T, 2,000 ¥/T, 500 ¥/T

Operating costs per hour = 5,000 ¥/T, 2,000 ¥/T

Costs per ton of byproducts = 20,000 ¥/T, 10,000 ¥/T

(2) Order of calculations

$$1 \rightarrow 2 \rightarrow 3 \rightarrow 4 \rightarrow 5 \rightarrow 6 \rightarrow 7 \rightarrow 8 \rightarrow 9 \rightarrow 10$$

(Product costs will be calculated by sequentially adding operation, overhead processing, and other costs to material costs)

(3) Mechanism of calculations

"Horizontal multiplication and vertical summing-up"

| | | | | |
|---|---|---|---|---|
| **Pipe Mill** | Quantity of Materials | Plate D | 50,000 ¥/T | = 60,000 ¥/T x 0 50,000 ¥/T x 1 + 40,000 ¥/T x 0 |
| | | Plate E | 40,000 ¥/T | = 60,000 ¥/T x 0 50,000 ¥/T x 0 + 40,000 ¥/T x 1 |
| | Quantity of Semi-Products from Previous Process | Pipe A | 50,650 ¥/T | = 1,000 ¥/T x 1 + 2,000 ¥/T x 0 + 500 ¥/T x 0 + 5,000 ¥/H x $\frac{1}{100\ \text{¥/H}}$ + 2,000 ¥/H x 0 + 20,000 ¥/T x (-0.01) + 10,000 ¥/T x (0.02) + 50,000 ¥/T x 1 + 40,000 ¥/T x 0 |
| | | Pipe B | 42,556 ¥/T | = 1,000 ¥/T x 1 + 2,000 ¥/T x 0 + 500 ¥/T x 0 + 5,000 ¥/T x $\frac{1}{90\ \text{¥/H}}$ + 2,000 ¥/H x 0 + 20,000 ¥/T x (-0.01) + 10,000 ¥/T x (-0.03) + 50,000 ¥/T x 0.2 + 40,000 ¥/T x 0.8 |
| | | Pipe C | 39,863 ¥/T | = 1,000 ¥/T x 1 + 2,000 ¥/T x 0 + 500 ¥/T x 0 + 5,000 ¥/T x $\frac{1}{80\ \text{T/H}}$ + 2,000 ¥/T x 0 + 20,000 ¥/T x (-0.02) + 10,000 ¥/T x (-0.08) + 50,000 ¥/T x 0 + 40,000 ¥/T x 1 |
| | Quantity of Products | Pipe A | 52,604 ¥/T | = 1,000 ¥/T x 0 + 2,000 ¥/T x 0.2 + 500 ¥/T x 1 + 5,000 ¥/H x 0 + 2,000 ¥/H x $\frac{1}{100\ \text{T/H}}$ + 50,650 ¥/T x $\frac{1}{0.98}$ + 42,556 ¥/T x 0 + 39,863 ¥/T x 0 |
| | | Pipe B | 52,604 ¥/T | = 1,000 ¥/T x 0 + 2,000 ¥/T x 0.6+ 500 ¥/T x 1 + 5,000 ¥/H x 0 + 2,000 ¥/H x $\frac{1}{80\ \text{T/H}}$ + 50,650 ¥/T x 0 + 42,556 ¥/T x $\frac{1}{0.96}$ + 39,863 ¥/T x 0 |
| | | Pipe C | 46,825 ¥/T | = 1,000 ¥/T x 0 + 2,000 ¥/T x 1 + 500 ¥/T x 1 + 5,000 ¥/H x 0 + 2,000 ¥/H x $\frac{1}{60\ \text{T/H}}$ + 50,650 ¥/T x 0 + 42,556 ¥/T x 0 + 39,863 ¥/T x $\frac{1}{0.90}$ |
| **Sales Plan** | Quantity of Final Products | Pipe A | 52,604 ¥/T | = 60,000 ¥/T x 0 + 50,000 ¥/T x 0 + 40,000 ¥/T x 0 + 52,604 ¥/T x 1 + 46,054 ¥/T x 0 + 46,825 ¥/T x 0 |
| | | Pipe B | 46,054 ¥/T | = 60,000 ¥/T x 0 + 50,000 ¥/T x 0 + 40,000 ¥/T x 0 + 52,604 ¥/T x 0 + 46,054 ¥/T x 1 + 46,825 ¥/T x 0 |
| | | Pipe C | 46,825 ¥/T | = 60,000 ¥/T x 0 + 50,000 ¥/T x 0 + 40,000 ¥/T x 0 + 52,604 ¥/T x 0 + 46,054 ¥/T x 0 + 46,825 ¥/T x 1 |
| | | Plate Mill | 60,000 ¥/T | = 60,000 ¥/T x 1 + 50,000 ¥/T x 0 + 40,000 ¥/T x 0 + 52,604 ¥/T x 0 + 46,054 ¥/T x 0 + 46,825 ¥/T x 0 |

**Figure 8.9B**

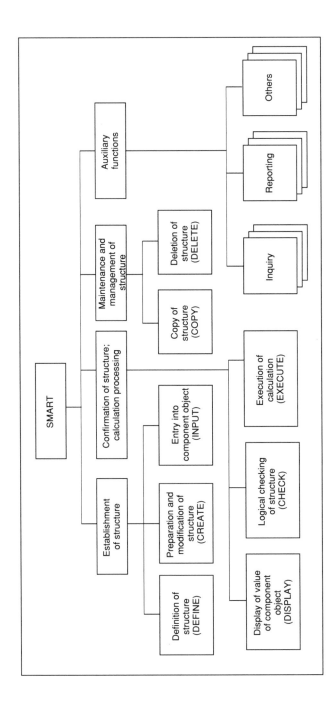

**Figure 8.10 Summarized Functions of SMART**

# PART II

## Profit Planning and Control Systems in Japan

# 9

## Management Control Systems in Japan*

*Yasuhiro Monden, Institute of Socio-Economic Planning,*
*University of Tsukuba*

Management control is a mechanism for managers to control their subordinate managers, thereby achieving organizational goals. This is an abbreviated phrase for management planning and control. Such a process is supported by many kinds of systems, but we will take the management accounting system as the primary one. The best way to understand the features of a Japanese management control system is with a case study of a typical Japanese company. Thus, we will describe in detail the divisionalized planning and control system of Matsushita Electric Industrial, Ltd.

Matsushita launched its divisionalized system in May 1933. General Motors and Du Pont introduced divisional systems in the United States in 1921 and Westinghouse, a pioneer in the electrical industry, introduced such a system in 1935, two years after Matsushita's. Although this system was invented in the United States, Matsushita invented the same system independently at almost the same time in the Far East. Therefore, this chapter calls the reader's attention to common points found in excellent companies worldwide.

* Reprinted with permission from *Innovations in Management: The Japanese Corporation*, Y. Monden, R. Shibakawa, S. Takayanagi, T. Nagao, Eds., (Atlanta: Institute of Industrial Engineers, 1985).

Matsushita's founder, Konosuke Matsushita, says that his company's divisional system was created from the notion of "optimally scaled business"; that is, everyone has some limitations in managing ability, so the optimal scale in business for a person to manage effectively must be found. Therefore, when his company entered new fields and Matsushita could not be involved in all of them himself, he selected a suitable person for each field, delegating authority — from production to sales — to each, and thus enhancing the management ability of the company as a whole.

In such a decentralized system, however, the president must have some way to control divisional managers. The management control system is a means to this end. Matsushita has many kinds of management control, or management accounting, systems. As shown in Figure 9.1, they can be classified in two ways:

- *For top management to control divisional managers:* Divisional planning, internal capital, and monthly accounting settlement systems.
- *For divisional managers to control departmental managers:* Budget and monthly accounting settlement systems.

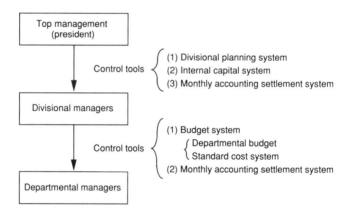

**Figure 9.1 Management Control Systems at Matsushita**

Although these systems may seem similar to methods used in Western countries, Matsushita's system has unique points, including the "king-sealed document" (divisional plan outline), a centralized accounting staff, an internal capital system, and a participative approach to investigating variances and improvements. The internal capital system described here is Matsushita's invention. Matsushita's strength lies in faithfully implementing an ordinary, textbook-like system with cooperation from top management down through workers.

**Divisional Planning System.** The divisional planning system is one of the most important pillars in Matsushita's divisionalized organization. It directs each division to make its own plan from which the corporate plan of the entire company can be prepared.

The divisional plan is a one-year business plan positioned in the first year of a middle-range plan. It consists of several planning outputs:

1. Production plan.
2. Sales plan.
3. Budgeted profit-and-loss statement.
4. Capital expenditure plan.
5. Budgeted fund statement (statement of source and application of funds).
6. Budgeted balance sheet.
7. Working capital sheet.

The steps in this divisional planning process are shown in Figure 9.2.

*Step 1. Announcement of the basic corporate policy:* The president announces this at the beginning of each year, in the presence of all divisional managers, presidents of cooperative companies in the Matsushita group, executives of overseas affiliated companies, and labor union leaders. Tens of thousands attend. Announced corporate policy, expressed verbally, is somewhat abstract, but emphasizes Matsushita's situation for the coming year, and the intention of overcoming difficult environments and improving policy or ambition. The policy statement becomes a kind of slogan for Matsushita employees. Recent slogans have included:

- "Positive attack with the mind of original establishment" (1978, the company's sixtieth anniversary)
- "Aiming at the top of the electronics industry" (1979)

*Step 2. Instruction of the divisional guideline:* Because the basic corporate policy is abstract, the president gives the contents of the divisional planning guide (also called the "president's policy") to divisional managers about two months before the formal accounting period. The guide includes the increases in sales rate, wage costs, and so forth.

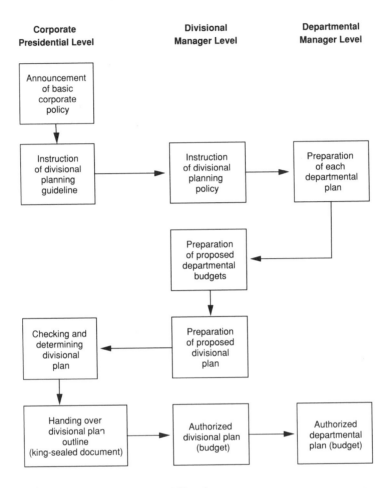

**Figure 9.2 Steps for Divisional Planning**

*Step 3. Instruction of the divisional planning policy:* To achieve the president's policy, each divisional manager will determine his or her own divisional planning policy and instruct departmental managers on production, sales, inventory, market share, cash collection and payment, profit, new-product development, product prices, cost-reduction targets, facilities, human resources, support to vendors, and so forth.

*Step 4. Preparation of each departmental plan:* Based on the divisional manager's planning policy, each departmental manager will, in turn, make departmental plans for sales, production, purchasing, engineering, administration, human resources, facilities, etc. For example, production's departmental plan includes plans for many manufacturing and subsidiary manufacturing departments. Since this phase is the core of the annual divisional planning, such planning starts about three months before the accounting period.

*Step 5. Preparation of the proposed departmental budget:* The divisional manager and accountants check each departmental plan for costs and benefits before preparing the proposed departmental budget.

*Step 6. Preparation of the proposed divisional plan:* The proposed departmental budget will be finally integrated as a divisional profit budget and fund budget to be proposed to the corporate central office.

*Step 7. Checking and determining divisional plans:* At the central office, each director checks divisional plans in detail; for about a month, the corporate accounting office also checks them. For some divisions, the president evaluates whether his policy has been properly incorporated.

When the central office has approved the divisional plans, they will be summarized as a corporate business plan (corporate master budget). After the president approves this plan, the corporate and divisional plans (budgets) will be determined and the divisional plan will be authorized at a meeting of executive directors (see the last two steps in figure 9.2).

*Step 8. Handing over the divisional plan outline:* The essential points of the authorized divisional plan will be handed over, as the divisional plan outline sheet, by the president to each divisional manager. This sheet is also called the king-sealed document.

This handing-over ceremony is very Japanese; the king-sealed document is regarded as a contract between the president and the divisional manager. Achieving the divisional plan is a must for the divisional manager.

As shown in Figure 9.3, the king-sealed document specifies only the essence of the divisional plan; that is, the sales amount, the budgeted profit, and the internal capital fund. The percentage for payment to the corporate office, however, is determined as a fixed rate (3 percent) of the division's sales, a rate common to all divisions. Each divisional manager is responsible for attaining only the written items of the king-sealed document. The method used to achieve this

To the divisional manager

Mr. _____

From President
Toshihiko Yamashita
(Sealed)

I will transmit your divisional plan outline as follows. In order to attain these essential points, you shall display your autonomous management responsibility.

1. Responsible sales amount for the current year:  ¥ _____
2. Responsible profit amount for the current year:  ¥ _____
3. Responsible profit ratio to sales for the current year:  10%
4. Amount of payment to the corporate office:  3% of sales
5. Internal capital for the current year:  ¥ _____

(Comment by the president)

I will approve your proposal of increasing the workforce in your division in order to promote your divisional project _____ .
By attaining your plan you shall realize the budget profit.

**Figure 9.3  Divisional Plan Outline (or "King-Sealed Document")**

agreement is delegated to the divisional manager, a point unique to Matsushita's budget systems.

***Accounting Staff for Centralized Management.*** At Matsushita, the accounting staff has about 1,500 members. Only 100 work at the corporate central accounting department. The rest belong to divisions and other affiliated companies that are profit centers.

The divisional planning system coupled with the monthly evaluation system form a management control system to support the divisional organization of Matsushita. The accountants at both the central accounting department and each divisional (and subsidiary) accounting department help the divisional managers make their divisional plans and measure the monthly results. Therefore, the accounting staff at Matsushita functions as a subject of the management control system. In a sense, the accounting staff is a tool of *centralized management* (of the president), while *decentralized* decision-making authority is delegated to each divisional manager.

When a divisional manager makes divisional planning policy (step 3), the accounting department will participate in determining the production, sales, new-product development, capital expenditure, cost reduction, and advertising and promotional plans. The accounting staff also supplies the necessary data to various departments within the division for their planning activities.

When preparing the departmental budget, the division accounting staff gives advice on estimating the product costs, determining the standard costs, and measuring the actual costs. Accountants even participate in monthly production sales and new-product meetings. When developing and designing new products, accountants play an especially important role in estimating expected costs and computing target costs. Accountants also suggest areas for cost reduction by computing the variance between standard and actual costs. To play such a central role in promoting cost reduction, accountants must have knowledge of products, materials, and so forth.

In the monthly accounting settlement system, the monthly result is measured and compared with the divisional plan. The corporate center can thus judge divisional performances and decide whether action (dispatching additional people, suggesting proposals for improvements, etc.) is necessary.

***Damlike Management and Nondebt Policy.*** An important business philosophy of Matsushita is "independent business" — that is, business done independently and autonomously with regard to funds and/or R&D ability. While most Japanese companies relied on bank loans during their postwar growth, Matsushita was unique in its nondebt financial policy. It has no bank loans.

Why does Matsushita keep its nondebt policy? This is Matsushita's philosophy of damlike management — a company should have buffers in every aspect of business to enable it to adapt to changes in the environment and maintain steady growth. These buffers can include dams for facilities, funds, human resources, inventory, technology, and R&D. Such dams, however, are not equivalent to wasting excess capacities in facilities and inventory based on unexpected lower demand.

On the other hand, a company that relies on bank loans — and has excess liabilities — will experience poor performance when interest rates go up. To grow even during difficult economic or financial times, a company should hold its owned capital and avoid relying on debt. Accumulating surplus within the company is especially necessary.

Considering this financial policy, each division should be managed by relying only on its owned capital. Thus, the concept of *divisional internal capital* was introduced by Matsushita for implementing decentralized fund management. The divisional capital concept clarifies the separation between divisional owned capital and divisional short-term borrowing and surplus.

At Matsushita, two kinds of responsibility and authority are delegated to each divisional manager: *profit* management and *fund* management. The purpose of profit management is, of course, to increase profits from appropriate production and sales. This is not, however, the only objective. The prompt, accurate collection of accounts receivable and the prompt, accurate payment of accounts payable are important responsibilities of divisional managers. The proper application of funds is also the responsibility of each division.

*Internal Capital System.* The most unique point in Matsushita's management accounting system is its internal capital system. Internal capital is a fund necessary for each division to promote its business. Suppose a certain division is installed. The central office then gives it the necessary fixed assets and working capital and delegates to the manager the authority for managing this capital. The internal capital is basically the sum of these fixed assets and working capital.

To measure this working capital, Matsushita applies a standard value, against which the actual amount is compared and judged; necessary amounts of each item in current assets and current liabilities, corresponding to the budgeted sales or production level, are computed. For example, the standard amount of accounts receivable is computed by assuming its turnover (staying) period to be a month. The standard amount of accounts payable can be measured by assuming that the material to total manufacturing costs ratio is 50 percent and the turnover period is 35 days (see Figure 9.4).

Now look at the rules of the internal capital system in summarized form.

1. Structure of internal capital (see Figure 9.5) *where* reserves consist of the reserve for retirement allowances and the employees' deposits received.

| Account Title | | Computation Basis for Standards | | Standard Amount (Yen) | Ratio to Monthly Sales |
|---|---|---|---|---|---|
| | | Basis | Computations | | |
| Current Assets | Notes Receivable | Ratio of notes: 30%<br>Sight of notes: 90 days | (Sales)<br>$100 \times 30\% \times \dfrac{90 \text{ days}}{30 \text{ days}}$ | 90 | Months 0.90 |
| | Accounts Receivable | Turnover period: 30 days | (Sales)<br>$100 \times \dfrac{30 \text{ days}}{30 \text{ days}}$ | 100 | 1.00 |
| | Finished Products | Ratio of cost of sales: 70%<br>Turnover period: 30 days | (Sales)<br>$100 \times 70\% \times \dfrac{30 \text{ days}}{30 \text{ days}}$ | 70 | 0.70 |
| | Work-in-Process | Ratio of manufacturing cost: 70%<br>Turnover period: 3 days | (Production)<br>$100 \times 70\% \times \dfrac{3 \text{ days}}{30 \text{ days}}$ | 7 | 0.07 |
| | Materials | Ratio of materials: 50%<br>Turnover period: 15 days | (Production)<br>$100 \times 50\% \times \dfrac{15}{30}$ | 25 | 0.25 |
| | Other Current Assets | Sales amount 3% | (Sales)<br>$100 \times 3\%$ | 3 | 0.03 |
| | Total: A | | | 295 | 2.95 |
| Current Liabilities | Notes Payable (Materials) | Ratio of materials: 50%<br>Ratio of notes: 10%<br>Sight of notes: 90 days | (Production)<br>$100 \times 50\% \times 10\% \times \dfrac{90}{30}$ | 15 | 0.15 |
| | Accounts Payable | Ratio of materials: 50%<br>Turnover period: 35 days | (Production)<br>$100 \times 50\% \times \dfrac{35 \text{ days}}{30 \text{ days}}$ | 60 | 0.60 |
| | Other Current Liabilities | Sales amount 35% | (Production)<br>$100 \times 35\%$ | 35 | 0.35 |
| | Total: B | | | 110 | 1.10 |
| | Balance: A − B = working capital | | | 185 | 1.85 |

**Figure 9.4 Structure of Standard Working Capital**

Internal capital = standard working capital
                 + fixed assets
                 − reserves

*where* reserves consist of the reserve for retirement allowances
and the employees' deposits received.

2. The interest amount for internal capital is computed at 1 percent
per month, and should be paid to the central office each month.
3. To cover central office expenses, 3 percent of each division's sales
must be paid to central headquarters. After deducting this payment, divisional *net profit* should be 10 percent of sales.
4. Divisional net profit should be disposed of as 60 percent for dividends and taxes, and 40 percent for earned surplus. The amount
corresponding to dividends and taxes should be paid to the central
office during the next period by the monthly allotted amount.
5. The investment for additional necessary working capital and fixed
assets, after a division has been launched, should be based on the
divisional owned fund (the divisional earned surplus and accumulated depreciation).
6. If the divisional owned fund is insufficient for such additional requirements, or if the fund shortage for paying suppliers is temporary, the division can borrow from the central office (after receiving
permission), and should repay the center after a certain period
of time.

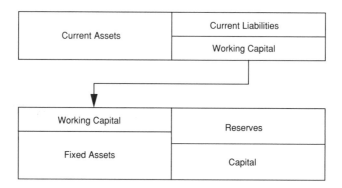

**Figure 9.5 Structure of Balance Sheet at Matsushita**

Annual sales = ¥ 50 billion
Internal capital = ¥ 10 billion
Divisional operating profit = ¥ 7.7 billion

Then,

Divisional net operating profit = divisional operating profit
                                    − corporate expense
                                    (= annual sales × 0.03)
                                    = 7.7 − 50 × 0.03
                                    = ¥ 6.2 billion

Divisional net profit before tax = divisional net operating profit
                                    − interest for internal capital
                                    (= internal capital × 0.12)
                                    = 6.2 − 10 × 0.12
                                    = ¥ 5 billion

Divisional earned surplus = divisional net profit before tax
                                    − dividend and tax
                                    (= divisional net profit
                                          before tax × 0.60)
                                    = 5 − 5 × 0.60
                                    = ¥ 20 billion

Of course, the actual balance sheet of a division deviates from the standard balance sheet described in Figure 9.5. For example, the actual amounts of cash-and-deposit accounts may be larger, corresponding to the actual amount of earned surplus shown in Figure 9.6.

If there is a deviation from the standard balance sheet (BS) in the form of a fund shortage because of overstock in inventory and excess period of accounts payable, the division cannot postpone the payment to suppliers. Matsushita has a rigorous rule for complete payment by the end of each month. The division must report this shortage to the accounting department of the central office (called the Matsushita Bank) because no division is permitted to borrow from outside city banks. Thus, a shortage of funds at any division is automatically reported to the central office. Then, Matsushita Bank grants a loan to the division because it cannot create trouble for outside suppliers. But the bank examines its causes, and the division must propose countermeasures for fund shortages and repay the loan by an agreed upon day.

| Sales Credit | Payables |
|---|---|
| | Short-Term Debt |
| Inventory Assets | Reserve for Retirement Allowances |
| | Employees' Deposits Received |
| | Internal Capital |
| Fixed Assets | Internal Earned Surplus |
| Cash and Deposit | |

**Figure 9.6  Actual Balance Sheet of a Division**

On the other hand, if a division has excess cash, it can deposit it in an outside bank. But if the amount is relatively large, the division will deposit the cash in the Matsushita Bank because its interest rate is a little higher than that of outside banks. As a result, money on deposit is *automatically* absorbed by the Matsushita Bank. Money shortages and excesses at any division can be centrally controlled by the Matsushita Bank.

Until 1982, any divisional earned surplus that was the accumulated residual of each year's divisional net profit was used by the divisional manager for reinvesting in new products or securities. In November 1982, the system was changed to prevent a division from earning huge interest revenues from its financial investment in securities. Before this change, for example, some divisions earned half their net profits this way. In the changed system, out of the divisional retained surplus, most of the fund (except the amount needed for operating activities) is withdrawn by the central office. As a result, the cash and deposits of each division was reduced, on average, to 8 percent of its past amount.

When a division wishes to take on a new project requiring extensive extra funds, the central office makes financial assistance available if the president approves. Thus, a large investment from the corporate portfolio is made and managed by the central office.

***Evaluating Division Manager Performance.*** At Matsushita, each divisional manager is evaluated in terms of profit relative to sales in the annual accounting settlement. There are four ranks:

- Rank A: not less than 9 percent
- Rank B: not less than 6 percent
- Rank C: not less than 4 percent
- Rank D: less than 4 percent

Divisional performance is evaluated for each period and officially announced. If rank D persists for two years at a division, its divisional manager is transferred.

It is often said that measurement of only the profit rate may induce divisional managers to avoid risky projects or investments. President Tochihiko Yamashita feels that such cautiousness does not necessarily result in a negative effect for one period of performance; however, if such a conservative policy continues for a few periods, it *will* negatively influence the profit rate of the division.

When measuring the profit rate for divisions, interest revenues are excluded because the profit acquired as a "maker" is most important for Matsushita. Matsushita is basically a manufacturer, not a bank; a manufacturer should earn its profit by providing goods of high quality at low cost.

***Monthly Accounting Settlement.*** At Matsushita, the monthly accounting measurement of performance is calculated in almost the same way as an annual settlement measurement. Called a *monthly accounting settlement*, this system is used with the divisional plan of the month in question. A special feature is that the monthly settlement is made on the twentieth of the month, and all reports are prepared at that time for comparison with that month's divisional plan. The monthly accounting settlement is used in two ways. First, the corporate central office uses it as a measure of divisional performance to control the division. Second, the divisional manager uses it to control performance of various departments.

When monthly performance is measured, it is analyzed by comparing it with plans, and it is used to revise the performance expectations for future months (feedforward control). Performance is also compared with that of the prior three years and the projected three years. Further comparisons are made of different products, departments, and companies in the same industry.

The monthly accounting settlement within a division at Matsushita has two purposes: (1) profit management and (2) invigorating the division by instilling managerial consciousness in each responsible person in the budget unit. The steps to achieve these goals are:

1. Measuring the results.
2. Finding problems.
3. Sharing problems with managers of related departments. (The problem should be considered by not only the department in question, but by all related departments.)
4. Resolving the problems.
5. Examining the results of improvements.

Thus, the principal aim of the monthly accounting settlement is to act as feedback control for improvements. It is not a means of accusing a person of creating problems. The monthly performance analysis is a means of sharing problems with all people concerned and eliciting ideas for improvements. The reward or sanction function (incentive system or merit rating system) is separated from the feedback control for future improvement.

Probably the most important factor in the effective use of this system is top management's interest. Without a strong commitment to effective use of this system, the performance measurements are merely useless figures.

***Performance Check Meeting: Participative Approach.*** When the monthly accounting settlement has been made, responsible persons from all budget units meet at a performance check meeting. A budget unit's figures must correlate closely to related budget units. For example, consider the reasons for inefficiency on an assembly line, excluding human and machine factors:

- *Sales:* Unstable orders, frequent changes of products, etc.
- *Material suppliers:* Delays in parts delivery, instability of parts precision.
- *Engineering:* Problems in product design; troubles in machines, meters, and tools; etc.
- *Operations management:* Problems in production control of the entire factory.

Merely pointing out defects is not enough. The problem must be solved by all those involved. Through such a participative approach, mutual understanding and cooperation between direct and indirect departments (such as product design and production control) can be achieved. In the performance check meeting, each person responsible for a budget unit is equal to others and talks as freely about problems of other sections as his or her own. Through the analysis and discussion, each section's responsibility is defined.

Finally, more important than the monthly accounting measurements, are the daily analysis of results and prompt action to correct problems, which evaluate the monetary results of each day's actions and examine countermeasures from a total perspective.

***Budget System for Cost Control.*** To prepare the divisional plan and implement it, Matsushita uses a departmental budget system at each division. The budget system is used to inform all division levels of top management's policy. It achieves this by specifying concrete figures with reasonable objectivity, and highlighting each department's performance in reaching its target. In this way, top management controls the activities of each department. The purpose of the budget system is to control costs, performing part of the function of divisional profit management. The budget system controls cost-causing activities in each department of a division. Therefore, this system is a subsystem of the overall divisional planning system.

The budget system consists of two elements: a departmental budget and standard cost accounting (or standard cost). These two elements are closely related when it comes to controlling costs (see Figure 9.7).

A budget is a monetary expression of the period activity plans of each department. This departmental budget amount is divided by its period activity level to compute the labor or machine rate and to incorporate the standard cost of a product into a unit. Then the divisional

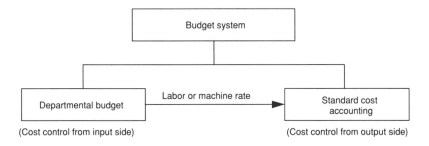

**Figure 9.7  Elements of a Budget System**

plan is prepared. Here, both departmental budget and unit standard costs are based on the same figure. Therefore, to prepare an accurate rate or standard cost, budgets must be carefully prepared. Since preparation of a good budget is a prerequisite for making a divisional plan, the total system is called the budget system instead of the standard cost accounting system.

The procedure for preparing the divisional plan by using the budget system is shown in Figure 9.8, which we now examine in detail.

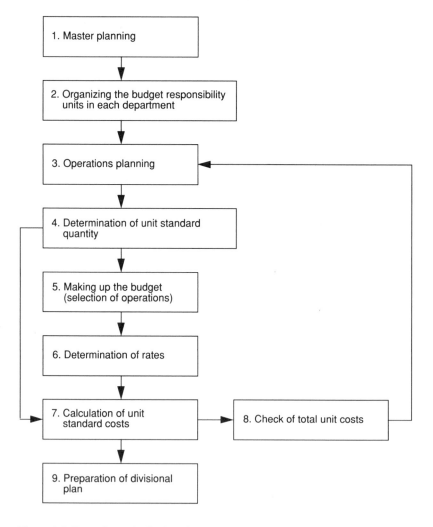

**Figure 9.8 Procedure of a Budget System**

- *Master planning (sales, inventory, and production planning conducted by the division's top planning office):* The first planning area is sales, which will be segmented into sales channels, main customers, and product types.
- *Organizing the budget responsibility unit (the start of departmental planning):* "Department" in department budget planning does not mean the existing line organization; it implies functional units that make up the budgets. For example, if a material section had three functions, such as purchasing, warehousing, and checking, the budget responsibility units would be classified into three departments.

When a budget unit has been determined, one person responsible for the budget amount must be appointed to the unit. He or she is not necessarily a manager, but must assume responsibility for the function in question and provide reasons and countermeasures for any variance between the budget and the results. This person will prepare the budget for this particular function without having to make up a specific budget amount. Decision authority is truly delegated to this budgeting person.

- *Operations planning:* The person responsible for each budget unit must make various operations plans and estimate the value of each. Figure 9.9 is an example of an operations plan.

  In the Contents of Operations column, various operation plans are written. The Input column asks for resources required for each operation; the necessary expense and labor should be entered for each operation. The Output column asks for the expected effect from the input. Examples of the output are reductions of costs or labor.
- *Determining standard quantity per unit:* This forms the basis for establishing each department's necessary activity level. It includes the process yield rate and the necessary labor hours or material quantity per unit of a product.
- *Developing the budget:* The divisional manager examines the operations plans to compare costs and benefits. Costs are "inputs" and benefits are "outputs" in the operations plan sheet in Figure 9.9. If an operation is not attractive from this viewpoint, the divisional manager decides whether to change or abolish it. Care should be taken, however, that future needs are not ignored for immediate profits. Thus, the divisional manager will complete the budget by examining the operations plan sheet and revising, cutting, or adding operations plans.
- *Standard costing procedure for divisional planning:* When each departmental monthly budget is prepared, the standard costing rate (such as labor hours or machine hours) is computed to determine standard unit costs of each product. This standard unit cost will be incorporated into the overall divisional plan proposed to the president.

Year 19__                                    Budget responsibility unit number _____

| Number | Contents of Operations | Schedules | | Input | Output | Notes | Total |
|---|---|---|---|---|---|---|---|
| | | Former Period | Later Period | | | | |
| | | | | | | | |

**Figure 9.9 Operations Planning Sheet**

Finally, the performance variance analysis for each budgeting unit will be made through a participative method including all employees concerned. At this point, the monthly accounting settlement system will be connected to the budget system.

### References

1. Hata, K., *Zen-in keiei no bazzet sisutemu* (Budget System by Participative Management). (Tokyo: Diamond Publishing Co., 1982).
2. Hino, S., *Matsushita keiri daigaku no hon* (Matsushita Accounting College). (Tokyo: Jitsugyo-no-Nippon Sha., 1982).
3. Majima, H., *Matsushita Denki no jigyobusei* (Divisionalized System of Matsushita). (Tokyo: Nippon-Jitsugyo Shuppan, 1978).
4. Matsumoto, K., *Matsushita Denki no keiei kyoiku* (Management Education of Matsushita). (Tokyo: Diamond Publishing Co., 1981).
5. Matsushita Electric Industrial Co., Ltd., 1976, *Genka kanri: jizen keisan hen* (Cost Control: Ex Ante Calculation). (Osaka: Accounting Department). (Unpublished).
6. _____ . 1976. *Genka kanri: jigo keisan hen* (Cost Control: Ex Post Calculation). (Osaka: Accounting Department) (Unpublished).

7. _____. 1981. *Matsushita Denki no genka kanri* (Cost Control of Matsushita). Presented at Conference of Japan Cost Accounting Association, Osaka, Accounting Department.
8. Matsushita, K., *Jissen keiei tetsugaku* (Practical Management Philosophy). (Kyoto: PHP Kenkyusho, 1978).
9. Nishiyama, K., "*Jissen teki kanri kaikei no hōkō*" (Direction of Practical Management Accounting). *Keiei Jitsumu* (February 1983): 20-26.
10. Nishizawa, O., "*Kōshueki no gendō ryoku: Matsushita Denki no jigyobusei kaikei* (Motivating Power for Big Profit: Divisional Accounting at Matsushita). Part 1. (*Diamond Harvard Business*, March-April 1981): 38-47.
11. _____. "*Kōshueki no gendō ryuku: Matsushita Denki no jigyobusei kaikei*" (Motivating power for Big Profit: Divisional Accounting at Matsushita). Part 2. (*Diamond Harvard Business*, May-June 1981): 76-84.
12. Ohno, T., *Matsushita Denki no gijyutsu senryaku* (Engineering Strategy of Matsushita). (Tokyo: Nikkan Shobo, 1980).
13. Okumura, A., *Nippon no top manejiment* (Japanese Top Management). (Tokyo: Diamond Publishing Co., 1981).
14. Pascale, R.T., and A.G. Athos, *The Art of Japanese Management* (New York: Penguin Books, 1982).
15. Takamiya, S., B. Hijikata, and I. Sonoya, eds., *Nippon teki keiei to dōtai soshiki* (Japanese Management and Dynamic Organization). (Tokyo: Maruzen, 1973).
16. Yamaichi Securities Co., Ltd., *Matsushita Denki no kenkyu* (Research in Matsushita). (Tokyo: Toyo-Keizai Shinposha, 1981)

# 10

## Performance Measurement Techniques and Goal Setting: A Comparison of U.S. and Japanese Practices*

*Michiharu Sakurai, School of Business, Senshu University*

*Larry N. Killough and Robert M. Brown, Professors,*
*Virginia Polytechnic Institute (VPI)*

If you travel the U.S. and ask top businessmen about their problems, you'll hear this comment again and again: "We're falling behind our foreign competition." Press the point and it turns out that what American executives worry about most is not foreigners in general but specifically the Japanese. (*Forbes*, July 4, 1983).

No doubt, the pre-eminence of the U.S. industrial complex is being seriously challenged. Industries such as auto and steel which were once hailed as examples of U.S. industrial strength, have seen their dominance over world markets fade. And now the battle lines have been drawn with respect to the electronic and computer industries.

Many reasons have been given for the decline of certain U.S. industries, and these arguments will not be reiterated here. As Mechlin

---

* The basic idea of this paper was outlined in the October 1983 issue of *Kigyokaikei* in Tokyo, Japan, and extended from ideas formulated with Larry N. Killough and Robert M. Brown when Michiharu Sakurai was at the Virginia Polytechnic Institute.

and Berg (1980) suggest, however, at least one culprit may be the heavy reliance of U.S. businesspeople upon the return-on-investment (ROI) measure. They point out that ROI has led managers to place more and more emphasis on short-run profitability, which has brought about a decrease in R&D investment, with a corresponding restriction on innovation.

As would be expected, substantial similarities exist between the management control theory and practices of U.S. and Japanese companies. In this chapter, we will examine the differences not the similarities observed in performance measurement and goal setting. The method of analysis will be the examination of surveys done in each country. These results are interpreted in light of the authors' knowledge of how industries operate in the respective countries.

*Performance Measurement and Goal Setting in the United States.* Return on investment (ROI) and residual income (RI) are the two performance measures most often mentioned in the literature and textbooks. ROI is defined as *profit divided by investment*, and RI as *profit less some capital charge*. In the one case, you get a percentage, in the other, a dollar amount. Which is the better measure is open to discussion. Most writers prefer RI, while most businesspeople prefer ROI. Dearden (1969), Mauriel and Anthony (1966), Reece and Cool (1978), and Solomons (1965) all agree that RI is conceptually superior to ROI as a measure of investment center financial performance. In spite of its apparent deficiencies, most major decentralized companies in the United States continue to use ROI for measuring divisional performance. The often-cited 1966 survey by Mauriel and Anthony indicates that out of the companies with investment centers, 52.3 percent use ROI only, 41.5 percent use both, and only 6.2 percent use RI exclusively.

The most recent survey by Reece and Cool (1978) indicates that not only is ROI still in wide use but its use may be on the increase. They found that 65.1 percent of respondents with investment centers were using ROI exclusively, as opposed to the 52.3 percent in the Mauriel and Anthony study. A comparative list for these surveys is shown in Table 10.1.

It seems to us that most U.S. companies use ROI not only in performance evaluation, but also in corporate goal setting. For example, the Reece and Cool survey also shows that more than 70 percent of the companies that use ROI set an ROI target for their investment centers. Essentially, this suggests that a majority of U.S. companies use

| Name | Mauriel and Anthony[*1] | | Reece and Cool[*2] | |
|---|---|---|---|---|
| Measure | Company | Percent | Company | Percent |
| ROI only | 838 | 52.3% | 299 | 65.1% |
| Both ROI and RI | 665 | 41.5 | 128 | 27.9 |
| RI only | 100 | 6.2 | 9 | 2.0 |
| Others | — | — | 23 | 5.0 |
| Total | 1,603 | 100.0 | 459 | 100.0 |

[*1]Source: Mauriel, John J. & Anthony, Robert N., (1966).
[*2]Source: Reece, James S. & Cool, William R., (1978).

Table 10.1 Divisional Performance Measures in the United States

ROI for setting corporate goals. Japanese companies, on the contrary, use ROI differently in both performance evaluation and corporate goal setting.

*Performance Measurement and Goal Setting in Japan.* Japanese managers tend to use a variety of performance measures. In addition to various profit measures, they make extensive use of productivity, growth of sales, and growth in market share. A survey by Tsumagari and Matsumoto (1972) indicates that only 69.8 percent (97 companies out of 139) use profit as a measure of divisional performance. Others use productivity, sales, market share, or reduction of cost (see Table 10.2).

An affiliated company structure is more prevalent in Japan than divisionalization. This must be considered when comparing the divisional performance measures of Japan and the United States. An *affiliated company* is defined as a separate entity (or company) controlled by a parent company holding over 50 percent of the affiliated company's common stock. Even in the case of the affiliated company structure, there is a tendency for management to make use of different performance measures. According to a survey by Miyamoto and Matsutani (1982), growth and productivity are important factors in measuring the performance of Japanese affiliated companies. As Table 10.3 shows, profit is also very important, although Japanese managers are much more concerned with absolute profit as opposed to a profit ratio. Table 10.4 further illustrates the importance placed on

| Performance Measures | Number of Companies | | Percent | |
|---|---|---|---|---|
| Companies with Definite Measures | 111 | | 36.2% | |
| Profit Rate | | 97 | | 69.8% |
| Sales/Growth Rate | | 56 | | 40.3 |
| Market Share | | 5 | | 3.6 |
| Productivity | | 30 | | 21.6 |
| Cost Reduction | | 18 | | 12.9 |
| Others | | 17 | | 12.2 |
| Companies with No Definite Measures | 28 | | 9.1 | |
| **Subtotal** | **139** | **223*1** | **45.3%** | **160.4%1** |
| Companies with No Divisionalization | 127 | | 41.4 | |
| No Response | 41 | | 13.3 | |
| **Total** | **307** | | **100.0** | |

*1Multiple answers of companies with definite measures.
Source: Tsumagari, Mayumi and Matsumoto, Joji, (1972).

**Table 10.2 Divisional Performance Measures in Japan**

periodic profit and sales amounts as opposed to ROI. Only 16.9 percent of the companies use ROI as a performance measure. On the other hand, 48.5 percent of the companies use periodic profit.

As previously indicated, ROI is used extensively in the goal setting function of U.S. corporations. A similar use does not appear to exist for Japanese companies. As shown in Table 10.5, periodic profit ranks first among Japanese companies. ROI ranks second, but only 15.8 percent of the companies surveyed use this measure. Return on sales is used by 12.6 percent of the companies, and ranks third.

Table 10.6 indicates the differences between the United States and Japan in the use of ROI to set corporate goals. In this survey, the United States considers ROI twice as important. The goal of increasing stock prices is also more important in the United States. New product development and market share appear to be key factors in goal setting for Japanese companies.

**Reasons for the Differences.** The approach to measuring performance and goal setting is considerably different in Japan. In particular,

| Measures \ Whole or Partial | Performance Measure | |
|---|---|---|
| | Overall | Specific |
| Profitability | 80.2% | |
| Periodic Profit | | 85.1% |
| Return on Total Assets | | 42.1 |
| Return on Equity | | 24.6 |
| Others | | 8.8 |
| Growth (Profit) | 59.9 | |
| Growth (Sales) | 45.7 | |
| Sales Volume | | 92.1 |
| Market Share | | 18.4 |
| Others | | 52.7 |
| Productivity | 40.1 | |
| Stability | 36.4 | |
| Contribution | 34.6 | |
| Society | | 20.2 |
| Good Labor and Management Relations | | 28.1 |
| Others | | 6.1 |
| **Total (144 Companies)** | 296.9*1 | 378.2*1 |

*1Multiple answers.
Source: Miyamoto, Kuniaki and Matsutani, Seiji, (1982).

**Table 10.3  Performance Evaluation of Affiliated Companies**

| | Company | Percent |
|---|---|---|
| ROI | 23 | 16.9% |
| Periodic Profit | 66 | 48.5 |
| Dividends | 15 | 11.1 |
| Others | 32 | 23.5 |
| **Total** | 136*1 | 100.0% |

*1Multiple answers
Source: Aoki, Shigeo, (1975).

**Table 10.4  Performance Measures of Affiliated Companies**

| | Past | Present | Future*1 |
|---|---|---|---|
| Operating Profit | 6.7% | 5.5% | 3.8% |
| Ordinary Income (EBT) | 38.7 | 47.3 | 35.4 |
| Net Profit After Taxes | 17.9 | 17.4 | 13.5 |
| **Periodic Profit Subtotal** | 63.3 | 70.2 | 52.7 |
| Return on Total Assets | 12.4 | 13.9 | 28.3 |
| Return on Owner's Equity | 0.6 | 0.8 | 2.9 |
| Return on Capital Input | 1.1 | 1.1 | 1.6 |
| **ROI Subtotal** | 14.1 | 15.8 | 32.8 |
| Return on Sales | 20.5 | 12.6 | 11.8 |
| Internal Rate of Return | 1.2 | 0.7 | 1.8 |
| Others | 0.9 | 0.7 | 0.8 |
| **Total** | 100.0% | 100.0% | 100.0% |
| **Total (Companies)** | 1,000*2 | 996*2 | 992*2 |

*1"Future" refers to five or ten years from now.
*2The number of responding companies.
Source: The Economic Planning Agency (1976).

**Table 10.5  Changes in Corporate Goals**

| Corporate Goals | United States | Japan |
|---|---|---|
| ROI | 2.43*1 | 1.24 |
| Rising Stock Price | 1.14 | 0.02 |
| Market Share | 0.73 | 1.43 |
| Improved Product Portfolio | 0.50 | 0.68 |
| Rationalization of Logistics System | 0.46 | 0.71 |
| Improved Net Worth | 0.38 | 0.59 |
| New Product Development | 0.21 | 1.06 |
| Increased Company Recognition | 0.05 | 0.20 |
| Improved Working Conditions | 0.04 | 0.09 |

*1These numbers refer to average score importance (1 = 3 points, 2 = 2 points, 3 = 1 point, others = 0) in 227 U.S. companies and 291 Japanese companies. Companies contacted were America's Fortune 1000 and large businesses listed on the Tokyo stock market (1,031).
Source: Kagono, Tadao, (1980).

**Table 10.6  Comparing Corporate Goals in the United States and Japan**

Japanese companies seem to have made little use of ROI. They have employed instead the older measure of periodic profit. A number of factors may have caused this preference, the most significant being:

1. Reluctance of top management in Japan to change management control systems.
2. Institutional differences that make periodic profit significant, such as the absence of significant stockholder strength and different organizational arrangements.
3. High economic growth, inflation, and financing alternatives.

**Reluctance to change.** Some Japanese academics have suggested that Japanese top management's reluctance to change has placed Japan behind the United States in developing management control techniques. The absolute profit measure is certainly one of the oldest forms of performance measurement, but it appears to be a rather incomplete measure for management control purposes in today's environment. Consequently, management personnel using it as a management control technique may be perceived as unsophisticated. For example, a panel discussion on divisional performance at the Japan Accounting Association's annual meeting a few years ago asked why most top executives at large Japanese corporations make such little use of ROI. A panel member replied that the top manager in question must be rather backward. This is a typical view, especially in academia, of Japanese management. While it may be partially true that Japanese top management is unlikely to use quantitative techniques and control systems, it is doubtful that ROI techniques are not used simply because of lack of sophistication.

**Institutional differences.** Institutional differences focus on three perceived factors: autonomy, employee/employer relations, and stockholder strength. Evidence indicates that Japanese corporations give relatively little autonomy to their divisions. This lack of autonomy reduces the significance of measures such as ROI and increases the importance of less encompassing evaluation and goal setting measures, such as sales volume, return-on-the-dollar volume of sales, and possibly periodic profit. Even for those Japanese organizational structures where autonomous relationships do exist, such as in the affiliated company, the use of ROI is not nearly as prevalent as in the United States. This means that we cannot simply attribute the low use of ROI in Japanese companies to the fact that most divisions do not have the degree of autonomy that exists in their U.S. counterparts.

A fundamental principle of company policy in Japan is to attempt to measure success over the long run. This is closely related to the lifetime employment system of Japanese companies. Under this system, an employee is rewarded for long-term performance rather than short-term achievements. The notion of emphasizing profit only, especially ROI, misdirects managerial effort toward short-term results rather than long-term profitability.

In the United States, the influence of stockholders tends to be much greater. As a result, earnings per share (EPS) and ROI have become key indicators. The strength of stockholders in Japan is weak due to a debt-oriented capital structure. As a consequence, it seems to us that most Japanese managers are not pressured to place more importance on short-term profit measures such as ROI.

In summary, some authorities attribute Japan's low use of ROI to the fact that managers in most Japanese divisions have minimal authority. Others cite the low stockholder influence. These reasons, nevertheless, do not fully explain why managers in Japanese companies make little use of ROI. Other reasons appear to be economic in nature.

**High economic growth, inflation, and financing alternatives.** The high economic growth between 1955 and the early 1970s led Japanese management to expand its scale of operations considerably. The huge amount of funds required for this expansion was obtained through debt financing, chiefly bank loans. The tax laws of Japan, like those of the United States, treat interest paid on borrowing as an expense. This makes it generally more advantageous for an enterprise to borrow money than to increase its capital and bear the burden of added dividends.

During this period of high economic growth, companies did not find it difficult to bear large interest burdens. It was usually possible for them to achieve adequate profit margins by using the borrowed money to expand business operations. Since there has been little fear of bankruptcy, most Japanese companies have been able to borrow money easily from banks, and most banks have ample funds to lend because the Japanese people typically put their surplus money into banks rather than other investments.

Due to this special feature of Japanese financing alternatives, the average net worth ratio of Japan's principal corporations dropped to less than 20 percent in 1973, and this tendency has continued until today. The corresponding figure for the United States as of the end of 1973 was 52.1 percent. The return on total capital was lower for most Japanese companies. Due to the leverage effect, however, the return on owner's equity was higher than that of U.S. companies (see Table 10.7).

| | Return on Total Capital*¹ | | Return on Owner's Equity | |
|---|---|---|---|---|
| | Japan | United States | Japan | United States |
| 1963 | 7.5 | 11.2 | 16.4 | 18.1 |
| 1964 | 8.1 | 11.9 | 15.4 | 19.4 |
| 1965 | 7.6 | 12.8 | 13.1 | 21.3 |
| 1966 | 8.7 | 12.8 | 18.0 | 21.9 |
| 1967 | 9.2 | 10.9 | 22.5 | 18.8 |
| 1968 | 9.0 | 11.4 | 22.8 | 20.3 |
| 1969 | 9.2 | 10.7 | 25.3 | 19.6 |
| 1970 | 8.6 | 8.6 | 22.6 | 15.5 |
| 1971 | 7.0 | 9.1 | 15.2 | 16.2 |
| 1972 | 7.6 | 10.0 | 18.8 | 17.9 |
| 1973 | 8.9 | 11.5 | 27.8 | 21.1 |
| 1974 | 8.2 | 10.9 | 18.4 | 21.5 |
| Average | 8.3 | 11.0 | 19.7 | 19.3 |

*¹Numerator is operating profit.
Source: Bank of Japan, Financial Statement Analysis of Major Firms and "Quarterly Financial Report."

**Table 10.7 Comparing ROI and Net Worth Ratio in the United States and Japan**

High economic growth coupled with the high rate of inflation between 1950 and the early 1970s convinced most Japanese executives that rapid expansion of their production capacity was the best way to ensure business survival. By expanding at a rapid rate, capital gains were available if management actively invested their resources in land, equipment, and machines. Low-cost bank loans practically ensured that companies would expand their production capacity.

Because of these Japanese characteristics, most companies still tend to invest in new markets, even if these investments have an adverse effect on short-term profitability. During periods of high economic growth, companies experiencing low growth tend to go out of business. Consequently, top managers in Japan think that maximizing earnings before taxes is the best corporate goal and the best performance measure.

We would be remiss if we failed to mention that rate of return on the dollar volume of sales is a popular performance measure in Japan. Many prominent companies, such as Toyota and Matsushita, consider return on sales to be an integral part of their evaluation and goal-setting process. This measure is often criticized because it ignores the question of how much investment it may have taken to produce either the sales or the income. We think it is widely used by Japanese companies for three basic reasons:

1. Return on sales avoids the problems associated with valuing the investment base, which is necessary if a company is using ROI.
2. Most companies using return on sales have separate measures for controlling individual assets.
3. Companies feel that a return-on-sales measure of the profitability of individual products is more relevant to planning than overall return on investment. For example, Toyota believes that return on sales is a more useful comparison of profitability for each type of car.

*Conclusion.*    Although ROI appears to be firmly entrenched in the United States, evidence suggests that some U.S. companies may have lost their initiative and competitive position by placing too much importance on short-term maintenance of ROI. For example, General Motors' principal pricing goal is known as "pricing for return on product investment." Therefore, during the 1974-1975 recession, the auto industry raised prices an average of $1,000 while sales fell by 25 percent (Monroe, 1979). During the same period, most Japanese automobile companies expanded their productive capacity despite decreasing returns on investment.

As previously stated, Mechlin and Berg concluded that management's continued use of ROI placed primary emphasis on short-term profitability. This emphasis led to innovation restrictions because of reduced R&D investment. It might be that the United States could have expanded its economy much more if most companies had not used ROI to measure performance and set corporate goals. Conversely, Japan would have been unable to expand its economy if it had hesitated to commit large amounts of money to new markets simply because they required R&D expenses that result in a low short-term ROI.

Now that Japan's economy is shifting to a low growth pattern, the attitude of business toward capital investment has become more conservative. It therefore seems safe to predict that future trends in financing will gravitate toward internally generated funds. In fact, the average net worth ratio of Japan's principal corporations rose to 24.16 percent in 1986, a postwar high, after sinking to a 1976 low of 15.65 percent. In addition, many Japanese are beginning to invest their money in stocks rather than bank it. The result is a rapid increase in the strength of the Japanese stockholder. Furthermore, the inflation rate is negligible (the 1986 CPI was 0.6 percent).

One can infer from Table 10.5 that most Japanese managers appear to be moving toward an ROI rather than a periodic profit orientation, and most Japanese management must be conservative in investing their money in R&D. Such inferences, however, are misleading. Japanese managers generally are not using ROI, and investment in R&D has not decreased, even in recent periods. On the contrary, R&D investment has risen to 2.60 percent as a percentage of GNP in 1984. The increasing rate was 18.5 percent in Fujitsu, 15.0 percent in NEC, 13.8 percent in Honda, and 12.0 percent in Hitachi, to name a few.

In a survey of 32 Japanese companies in 1984, the profit goals they used in profit planning are shown in Table 10.8. The result clearly indicates that many Japanese managers are using ROS instead of ROI.

| Profit Planning Goals | Number of Companies |
|---|---|
| ROI | 4   (12.5%) |
| Periodic profit | 5   (15.6) |
| Return on sales | 23   (71.9) |
| Total | 32 (100.0%) |

Table 10.8  Profit Planning Goals in 32 Japanese Companies

And the result was representative of Japanese companies. When Sakurai examined pricing practices in 1986, 394 of 740 large manufacturing companies responded to a mail survey. The results, based on the 52.3-percent response rate (Sakurai, 1986), are shown in Table

10.9. Only 12 companies were using ROI, while more than 45 percent of the respondents were using ROS.

| Pricing Method | Number of Companies |
|---|---|
| Full cost plus profit | 108  (34.9%) |
| Conversion method | 28    (9.1) |
| ROI | 12    (3.9) |
| ROS | 143  (46.3) |
| Others | 4    (1.3) |
| No answer | 14    (4.5) |
| **Total** | 309 (100.0%) |

**Table 10.9  Pricing Practices in 394 Japanese Companies**

Everyone knows ROS is theoretically inferior to ROI because ROS does not consider turnover of capital. Yet many Japanese managers use ROS. The essence of their approach lies in separating ROI into two parts, ROS and turnover. By doing this, they can obtain separate measurements, and thus avoid ROI weaknesses such as the negative management attitude toward investing large sums of capital re-sources in new investment and R&D.

### References

1. Aoki, Shigeo *Management Control and Accounting in Affiliated Com-pany* (Tokyo:  Zeimukenkyukai Publishing Department, 1975), p. 259. The number of responding companies was 85.
2. Dearden, John "The Case Against ROI Control," *Harvard Business Review*, May-June 1969, p. 124.
3. Economic Planning Agency, *Survey on Searching Business Behavior*, Printing Office at Ministry of Finance, 1976. In this paper, *profit* in-cludes ROI, return on the dollar volume of sales, or periodic dollars of profit. Periodic dollars of profit are mostly used for expressing earnings before income tax (EBIT), but can also mean net profit after tax and, in rare instances, operating profit. When compara-ble to EBIT, it means a rough approximation of residual income (RI) because the owner's capital ratio of Japan's corporations is usually less than 18 percent, which is negligible as capital cost.

Regarding surplus, most Japanese top management include opportunity cost in their calculations only when unavoidable.

4. Kagono, Tadao "Comparison of Corporate Strategy and Organization between the United States and Japan," *Japanese Business,* 1980, p. 178. For more details, see Kagono, Tadao, Nonaka, Ikujiro, Sasakibara, Kiyonori, and Okumura, Akio, *Comparison of Business Between the United States and Japan,* Nippon Keizai Shimbunsha (Japan Economic Newspaper Co. Ltd,), 1983, p. 25.

5. Kono, Toyohiro, *Example of Long-Range Business Planning,* (Tokyo: Dobunkan Publishing Co., 1978), p. 42.

6. Mauriel, John S., and Anthony, Robert N. "Misevaluation of Investment Center Performance," *Harvard Business Review,* March-April 1966, pp. 100-102. Of the largest companies in the United States, 2,658 responded. From these, 1,803 reported using investment centers.

7. Mechlin, George F., and Berg, Daniel "Evaluating Research: ROI Is Not Enough," *Harvard Business Review,* September-October 1980, pp. 93-99.

8. Miller, Elwood L. *Responsibility Accounting and Performance Evaluations* (New York: Van Nostrand Reinhold, 1982), pp. 100-129.

9. Miyamoto, Kuniaki, and Matsutani, Seiji "Survey of Management Control Systems in Japanese Affiliated Companies," *Business Accounting,* November 1982, pp. 95-96. Out of 1,050 listed in the Tokyo Stock Market, 144 companies (13.75 percent) responded.

10. Monroe, Kent B. *Pricing: Making Profitable Decisions,* (New York: McGraw-Hill, 1979), p. 216.

11. NAA Tokyo Chapter *The 1967 Survey on Business Planning,* (Tokyo: Kigyo Keiei Institute, 1967), pp. 13-14.

12. Reece, James S., and Cool, William R. "Measuring Investment Center Performance," *Harvard Business Review,* May-June 1978, pp. 29-30. Out of the *Fortune* 1000 companies for 1976, 62 percent responded.

13. Sakurai, Michiharu, "Empirical Research on Japanese Pricing Practices: A Comparison with American and Canadian Companies," *Senshu Keigeigakuronsyu* (*Sensyu University Journal*), September 1986, No. 42, p. 18.

14. Solomons, David, *Divisional Performances: Measurement and Control,* (New York: Financial Executive Research Foundation, 1965), p. 64.

15. Tsumagari, Mayumi and Matsumoto, Joji, *Japanese Business Budget,* (Tokyo: Japan Productivity Center, 1972), p. 226. Out of 827 companies, which consisted of companies listed on the Tokyo Stock Market (772) and foreign-affiliated companies (55), the number of respondents was 307 (37 percent).

# 11

## Full Cost-Based Transfer Pricing in the Japanese Auto Industry: Risk-Sharing and Risk-Spreading Behavior*

*Yasuhiro Monden, Institute of Socio-Economic Planning, University of Tsukuba*
*Teruya Nagao, Information and Decision Sciences, University of Tsukuba*

Our purpose in this chapter is to describe the risk-sharing and risk-spreading behavior found between producers of finished automobiles and producers of automobile parts in Japan. We will show how the automaker seeks to motivate the parts manufacturer's commitment to invest in necessary parts production for new car models through risk-sharing arrangements. In analyzing risk management, we will focus on the parts transfer-pricing scheme between automobile and parts manufacturers.

The automobile industry at this level consists of automakers (final car assembly) and part suppliers. In introducing a new model

* A revision of a paper first published in *Journal of Business Administration*, 1987/ 88, Vol. 17, Nos. 1 & 2, pp. 117-136). Reprinted with kind permission of the University of British Columbia.

car, automakers ask parts manufacturers to invest in the parts suitable for the new model. Thus, the part supplier must invest in appropriate facilities to make the parts and, as a result, accrues the fixed costs of these facilities.

Assuming that this particular investment project promises a high expected return, the part supplier still risks covering the fixed costs of the investment. Whether or not the supplier can cover the fixed costs of parts for a new model car depends on the evolving market demand for the model. The automaker also risks certain fixed costs for a new model production run. In other words, the automaker and the part supplier both risk covering certain segments of total fixed costs in new model car production.

If the supplier's management feels it is impractical to cover the total incremental fixed costs needed, the supplier may not make an adequate investment in the production facilities for this part. If the automaker provides a subsidy in such a situation, the part supplier's risk is defrayed and production becomes more likely. In this case, a certain degree of risk shifts from the supplier to the automaker. The supplier, however, cannot expect as much profit later if the new car model is successful. On the other hand, if the part supplier feels justified in covering the total fixed costs, there is no need for auto-maker subsidies. In such a case, risk does not shift to the automaker, and the supplier's expected profit is higher.

In both cases the automaker's purpose is *to motivate the parts manufacturer to make a commitment to invest in production*. In this way, the parts necessary for a new model car can be obtained. In the Japanese auto industry, such risk-management control systems utilize transfer pricing for auto parts. We will describe how a certain system of subsidies and transfer prices can bring about risk sharing between the automakers and the part suppliers.

Transfer pricing is often based on a "full cost plus markup" method. When based on the full-cost principle, the actual fixed overhead cost per unit of the transferred product will vary, depending on its sales volume. Therefore, the predetermined transfer price may not cover total fixed costs. Thus, under full cost-based transfer pricing, there is the persistent risk of uncovered fixed costs.

The risk-sharing behavior of a divisionalized firm was first analyzed by Kanodia (1979). Loeb and Magat (1978) and Harris, Kriebel and Raviv (1982) have also characterized the systems of profit allocation and transfer pricing among divisions and central head-quarters under *asymmetric* information situations. We will not examine the optimal full-cost transfer pricing system in the presence of either full or asymmetric information, but we will describe how supplementing such a system with direct subsidies allows risk sharing to occur.

First, we will introduce institutional aspects of general transfer-pricing practices for Japanese auto parts, and then describe these practices in a set of hypothetical examples. Description of the institutional arrangements is based on Asanuma (1984) and Monden (1983, 1986).

*Characteristics of Vertical Relationships in the Auto Industry.* Development programs for both new cars and fully revamped models normally take about 36 months. During this development period, the specifications and blueprints of parts, part prices, and target costs of parts manufactured in-house as well as purchased parts are determined. The part supplier and part price, which the authors call the "transfer price," are usually determined just before trial mass production, six to nine months before general mass production begins.

This part price will be used as a base price throughout the period of the part's mass production. As conditions change, however, price adjustments may be reached, usually at six-month intervals. Production periods for parts normally run four years for a full model change and two years for a minor model change. It should be noted that the engine and transmission are not necessarily changed for a full model change. Once orders are placed with a supplier to make a certain part, he or she is hired for the full four- or two-year production cycle.

Compared to the frequency of price adjustments, quantity adjustments are made more often. First, to determine the initial base price, the estimated sales quantity of a part will be projected for the model life. Then, quantities will be computed monthly, and requisitioned by applying the material requirement planning system to the master production schedule of finished automobiles, based on quantities estimated by the dealerships. In addition, minor quantity adjustments may be made daily, based on daily orders from the dealers, four days or a week before car production begins.

This daily adjusted quantity is transmitted to the supplier by using the *kanban* system of sequence scheduling cards for the mixed parts assembly line. The result is the just-in-time (JIT) production of cars, in the required models and quantities at the exact time they are needed.

To summarize the nature of vertical relationships in the Japanese auto industry, the overall customer-vendor relationship is generally unlimited in duration. At the least, the part supplier's position of selling a specific part to the automaker will be maintained for the model life of the part. The price of the part, however, may be adjusted every six months through negotiation, and the general contract for a specific part may be discontinued after four years, in the case of a full model change, or after two years, in the case of a minor model change. In this sense, a "market" can be seen at each six-month interval, and again at each contract's expiration date.

Thus, the Japanese auto industry is an institutionalized system with both strong vertical relationships and competitive market characteristics. The authors call this system "market-adjusted organizational cooperation" or a "market-adjusted coalition."[1] In this sense, we use the term *transfer price* rather than *market price*.

In such a system, the autonomy of decisions by each supplier is weakened, and quantity decisions are made by the automaker. A fixed and continuous relationship as a part supplier will be created, however, to minimize various transaction costs. Since the automobile manufacturer is free to discontinue contracts at their expiration date, the manufacturer can decrease management costs, which may take the form of a part supplier's reluctance or inability to adopt requested environmental and technical innovations. On the other hand, a part supplier maintains autonomy in the following areas:

- *Improvement activities and rationalized investment*: Improvements may be made in (1) working methods that reduce labor hours, (2) the utilization of materials and machines, and (3) facilities investments that reduce fixed labor costs.
- *Value engineering (VE) and value analysis (VA) resulting in design improvements*. Parts can be reformed and materials exchanged while still maintaining the same function or quality level, thereby reducing the number of processes and the material costs. VE is conducted before, and VA after, mass production of the model begins.

As noted above, negotiations on part prices will be conducted between the supplier and the automaker every six months. In cases of improvements or savings, however, the total surplus created must be shared between the part supplier and the automaker. Otherwise, the supplier will lose incentive. Any surplus achieved through improvements may be (1) shared by the supplier, (2) retained in full by the supplier for six months or a year, or (3) absorbed in full by the automaker for the time being, but evaluated during the regular price negotiations with preference shown to the part supplier in question over competitive suppliers.[2]

*Two Types of Part Suppliers.* The part price, or transfer price, of a part supplied from a vendor to an automaker is determined and altered in one of two ways, depending on the type of part supplier. Part manufacturers can be divided into two general groups (Asanuma, 1984). The first has responsibility for machining and part production manufacturing services, without involvement in design. In Japan, this is known as a *taiyo-zu*, or "borrowed-blueprint" maker. In such cases, the automaker designs the part and farms out the production work.

The second type of part supplier sometimes develops parts, submitting blueprints to the automaker. If the designs are approved, the supplier can provide both design and manufacturing services to the automaker. In Japan, such a supplier is called a *shonin-zu*, or "approved-blueprint" maker. Typically, borrowed-blueprint makers supply the small pressed parts surrounding the auto body, while approved-blueprint makers produce specialized parts, such as the battery, carburetor, electronic apparatus, ball-bearings, tires, and brakes.

Automakers and part suppliers can withhold information from one another. In practice, however, this asymmetric information-sharing, or risk-sharing, in Japan is rare. For the borrowed-blueprint maker, there is a *symmetry of information*, in which the automaker's purchasing department is well aware of the part supplier's facilities, capacity, workforce, costs, and required labor hours for each part. The automaker allocates orders with full knowledge of each supplier's plant capacity. Because the supplier's internal information is well known, and also because the supplier lacks the ability to develop the part or parts in question, his profits tend to be smaller.

On the other hand, an *asymmetry of information* exists between the approved-blueprint supplier and automaker; that is, the details and breakdown of part costs are not fully disclosed to automakers because the supplier is a developer of the part. Therefore, he can enjoy larger profits in negotiating prices. The transfer price proposed by such a supplier may be regarded as data implicitly disclosing the supplier's true state (Harris, Kriebel, and Raviv, 1982).

In practice, however, many part suppliers lie between these two types of vendors. In such cases, parts are developed and designed jointly by both the automaker and the supplier. Interior parts are often produced this way. While the plastic parts around the dashboard are generally designed by the automaker, seats are often produced with design approval. In fact, both kinds of parts may be *developed cooperatively* once their general style is approved.

***Two Types of Risk Arrangements Between an Automaker and Part Supplier.*** The transfer price of a certain part is calculated by the formula in Table 11.1. This formula is essentially based on the full-cost-plus-markup approach. From the formula, let's examine how the die cost average (e) is calculated.

---

Transfer price = (a + b + c + d) + e + (f + g + h)

a = Materials cost
b = Purchased parts cost
c = Outside processing costs
d = In-house processing costs
    (direct labor costs + overhead costs)
e = Die cost (depreciation cost of the dies)
f = Sales costs + administrative costs
g = Target profit
h = Savings through proposed improvements

---

**Table 11.1  Transfer Price of a Pressed Part**

The legal duration, based on depreciation for tax purposes, for die presses in Japan is two years. Estimated production levels for the two-year period must be projected to determine the die cost. Thus, the automaker must inform the part supplier of the estimated output level in a form of, for example, "20,000 units per month for the next two years."

Assume the estimated production quantity of a part is 480,000 units (20,000 units × 24 months). Therefore, the die cost per unit part will be:

$$e = \frac{x}{480,000} \text{ , where } x = \text{total cost of dies purchased}$$

The die cost of a part's transfer price is an interesting point in Japan. How die cost is handled depends on the part supplier's function, that is, whether he or she is responsible for manufacturing only, or for both design and manufacturing. If the (e) amount calculated by the supplier is accepted and production of the part is stopped after two years because of a model change, a borrowed-blueprint maker might be faced with one of two situations:

1. If car sales were below estimated levels, the cumulative output of the part at the end of two years may be less than projected, say, only 380,000 units. Where the (e) value was set to compensate for total die depreciation costs over 480,000 units, a portion of the die costs is unrecovered (in this case 20.8 percent or 100,000/480,000). In this situation, the automaker generally will compensate the supplier for the unrecovered depreciation cost. This arrangement is, in essence, a contract in which the automaker ("principal") provides full insurance to the supplier ("agent") against unforeseen fluctuations in demand. In other words, the automaker covers the risk by giving a "lump-sum subsidy" to the supplier. This subsidy may be interpreted as an increase in transfer price value at the end of the period.

2. Suppose, however, that car sales were better than expected, increasing the cumulative output level to 480,000 units after only 18 months (six months earlier than expected). In this situation, the transfer price must be reduced by the amount of the unit die cost through renegotiation. As a result, the supplier generally cannot enjoy any extra profit for selling more parts than budgeted.

In the above situations, we assume that the part is used only for a specific car of a particular automaker.

In summary, the flexibility of the value of the transfer price depends on customer demand for the assembled car. The borrowed-blueprint maker will have neither a loss nor extra profit in terms of die-cost compensation. It is the automaker who either absorbs the loss or enjoys extra profit — because the automaker carries the risk. This situation, therefore, implies that the part supplier receives a subsidy equivalent to the total die costs. Similarly, aluminum die and mold subsidies are based on number of pressings, and specialized machine subsidies are based on estimated production quantity over the legal depreciation period of four years.

Another rule applies to the approved-blueprint supplier: The risk of investing in dies for parts should be undertaken by the part supplier, thereby making part price changes independent of the automaker's demands.

This rule assumes that the part in question is one commonly used by various automakers, making the risk from unforeseen demand fluctuations spread out over a number of manufacturers. If production of a certain part consists of something used exclusively by a particular automaker and something used commonly by many automakers, the former portion cost is guaranteed, while the latter portion cost has no such assurance.

*A Simple Illustration of Risk Management Schemes.* We shall now present a few models to illustrate the essentials of our discussion. Our illustrations will be presented in extremely simplified components — a linear utility measure and simple Bernoulli probability distribution. More sophisticated and formal arguments of our assertions can be presented with a variety of utility and probability terms, but not within the scope of this chapter.

**Proposition 1.** Suppose a part supplier expects to realize profits that will fluctuate because of uncertain market demands for automobiles. Also assume that, although the supplier holds total risk, the automaker chooses to share the supplier's risk by subsidizing a portion of the investment. In this way, fluctuations in the supplier's profits will be reduced, while expected profit remains unchanged. The supplier's risk is reduced, thus ensuring a more positive use of profits and perhaps inducing him or her to accept a contract with the automaker.

**Illustrative model for proposition 1.** *Assumption 1:* We assume that the utility (U) felt by the supplier for the monetary amount of profit (Y) can be depicted by the following simplified function:

$$U = Y \text{ for } Y \geq 0$$
$$U = kY \text{ for } Y < 0$$

where, k is arbitrarily set at 4 in all the following cases.

where k is arbitrarily set at 4 in all the following cases. The concavity of the above utility functions implies that part suppliers are susceptible to high losses.

*Assumption 2:* We may specify the situation of the supplier as yielding high profit and low profit with equal probability. At high demand, the sales quantity of the part should be 255 units; at low demand, 245 units.

We shall now present three cases: cases I(a) and I(b) for describing the situation of a borrowed-blueprint maker, and case II for that of an approved blueprint maker. We will begin by demonstrating how the standard deviation of profits will be reduced when a subsidy is received.

**Case I(a).** *Assumption 3:* Suppose the supplier has the following data for making the parts in question.

- Unit variable costs = $2.00
- Fixed costs A = $690.00
- Fixed costs B = $300.00
- Unit margin = $0.04

(i) At average demand of high sales (225) units and low sales (245 units):

$$\text{expected sales quantity} = \frac{(225 + 245)}{2}$$

$$= 250 \text{ units}$$

$$\text{transfer price} = \$2 + \frac{\$690 + \$300}{250} + \$0.04$$

$$= \$6$$

$$\begin{aligned}
\text{average profits} &= \text{transfer price} \times \text{volume} \\
&\quad - (\text{total variables costs} + \text{fixed costs}) \\
&= \$6 \times 250 - (\$2 \times 250 + (\$690 + \$300)) \\
&= \$10
\end{aligned}$$

Using the transfer price of $6.00, we will achieve the following two profit possibilities.

(ii) If high demand = 225 units:

high profits      = transfer price × volume − total costs

$$= \$6 \times 255 - (\$2 \times 255 + (\$690 + \$300))$$

$$= \$30$$

**(iii) If low demand = 245 units:**

low profits      $= \$6 \times 245 - (\$2 \times 245 + (\$690 + \$300))$

$$= -\$10$$

Since we assume a situation where only high and low profits occur with equal probability, the standard deviation of profit $S_1$ ($y_1$) will be:

$$S_1(y_1) = \sqrt{\frac{((-\$10 - \$10)^2 + (\$30 - \$10)^2)}{2}}$$

$$= \$20$$

We then get

$$E(U) = \frac{1}{2} \times 4 \times (\$10 - \$20) + \frac{1}{2} \times 1 \times (\$10 + \$20)$$

$$= -\$5$$

Here, the part supplier's negative expected utility of profit implies that he would be reluctant to undertake production. (See Figure 11.1.) However, if the automobile manufacturer subsidizes the part supplier, as done in Japan for borrowed-blueprint makers, the figures in the example will be changed as follows.

**Case I(b).** *Assumption 4:* Suppose that fixed cost B is a die cost and will be compensated in full by a subsidy from the automaker.[3]

(i) The transfer price and total revenue at average demand will essentially be:

$$\text{Effective transfer price} = \text{unit variable costs (\$2.00)}$$
$$+ \text{ unit fixed costs A} \left( \frac{\$690}{250 \text{ units}} \right)$$
$$+ \text{ unit margin (\$0.04)}$$
$$= \$2 + \$2.76 + \$0.04$$
$$= \$4.80$$

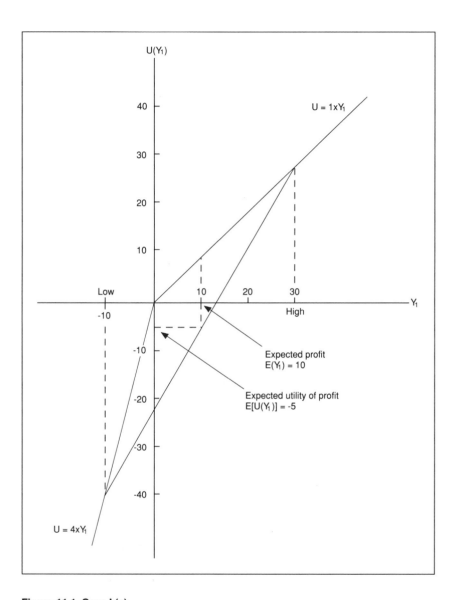

**Figure 11.1 Case I (a)**

$$\text{Total average revenue} = \text{transfer price}$$
$$\times \text{ average volume} + \text{subsidy}$$
$$= \$4.80 \times 250 + 300$$
$$= \$1,500$$

Average profits          = average revenue − average expenses

                         = \$1,500 − \$2 × 250 + (\$690 + 300)

                         = \$10

(ii)    If high demand = 255 units:

High profits          = (\$4.80 × 255 + \$300)

                      − \$2 × 255 + (\$690 + \$300)

                      = \$24

(iii) If low demand = 245 units

Low profits          = (\$4.80 × 245 + \$300)

                     − \$2 × 245 + (\$690 + \$300)

                     = − \$4

Again, since we are assuming that high and low profits will accrue with equal probability, the standard deviation of profit $S_2(y_2)$ will be:

$$S_2(y_2) = \sqrt{\frac{((-\$4 - \$10)^2 + (\$24 - \$10)^2)}{2}}$$

       = \$14

Comparing case I(b) with case I(a), you will notice that the standard deviation was reduced to \$14.00 from \$20.00 while expected profits remained unchanged. Here we see the reduced risk of the supplier, who can receive a subsidy in compensation for certain fixed costs, while fluctuations of sales quantities remain unchanged.

The automaker can subsidize the supplier's investment on the condition that the automaker's preference is risk-neutral or less risk-averse, enabling him or her to absorb a portion of the supplier's risk. Aversion to risk might be reduced for the Japanese automaker because of his or her scale of operation and financial arrangements with the domestic banking community. We can calculate the expected utility for this modified situation:

$$E(U) = \frac{1}{2} \times 4 \times (-\$4) + \frac{1}{2} \times 1 \times \$24$$

$$= \$4$$

Since the expected utility is of positive value, the supplier might decide to invest in this contract. (See Figure 11.2.) The decision differs because a portion of the risk is shifted away from the supplier to the automaker through subsidization. In other words, the automaker guarantees recovery of die costs, while the part supplier still bears the risk of the other items shown in Table 11.1. But the automaker, as a result, can induce the supplier to participate in a coalition for manufacturing a new car model.

We now turn case II, where we present a different type of supplier, one who has already contracted to supply a certain part to automaker I, and is now considering whether or not to sign a new contract to supply automaker II with the same part.

**Proposition 2.** If a part supplier already has contract I with a certain automaker,[4] he or she is likely to accept another independent contract II with a second automaker, even though there is no subsidy for this additional contract. It does not seem worthwhile to accept contract II unless contract I is already in process. The degree of risk aversion or risk tolerance has decreased because of the ability to diversify risk over two manufacturers. As a result, the expected utility of contract II plus existing contract I tends to be positive. The variable coefficient of total profits from contracts I and II becomes smaller when both contracts are adopted, implying a reduction in risk.

**Illustrative model for proposition II.** *Assumption 5:* For simplicity, we assume the same utility function as assumption 1, and the same distribution of profits as assumption 2, for both contracts I and II. We also assume that they are independent (that is, not correlated) so that we have a joint distribution, as in Table 11.2. Thus,

Profit from contract I:     $Y_1$

Profit from contract II:    $Y_2$

Total profit:    $Y = Y_1 + Y_2$

Utility function:    $U(Y) = U(Y_1 + Y_2)$

$$= 1 \times (Y_1 + Y_2) \text{ for } Y_1 + Y_2 \geq 0$$

$$\text{or } 4 \times (Y_1 + Y_2) \text{ for } Y_1 + Y_2 \leq 0$$

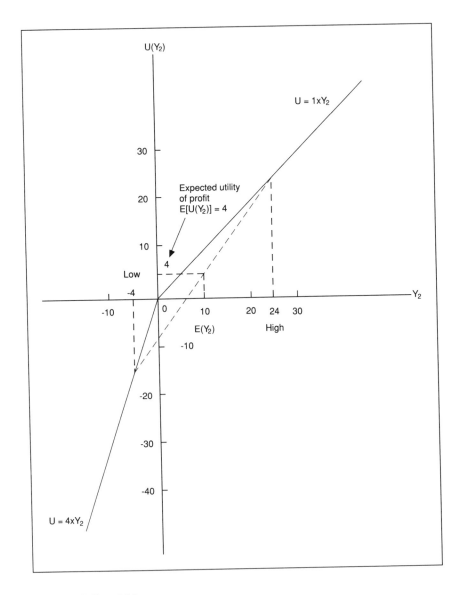

**Figure 11.2  Case I (b)**

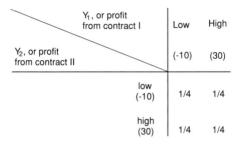

**Table 11.2  Joint Probability Distribution, Case II**

**Case II data.** *Assumption 6:* The cost data and unit margin for contracts I and II are the same as in assumption 3. Therefore,

Expected profit from contract I:  $E(Y_1) = \$10$
Standard deviation of profit from contract I:    $S_1 = \$20$
Expected profit from contract II:  $E(Y_2) = \$10$
Standard deviation of profit from contract II:    $S_2 = \$20$

Thus, the distribution of joint profits $(Y_1 + Y_2)$ and total utility $U(Y_1 + Y_2)$ accruing from contracts I and II will be as depicted in Figure 11.3. For example, at a point $(\text{high}_1, \text{low}_2) = (30, -10)$ since $(\text{high}_1 + \text{low}_2) = 20$, the total utility $(U)$ will be: $U = 1 \times Y = 1 \times (Y_1 + Y_2) = 1 \times (30 - 10) = \$20.00$.

As such, the calculation of expected utility for case II (the approved-blueprint maker) will be:

$$E[U(Y)] = \sum_{n=1}^{4} p_i k_i (Y^i_1 + Y^i_2)$$

where $k_i = 1$ for $Y_1 + Y_2 \geq 0$

$k_i = 4$ for $Y_1 + Y_2 < 0$

$p_i$ = probability for joint profit state i

Therefore,

$$E[U(Y)] = \frac{1}{4} \times 1 \times (\text{high}_1 + \text{high}_2)$$

$$+ \ \frac{1}{4} \times 1 \times (\text{high}_1 + \text{low}_2)$$

$$+ \ \frac{1}{4} \times 1 \times (\text{low}_1 + \text{high}_2)$$

$$+ \ \frac{1}{4} \times 4 \times (\text{low}_1 + \text{low}_2)$$

$$= \frac{1}{4} \times 1 \times [(\$10 + \$20) + (\$10 + \$20)]$$

$$+ \frac{1}{4} \times 1 \times [(\$10 + \$20) + (\$10 - \$20)]$$

$$+ \frac{1}{4} \times 1 \times [(\$10 - \$20) + (\$10 + \$20)]$$

$$+ \frac{1}{4} \times 4 \times [(\$10 - \$20) + (\$10 - \$20)]$$

$$= \$5$$

As a result, the approved-blueprint maker will decide to accept contract II.

The reason we have a positive value of expected utility is that we achieved risk spreading. When the part supplier accepts both contracts I and II as diversified investments, then expected profit from joint contracts is:

$$E(Y_1 + Y_2) = E(Y_1) + E(Y_2)$$
$$= \$10 + \$10$$
$$= \$20$$

The standard deviation of profits from the joint contracts is:

$$S(Y_1 + Y_2) = \sqrt{S_1(Y_1)^2 + S_2(Y_2)^2 + 2S_1(Y_1) \times S_2(Y_2) \times r}$$
$$= \sqrt{(\$20)^2 + (\$20)^2 + 2 \times \$20 \times \$20 \times r}$$
$$= \$28.30 > S_2(Y_2)$$
$$= \$20$$

where r (the correlation coefficient) is assumed to be zero.

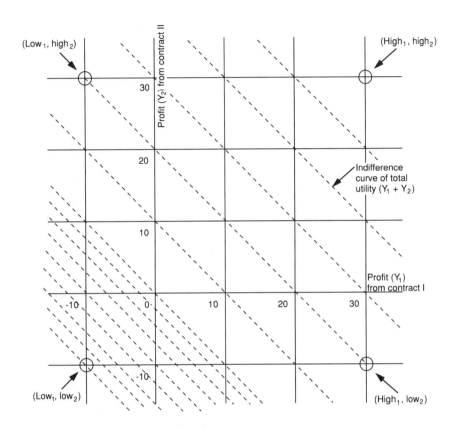

**Figure 11.3 Distribution of Profits of Contracts I and II**

Thus, the variation coefficient $S(Y)/E(Y)$ was reduced to 1.41

$$\frac{(28.3}{20)}$$

from the original 2

$$\frac{(20}{10)}$$

in just the single investment in contract I or II. This reduction in the variation coefficient was caused by risk spreading (instead of risk sharing) through the simultaneous adoption of two contracts.

Another reduction in the variation coefficient implies decreased risk on the supplier's side.

Finally, we shall modify Assumption 5, which states that the distribution of Y1 and Y2 are independent, and test for the probability of Y1 and Y2 being somewhat correlated. (See Table 11.3.)

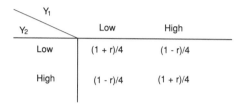

|       | Y₁ |        |         |
|-------|-----|--------|---------|
| Y₂    |     | Low    | High    |
| Low   |     | (1 + r)/4 | (1 - r)/4 |
| High  |     | (1 - r)/4 | (1 + r)/4 |

**Table 11.3  Joint Probability Distribution, Case II (b)**

If the correlation

$$\text{coefficient } (r) = \frac{1}{3}, \text{ then } E[U(Y)] = 0$$

Conversely, if outcomes of Y1, Y2 have negative correlation, say,

$$(r) = \frac{1}{2}, \text{ then } E[U(Y)] = \$12.50$$

Therefore, it follows that the breakeven point in the values of the correlation coefficient is ⅓, if we assume all things being equal. In all likelihood, automakers need not share manufacturing risk to motivate a part supplier to participate in new car model manufacturing.

*Conclusion.* We have set out to clarify the different types of part suppliers, the interrelationships between such suppliers and automakers, and overall risk-bearing behavior within the Japanese automotive industry. The distinct differences in automaker relationships between borrowed-blueprint and approved-blueprint part suppliers, along with certain risk-sharing arrangements described here (such as the treatment of uncovered fixed costs), may be more prevalent in Japan than elsewhere. We have also paid particular attention to the formulation of transfer pricing based on full-cost consideration, and the transfer price flexibility used by automakers to stimulate supplier investment.

In summary, the risk of the borrowed-blueprint maker will be reduced by risksharing with the automaker, which motivates the supplier to accept the contract. On the other hand, the approved-blueprint maker can enter into multiple contracts and reduce risk on any contracts after the first. This behavior is also explained by the concept of risk spreading, a risk that need not be shared by automakers.

## Notes

1. Imai et al. (1982) call this system an "intermediate organization." It may be considered a hybrid of a "syndicate" (defined by R. Wilson) and a "team" (defined by J. Marschak and R. Radner), where the whole system is regarded as a syndicate, with each company in it considered a team.
2. North American auto companies have maintained a high in-house manufacturing ratio of steel products and unit, or main assembly, parts. Although this approach may contribute to reduced market transaction costs, it could simultaneously increase management costs. Recently, their in-house manufacturing ratio has begun to decrease.
3. The value of the transfer price will be decreased by the amount of unit die costs when the expected sales are realized earlier than planned. Also, the uncovered depreciation cost of dies will be compensated by the automaker when the sales are below those expected. Therefore, such a convention implies that the part supplier receives a subsidy equivalent to the die cost.
4. Although the expected utility of contract I itself is negative, the reader can assume that its negative value of utility is discovered only after the contract is adopted.

## References

1. Asanuma, B. (1984). *Jidosha sangyo niokeru buhin torihiki no kozo: chosei to kakushinteki tekio no mechanism*, ("The Organization of Parts Purchases in the Japanese Automotive Industry"), *Kikan Gendai Keizai*, No. 58, pp. 38-48.
2. Harris, M.; Kriebel, C. H.; and Raviv, A. (1982). "Asymmetric Information, Incentives, and Intrafirm Resource Allocation," *Management Science*, Vol. 28, No. 6, pp. 604-620.
3. Imai, K.; Itami H.; and Koike, K. (1982). *Naibu-soshiki no neizaigaku* ("Economics of Internal Organization") (Tokyo: Toyokeizai-Shinposha Publ.)
4. Kanodia, C. (1979) "Risk-Sharing and Transfer Price System Under Uncertainty," *Journal of Accounting Research*, Vol. 16, No. 1, pp. 103-121.

5. Loeb, M., and Magat, W.A. (1978). "Soviet Success Indicators and the Evaluation of Divisional Management," *Journal of Accounting Research*, Vol. 16, No. 1, pp. 103-121.
6. Monden, Y. (1983). *Toyota Production System* (Norcross GA: Industrial Engineering and Management Press).
7. Monden, Y. (1986). "Total Cost Management System in Japanese Automobile Corporations," *Applying Just-In-Time: The American/Japanese Experience* (Norcross, GA: Industrial Engineering and Management Press), pp. 171-184.

# 12

## Profit Management at Kyocera Corporation: The Amoeba System

*Kazuki Hamada, School of Commerce, Seinan Gakuin University*
*Yasuhiro Monden, Institute of Socio-Economic Planning,*
*University of Tsukuba*

Kyocera Corporation is a Japanese manufacturing company that produces sophisticated ceramic materials, industrial ceramics, semiconductor parts, and so forth, for the electronics industry as well as consumer products such as electronic equipment, optical precision instruments, and cameras.

Its financial situation is excellent. Statistics, based on financial statements made public in March 1986, show that Kyocera's profit is much greater than average for the overall electronic instruments industry. With its high rates of return, Kyocera uses profits to pay off its liabilities and adds surplus funds to its current assets. In Table 12.1, net profit rates on sales and total assets are shown as profitability indicators, while current ratios of assets, liabilities, and net worth are indicators of liability and stability.

The percentages of each asset to total assets show that the ratios of quick assets to current assets are large, while fixed assets are small. The ratios of liabilities to net worth are high, although these ratios are characteristically low in Japanese firms. This fact suggests that Kyocera seeks to make its net worth as high as possible.

Units in Percentages

| | Kyocera | | | Average Values in Similar Electronics Industries[2] | | |
|---|---|---|---|---|---|---|
| | 1984 | 1985 | 1986 | 1983 | 1984 | 1985 |
| Sales net profit ratio $= \dfrac{\text{net profit}}{\text{sales}}$ | 10.94 | 11.16 | 7.88 | 5.47 | 5.85 | 4.75 |
| Rate of net profit on total assets $= \dfrac{\text{net profit}}{\text{total assets}}$ | 10.14 | 10.02 | 5.90 | 6.67 | 7.03 | 4.87 |
| Current ratio $= \dfrac{\text{current liabilities}}{\text{current assets}}$ | 377.74 | 319.41 | 448.21 | 188.79 | 197.59 | 219.66 |
| Ratio of liabilities to net worth $= \dfrac{\text{liabilities}}{\text{net worth}}$ | 78.97 | 76.38 | 83.97 | 52.13 | 54.37 | 58.46 |

Daiwa Securities Institute, "Analyst's Guide," August 1986.

[1] Kyocera settles accounts in March.

[2] "Fiscal year" indicates an accounting period from April 1 of one year through March of the following year (e.g., fiscal 1985 falls between April 1, 1985, and March 31, 1986).

**Table 12.1  Net Profit, Assets, and Liability Ratios of Kyocera Corporation**

Kyocera has attained great profits while maintaining an excellent financial condition. One secret of Kyocera's success is its radical cost reduction management. It has taken every opportunity to cut costs, more than is usually considered necessary. Radical cost reductions have been possible because of the management system Kyocera has developed to instill a thorough cost reduction mentality in every employee. This unique management system is called the "amoeba system."

The system's smallest units are called "amoebas" because each performs similarly to this simple microorganism. An amoeba is a single cell, flexible in shape, that multiplies by cell division. It can absorb food through many parts of its body. Kyocera's "amoeba" is similarly flexible regarding work quantities. When it has a large amount of work or many kinds of tasks, it divides into smaller units. It moves from one section of the factory to another, breaking itself down when necessary. If factory work quantities decrease, members of the amoeba join other amoebas, or departments, such as the sales department.

This Kyocera amoeba is also a unit of the independent profit system and bears profit responsibility. To increase profits, amoebas use their own discretion when tackling cost reduction problems, for example. These independent cost reduction activities are considered by Kyocera to be the best feature of its profit management system. The purpose of this chapter is to examine Kyocera's revolutionary "amoeba system" in terms of management, as well as management accounting.

*Features of Kyocera's Amoeba System.* Kyocera's amoeba was a result of pursuing the merits of being small. The smaller or simpler a unit is, the more easily it can discover even a small elusive loss, and the higher its efficiency, as long as adjustments are made effectively among the other units. "The amoeba management system enables Kyocera to take full advantage of Japan's deep-rooted system of small- and medium-sized companies," explains Kyocera's president Kazuo Inamori.

An amoeba is usually composed of three to 50 members. In the manufacturing area, the amoebas are divided according to each process of the production line. In the sales area, they are allotted to each section of a particular product according to region. This chapter deals mainly with manufacturing amoebas.

Kyocera has some 400 amoebas, each controlled by a supervisory division. There are about 50 divisions controlled by a division headquarters. Figure 12.1 illustrates Kyocera's organizational structure. For example, the headquarters of the commodities division controls cutting tools, jewelry, and biomaterials, while the headquarters of the electronic instruments division governs electronic components and equipment.

The Yashica division headquarters, established when Kyocera absorbed Yashica Corporation in 1983, is located in Kyocera's Okaya Plant. It has features of both the amoeba system and the Toyota production system, or just-in-time (JIT). The Toyota production system is a Japanese production management system well known for effectively eliminating wastes. Before its takeover by Kyocera, Yashica Corporation adopted the Toyota production system. Consequently, Yashica division headquarters has features of the two management systems.

At Kyocera, an amoeba adopts an independent profit system, even though it is small in scale. This system will work only if each

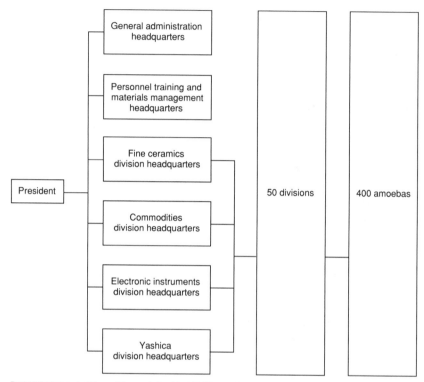

Ryuichi Kunitomo, *Ambitions of Kyocera's President*, (Pal Press, 1986), p. 55.

**Figure 12.1 Kyocera's Organizational Structure**

amoeba is given the authority and responsibility to compute its own profit statistics. Satisfactory transfer prices must be determined, therefore, because they influence the performance of the amoebas.

Transfer prices are usually established by considering market prices, full cost plus profit, partial costs plus profit, and opportunity costs or shadow prices. At Kyocera (where trades of intermediate products produced by each amoeba occur among amoebas at their discretion), trade prices, trade volume, delivery dates, and other conditions are negotiated by the amoebas concerned. These business dealings differ remarkably from the one-on-one negotiations conducted in Japan by many companies. While one amoeba searches among the others for one to supply its needs most advantageously, other amoebas are doing the same. Amoebas are always on the lookout for a better buyer for their intermediate products. Another Kyocera characteristic is that many amoebas produce the same or similar intermediate products.

Competition among amoebas, therefore, is keen. Each amoeba and its members strive to cut costs and improve the quality of their products. This internal competition, in fact, is often sharper than Kyocera's competition with other companies. A buyer amoeba rejects any vendor amoeba's products that are even slightly higher in price or a little lower in quality than it requires. Delivery delays are out of the question. This practice introduces external market procedures into the company's internal production system.

This environment of severe competition and negotiation (1) encourages amoeba members to produce better quality and low cost goods, (2) makes them aware of the importance of cost control, and (3) teaches them about business. The "production, cost, and business consciousness" of Kyocera workers is continuously raised.

Kyocera's amoebas are also authorized to trade intermediate products with outside companies, even in the intermediate processes. When trade conditions offered by internal vendors are unreasonable, the buyer amoeba will search for a satisfactory supplier outside Kyocera. This means that members of an amoeba must be well informed not only about other amoebas' activities, but also about the external markets. If members have nothing to do in their amoeba, they go outside and look for business among competing companies. Consequently, they find themselves competing with other amoebas, as well as with other companies. This is called a "two-stage structure of competition."

Another feature of the amoeba system is member trading. Heads of amoebas lend and borrow members, thereby eliminating losses caused by surplus labor. This differs with other Japanese companies, in which workers are usually assigned to a certain section and have difficulty moving from one to another. At Kyocera, a performance evaluation method was developed to facilitate the transfer of amoeba members. This method will be explained in the next section.

We will now discuss ways in which Kyocera's amoebas multiply, disband, and form new units. Amoeba division and breakup are considered in terms of (1) output and (2) the worker's added value per hour. The following three cases are typical when considering whether or not to divide or disband an amoeba:

1. When output is low, and the added value per worker and per hour is high:  since efficiency in this case is considered high, the amoeba

must multiply. When it is too big, its mobility decreases, and it no longer has the advantages of being small. The amoeba will then be divided or reduced in scale.

2. When both output and the added value per worker and per hour are high: the amoeba, in this case, remains as it is.

3. When output is high, and the added value per worker and per hour is low: to increase efficiency in this case, the amoeba must scale down its members or rearrange its organization. If this still is ineffective, the amoeba must disband.

Besides the three mentioned above, we could consider a case in which both output and the added value per worker per hour are low. Such a case, however, has never occurred at Kyocera.

Amoeba division and breakup are everyday occurrences at Kyocera. When needed, a new amoeba is formed instantly. As Mr. Inamori puts it, "Development is the continued repetition of construction and destruction." Under these circumstances, neither age nor training is essential to become the head of an amoeba. What matters is one's faculty for the job. If judged unsuitable, a head is replaced immediately. Note also that *head* is only a title. It does not guarantee a higher wage than other amoeba members.

These are the features of Kyocera's amoebas, units that have developed many and various ways to cut costs. These features are all the more distinctive because their activities are so different from those of small groups in similar companies. Certainly, amoebas and other small groups are similar in scale, but the performance goals of the other small groups are often vague. They usually have little or no responsibility, are disorganized, and may not even be officially recognized within their company.

The members of Kyocera's amoebas, in contrast, perform according to rules, specified purposes, and clear plans and policies. They also assume responsibility for their activities, making amoebas officially part of Kyocera's organizational structure. They are expected to compete with one another, both inside and outside the company.

***The Performance Evaluation Method of the Amoebas.*** The performance of an organization is generally evaluated by assessing the degree of achievement of realized value in view of its goal. The result of the assessment is regarded as the unit's performance of managerial responsibility. Its profit and cost responsibilities are clarified, depending on whether or not the result is controllable and, if so, how.

While including these factors, Kyocera views performance evaluation as a motivating tool to stimulate competition among the amoebas. It also serves to point out when to divide or disband the amoeba, or form a new one. The evaluation plays an important role in deciding whether or not an amoeba system functions effectively.

An amoeba is evaluated by two criteria, one being added value. The added value of an amoeba is the value of its production, and represents net production. This value-added criterion is one of Kyocera's remarkable features. In contrast, performance evaluation in other Japanese companies is either profit, output, cost, or rate of return on investment.

The added value per hour at Kyocera is computed as follows:

*Step 1.* Total amount of shipment – purchasing costs from the company's other amoebas = total output

*Step 2.* Total output – (purchasing costs from outside the company + operating costs + general administrative costs) = deduction of sales

*Step 3.* $\dfrac{\text{Deduction of sales}}{\text{total labor hours}}$ = added value per hour

As stipulated by Kyocera, the operating costs mentioned above are the margin, or 10 percent of the total amount of production, to be paid to the sales department. General administrative costs include supplies, light and heating, transportation, traveling expenses, rent, depreciation, and others. The deduction of sales stands for the added value created by the amoeba.

Generally, added value is computed by the deduction method or the addition method. The former computes added value in terms of production; the latter in terms of allocation or distribution. The choice of methods depends on the purpose. Kyocera chooses the deduction method, putting it in terms of added value.

The added value per worker and per hour of each amoeba is computed daily, and the results officially announced. This management tool makes amoeba members aware of their daily situation. These daily results are summarized in the accounting table drawn up monthly by each division.

Each column of the table shows the computed value per hour of an amoeba. The total columns present the results of all the amoebas belonging to a division. Each amoeba's result is scored or given numerical points, and this information is announced to all employees. The following shows how an amoeba computes its scores:

$$1. \quad \frac{\text{Deduction of sales}}{\text{total labor hours}} = \text{score}$$

$$2. \quad \frac{(\text{Deduction of sales}}{\text{total output} \times 100} = \text{score}$$

$$3. \quad \frac{\dfrac{(\text{Total output}}{\text{total labor hours}}}{2} = \text{score}$$

4. Management results of an amoeba = total score

Score evaluation:
A rank = over 15,000 points
B rank = over 13,000
C rank = over 10,000
D rank = over 7,000
E rank = less than 7,000

As previously stated, three items and their total are expressed numerically to reach as fair a comparison as possible of the amoebas of different processes. In this way, announcing the scores of all the amoebas serves to raise overall employee morale at Kyocera. Through their competitive spirit, individual members come to understand the importance of cost control.

Another criterion of Kyocera's performance evaluation is the achievement of monthly and yearly sales targets. These targets are set by each amoeba after considering past results and future economic possibilities. Once established, the target can be revised by the manager. In any case, approved or revised, the monthly target is decided officially and, based on this target, the rate of the amoeba's progress toward the target is announced every day.

These two criteria — added value per hour and achievement rate of the target — reflect the recognition of the necessity of (1) increasing output or sales and (2) reducing costs. To evaluate performance, Kyocera uses delivery and shipping slips as records.

The results of the performance evaluations are used to improve future performance. Therefore, results are carefully reviewed, and policies for improving performance are discussed and decided. Kyocera's structure is designed to invite full and frank discussion about results and policy. Kyocera attempts, at the same time, to make the performance evaluation method as easy to understand as possible so that all amoeba members can participate. This is why managerial control in terms of dollars is valued more than production quantities — it facilitates the calculation of profit and loss, a more convincing standard.

**Standardizing the Operation and Cost Reduction System.** The heart of Kyocera's management problem is cost reduction — encouraging the amoebas to improve operations to increase the value added per hour. The challenge is how to standardize operations, while still giving each amoeba independence.

Different intermediate products require different operations standards. Standards are set to meet the highest — not the average — requirements. In addition, standard operations specify how to (1) prevent overproduction, (2) process low-quality products, (3) eliminate wasted labor power and time, and thereby (4) facilitate an amoeba member's mobility, and (5) improve the output rate. To eliminate substandard products that hurt the subsequent processes, quality inspections are built into the final stage of each process as well as into each amoeba. Kyocera specifically stresses quality improvement, and therefore standardizes quality inspection operations to achieve total quality control.

Kyocera also arranges its machines to shorten transport distance between processes, achieve zero inventories between processes, and reduce idle hours. To eliminate wasted time, for example, one worker simultaneously operates two or three machines. To encourage amoeba members to propose better operating methods, a suggestion system has been established. In fact, many employee proposals have been put into practice.

To summarize, Kyocera is fully aware that production control consists of product control and people control. Great importance is attached to the latter. Kyocera therefore asks its divisions to control their amoebas, even though they are given a free rein. Figure 12.2 explains Kyocera's production management system. In overseeing their

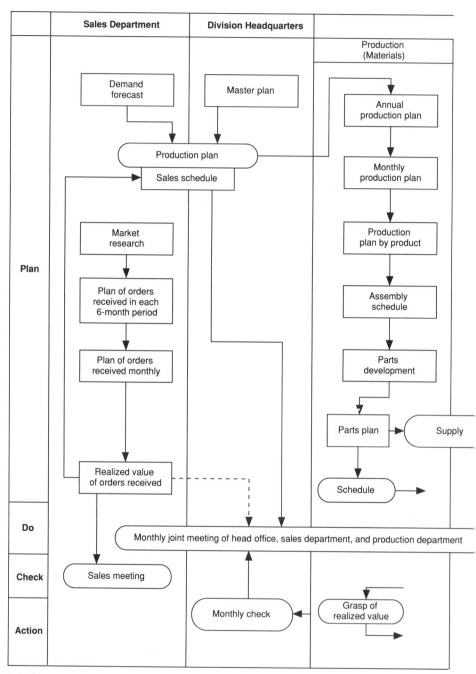

Ryuichi Kunitomo, "Kyocera's Amoeba System", (Pal Press, 1985), p. 131.

**Figure 12.2  Kyocera's Production Management System**

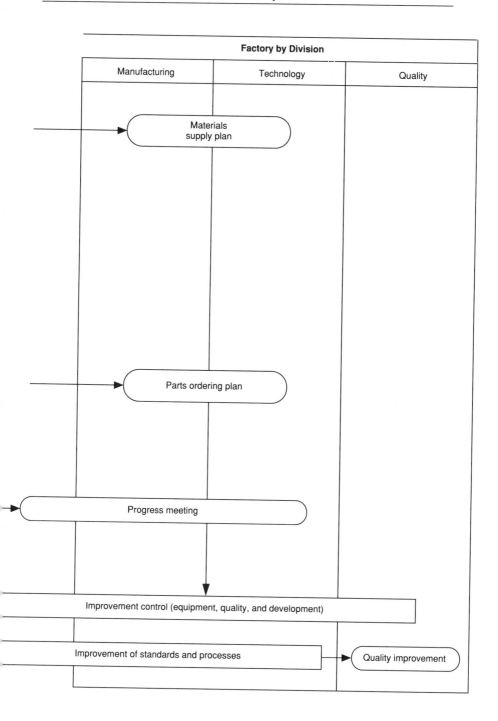

amoebas, the divisions are required to check on the following four points:

1. *Production capacity:* Does amoeba capacity meet the requirements?
2. *Production schedule in view of the delivery date:* Do product-assembly plans consider supply of materials, initial production quantity, and delivery date?
3. *Members' improvement activities:* Do amoeba activities clarify the work's progress and facilitate discovery of defective products? Can they correct irregularities at once?
4. *Volume of inventory:* Can inventory quantities handle any irregularities that might occur in points 1, 2, and 3?

**The Amoeba Management System Versus the Toyota Production Management System.** Kyocera's amoeba system and the Toyota production system have the same goals — to increase efficiency and reduce costs. They were also both developed to fill the need felt by people on the job. Both systems have achieved appreciable results in terms of effectiveness, though they differ in the scale of production.

The Toyota production system attaches particular importance to process control and eliminating waste. This is reflected in the motto "just-in-time." Just-in-time (JIT) production incorporates the "subsequent process receiving system," devised to prevent overproduction by matching the production quantity of the preceding process to the requirements of the subsequent processes. Toyota has also standardized operations for each worker to maintain an adequate balance throughout the production line. By standardizing operations, Toyota seeks an overall improvement of the entire factory's efficiency. *Kanban* is a technique used to adjust the activities of the processes. A particular kanban indicates a particular operation, and characteristically moves along with the product as it is being processed.

Kyocera's amoeba system, on the other hand, allows amoebas to trade not only their intermediate products, but also their own members for the sake of balance. This is a system for personnel management as well.

When receiving orders for its products, Toyota has its production instructions flow in the opposite direction — starting with the final process. The final process orders the exact quantity of the intermediate products they need from the second to last process, which then does the same with the third to last process. In this way, production orders proceed backward up to the initial process.

In Kyocera's amoeba system, orders received by the sales department are passed directly to the amoeba of the final process. The rest of the amoebas in the preceding processes are given free rein, however, concerning the matter. This point differs remarkably from Toyota's system.

We have mentioned that Yashica manufactured optical precision instruments when it was absorbed by Kyocera in 1983. It is now Kyocera's Okaya Factory, with a management system embracing several features of both the Toyota and amoeba systems:

1. Process control is exercised under the Toyota production system.
2. In the lowest and smallest units of production, the amoeba system is adopted.
3. Intermediate products are traded among the amoebas inside the company.
4. Performance results based on the added value per person and per hour are announced at the beginning of each month.
5. Unlike other Kyocera amoebas, Okaya's amoebas do not trade intermediate products with any outside suppliers.

In short, Yashica's management system is remarkably different from Kyocera's original amoeba management system.

**Conclusion.** This chapter has dealt with the features of Kyocera's amoeba and profit management systems. Every amoeba has different features and develops different activities, but they all share the same purpose — cost reduction. The amoeba system is original — developed after reflection on the strengths and weaknesses of conventional management systems.

To make it work more effectively, Kyocera developed the performance evaluation method in terms of added value, and has attempted to instill in every employee the idea of "cost consciousness." When handled effectively, this performance evaluation method encourages amoebas to compete with one another, consequently reducing the total costs of the entire company. Because Kyocera is successful in applying this principle, it enjoys a reputation as an outstanding company showing great profits.

At present, Kyocera is reinforcing its sales network — because, although it produces many kinds of products, it is basically a manufacturer of fine ceramics. This industry is still in its first stages of growth, which means that more and more companies will make inroads.

Another problem is in the field of IC packages — what Kyocera considers its specialty. IC packages are made either of fine ceramics or plastics, and plastics are invading the market share of ceramics. To cope with the situation, Kyocera intends to shed its conventional business lines, which are dominated by the market situation of the IC packages. It seeks to be an independent and invincible enterprise.

### References

1. Daiwa Securities Research Institute. (1986) "Analysts' Guide."
2. Inamori, Kazuo. *How Shall We Live in the Age of Zero Growth?*, Unpublished.
3. Kunitomo, Ryuich. (1985) *The Amoeba System at Kyocera.* Pall Press.
4. Kunitomo, Ryuich. (1986) *Ambitions of Kyocera's President Inamori.* Pall Press.
5. Kyocera Corporation. (1985, 1986) *Annual Report.*
6. Monden, Yasuhiro. (1986) *Toyota Production System.* Kodansha. Murata, Yasuji. (1986) *Amoeba Strategy.* Gyosei.
7. NIKKEI. (1986) *Annual Corporation Report.*
8. Ohno, Taiichi, and Monden, Yasuhiro. (1983) *New Developments in the Toyota Production System.* Japan Efficiency Association.

# 13

## Decision Support Systems
## Based on a Structured Matrix[1]*

*Kyosuke Sakate, Professor of Accounting, Soka University*
*Takayuki Toyama, Senior Industry Specialist, IBM Japan*

The planning function in Japanese businesses has grown in importance in recent years. Due to the rapid and continuous environmental changes of business organizations, however, the role of planning often has not been defined satisfactorily. Conventional profit planning, for example, has limitations of speed, accuracy, and consistency — limitations that become apparent as markets become more global, more complex, and more dynamic. What business requires is the ability to make comparative studies and forecasts quickly, accurately, and consistently. In addition, management requires the ability to make studies based on changes in the marketing structure and sensitivity analysis based on changes in the initial data.

In the profit planning process, management typically must account for:

- Profit fluctuations caused by differences in the costs of each product type.

---

* A revision of a paper first published in the APL 1988 Conference Proceedings, (Vol. 18, No. 2, Dec. 1987). Original material and artwork reprinted with kind permission of the Association for Computing Machinery.

- Profit fluctuations caused by differences in the quantities sold of each product type.
- Sales fluctuations caused by differences in the sales prices of each product type.
- Profit fluctuations caused by differences in foreign exchange rates.

Is it possible to meet all these requirements? It should be noted that the amounts of data normally required would be vast, and the algorithms can be prohibitively complicated.

To deal with their dynamic new environment, business managers need Decision Support Systems (DSS) that are easy to visualize and manipulate. The validity of the planning function in a specific organization must be judged by its adaptability to management's needs, even when management itself is unable to specify its informational needs in the decision-making process. The planning function when used as a DSS should include computational support. When computational algorithms are predetermined, tasks assigned to planning models are relatively easy to complete. In this case, the adaptability of the models implies timeliness and exactness in the information derived. In contrast, when the algorithms are selected as alternatives in the planning stage, it implies the system's effectiveness in expanding management's problem-searching and problem-solving abilities. In both cases, a DSS should reflect the organization's essential structure. After interpreting new information, management may even decide to change the structure of the organization itself.

In this chapter, we intend to demonstrate the remarkable contribution of the structured matrix approach toward creating a DSS in the profit planning area. This approach originated in the accounting area of West Germany's iron and steel industry. The system's software-generating capacity has been expanded and refined though the cooperation and activities of IBM Japan, other leading Japanese corporations, and various researchers.[2]

The advantages of the structured matrix approach to designing a DSS include easy system maintenance and updating, simplified performance of calculations, and an enhanced ability to integrate business activities, logic, and computer processing. The key to the effectiveness of a structured matrix DSS is its simplified but comprehensive graphic display of data. In particular, systems based on a structured matrix have the following benefits:

- *Visibility:* The logic behind both business activities and computer processing can be grasped comprehensively at a glance.

• *Clarity:* We can trace in detail how data are processed, avoiding so-called "black box" computer processing.
• *Program-free simulation:* "What-If" simulations can be undertaken without formulating equations and programming replacements.

Our readers may find that the sophisticated structured matrix, coupled with computer science and software technology, will successfully help to develop a powerful DSS.

To demonstrate how a structured matrix DSS can work, we will look at profit planning based on a structured matrix software package called MATPLAN. The principles of laying out a structured matrix and of performing calculations based on the matrix will be discussed, and an example based upon purchasing operations in the automobile industry will be offered. The concept of a hierarchical table will be introduced to demonstrate the graphics sophistication and computational flexibility attainable with the structured matrix approach. Finally, a few practical extensions of the structured matrix will be discussed.

**MATPLAN Profit Planning Based on the Structured Matrix.** The structured matrix was originally proposed by O. Pichler in West Germany to represent complicated chemical processes simply. Since then, the matrix has been developed and refined as a general approach for building business models by mapping an organization's complicated technological and organizational features. In the course of the matrix's development, it has been demonstrated in the iron and steel industries that cost accounting methods can be improved by reflecting on the causality among cost-determining variables and costs.[3]

Instead of getting involved in further detail, let's begin with a simple introduction to a break-through technology which resulted in the structured matrix software package MATPLAN. MATPLAN is an interactive program based on the structured matrix approach. Because of its generality and flexibility, MATPLAN is being used in various areas of DSS applications. Although MATPLAN and the structured matrix are not identical, for want of space we will treat them as synonymous.

**Principles of table layout and calculation.** The structured matrix in Figure 13.1 is subdivided into three areas: a top margin, center, and left margin. In the top margin, there appear several row vectors, A, B, C, and D, representing input information about the production process. In the center, there appear several normal matrices, M1, M2,

M3, and M4, whose column dimensions conform to the dimension of corresponding row vectors in the top margin, and which represent, roughly, certain transformation of the inputs. In the left margin, there appear several column vectors, C, D, and E, representing final and intermediate outputs of the production process. In general, each vector that appears in the left margin is the result of a simple process of matrix multiplication and addition.

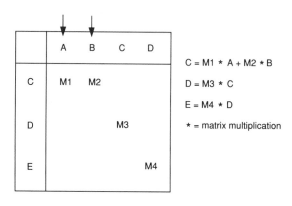

**Figure 13.1  Calculation Sequences in a Structured Matrix**

For each left margin vector, certain of the matrices in the center are multiplied by corresponding vectors in the top margin and then added together according to simple equations. For example, in Figure 13.1's example we may assume that:

$$C = M1 * A + M2 * B$$
$$D = M3 * C$$
$$E = M4 * D$$

The normal rules of matrix multiplication (*) apply. The same vector may of course appear in both the top and left margins, indicating that some inputs may go through a series of transformations in a given production process.

**Simple introduction by table form.** In Figure 13.2 there appears a simple illustration based on the automobile industry. We will calculate (1) the number of cars produced, (2) the amount of materials used, and (3) the total cost of materials.

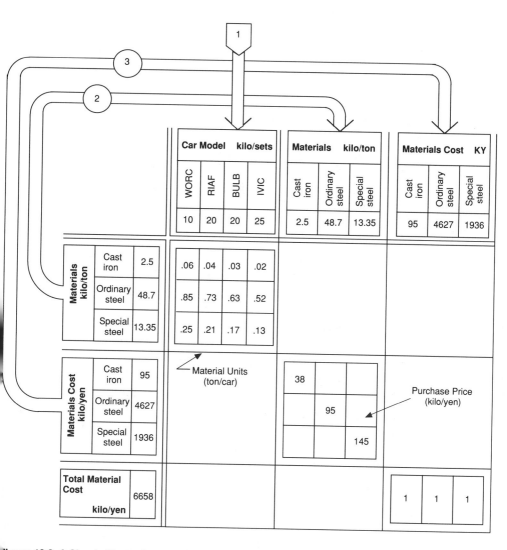

**Figure 13.2  A Simple Illustration of Purchasing in Car Manufacturing**

Let vector A represent the number of cars produced, by model. In the table, the vector is represented visually as block A, *variety of cars produced*. There are four car models altogether, and the number of each model produced appears below the model name.

Let vector B represent the amount of each material input used to produce all cars of all models. In the table, the vector is represented as block B, *amount of material used*. There are three material inputs altogether. Note that B appears both on top and in the left hand margin of the structured matrix, indicating a sequence of transformations in the production process.

Let vector C represent the cost of each material input. In the table, the vector is represented as block C, *the cost of material used*. Like vector B, vector C appears both on top and in the left hand margin of the structured matrix.

Let vector D represent the total cost of production. In the table, the vector is represented as block D, *total cost*.

Let Matrix M1 represent material units expressed in (tons/car) for each material used to produce each car model. In the table, the matrix appears as block M1, *amount of material (ton/car)*. To make the structured matrix more user friendly, the figures in the block are actually an inversion of M1, to suggest visually the correspondence between elements of A and M1. For the same reason, the values for M2 and M3 also appear in inverted form in the table.

Let Matrix M2 represent the purchase price of each material expressed in terms of yen/ton. M2 appears as block M2 in the table.

Let Matrix M3 be a unit vector, a conceptual device necessary to facilitate addition of total production costs. M3 appears as block M3 in the table.

To calculate the total cost of production, we begin at arrow 1 and calculate *amount of material* in the following manner:

$$A * M1 = B$$

The values contained in B are entered in both the left and margin and the top of the structured matrix, as indicated by arrow 2. Then the cost of each material used is calculated thus:

$$B * M2 = C$$

The values contained in vector C are entered in both the left hand margin and the top of the structured matrix, as indicated by arrow 3. Then total costs of production are calculated thus:

$$C * M3 = D$$

The results of these calculations are shown in Table 13.1.

| WORC | $10 \times 0.06 = 0.60$ | $10 \times 0.85 = \quad 8.50$ | $10 \times 0.25 = \quad 2.50$ |
| RIAF | $20 \times 0.04 = 0.80$ | $20 \times 0.73 = 14.60$ | $20 \times 0.21 = \quad 4.20$ |
| BULB | $20 \times 0.03 = 0.60$ | $20 \times 0.63 = 12.60$ | $20 \times 0.17 = \quad 3.40$ |
| IVIC | $25 \times 0.02 = 0.50$ | $25 \times 0.52 = 13.00$ | $25 \times 0.13 = \quad 3.25$ |
| | Cast iron = 2.50 | Ordinary steel = 48.70 | Special steel = 13.35 |

**Table 13.1 Material Needed To Produce Each Car Model**

**A table with two-level hierarchy.** If this table were to represent 100 car types and 100 varieties of operating items, the table would be enormous. So, in MATPLAN, a table can be divided into blocks and each block given a name. To control the division into blocks, an arrangement table, called a "macro table" is used, as well as tables, called "micro tables," expressing what is inside the blocks. The composition of a hierarchical macro/micro table is illustrated in Figure 13.3.

**An illustration of profit planning.** *Assumption:* Suppose the planning department of an electric appliance manufacturer who sells stereos, TVs, and VCRs in the United States as well as Japan is requested by top management to prepare a statement of estimated sales and gross margin for the coming fiscal period. The department's staff has contacted involved departments to obtain the data listed in Table 13.2.

We can express the profit planning problem presented in Table 13.2 in terms of a hierarchical structured matrix, which appears in Figure 13.4. Figure 13.4 is drawn in two dimensions with mixed macro and micro tables appearing in the same plane. Figure 13.4 can only suggest the many levels of complexity that may be handled by a hierarchical structured matrix. But if you can imagine that different

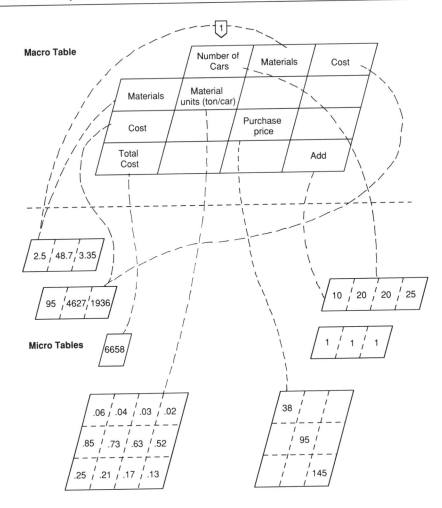

**Figure 13.3  Conceptual Structure of a Hierarchical Table**

| | Sold (in sets) | | Unit Sales Price | | Production Cost (¥ 10,000) |
|---|---|---|---|---|---|
| | Domestic | Export | Domestic (¥ 10,000) | Export ($) | |
| Stereo | 150 | 50 | 10 | 1,000 | 6 |
| TV | 200 | 100 | 5 | 400 | 3 |
| VCR | 100 | 50 | 10 | 700 | 6 |

Assumed foreign exchange rate:  ¥ 160 = $1

**Table 13.2  Initial Profit Planning Data**

product types consist of hundreds of different product components with different cost behaviors, you will understand why current programming approaches are not practical.

***Practical Extension of the Structured Matrix Concept.*** Having described the fundamentals of the structured matrix, we can summarize the basic concepts, which are built into the system, as follows:

- A hierarchy with table nesting and block processing.
- The ability to express relationships within the total "macro" matrix as well as within "micro" matrix blocks.
- A network of data processing sequences.
- Linear processing in calculation sequences.

These elements show the power of the structured matrix as a tool. The end user is given a visual image of the causality of applications processing. Decision support systems based on structured matrices are also tough enough to build viable Management Information Systems (MISs). Twenty years ago, MIS faltered because of the expense and lack of suitable computer technology. To create efficient software, we have introduced various concepts into MATPLAN. Some of these extensions will now be discussed.

**Cost control models.** Up to this point, we have illustrated the structured matrix approach with applications to profit planning. With simple changes in rules of calculation, the same basic matrix may be used to create a cost control model.[4]

**Structured matrix chaining.** Perhaps the most exciting extension of the structure matrix approach is chaining, a process which connects one structured matrix to another. Chaining facilitates multi-user modeling that can be coordinated across the functional areas of the corporation. Structured matrices can be chained in four ways:

1. Spatially, in a plane
2. By time series
3. Spatially and by time series together
4. By transferring a matrix from one use to another

With these procedures, users in Japan have designed several important applications:

- Companywide profit planning and budgeting systems
- Production planning systems
- Cost management systems
- Plant-wide planning systems for materials

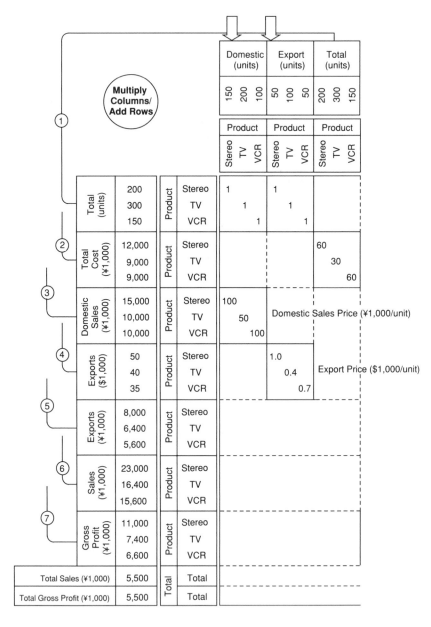

**Figure 13.4 The Profit Planning Model of an Appliance Manufacturer**

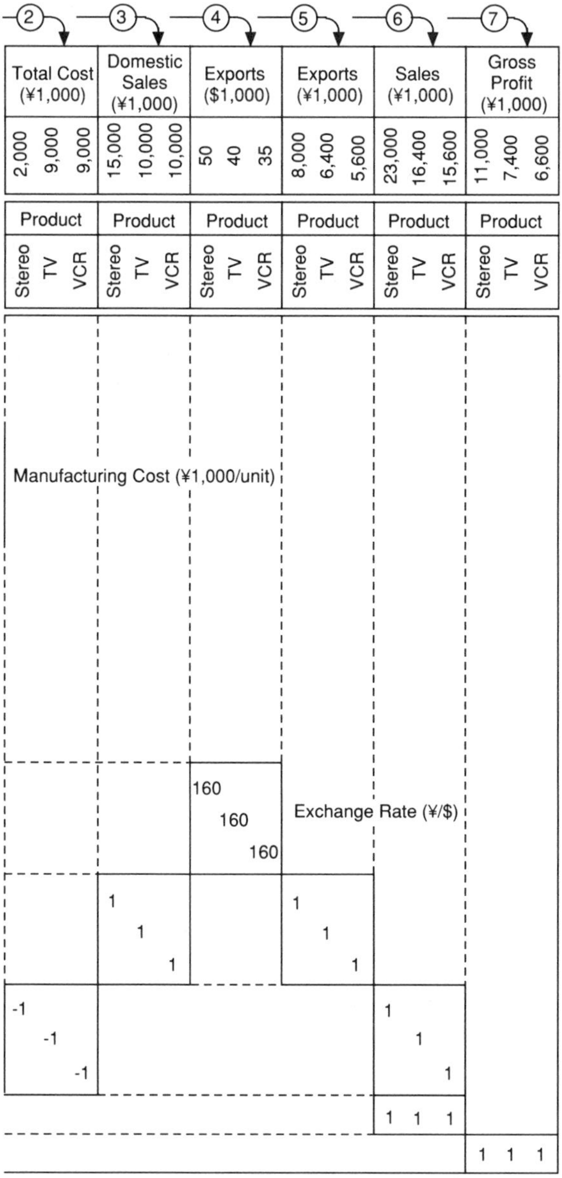

(2) (3) (4) (5) (6) (7)

| Total Cost (¥1,000) | Domestic Sales (¥1,000) | Exports ($1,000) | Exports (¥1,000) | Sales (¥1,000) | Gross Profit (¥1,000) |
|---|---|---|---|---|---|
| 2,000 9,000 9,000 | 15,000 10,000 10,000 | 50 40 35 | 8,000 6,400 5,600 | 23,000 16,400 15,600 | 11,000 7,400 6,600 |
| Product | Product | Product | Product | Product | Product |
| Stereo TV VCR | Stereo TV VCR | Stereo TV VCR | Stereo TV VCR | Stereo TV VCR | Stereo TV VCR |

Manufacturing Cost (¥1,000/unit)

160
160
160

Exchange Rate (¥/$)

1
1
1

1
1
1

-1
-1
-1

1
1
1

1 1 1

1 1 1

Some applications, in which different tasks are assigned to different staff members, have been thought too difficult to computerize by traditional programming methods or simulation language. Systems built by the traditional method seem to be satisfactory as long as they are used within the scope of their actual developers. If you try to link separate individual tasks as components in a multi-user application involving ten or more people, you will find it almost impossible. A hierarchical table based on simple chaining of structured matrices overcomes this difficulty. With a system built upon chained structured matrices, each individual involved in a multi-user application can actually visualize, manipulate, and communicate the contents of tables in which various individual component applications are expressed. Two MATPLAN installations are discussed briefly below to give an idea of what can be accomplished with this approach.

**Two sophisticated MATPLAN installations.** *Case 1: Consolidated profit planning.* The results of a multi-user application to profit planning appear in Figure 13.5. In this case, each structured matrix (shown as a rectangle) is developed and maintained by a single user. Results generated by each user of the system are sent to a manager in charge of corporate profit planning through normal lines of communication. Having received the models and data, the profit planner chains the individual models into a single corporate model. The corporate model can be used to conduct thorough-going "What-If" case studies during the planning process. The corporate model also provides planning feedback for each unit of the company as well as top level management, and leads to more intelligent discussion and ultimately to better planning for the company.

*Case II: Multi-site profit planning.* Figure 13.6 shows the results of an exercise in corporate contribution profit planning. The exercise covered all divisions and plants of a single firm and was implemented nationwide. In this case, each division and plant has profit responsibility, and each site can select the structure of models to send. The divisions discuss their profit goals and how to achieve them by sending each other data and models to manipulate. Large corporations can have as many as 50 divisional profit centers, making the usual data linkages insufficient for real profit planning. With hierarchical tables based on structured matrices, implemented with MATPLAN software, corporate management can link the different

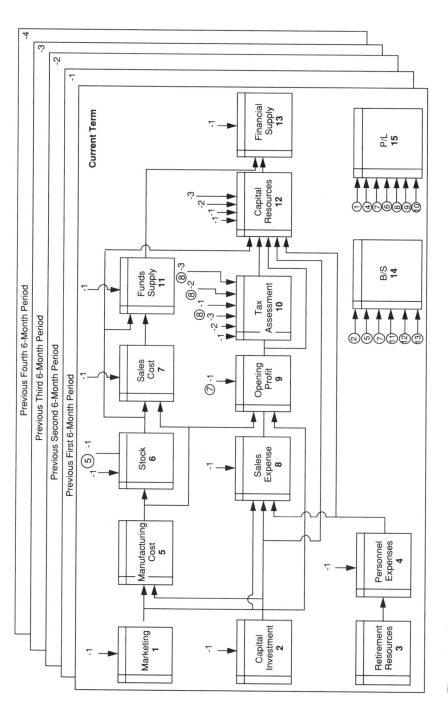

**Figure 13.5 Consolidated Short-Term Profit Planning**

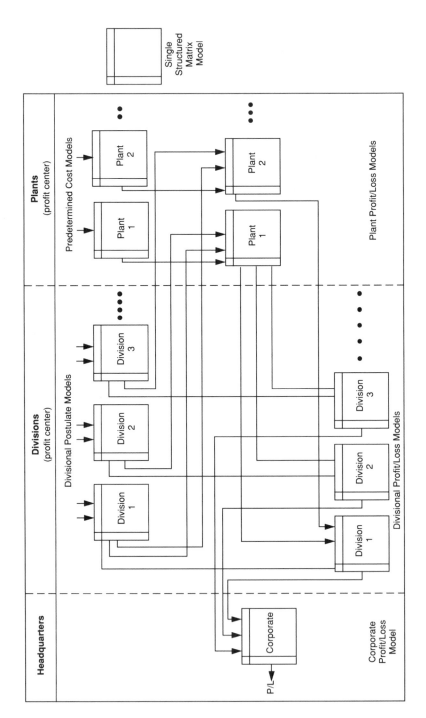

**Figure 13.6  Contribution Profit Planning in a Multi-Site Company**

ways different people handle their planning activities. Most models tend to be standardized, but sensitivity analysis is possible due to MATPLAN's flexibility.

**Summary.** As the reader knows, in planning it is important not only to consolidate the logic of corporate activities, but also to create computer systems capable of following the human way of thinking. An interactive computation system must be achieved to facilitate the creation and modification of models. Such a system must also provide a flexible simulation capability that will reflect environmental changes of an organization and management's response to them.

The structured matrix approach attracted attention, even before computers, as a method of applying human thinking and reasoning. The strengths of structured matrix systems are:

- Short development times
- No need for programming
- Ease of restructuring models
- Incorporation of non-linearity in extended structured matrices

MATPLAN has already made strides in the right direction. The examples shown in this paper are only a few of the applications we have developed. In a recent development, a new structured matrix package, MATPLAN2, has been developed as a user friendly all-purpose program to express the complicated relations, for example, of financial and material values and time utilization. To these ends MATPLAN2 incorporates the following elements:

- Graph theory
- Networked data flows
- Functional arrays
- Application visibility by end users

MATPLAN2 is applicable in the following activity areas:

- Cost accounting, and other areas comprising a complicated structure with simple logic.
- Finance, overall cost, variable cost, and other areas requiring systematization from multiple points of view.
- Profit planning systems, and other management support systems in which we need to analyze segments while maintaining an overview of the system.
- Budgeting, ALM, sales targeting, and other areas that carry out planned versus actual analysis and studies based on end data.

• Almost all planning areas, allocation planning, and cost allocations corresponding to organizational changes and other areas in which logic is changed frequently.

In summary, structured matrix is a tool that allows management to cope with the basic requirement of human thinking — the demand for simplification of events no matter how complicated they may be. MATPLAN and MATPLAN2 connect computer technology with a vehicle for human expression. It also gives application know-how the transferability essential to artificial intelligence and may serve as a starting point for fruitful experimentation with logic bases of artificial intelligence systems. This software has the potential to bring a human touch to the computer environment.

### Notes

1. The authors are indebted to many for giving constructive criticism when adopting the structured matrix approach to their business planning. Their assistance along with that of IBM Japan's information specialists turned the software technology into a practical implementable tool. The following companies participated in the revision process:

   Daishowa Paper Mfg. Co., Ltd.
   IBM Japan Co., Ltd.
   Kawasaki Steel Corporation
   Kobe Steel Ltd.
   Kubota Ltd.
   The Mitsui Trust & Banking Co., Ltd.
   Nippon Kokan Co., Ltd.
   Shionogi & Co., Ltd.
   Sumitomo Metal Industries Ltd.
   Teijin Ltd.
   Torey Co., Ltd.

   And various other group corporations such as Mitsubishi Chemical Group.

   The authors are also grateful to the West German academic researchers and industries who developed the original structured matrix model. Their contributions are listed at the end of this paper. Special thanks goes to Professor Tetsuo Kobayashi of Kobe University who introduced the theory to Japan and led us to the successful development of structured matrix applications.
2. See the references in note 1.

3. In Japan, we independently found the same idea valuable in expressing the linkage of management systems with cost systems, and even as a non-programming approach to solving problems without expanding the semantic gap between computer programming and its applications.
4. A bi-linear calculation model for planning and control has been developed in Japanese companies. Information sources are noted in the references at the end of this chapter.

## References

*Books:*

1. Lassman, G. (1968). *Die Kostenund Erlosrechnung als Instrument der Planung und Kontrolle in Industriebetrieven*. Verlag Stahl und Eisen.
2. Frank, R. (1972). *Betriebsmodelle*. Berthel-Verlag.
3. Wittenbrink, H. (1975). *Kurzfristige Erfolgscrechnung und Erfolkskontrolle mit betriebsmodellen*. Wiesbaden.
4. Walter, K.-D. (1977). *Gestaltung und Verwirklichung Linearer Modelle zur Unternehmensplanung*. Bochum: Studienverlag Dr. N. Brockmeyer.
5. Betriebswirtschaftliches Institute der Eisenhuttenindustrie (Bearbeitet) *Richtlinien fur das Betriebliche Rechnungswesen der Eisen und Stahlindustrie*. (1976). Dusseldorf.
6. Kobayashi, T. (1973). *Cost Accounting: The Theory and Calculative Examples* (in Japanese). Tokyo: Chuou Keizai Corporation.

*Articles:*

1. Franke, R. "A Process Model for Costing," *Management Accounting*, January 1975, pp. 45-47.
2. _____ . "Costing with Matrix Analysis," *Management Accounting*, April 1976, pp. 44-46 and p. 53.
3. Kobayashi, T. "Development of Cósting Models in West Germany (in Japanese)," *Kigyoukaikei* ("Accounting"), May 1973, pp. 104-118.
4. _____ . "Costing Models Based on Structured Matrix (in Japanese)," *Industrial Accounting*, March 1979, pp. 13-20 and April 1979, pp. 61-68.
5. _____ . "Costing System Based on Structured Matrix (in Japanese)," *Industrial Accounting*, March 1979, pp. 13-20 and April 1979, pp. 61-68.
6. _____ . "Management Accounting Standard for the Iron and Steel Industry in West Germany (in Japanese)," *Industrial Accounting*, May 1979, pp. 60-77.
7. Tamaki, T. "Structured Matrix System applied for Cost Control (in Japanese)," *Operations Research*, August 1983, pp. 22-29.

8. Toyoma, T. and Aikawa, M. "An Approach to Management Information System based on Structured Matrix (in Japanese)," *Operations Research*, July 1982, pp. 32-38.

9. Toyoma, T., and Yasuda, M. "Innovation of Decision Support System-MATPLAN based on Structured Matrix Supported by APL," *APL 88 Conference Proceedings*, pp. 318-328.

10. Toyoma, T. and Shinohara, S. "Towards Integrated Decision Support System Based on Implemented Examples," *1988 IIASA International Conference Proceedings*, International Institute for Applied System Analysis, forthcoming.

*IBM Japan Publications (in Japanese):*

1. *Executive Guide — Cost Planning and Accounting using Matrices* — COSTMAT N: GE18-6019-1.

2. *Application Guide — Cost Planning and Accounting using Matrices —* COSTMAT N: GE18-6017-2.

3. *System and Installation Guide — Cost Planning and Accounting using Matrices —* COSTMAT N: GE18-6020-2.

4. *Guide for Cost Control using "Structured Matrix"* N: GE18-6042-0.

5. *The 12th IBM Process Industry MIS Symposium (1980) Report*, "Application of Matrix Techniques in Cost Control Systems" by Y. Fukuhara and N.Mizuta (Technology Dept., Kobe Works, Kobe Steel Works, Ltd.).

6. *IBM Manufacturing/Process Industries Management Planning System Seminar (1980) Report*, "A Structured Matrix Approach to a Management Control System" by T. Toyama, IBM Japan.

7. *User's Guide — Matrix System for Planning and Analysis (Material)* Program No.: 5788-J DH N: SB10-7367-00.

8. Brochure — *Matrix System for Planning and Analysis* (MATPLAN) N: GB18-0095-0.

9. IBM Review 91 1983 (DDS Edition) Reports:
   • "Applying the Structured Matrix in a Cost Control System" by H.Sugiura and Y. Yoshikawa (Systems Dept., Fukiyama Works, Nippon Kokan K.K.).
   • "Profit Planning System based on MATPLAN" by F. Nakamura Finance Dept., Sionogi Pharmaceutical Co.).

# 14

## Profitability Analyses of Yen Appreciation: A Case Study

*Tamio Fushimi, School of Business Administration, Keio University*

Most top managers of Japanese companies were forced recently to examine closely the effect of the severe yen appreciation on their businesses. "Hoshikawa Inc." (the company name is fictitious) confronted problems almost identical to those many Japanese companies are now facing. Though the Japanese business environment has changed a lot during this decade, the context in which rapid yen appreciation affects profitability is relevant to many international businesses.

This chapter first introduces the summary of the Hoshikawa case, then presents appropriate analyses of profitability aspects from it. Applicable models with mathematical equations are presented.

**Summary of the Case Study.** In the spring of 1978, the Corporate Planning Office of Hoshikawa Inc. had to determine the effect of the recent and sudden yen appreciation on business, and decide quickly and firmly to either modify its international marketing policy or continue exports as usual. The "Nixon Shock" in August 1971 triggered a major change in foreign exchange markets: the fixed rate system was suddenly substituted for a floating rate system. When the Smithsonian

System was adopted at the end of 1971, the dollar returned to a fixed rate for a short period. This system, however, was abolished in 1973, and Japan and other countries re-adopted a floating rate system. In October 1973, the oil crisis contrived by the Middle Eastern oil producers destabilized the yen again, and put pressure on the foreign exchange market in Tokyo to sell yen. Exchange stabilization measures by the Japanese government and the Bank of Japan, as well as the U.S. support of the dollar, contributed to the restabilization of the yen, which then hovered between ¥280 and ¥300 to the dollar for the next few years.

At the start of 1977, the Klein Statement fueled European and U.S. dissatisfaction over Japanese foreign market policies, particularly U.S. government and corporate criticism of the Japan-U.S. trade imbalance. By June 1977, the yen rate had climbed past the ¥270 mark; it remained there that summer. From autumn, the rate began rising steadily, going past the ¥240 mark in February 1978, the value at which the Bank of Japan had been expected to prop the yen.

Yen has been remarkably appreciated after the "G5" consensus in autumn 1985, and its rate in 1988 is ¥125 per dollar. Although the following discussion is not dealing with such a remarkable figure, it will hold, even in this extreme situation.

It was at this time that the head of the Corporate Planning Office decided to investigate the effects of the appreciating yen on business. The major business of Hoshikawa Inc. was the production and sales of processed food products, the main ingredients of which were imported grains. These grains came mostly from the United States and were paid for in dollars. The company had three product departments that required different materials. Though the export ratios and cost structures of the three departments differed, the cost component ratios of the respective products within each department were similar.

The Product Q Department was chosen as the model case because data for its product could be obtained easily and its markets were fairly stable. The monthly production and sales of product Q averaged 100,000 cases, of which 80 percent was domestic sales and 20 percent export sales. Since stock volume hardly varied, it was considered negligible for costs estimates. The net selling price for product Q was ¥12,500 per case for both domestic and export sales. In dollar terms, the export price was $50 per case. Since the exchange rate was ¥250 yen to the dollar, the yen price was ¥12,500 per case.

The estimated costs per case were calculated using average figures for the current two months:

- Direct raw materials: ¥5,000
- Supplementary materials, supplies, and other variable costs: ¥1,000
- Direct labor costs: ¥2,000
- Overhead costs (including depreciation): ¥1,800
- Selling and administrative expenses: ¥1,200
- Total costs: ¥11,000

Of the total costs, imports accounted for all raw materials and totalled $20 per case of product Q. All other costs and expenses were paid for in yen. Of the yen costs, supplementary materials, supplies, and other variable costs were proportional to production and sales volume. Direct labor costs, overhead costs, and selling and administrative expenses, on the other hand, were fixed monthly costs and were divided by the monthly production volume (100,000 cases) to get a cost-per-case figure.

Using these costs and revenue data, one of the staff of the Corporate Planning Office first prepared the following calculations. The monthly profit for product Q, based on an exchange rate of ¥250 per dollar, is:

$$(¥12,500 - ¥11,000) \times (80,000 + 20,000) = ¥150,000,000$$

A rise in the yen rate, however, would lower the monthly profit. For example, if the yen appreciated by 20 percent, the value of one dollar would become ¥250 × (1 − 0.2), or ¥200. If the export ratio remained the same as before, then the monthly profit would be:

- Domestic sales: (¥12,500 − ¥10,000) × 80,000
- Export sales: (¥10,000 − ¥10,000) × 20,000
- Total: ¥200,000,000 + 0 = ¥200,000,000

If the yen appreciated by 25 percent, the monthly profit would become:

- Domestic sales: (¥12,500 − ¥9,750) × 80,000
- Export sales: (¥9,375 − ¥9,750) × 20,000
- Total sales: ¥220,000,000 − ¥7,500,000 = ¥212,500,000

This example suggests that a 20-percent yen appreciation would reduce the monthly profit from export sales to zero, and a 25-percent yen appreciation would result in a net loss; the breakeven point would be 20 percent. Any further appreciation, barring any special management strategy, would warrant a termination of export sales if strict profitability were to be maintained.

Having heard these calculations and tentative conclusions, the head of the Corporate Planning Office pointed out a number of reservations, as well as additional demands. The questions are:

1. The calculation uses the full costing concept applied in the company's monthly financial reporting. What the corporate management and the staff want to know is a way to calculate the more significant effect on profitability in terms of management accounting. The conclusion that termination of exports are preferable when the yen rate appreciated beyond 20 percent comes from a lack of distinction between variable and fixed costs.

2. The calculations show that the profit of Product Q Department increases as the yen appreciation rate increases, but can't this relationship be accounted for by the current export ratio of 20 percent? Since the export rate of product Q was expected to rise in the future, how would that change the way the appreciating yen affects profitability? The office head wanted a simple way to find out what the change in effect would be.

3. The company handles a variety of products, each with its own cost structure and export ratio. Even in a single product department, these two factors are always likely to change as the production system is improved and the purchasing policy modified. Therefore, what the company wants is a general method of analysis that can be applied against a variety of cost structures and export ratios to provide a quick understanding of the effects of yen rate variations.

4. To be more exacting, the yen rate appreciation is not always reflected in direct proportion to the prices of imports or selling prices. Some of the savings in the costs of imports provided by a rising yen are easily absorbed at the distribution stage. It would probably be safer therefore to estimate such savings with a downward margin of 10 to 20 percent. Furthermore, the pressure to reduce prices in domestic sales during a high yen-to-dollar exchange rate could not be ignored.

*Calculating Monthly Profit by Analyzing Cost Factors.* Assuming Z to be the monthly operating profit before interest and tax of the Product Q Department for a month (hereafter referred to as monthly profit), then:

$$Z = \text{gross margin from domestic}$$
$$+ \text{gross margin from export sales}$$
$$- \text{fixed costs per month}$$

If $X$ is taken to be the rate of yen appreciation (or dollar depreciation), then the total profit $Z$ can be expressed by the following equations:

(1) $Z$ = (domestic) [¥12,500 − ¥5,000 (1 − $X$) − 1,000] × 80,000

   + (export) [(¥12,500 − 5,000) (1 − $X$) − 1,000] × 20,000

   − (fixed costs) 500 million

Here, the "domestic" and "export" in parentheses stand for the "gross margin from domestic sales" and "gross margin from export sales," respectively. Thus, if $X = 0$ ($1 = ¥250), then the total profit $Z$ is:

(2) $Z$ = (domestic) [¥12,500 − ¥5,000 − ¥1,000] × 80,000

   + (export) (¥12,500 − ¥5,000 − ¥1,000) × 20,000

   − (fixed costs) 500 million

   $Z$ = 6,500 × 80,000 + 6,500 × 20,000

   = 520 million + 130 million − 500 million

   = 150 million

Computing the monthly profit for a given yen appreciation rate of 20 and 25 percent, as discussed in the case, can be done using Equation 1 (see Figure 14.1). For a 20-percent yen appreciation [where $X = 0.2$ ($1 = ¥200)]:

(3) $Z$ = (domestic) [¥12,500 − ¥4,000 − ¥1,000] × 80,000

   + (export) [¥10,000 − ¥4,000 − ¥1,000] × 20,000

   − (fixed costs) 500 million

   $Z$ = ¥7,500 × 80,000 + ¥5,000 × 20,000 − ¥500 million

   = ¥600 million + ¥100 million − ¥500 million

   = ¥200 million

For a 25-percent yen appreciation, [where $X = 0.25$ ($1 = ¥187.5)]:

(4) $Z$ = (domestic) [¥12,500 − ¥3,750 − ¥1,000] × 80,000

   + (export) [¥9,375 − ¥3,750 − ¥1,000] × 20,000

   − (fixed costs) ¥500 million

∴ $Z$ = ¥7,750 × 80,000 + ¥4,625 × 20,000 − 500 million

   = ¥620 million + ¥92.5 million − ¥500 million

   = ¥212.5 million

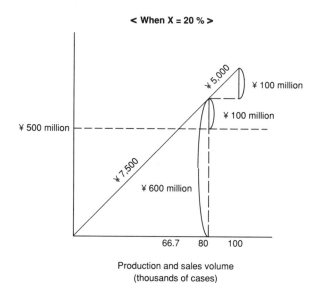

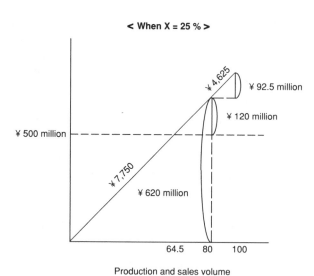

**Figure 14.1 Behavior of Total Profits**

**Profitability Formulation As Functions of Yen Appreciation Rate.** The calculations suggest that the total profit continues to rise, even when the yen rate appreciates beyond 25 percent. There is, however, no guarantee that total profit will rise indefinitely. To confirm this, Equation 1 is applied again, with the gross margin from domestic sales, gross margin from export sales, and the total profit expressed as functions of the yen appreciation rate, as follows (see Figure 14.2.):

(5) $Z$ = (domestic) [¥6,500 + 5,000 $X$ ] × ¥80,000
    + (export) [¥6,500 − 7,500 $X$ ] × 20,000
    − (fixed costs) ¥500 million
    = (domestic) ¥520 million + 400 million $X$
    + (export) ¥130 million − 150 million $X$
    − (fixed costs) 500 million

(6) ∴ $Z$ = ¥150 million + 250 million $X$

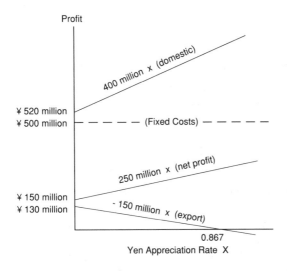

Figure 14.2  Profitability as Functions of the Yen Appreciation Rate

Equation 5 indicates that as $X$ increases, the gross margin from domestic sales increases, while the gross margin from export sales decreases. Since the rate at which the gross margin from domestic sales increases is greater than the rate at which the gross margin for export sales decreases, the total profit will show an increase. The gross margin for export sales is positive only when $X$ satisfies the following conditions:

(7) $\therefore$ ¥130 million $-$ 150 million $X > 0$

$$X < \frac{13}{15} = 0.867$$

This equation suggests that terminating exports is not preferable when $X$ is less than 86.7 percent. Note that this calculation does not take into account an increase in domestic sales to compensate for a decrease in exports.

### The Export Rate and Yen Appreciation Rate.

The Q Product Department considered in this case had a low export ratio of 20 percent. If the given product department had a higher export rate, however, how would the conditions change? To answer this question, further generalization and formulization of the problem may be tried.

If we let $d$ be the domestic sales ratio of the given product department, $e$ the export sales ratio (i.e., $d + e = 1$), and $N$ the monthly sales volume, the monthly profit $Z$ may be determined as follows:

(8) $Z$ = (domestic) $[(12,500 - 5,000) (1 - X) - 1,000] (1 - e) N$

+ (export) $[(12,500 - 5,000) (1 - X) - 1,000] \times eN$

$-$ (fixed costs) 500 million

= (domestic) $(6,500 + 5,000 X) (1 - e) N$

+ (export) $(6,500 + 7,500 X) eN$

$-$ (fixed costs) 500 million

(9) $\therefore$ $Z$ = $[6,500 + (5,000 - 12,500e) X] N - 50,000$

Equation 9 shows that an increase in the rate of yen appreciation results in an increase in $Z$, but only when the value of $e$ lies within the following range:

(10) $\therefore$ 5,000 $-$ 12,500$e > 0$

$$e < \frac{5,000}{12,500} = 0.4$$

It can be seen from Equation 10 that an increasing yen appreciation rate results in a larger total profit for export ratios less than 40 percent, while an increasing yen appreciation rate results in a lower total profit for export ratios greater than 40 percent. Figure 14.3 illustrates

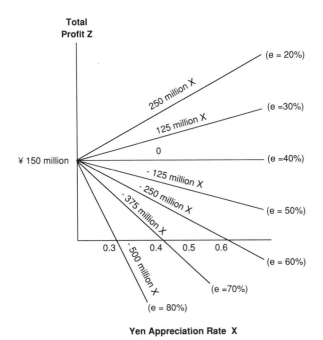

**Figure 14.3 Profit Functions for Various Export Rates**

the profitability functions for various export ratios, assuming that a department has the same cost structure as the Product Q Department.

*Application for Multiple Product Types.* In the analyses, the specified conditions about the cost structure (the dollar and yen components of variable costs) of the product were assumed. To apply these types of analyses to a variety of product departments, however, requires more generalized formulization.

Using a specified yen rate, let $p$ stand for the selling price of the given product, $v$ the variable cost ratio of the selling price with $v_1$ the dollar component (for example, important materials) and $v_2$ the yen component (for example, materials and services bought domestically) (i.e., $v = v_1 + v_2$), $C$ the fixed costs for the period to be analyzed, $N$ the total sales volume, and $e$ the export ratio. The total profit for the period may then be calculated with the following equation:

(11) $Z$ = (domestic) $p\ [1\ -\ v_1(1\ -\ x)\ -v_2]\ (1\ -e\ )\ N$

   + (export) $p\ [(1\ -v_1)\ (1\ -x\ )\ -v_2]\ eN$

   $-$ (fixed costs) $C$

The conditions for a positive gross margin from export sales are:

(12) $(1 - v_1)(1 - x) - v_2 > 0$

$$\therefore\ x < \frac{(1 - v_1 - v_2)}{(1 - v_1)}$$

We may test the equation by using the conditions given for the Product Q Department:

(13) $\quad x < \dfrac{(1 - 0.4 - 0.08)}{(1 - 0.4)} = \dfrac{0.52}{0.6}$

$$= 0.867$$

The results match those obtained in the numerical calculations illustrated in the case summary.

Using the Product R Department as another example, let the current selling price $p$ be ¥ 10,000, the dollar component of variable costs be ¥ 1,000 ($v_1 = 10\%$) and the yen component of variable costs be ¥ 3,000 ($v_2 = 30\%$). The condition for a positive gross margin from export sales is:

(14) $\quad x < \dfrac{(1 - 0.1 - 0.3)}{(1 - 0.1)} = \dfrac{0.6}{0.9}$

$$= 0.667$$

The results indicate that continuation of export sales is preferable when $X$ is less than 66.7 percent, while termination is preferable when $X$ is 66.7 percent or more. As suggested in Equations 11 and 12, it is possible to anticipate the yen appreciation rate $X$ for which termination of export sales becomes preferable without having to know the actual values for factors such as sales volume, export ratio, and selling price.

Let's consider the relationship between monthly profit and export ratio. In the case of a product with a given cost structure, what export ratio marks the point at which the rise in monthly profit that accompanies an appreciating yen changes to a decrease? To find the breakeven point, Equation 11 is modified as follows:

(15) $Z = PN [1 - v_1 (1 - x) - v_2 - (1 - v_1 (1 - x) - v_2)e$
$+ ((1 - v_1) (1 - x) - v_2)e - C$
$= PN [1 - v_1 - v_2 + v_1 x - ex] - C$
$= PN [1 - v_1 - v_2 + (v_1 - e) x] - C$

This equation may be used to obtain the boundary export ratio that marks the point at which the rise in monthly total profit accompanying an appreciating yen rate changes to a decrease:

(16) $(v_1 - e) x = 0$
$\therefore e = v_1$

The boundary export ratio $e$ equals the dollar component of the variable costs of the current selling price. To confirm the applicability of this equation, it may be applied to product $Q$:

$$e = \frac{5,000}{12,500} = 40\%$$

and to product R:

$$e = \frac{1,000}{10,000} = 10\%$$

To be more exact, the yen appreciation may not be reflected in direct proportion to imports or selling price. Assume, for instance, that the corporate staff estimates the savings in the costs of imports with a downward margin of $m_i$, and the pressure to reduce prices in domestic sales during a high yen-to-dollar ratio with a downward margin of $m_p$. In this case, Equations 11 and 15 should be modified as Equations 17 and 18 respectively, where $w = 1 - m_i$ and $u = 1 - m_p$.

(17) $Z = $ (domestic) $p [1 - v_1 (1 - wx) - v_2] (1 - e) N$
$+ $ (export) $p [(1 - ux) - v_1 (1 - wx) - v_2] eN$
$- $ (fixed costs) $C$

(18) $Z = PN [1 - v_1 - v_2 - v_1 wx - eux] - C$
$= PN [1 - v_1 - v_2 - (v_1 w - eu) x] - C$

The condition for a positive gross margin from export sales is:

$$1 - v_1 - v_2(y - v_1 w) x > 0$$

$$x < \frac{(1 - v_1 - v_2)}{(y - v_1 w)}$$

and the boundary export ratio where the rise in monthly profit that accompanies an appreciating yen rate changes to a decrease is:

$$(v_1 w - eu) x = 0$$

$$eu = v_1 w$$

$$\therefore e = \frac{v_1 w}{u}$$

Further development of these equations can be done as discussed.

# 15

## The Transition of Long-Range Planning Systems: The Case of NEC Corporation

*Toyohiro Kōno, Professor of Business Administration,*
*Gakushuin University*
*Yoshihiro Suzuki, Vice President, NEC Corporation*

Long-range corporate planning has evolved in Japan as the business environment has changed. The surveys conducted by Kōno during the past 20 years reveal clearly defined periods of activity, as can be seen in Table 15.1.

After World War II, Japan's economy had to be reconstructed. For companies, the reconstruction of destroyed factories was the first priority. Individual project planning was the activity of the 1950s. Long-range plans for rebuilding equipment were drawn up, but they were not comprehensive.

The 1960s marked a period of quantitative planning. Once Japan's economy entered a high-growth period, the government announced an aggressive national economic plan that greatly stimulated management behavior in general and business planning systems in particular. Comprehensive long-range planning was widely adopted among large corporations.

The planning was mostly quantitative because using capital investment for expansion was the most important strategy. To attain a

| Years | 1950 | 1960 | |
|---|---|---|---|
| Environment | Economic Reconstruction | High Growth Period | |
| Long-Range Plan | 1. Long-range projects plans → | 2. Forecasting and quantitative → | 3. Allocation of goals and quantitative |
| | Long-range plan for projects<br>Centralized planning | Comprehensive<br>Build up approach<br>Emphasis on capital investment | Quantitative<br>Allocation of goals<br>Emphasis on capital investment |

| Years | 1970 | 1974 | 1978 |
|---|---|---|---|
| Environment | From High to Stable Growth | Oil Crisis | Stable Growth |
| Long-Range Plan | → 4. Strategic and all inclusive | → 5. Rationalization oriented | → 6. Strategy oriented |
| | All inclusive strategy | Emphasis on cost reduction | Aggressive long-range strategy plus Medium-range plan |
| | Important strategies are separately considered | PPM and contingency plan were studied | Corporate level strategies are important |
| | Interactive or build up approach | Interactive | Strategic planning department is strengthened |
| | Two long-range plans<br>Use of simulation | | |

**Table 15.1  Transition of Long-Range Planning System**

balance of goals, it was necessary to integrate capital investment through a long-range profit plan. Many specialized companies had forecasting plans, which clearly identified the financial results of capital investment as well as the gaps between needs and available capacity. On the other hand, many diversified companies had goal-clarifying plans. Upper management assigned goals to each department, which in turn drew up quantitative plans to implement the goals from the bottom up.

From 1970 to 1974, the emphasis was on projects — of which there were too many. While the economy continued growing at a high rate, the demand structure was changing. Quantitative planning started emphasizing project-market strategy. In Table 15.2, we notice that the comprehensive problem-solving type plan [A(4)] increased in 1970. Many companies, however, took up too many issues. Their priorities were unclear, and resources were not allocated appropriately. The important strategies tended to be built outside the long-range planning process. To overcome these defects, some companies implemented a two-plan system: (1) the long-range strategic plan and (2) the medium-range plan. In the latter, computer simulation was frequently applied.

The years 1974 to 1977 brought a suspension of long-range plans. The oil crisis resulted in increased uncertainty. Table 15.2 shows a response ratio for 1976. The companies that resumed long-range planning stressed cost-reduction plans. The growth-share matrix model attracted a large amount of attention as a tool for rationalization. The plan's timeline became shorter due to the uncertainty.

As the economy entered a low-growth period following 1976, Japanese companies began to notice that rationalization planning alone was too defensive. To take advantage of the new emerging opportunities, they needed to take positive action. The increase of goal-clarifying plans [A(2)] and an increasing emphasis in 1979 on projects and quantitative-consolidation plans [B(3)] indicate this awareness. Many successful companies selected five to ten key strategic issues around which they built their long-range strategy. At the same time, they developed medium-range plans to integrate these strategies and the allocation of resources. Long-range strategies were implemented from the head office using a top-down or interactive approach.

This description is a simplified account of the transitions in Japanese corporate planning systems over the past 30 years. The

| Year | | 1963 | 1965 | 1967 | 1970 | 1976 | 1979 | 1985 |
|---|---|---|---|---|---|---|---|---|
| **Number of Companies** | | 254 | 298 | 268 | 160 | 57 | 327 | 384 |
| **Response Ratio (%)** | Percent | 17.9 | 23.6 | 25.8 | 25.0 | 13.8 | 28.4 | 25.1 |
| **Characteristics** | A (1) Forecasting | 22% | 17% | 23% | 14% | 14% | 19% | 21% |
| | (2) Clarifying goals, without details | 41 | 44 | 43 | 23 | 16 | 46 | 39 |
| | (3) Individual problem solving | 8 | 2 | 2 | 1 | 0 | 3 | 2 |
| | (4) Comprehensive, including all of the above | 34 | 36 | 32 | 61 | 68 | 30 | 37 |
| | B (1) Mostly quantitative | | | 53 | 46 | 46 | 41 | 40 |
| | (2) Emphasis on projects | | | 3 | 3 | 7 | 10 | 9 |
| | (3) Emphasis on projects and also quantitative consolidation | | | 37 | 46 | 51 | 46 | 51 |
| **Time Horizon** | (1) Over 10 years | 1 | 1 | 1 | 1 | 2 | 2 | 0 |
| | (2) 10-7 years | 6 | 5 | 5 | 13 | 4 | 4 | 1 |
| | (3) 5 or 6 years | 50 | 53 | 59 | 60 | 56 | 34 | 32 |
| | (4) 4 years | 3 | 3 | 5 | 2 | 2 | 5 | 5 |
| | (5) 3 years | 30 | 29 | 35 | 29 | 32 | 47 | 56 |
| | (6) 2 years | 6 | 4 | 6 | 1 | 5 | 5 | 4 |

Comparison of Kōno's seven mail surveys over the past 23 years.

**Table 15.2 Transition of Long-Range Planning System in the Past 20 Years (Survey Analysis)**

changing planning systems have been tied in with the changing environment and the resulting changes in corporate strategies. Experience and improved technical knowledge for planning has been another strong force behind the change. NEC Corporation's long-range planning system typifies the planning systems of diversified Japanese corporations. It has the following characteristics:

- Originally a quantitative and forecasting system, it was recently changed to emphasize new projects and apply quantitative integration using computer simulation.
- Projects are divided into division- and corporate-level strategies (i.e., the corporate business plan).
- The company has a strong corporate planning division to analyze corporate strengths and weaknesses and propose corporate-level strategies. It also plans guidelines for divisions.
- It uses a computer simulation comprised of models for each division. The model is used in an interactive operation.
- It uses the product portfolio matrix with the model adjusted to NEC's specific needs. Because of the need for greater strategic flexibility, the model is used only informally at present.

*The Case of NEC Corporation.* NEC Corporation, founded in 1899, is a leading worldwide supplier of a broad range of communications systems and equipment — computers and industrial electronic systems; electron devices, including semiconductor devices; and home electronics products. It is also a provider of information services. With a total workforce of approximately 102,500, NEC and its subsidiaries and affiliates operate 53 plants in Japan and 25 plants in 12 other countries. NEC maintains 37 subsidiaries in Japan and 50 subsidiaries and affiliates in 22 other countries for manufacturing, marketing, service, and research operations. In fiscal 1988, sales were $21.9 billion (¥2,700 billion).

In 1977, NEC announced its synergistic concept of "C&C," or the integration of computers and communications. It has since focused its research and development, production, marketing, and service activities on this concept to be positioned well in the diversified world market.

"C&C" is a corporate logo expressing NEC's desire to help create a humanistic society through the integration of computers and communications. NEC wants to supply equipment, systems, and services in the information-intensive age. Figure 15.1 shows the transition of NEC's product mix toward the C&C concept.

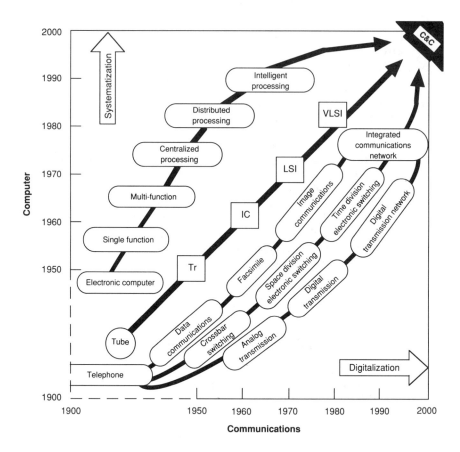

**Figure 15.1  Development of Computer and  Communications (C & C)**

*The Organization for Strategic Decisions.*  NEC's organizational structure is composed of:

1. *Product divisions and customer-oriented marketing departments:* The organizational structure is a mixture of operating and marketing divisions. An operating division is organized around specific products and technologies. Each operating division has full profit responsibility and the freedom to operate like an independent company. Several operating divisions combine to form an operating group, which is directed by a senior executive. The operating group integrates the activities of its operating divisions.

   The marketing function is separate from the operating divisions and is organized by customer or area. As the agents of the operating divisions, the marketing divisions and branch offices are responsible for sales. This system is useful for a customer-oriented integration of sales activities. Clear responsibilities also affect strong sales activities.

2. *Senior executives responsible for broad areas of operations:* Generally, authority tends to be concentrated in upper management under the traditional hierarchical organization. This concentration of power can threaten a large organization because upper managers have many decisions to make. On the other hand, the operating division system tends to develop centrifugally. NEC installed a system in which several senior executives have responsibility for some broad areas of management. The activities of operating divisions tend to be centrifugal because of the inherent delegation of authority. To carry out NEC's integrated strategy, centralizing forces are needed. When certain decisions exceed the capacity of the CEO, authority is shared with senior executives to balance the centrifugal and centripetal forces of groups and divisions under the president.

3. *Top management organization — the senior executive committee and the corporate management committee:* At NEC, two top management organizations are important decision-making bodies that perform strategic decision-making and integrating functions. The senior executive committee is composed of about ten senior vice presidents who freely discuss important strategic issues. The corporate management committee reviews operating issues and is composed of approximately 20 vice presidents, including members of the senior executive committee. The two committees meet alternately every other week. These executive committees are forums for the discussion and review of key issues. They are vehicles for the exchange of ideas and opinions needed to reach the consensus for final decision making.

4. *Frequent use of project teams:* New projects are studied by project teams horizontally composed of members from a number of divisions. This flexible system was instituted in 1965 as a means of revitalizing the company organization. Team members usually work part-time on the project and report to their managers for daily operations. The project leader, however, directs work concerning the project. Recently, under the slogan of C&C, there has been a greater emphasis on pooling the knowledge of two or more operating groups. This has increased the number and importance of companywide project teams.

5. *The corporate planning division and its role:* The corporate planning division prepares corporate-level strategy while supporting and coordinating the long-range planning of operating and other divisions. The five roles of the corporate planning division are:
   a. To analyze NEC's macroeconomic environment. This includes

analyzing the political and economic environment and monitoring future trends. Impacts of these trends are evaluated and disseminated to the divisions concerned.
b. To formulate medium-range plans. This means consolidating the medium-range planning of all units and developing a planning system to help the line divisions build their medium-range plans.
c. To prepare corporate-level strategic plans. This involves monitoring the rapidly changing environment, planning department surveys, analyzing corporate strategic issues.
d. To increase NEC's competitive power by initiating plans to reinforce the company's resource structure, promoting ways to attain the objective, and formulating plans to enhance productivity and review their implementation.
e. To assist the two top management committees by scheduling, arranging subjects for review, and recording the proceedings.

*The History and Features of Medium-Range Planning.* All organizations, not just business enterprises, must establish clear policies to let people know their purpose and shared values. At NEC, this corporate philosophy is the C&C concept. Because people participate in business for various reasons, the business management system acts as a motivational tool to encourage members to want to attain the corporation's goals and philosophy. The management planning system is an important feature of this tool.

There are four aspects of business planning: (1) a plan is classified by subject — a comprehensive plan covers the entire company while a partial (or individual) plan covers a specific division or a certain project; (2) a plan is classified by its contents — whether it is strategic or tactical in nature, whether it changes the business structure or management process; (3) planning is classified into long-, medium-, and short-range time lines; and (4) planning can be classified into a period plan or project plan, whether or not it is consolidated over a certain period. These four aspects enable us to classify NEC's medium-range planning as general, strategic, and medium-range period planning. Medium-range planning is developed for four reasons:

1. To reach a consensus on the business environment (i.e., political, economic, marketing, and technological trends).
2. To examine strategic issues that affect NEC's product market.
3. To coordinate the goals of all units with the corporation.
4. To forecast medium-range demands for corporate resources and the means to provide them.

Medium-range planning at NEC started in 1966 when each division's five-year, long-range plan was formulated and presented to the president. Since then, in what is called a rolling form, planning has been conducted and revised each year by adding another year. During this period, high growth was the goal of all divisions, and numbers-oriented, long-range planning was established. The view was that the more each business grew, the more NEC's overall performance would rise. Plans were based on a bottom-up approach.

The devaluation of the dollar in 1971, coupled with the 1973 oil crisis, made us review our long-range planning. Because we needed a method to overcome the immediate difficulties confronting us rather than a plan for the future, long-range planning was suspended. We lived from day to day.

When the company solved its problems in 1976, long-range planning, which was renamed medium-range planning, began again. The name was changed because upper management felt that ten years was a suitable length of time for a long-range plan. Three- or five-year plans, however, were better termed medium-range. At present, this applies not only to our company but also to NEC's domestic and foreign subsidiaries and affiliates. The goal is to establish an NEC group vision.

*The Relationship Between Medium-Range Planning, Project Planning, and the Budget.* The medium-range or three-to-five-year plan differs from an annual budget. It encompasses the entire company and all activities of its business groups over the period in question. Project planning, on the other hand, deals with specific projects. The relationship among the three plans, however, is close. The medium-range plan integrates the three-to-five-year project plans of each division, while the budget plan is a short-range (yearly) general plan.

We want to emphasize that NEC's medium-range plan is comprised of a number of strategic project plans making up the core of the period plan. Before the oil crisis, long-range plans were merely quantitative. Important project plans that had a large impact on the company as a whole are called corporate business plans (CBPs). They are at the heart of medium-range planning.

*The Process of Formulating the Medium-Range Plan.* The first step toward medium-range planning is to construct a forecast of the environment and set guidelines for the entire company. The complexity and speed of change is increasing: technology advances, the scale of economic activity grows, and society becomes more complex. This growing level of uncertainty increases the importance of analyzing the world environment, the Japanese economy, and industrial trends. Accurate analysis of the environment, in fact, is the premise of successful medium-range planning.

**Guidelines.** Following the environmental analysis, guidelines for future profits and losses, the flow of funds, and a product and market structure are formulated. For this reason, we examine the surroundings of individual operating units, market trends, and so on; estimate the results of ongoing project plans; and set goals. This work is done mainly by the corporate planning division.

1. *Business environment analysis:* The business environment analysis describes the impact of the world or Japanese economy on business management and industrial trends. We first analyze the basic problems of the world economy and the trends of the advanced nations, developing countries, and the Communist bloc. In the Japanese economy, we examine the factors with a future impact on the pattern of economic growth; changing demand structure; exchange rate of the yen; prospect of rising wages; price trends, including wholesale prices and the cost of living; and interest rates. In industry, we study production changes, the direction of the international division of labor, and investment trends of major industries in plant and equipment. We next look at electronic trends — communication systems, computers, electronic devices, and home electronics products. We examine how the changes in domestic demand, overseas market, and supply of key resources will affect business management. These analyses are usually conducted by the corporate planning division in conjunction with the appropriate divisions.

2. *Establishing guidelines:* Guidelines are drawn based on the forecast of the environment. At its core are the financial plans. We estimate the business resources input after analyzing the company's existing situation. We break it down by business groups and estimate the profit based on such resources planning.

   This stage does not reflect the intention of operating groups because goals are established from the top down based on the overall corporate financial plan. They reflect rather standard goals. Guidelines made in such a way are presented to the business groups on only important indexes such as the rate of return on total capital. We think that showing too many numerical values prevents divisions from formulating original plans.

**Drawing up a business group's medium range plan.** Next, we design the medium-range plan for divisions or operating groups. Divisions draw up business images that reflect the business policy and, at the same time, examine its operating environment. Using trade information, the marketing division of each business group knows enough about the market situation to provide the planning information. The product division prepares a plan based on the orders received and a sales plan based on the demand trend. In addition, the profit index, flow of funds, rate of return, and turnover rate of assets are planned by the divisions based on orders and the sales plan. It is important to examine thoroughly medium-range strategic issues. For example, is it necessary to increase personnel to make an expected profit or build a new factory? Or, should we build a manufacturing plant overseas? Medium-range plans that include measures dealing with these problems are drawn up by division and reviewed by operating groups.

When plans are complete, upper management holds a review meeting. The medium-range plans of each operating group are examined from every angle and are linked to NEC's overall corporate medium-range plan. During these discussions, the prerequisites for achieving the goals, problems, and the degree of reliability of the plans emerge.

*A Simulation Model for Medium-Range Planning.* When the medium-range plan is formulated, each division and business group use the computer. To make the overall company plan, the planning department uses a computer simulation model to formulate the guidelines or to periodically review the medium-range plan of the operating groups. The prototype of this model was developed in 1970. Since then it has been improved and become a convenient tool for daily estimating.

The minimal planning unit of the model, shown in Figure 15.2, can be used to formulate guidelines using a top-down approach, and also to review and coordinate the medium-range plans of operating groups presented in a bottom-up approach. The input parameter of this system is 221 (initial value, 42; policy parameter, 179). Input by OCR sheet or direct input by time-sharing system (TSS) are available. Output is 13 simulation output on display and 22 final printed output by line printer. This is a conversational type simulation model by TSS that is quick and easy to use.

*Concentration Management and NEC's Product Profit Management.* The electronics industry, to which our company belongs, contains many high-growth areas. Although the future for the electronics industry

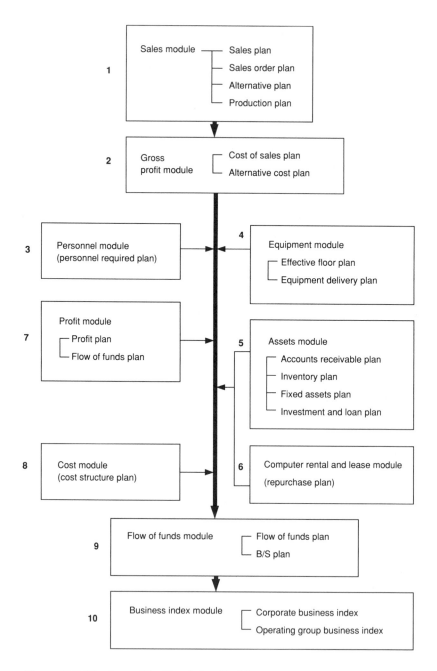

**Figure 15.2 Structure of the Simulation Model**

looks rosy, it is not possible to distribute corporate resources to every area equally. We have to allocate our limited resources selectively. At NEC, the resources needed for the growing semiconductor and information-processing divisions is enormous. Communication systems equipment is also a high-growth field compared to other industries. Moreover, it is a field now confronted with the technological change of digitalization, which demands adequate resources. It is not an exaggeration to say, in fact, that almost every division is in need of resources, a phenomenon also confirmed by the medium-range plan.

At the time the medium-range plan (which indicates the business strategy) is drawn up, the direction and priority of each business strategy should be clarified, with resources distributed to the high-priority areas. The tool used to promote this concentrated management is NPPM, NEC's version of product portfolio management (PPM).

**Strategic use of NPPM.** The purpose of PPM is to create an overview of the number of the corporation's businesses — to evaluate them and improve the product mix. When a corporation has several businesses, it is important to visualize and evaluate them in terms of market attractiveness and competitive position. Only then can ways to improve the entire business structure be discovered.

The aim of NPPM is to enhance strategic thinking at the division level. Each division is expected to know how to segment its own businesses, see the changing needs of its markets and customers and the movement of its competitors, and analyze its strengths and weaknesses. The corporate planning division provides several guidelines for investigating and extracting concrete strategic alternatives. With NPPM, it is simple to show the relative positions of businesses.

The NPPM matrix uses market attractiveness on the vertical axis and NEC's competitiveness on the horizontal axis. It has nine segments, which are shown in Table 15.3; the criteria are shown in Table 15.4.

NPPM applies the six steps shown in Figure 15.3. These are classified into: (1) the analytical (or business positioning) phase and (2) the strategic (or investigating) phase.

In the analytical phase, we first segment the businesses of each division. Then evaluation data are collected from past years. Lastly, by inputting the data into personal computers, the NPPM matrix is projected automatically. (See Figure 15.4.)

| Market Attractiveness ↑ | | |
|---|---|---|
| (Star)<br>Maintain and enhance the advantageous position | (Challenger)<br>Reinforce and expand | (Problem Child)<br>Raise market share |
| (Captain)<br>Maintain competitive advantage | (Weather Cock)<br>Stabilize | (Drop-Out)<br>Restrictively selective |
| (Cash Cow)<br>Recover invested capital | (Old Chicken)<br>Eat up | (Dog)<br>Minimize losses |

← **Company Strength**

**Table 15.3  NPPM Matrix Quadrants, Names and Characteristics**

| Market Attractiveness | | Business Strengths | |
|---|---|---|---|
| **Evaluation Index** | **Weight** | **Evaluation Index** | **Weight** |
| Market growth rate | 50 | Relative market share | 50 |
| Profitability of the industry | 30 | Profitability of the business | 30 |
| Market size | 20 | Size of sales | 20 |
| **Total** | **100** | **Total** | **100** |

**Table 15.4  Evaluation Indexes and Their Assigned Weights**

In the strategic phase of NPPM, whether it is balanced or not, the position of each business segment is reviewed. "The Guide to Business Balance" is provided in Figure 15.5 to help evaluate the positions. The direction and role of each business segment is thus clarified by comparison with the ideal NPPM matrix.

Next, individual strategies are compared with the ideal models for every business segment. "The Guide for Strategic Alternatives" shown in Figure 15.6 is prepared for every quadrant to indicate points of review and the sequence of investigation. The strategic alternatives are then evaluated and chosen based on the criteria, taking into account the risk involved, the probability of achievement, and the available resources.

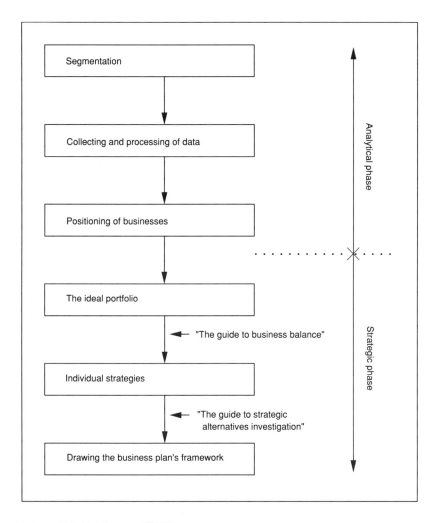

**Figure 15.3  The Steps of NPPM**

Finally, strategies are checked from two viewpoints: (1) whether or not they contradict each other and (2) whether or not the strategies are satisfactory compared to the ideal portfolio. Only then are the divisions' future NPPM matrices and concrete strategic plans determined. The results of the NPPM investigation are used as a framework for the medium-range or business plans. Action plans are drawn up with the business plans as a foundation.

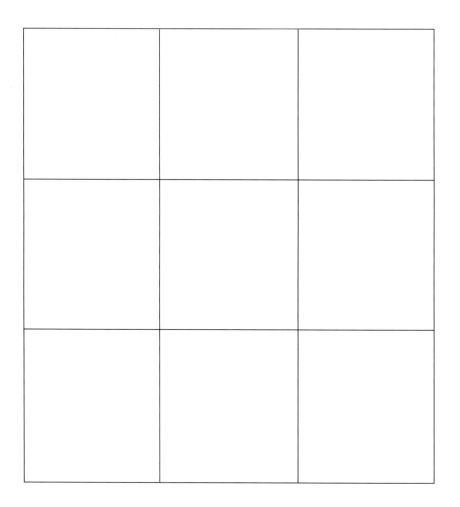

The size of the circle indicates the size of sales of segments.

**Figure 15.4 The Current NPPM Matrix**

**Recent NPPM application changes.** Under the new circumstances of a rapidly changing market structure and crossover technologies, the need for complete yet flexible decision making increased. We found the use of the NPPM method gradually decreased. PPM's basic concept — positioning businesses in light of markets, competition, and resources — remains important, however, even today.

This guide is to help investigate whether or not the entire division is balanced or not according to the described portfolio.

Divide the matrix into 4 quadrants; pattern the business distribution in 15 ways.

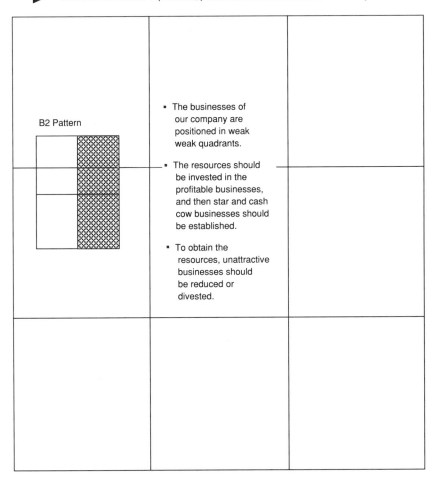

The size of the circle indicates the size of sales of segments.

**Figure 15.5  The Guide to Business Balance — An Example**

***Two Issues.*** There are two issues that NEC must confront: (1) the company may be getting too large, (2) the company is not yet sufficiently globalized. In 1981, NEC became a trillion-yen corporation, 82 years after its establishment. Five years later, in 1986, our company became a two-trillion-yen corporation. If NEC loses the

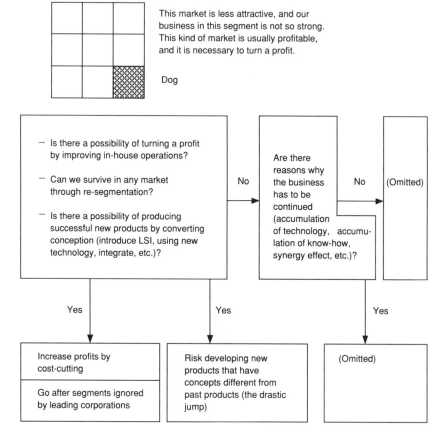

**Figure 15.6 The Guide for Strategic Alternatives — An Example**

ability to adapt to environmental changes, then, although the markets will continue to grow, our company will not. The issue is how to maintain and reinforce corporate adaptability, which tends to be weakened by expansion. At NEC, we have a saying: "A seemingly stable corporation contains the seeds of instability, while a seemingly unstable corporation can be stable." We feel that, even though, at a glance, a company may seem unstable, it can survive if it perpetuates innovation and creativity. It is necessary to establish an information system sensitive to change.

As NEC globalizes, intense competition with foreign companies is inevitable. Already, in fact, NEC's biggest rivals are IBM, the leader in information processing, and AT&T, the leader in communication systems. To preserve our competitive advantage with these two excellent companies, we must promote the globalization of our business and broaden the perspective of our people. First, it is necessary to promote local production. At present, 7,000 people — most of them U.S. citizens — work in our U.S. companies. Second, giving and encouraging an international perspective in our people is crucial. One way to attain this objective is to provide a training department that will increase employee's skills in international management.

### References

1. Kōno, Toyohiro. (1984). *The Strategy and Structure of Japanese Enterprises*. London: Macmillan Press.
2. Kōno, Toyohiro. (In press). *Long-Range Planning of Japanese Corporations*. London: Macmillan Press. The Japanese original was published in 1986 by Kobunkan Publishing Company in Tokyo.

# 16

## A Japanese Survey of Factory Automation and Its Impact on Management Control Systems

*Michiharu Sakurai, Professor of Accounting, Senshu University*
*Philip Y. Huang, CPIM, Associate Professor of*
*Management Science, Virginia Polytechnic Institute*

Factory automation (FA) has recently become an increasingly popular term in Japan. Generally speaking, FA can be defined as the automation of the factory through the use of flexible manufacturing systems (FMS), computer-aided-design/computer-aided-manufacturing (CAD/CAM), and office automation (OA). Of these three basic elements, FMS is the core of FA. Typically designed for mid-volume and mid-variety production, FMS integrates industrial robots, numerical control (NC) machines, and automated material handling systems using the concept of cellular manufacturing.

As a result of these technological innovations, continuous production in process-oriented industries such as steel, petroleum, and chemicals developed rapidly in Japan in the 1960s. Japanese assembly-oriented industries that produced a variety of products in medium to small volumes experienced numerous difficulties that have only recently been resolved. Due to the lack of consumer demand for product variety in the 1960s, the performance of these industries was rated quite low in Japan compared to other process-oriented industries.

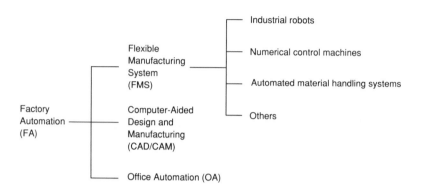

**Figure 16.1 The Relationship Between Flexible Manufacturing System (FMS) and Other Basic Elements of Factory Automation (FA)**

This situation started to change in the early 1970s, however, when assembly-oriented companies began attracting the attention of the business world. One reason for this development was the maturity of the Japanese consumer. By the time of OPEC's oil embargo, Japanese consumers were already demanding greater product variety. The demand for durable consumer goods was high, even by Western standards. To satisfy and further stimulate consumer demand, Japanese companies concentrated on specialized products.

The development and application of FMS has also contributed Japan's emphasis on mid-variety and mid-volume production. FMS has made it possible to automate the production process and thus reduce the direct labor cost. As a result, related industries have rapidly changed their production systems. New management control concepts suitable to these new production systems have also been developed simultaneously.

The object of this study is to discuss the change in management control systems due to Japan's introduction of FMS. A survey of 32 Japanese companies, mostly assembly-oriented, was conducted from 1984 to 1985. The majority of the surveys were on-site, as opposed to telephone interviews, to facilitate the discussion. Table 16.1 presents the distribution of these 32 industries by type. To further confirm our results, seven additional assembly-oriented companies were interviewed on-site in late 1985. Some of these interviewed companies have already implemented FMS, while others are still in the process of installation.

| Types of Industry | Number of Companies |
|---|---|
| Electrical | 10 |
| Motor vehicles | 6 |
| Machinery | 4 |
| Chemical | 3 |
| Precision devices | 2 |
| Food | 2 |
| Glass | 1 |
| Metal products | 1 |
| Other manufacturing | 3 |
| **Total** | **32** |

**Table 16.1  Industries Interviewed by Type**

*Impact of FMS on Labor Structure.* Productivity increases through reductions in direct labor costs have prompted interest in FMS — many companies have reported a significant reduction in direct labor cost through the use of FMS. To name a few, Toshiba Tungaloi has reduced direct labor costs from 70 to 16 percent, Niigata Engineering from 31 to 4 percent, and Yamazaki Iron & Steel from 25 to 12 percent.[1] Reduced direct labor costs have also been observed in other Japanese industries.[2]

FMS can reduce direct labor costs, which can be collected from and measured by production orders. At the same time, FMS can increase the indirect labor costs to be allocated. Consequently, FMS has drastically changed the cost structure of industries that have adopted it. Kenichi Ohmae commented on the net result of this change:

> FMS has changed traditional assembly-oriented industries such as automobile, appliance, semiconductor, and camera manufacturers, 25 percent or more of whose total cost structures traditionally were composed of labor costs. As a result of advanced production technology, automation, robot machining centers, and numerical controls, their labor content is now declining to something like 5 or 10 percent. In other words, the labor-intensive industries of yesterday are becoming capital intensive. According to Ohmae, they no longer absorb large amounts of labor.[3]

According, however, to some statistical data, Ohmae's view may not be correct. Our survey has indicated that the total labor cost content in overall manufacturing costs has decreased little, if any, in spite of the fact that the direct labor cost decreased significantly in the assembly-oriented industries. Table 16.2 displays the labor cost structure of four representative companies selected from both assembly-oriented and process-oriented industries. As indicated in this table, the percentage of labor cost in overall manufacturing cost has increased at Matsushita Electric and Nissan Motor, despite the fact that the direct labor force has decreased rapidly in the last two decades.

| Industry/Company | 1963* | 1973 | 1983 |
|---|---|---|---|
| Assembly-oriented | | | |
| Matsushita Electric | 13.2% | 14.6% | 14.6% |
| Nissan Motor | 6.7 | 8.8 | 9.9 |
| | | | |
| Process-oriented | | | |
| Nippon Oil | 9.3 | 2.4 | 2.0 |
| Nippon Kokan | 7.7 | 5.6 | 11.9 |

*Statistics are collected in March of each year.

**Table 16.2  Percentage of Labor Cost in the Total Manufacturing Cost**

There are four possible reasons that account for the increased percentage of labor costs in the total manufacturing costs of assembly-oriented industries:

1. Accompanying the decline in employment of skilled workers, there is a sharp increase in demand for monitoring and maintenance. Regardless of how automated the factories become, there is always a need for monitoring. In Japanese companies today, maintenance staffs are employed primarily to do the preventive maintenance required to minimize unscheduled machine downtime and maximize equipment utilization.
2. Although the demand for manual labor in automated factories is expected to continue decreasing in the future, the demand for innovative work such as software development and R&D activities has increased rapidly. For example, the Fuji plants of Fanuc Ltd. are well known, automated factories. As indicated in Table 16.3, total labor costs at Fanuc have not decreased since the completion

of their plants in December 1980, despite the decreasing number of field workers. This phenomenon is best stated by Mr. Inaba, president of Fanuc: "The number of software engineers in the R&D department is already half of the entire workforce and it will continue to increase in the future."[4]

3. Because of the life-time employment system, which is unique to Japanese society, companies have great difficulty dismissing their employees. Employees are not to be laid off, even if there is no work for them to do. Instead, employees are usually transferred to other departments such as maintenance, engineering, or marketing. These labor costs understandably become a burden to automated factories.

4. Since the early 1970s, the labor cost per employee has increased sharply. In addition to the general increase in blue-collar wages, the highly paid professionals enjoyed even greater increases in salaries. Indirect labor costs, however, have increased significantly in high-tech industries, regardless of the decreases in direct labor costs. As labor costs become indirect, there is a tendency to treat them as a capacity cost rather than an activity cost. As more professionals are employed by companies using FMS, new management tools are needed to measure and control indirect labor activities to improve their productivity.

*Changes in Management Control Systems.* The decreasing number of workers needed in an automated factory has caused a decline in the importance of the following management control systems: (1) direct costing, (2) the worker rate method, and (3) standard costing.

**Direct costing.** In addition to the declining direct labor cost, the main labor cost in an FMS company consists of paying those who work in maintenance, monitoring, R&D, and software development. These labor costs are basically indirect or fixed costs. Consequently, the variable portion of the direct costing tends to decrease, and material costs have become the only variable cost in direct costing.

In fact, only four of the 32 companies we interviewed still use direct costing. Two of these four are chemical companies that do not use FMS. Several executives have indicated that direct costing is a relic of the early 1960s and no longer suitable for today's business environment. For companies using FMS, "absorption costing becomes the only meaningful costing approach."[5]

**The worker rate method.** Traditional textbooks tell us that direct labor hours have been the accepted theoretical cost accounting method. This is true, however, only when the product is produced

| Cost Items | 1980 | 1981 | 1982 | 1983 | 1984 |
|---|---|---|---|---|---|
| Materials | 27,094 | 45,392 | 42,882 | 35,443 | 47,482 |
| Labor Cost | | | | | |
| Subcontracting[1] | 760 | 849 | 794 | 1,035 | 4,543 |
| Labor Cost | 2,373 (7.4%) | 2,699 (5.2%) | 3,172 (6.3%) | 3,428 (7.8%) | 3,733 (6.2%) |
| **Subtotal** | 3,133 (9.8%) | 3,548 (6.9%) | 3,966 (7.9%) | 4,463 (10.2%) | 8,276 (13.8%) |
| Manufacturing Expense | 1,659 | 2,756 | 3,356 | 3,869 | 4,070 |
| **Total Manufacturing Cost** | 31,886 (100%) | 51,696 (100%) | 50,205 (100%) | 43,776 (100%) | 59,831 (100%) |

[1]Expense paid to subcontractors for parts manufacturing. The material is usually given to the subcontractors with the purpose of saving the parent company's labor cost.
Source: *Securities Report* (similar to the U.S.'s *10k*)
(Units: Million Yen)

**Table 16.3  Percentage of Labor Cost in Total Manufacturing Cost — Fanuc Ltd.**

primarily by floor workers. With automation, in theory, the importance of the direct labor hour method diminishes, and that of the
machine rate method becomes more significant. Consequently, it is
no longer considered appropriate to use direct labor hours as a means
to allocate the overhead cost in automated factories. As Kimio
Kaneko of Oki Electric pointed out, to produce IC chips, companies
have to invest heavily.[6] The Japanese semiconductor industry is
therefore called the "money-gobbling industry." Compared to other
companies, and due to the large capital investment in FMS facilities,
the ratio of depreciation to labor costs increases dramatically, and the
percentage of overhead to total cost continues to climb. The semiconductor industry in Japan therefore tends to favor the machine rate
method. In fact, our survey has found that the machine rate method
has recently been introduced into companies such as NEC, Mitsubishi
Electric, and others.

The machine rate method has been strongly recommended to
high-tech industries in recent articles published in the United States.[7]
In the same articles, however, implementation problems of this
method were rarely discussed. Practical problems experienced by
many Japanese companies when implementing the machine rate
method are:

- How do we allocate the cost of idle capacity?
- If several machines are used, how do we choose the representative
  one?
- Even in an FMS environment, cost management by worker-hour is
  still important, not only for pure labor but also for maintenance
  work. How do we then devise a way to connect management by
  worker-hour to overhead cost allocation?

Due to the difficulty in solving these three problems, the number
of companies switching to the machine rate method is not as large as
we expected in Japan.

**Standard costing.** Standard costing was originally developed as
a control tool to improve factory efficiency. To improve worker efficiency, standard costing focused on controlling direct labor. The variance analysis of direct labor was therefore the most important of the
manufacturing cost variance analyses.

As previously discussed, the development of factory automation
has caused a decrease in the importance of standard costing as an efficiency control device. Since the ultimate goal is to achieve a worker-
free factory, it becomes meaningless in FA factories to establish standard

costs or to analyze the cost variance of direct labor. Moreover, the evolution of technology has lessened the relative importance of standard costing. Technological innovations have shortened the product's life cycle, as well as the improvement period of production methods. The stability of the production process, one of the more important conditions in implementing the standard costing method, has been reduced. Likewise, as the pace of technological innovation speeds up, the importance of production control activities in various production stages has diminished. Cost reduction at the product design stage has become more important.

Although standard costing has lost status in cost control due to automation and new technological innovations in assembly-oriented industries, it is still important in (1) furnishing data for preparing financial statements, and (2) simplifying and speeding up the computational procedure. Of the 32 companies interviewed, 26 still use standard costing. In short, our survey shows that the main role of standard costing in assembly-oriented industries has changed drastically from a cost control device to one that speeds up the preparation of financial statements and other financial accounting documents. This trend will continue as long as FMS is developing.

*Projecting Costs for Cost Reduction.* In the past, cost control activities in Japan were centered around maintaining and improving manufacturing cost. Standard costing had been the best control device for this purpose. As economic growth and expansion ceased, however, companies could no longer control production cost simply by using standard costing. The emphasis of cost management shifted therefore from controlling costs at the production stage to controlling costs at the design stage. The projected cost technique originated with Japanese automakers in the early 1970s, and was unknown to U.S. managers and researchers. It was introduced to the assembly-oriented industries such as makers of automobiles and household appliances during the first oil crisis, and is thought to have come from the concept of *management by objectives*. To implement a cost project, target costs must be established. The projected cost technique is also called the *target cost technique*. In Japan's major assembly-oriented industries, the projected cost method has already been firmly integrated into management control systems. Of the 32 companies interviewed, 18 (mostly manufacturers of automobiles, electronics, and machinery) had adopted the projected cost technique. Target costs are usually computed not in the accounting department, but in the R&D or engineering departments. The accounting departments of several companies, however, have actively participated in setting target costs and conducting variance analysis.

Although no standards have been established to implement projected costs, the following procedures developed in certain auto companies are provided as examples:

1. Identify the highest quality products that meet customer demands.
2. Establish target costs by applying value engineering (VE) and completing the process at the design stage.
3. Attain the target cost at the production stage using the standard cost.

From the viewpoint of managerial accounting, steps 2 and 3 are extremely important for the purposes of controlling and reducing costs.

After this first stage, the base cost of a product is established based on the status quo of each cost item. The target cost is then computed by subtracting the target profit from the selling price:

Target cost = selling price − target profit

The target cost is broken down into individual cost items, as indicated in the target cost sheet in Table 16.4.

The target cost is set based on one of the following three methods: (1) profit planning, (2) engineering planning, and (3) a combination of profit and engineering planning.[8] In every case, the production department should initiate the discussion of problems related to setting the target cost. The target cost typically is set for the total manufacturing cost. In some cases, however, it is limited to the conversion cost only.[9] Jun Saito of Atsugi Auto Parts Industries gives the following reason for this practice: "It is preferable to include only the conversion cost in the target cost because it enables management to focus on supervision."[10] Other reasons may include the diminished need for materials control, the repetition of the conversion process, and the spoilage rate.

The target cost is established to be attainable and motivate workers. It is authorized by top management. Foremen are responsible for carrying out the specific activities of the target cost. Control activities

| Number of Cars Produced | |
|---|---|

| Items | Base (Cost) | | Target (Cost) | |
|---|---|---|---|---|
| | Total | Per Car | Total | Per Car |
| Number of Workers<br>Direct Labor<br>Indirect Labor<br>Administrative<br>**Total** | Workers | Workers | Workers | Workers |
| **Number of Cars per Worker** | | Cars/<br>worker | | Cars/<br>worker |
| Conversion Cost<br>Running Cost<br>Wage<br>Utility<br>Supplies<br>Tools and Furniture<br>Defective Cost<br>**Total**<br>Fixed Expense<br>Maintenance Cost<br>Administrative<br>**Total**<br>Facility Related Cost<br>Depreciation<br>Property Tax<br>Insurance<br>**Total**<br>Amount Paid to<br>Subcontractors | $ | $ | $ | $ |
| **Grand Total** | | | | |

**Table 16.4  The Target Cost to Be Attained**

begin when manufacturing starts. Cost elements are reported regularly by the foremen, usually every one to three months. Cost variances are studied and corrective actions recommended to the cost reduction committee.

A comparison between the target cost and performance is made during the process of cost reduction activities. The comparison can occur as an integral part of the budget, or only in terms of quantity. In either case, the comparison differs from standard costing.

Generally, the projected cost method has been implemented chiefly in assembly-oriented industries because it is necessary for these industries to change models frequently. Projected cost is not suitable for process-oriented industries such as materials industries because, as pointed out by Shigeki Suenaga of Sumitomo Electric, "It is impossible for our industries producing wires and cables to attain the level of target cost by product design."[11] It should be recognized that certain industries are not suitable for projecting costs; however, since there is a general trend moving away from the standard costing toward the projected cost as a cost control technique, it seems to us that projected cost may be adjusted to suit other industries.

Projected cost is viewed as a cost reduction tool replacing standard costing, which is losing its importance as a cost control device. Projected cost can also be viewed as a tool promoting engineering cost techniques, such as total quality control (TQC), just-in-time (JIT), and value engineering (VE). The relationship between projected cost, budgeting, and other engineering cost techniques is shown in Figure 16.2.

**Engineering Cost Techniques.** A cost project cannot be implemented successfully in a company without the support of other tools such as engineering cost techniques. During the 1960s, several scientific management techniques, such as quality control (QC), economic order quantity (EOQ), and cost down (CD, or cost improvement), were introduced to Japan. In the 1970s, especially after the first energy crisis, these techniques were improved to meet the requirements of Japan's unique business environment. The improvements, such as the TQC, JIT, and VE, are currently adopted in Japan.

**Total quality control.** In 1966, Japan's Ministry of International Trade and Industry (MITI) published a statement entitled "Cost Management" to promote economic development. It illustrated the importance of quality control:

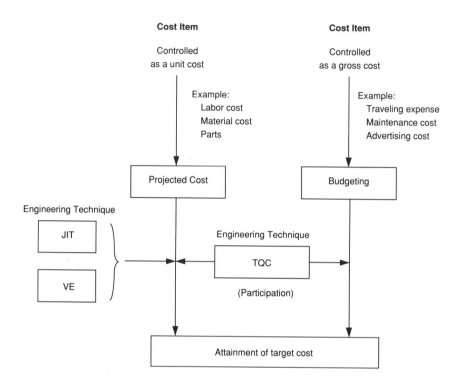

**Figure 16.2 Field Cost Improvement in Assembly-Oriented Industries**

Setting adequate quality standards and acquiring process stability by means of quality control contribute significantly toward increasing consumer trust through quality stability and fewer defects.[12]

This statement clearly indicates how hard Japan's government and business management sectors strived to build international confidence through improved quality in Japanese-made products, notorious in the 1950s for their inferior quality.

The fundamental difference between U.S. QC and Japanese TQC lies in the concept of *inspection*.[13] Unlike the Western QC systems that focus mainly on quality inspection, Japanese TQC concentrates on companywide quality control activities in which all employees in all departments participate. The autonomous activities of QC circles play an important role. While the goal of QC is closely related to production control, TQC is related to every area of business activity including engineering design. Consequently, TQC is an effective tool for implementing the target cost. All the companies surveyed in this study adopted the TQC system, despite the fact that several of them still use traditional QC terminology.

**Just-in-time.** In the 1960s, most Japanese companies began turning their attention to the EOQ analysis, which had originated earlier in the United States as an operations research technique. In Japan's *Cost Management* journal, MITI stressed the importance of EOQ as a cost engineering tool in 1966:

> In computing the optimal lot size, the sum of the annual setup cost and the annual interest cost of holding inventory should be at the minimal level by selecting the optimal lot size.

The premise of EOQ analysis is to hold certain amounts of inventory. Most Japanese companies, which suffered the effects of the energy crisis and needed badly to reduce cost, believe that inventory is the root of all evils. They want to reduce inventory levels to zero, if possible. This suggests that the trade-off analysis of EOQ is not suitable for typical Japanese companies.

While EOQ analysis is still useful for process-oriented industries such as iron ore and oil refining, it is almost useless to assembly-oriented industries. Although many process-oriented companies surveyed in this study still use EOQ analysis, none of the assembly-oriented companies did. They implemented just-in-time production instead — 19 of the 32 companies implemented JIT production. It should be noted that all the companies showed great interest in JIT. Several reasons why some companies do not use JIT are (1) difficulty in stabilizing the production process, (2) too many parts, (3) too small a production volume, (4) relatively low inventory holding costs, and (5) lack of subcontractors required by company policy. Three companies adopted an integrated system of material requirements planning (MRP) and JIT.

Small-lot production, a basic feature of JIT, can be attributed to (1) the social need for product variety, and (2) productivity problems from low-volume and high-variety production. JIT, an effective management tool for Japanese companies producing small to medium quantities of a large variety of products, should be viewed as a technique to increase the return on investment.[14] In short, JIT is a well-developed tool for both attaining the target cost in the projected cost and increasing the return on investment.

**Value engineering.** When the concept of VE was first introduced in Japan, it was used mainly as a management tool to control
purchasing activities. Now, however, the use of VE extends to the
control of all kinds of activities, not just purchasing. In the past, the
cost down (CD) technique (which is "Japanese-English" for reducing
cost through standard costing and other cost control techniques) was
an important tool for helping plant managers reduce cost. It was ineffective, however, due to the limited number of areas where CD can be
applied. While CD may improve the operation of part of the organization, it may also cause a decline in quality or a cost increase companywide. As a consequence, VE was introduced into Japan to overcome
CD's deficiency.

The fundamental difference between CD and VE is that the latter
is performed on a companywide basis. It can reduce cost without
reducing product quality. Consequently, a company as a whole can
benefit significantly by reducing costs in areas other than production,
even with a cost increase in a certain department.

To summarize, TQC, JIT, and VE have been effectively introduced into FMS companies in Japan. Without doubt, these
techniques will be implemented increasingly in the future.

**Return on Sales as a Target Profit.** Whether return on investment
(ROI) or residual income (RI) should be used as a measure of a division's performance has been a controversial issue in the United
States. While return on sales (ROS) has also been considered a measure, it has largely been ignored for a long time in the United States
because of the way capital investment is measured:

ROI = ROS × turnover

Income/Investment = Income/Sales × Sales/Investment

The use of ROI has been criticized by U.S. researchers because it
tempts division managers to avoid active investment.[15] Quite a few
U.S. managers, however, do use ROI as a measure of performance
evaluation. According to Reece and Cool (1978), 65 percent of the
companies they surveyed used ROI exclusively, 27.7 percent used
both ROI and RI, and only 2 percent used RI exclusively. It is important to note that the use of ROI is on the rise, as compared to the earlier Mauriel and Anthony survey.

In Japan, many researchers felt strongly that ROI should have more widespread management use because, at least theoretically, it was superior to RI and ROS. Most practitioners, however, continued to use the absolute profit amount, which is an approximate RI figure, for two reasons: (1) active investment can be compensated for capital gain from inflation during times of high economic growth, and (2) there was little or no pressure from stockholders. The use of the absolute profit amount as a performance measure consequently gained popularity in Japan in the high-growth period of the 1960s.[16]

ROS is frequently used by many companies, along with the absolute profit amount. According to the Economic Planning Agency's 1976 survey on measures of target profit, ROS was used by 12.6 percent of the 996 public companies, trailing behind the periodic profit (70.2 percent) and ROI (15.8 percent).[17] Our FMS survey indicated that there are quite a few FMS firms using ROS to measure target profit. The results of our findings are presented in Table 16.5, which indicates that ROS has been a more popular measure of target profit than ROI and periodic profit in FMS firms.

Reasons for using ROS differ from company to company. The following is a list of explanations compiled from our interviews:

1. ROS can clearly reveal the profitability of each product in a high-variety environment.
2. From the standpoint of cost benefit, it is almost impossible for companies producing low-volume and high-variety products to compute ROI for each product.
3. The amount of investment is relatively small compared to process-oriented industries.
4. For custom-made types of industries, which frequently use FMS, ROS is useful for making make-or-buy decisions.
5. ROI cannot be computed effectively in high-tech companies because the amount of capital investment fluctuates frequently.
6. Since the capital investment required for producing profitable products in the future is quite large, ROI can make a promising business look negative.
7. The use of ROS has a positive effect on workers and management alike.
8. ROS is easy to understand.
9. ROS can be effectively applied when there is a stable demand and little or no anxiety about a drop in sales volume.
10. ROS can be used safely when a company is not a division of another company.
11. Since the company is privately owned, there is little pressure from stockholders.

| Target Profit | Number of Companies |
|---|---|
| ROI | 4 |
| Periodic profit | 5 |
| ROS | 23 |
| Total | 32 |

Table 16.5  Target Profit in Profit Planning

There has been no evidence that companies using ROS are run recklessly. On the contrary, they are active and sound businesses. For example, Toyota and Matsushita use ROS as the target profit, taking into account the turnover by using other management tools. Toyota's just-in-time system can be viewed as a tool to increase turnover through reduced inventories. The internal capital system of Matsushita's divisionalization can be described as a tool for increasing each division's turnovers. Originated at Matsushita, this system has been popular in recent years as a unique technique for controlling division in Japanese companies. When the intracompany capital system is used, the headquarters allots each division a capital cost called an "opportunity cost." The real purpose of these management tools is to serve as supplementary means for companies using ROS.

The essence of these above approaches lies in separating ROI into two parts: ROS and turnover. By doing so, measures can be obtained separately, thus avoiding weaknesses of ROI, such as the negative management attitude toward investing large sums of capital resources in factory automation, and obscure denominator investment.

*Budgeting as a Management Control Device.* In coping with the relative decline of standard costing as a management tool, the budgeting system has become increasingly important as a comprehensive profit planning and control device; that is, cost control, in a strict sense, is losing its importance, while profit planning is on the rise in today's Japanese business world. There are two management functions in the budgeting system: planning and control. Though the control function is still important, the planning function is gaining importance in most of the companies we interviewed. Numerous managers told us that, while standard costing is losing its place as a cost control device, the budgeting system is taking its place as factory automation spreads. It is important to remember that the meaning of *control* in budgeting differs from that in standard costing. Variance analysis no longer plays a leading role in budgeting. Motivational control, however, is still important. This change, we believe, is closely related to the popularity of the budget system originated in Holland's Philips Corporation. The budget system, an integration of standard costing and budgeting, has been introduced into many Japanese companies, such as Matsushita and Victor.

The popularity of the budgeting system in Japan is a direct result of the rapidly increasing numbers of personnel and white-collar employees engaging in "brainwork" in Japanese factories. Traditional standard costing is no longer an effective tool for controlling employees. Motivational control through the budgeting system is far more effective. Since FMS makes brainwork more important, the budgeting system will continue to be an important management tool while the use of FMS spreads in Japan.

**Conclusion.** Factory automation through FMS has made steady progress in Japanese assembly-oriented industries. The ultimate goal of FMS is to have workerless factories that employ fewer direct laborers, and more supervisors and trained technicians. Consequently, the cost structure will undergo a significant change, resulting in lower direct labor costs and higher indirect labor costs. One problem in future cost management is discovering an effective tool that enhances white-collar employees' productivity.

The decline in importance of effective control over direct labor leads to the decline in importance of standard costing on one hand, and the increasing importance of budgeting on the other. In addition, TQC, JIT, and VE are frequently used to reduce cost in FMS firms. The importance of projected cost, an important tool for cost reduction, increases with the advent of management by objectives.

In the framework of projected cost, target cost is first computed by subtracting the target profit from target selling price. In this computational process, ROS plays a critical role by setting a minimum rate of return beforehand, so that management can project both the target selling price and cost level.

The introduction of FMS into Japanese assembly-oriented industries has caused great changes not only to the production system itself, but also to the management control system employed. The survey reported in this study confirms this trend. Since maintaining a high level of productivity is vital to the success or even survival of a company, it is management's responsibility to keep up with and take advantage of the new developments in management control systems.

## Notes

1. Economic Research Institute of Machinery Promotion; "International Comparison of Management in High Tech Industries," *ERIMP* (*Kikaishinkokyokai Keizaikenkyuujo*), March 1982, p. 92.
2. JMA Research Institute, *Robotization: Its Implications for Management*, Fuji Corporation, 1983.
3. Ohmae, Kenichi, *The Mind of the Strategist: Business Planning for Competitive Advantage*, (New York: Penguin Books/McGraw-Hill, 1982), pp. 189-190.
4. *Nikkei* (*Japan Economic Newspaper*), "High Tech Economics: An Interview with President Inaba," April 11, 1985.
5. Dilts, David M., and Grank W. Russell, "Accounting for the Factory of the Future," *Management Accounting*, April 1985, p. 37.
6. Kaneko, Kimio, "Cost Accounting for IC Factories," *Business Practice* (*Keieijutsumu*), February 1984, p. 32.
7. Seed III, Allen H., "Cost Accounting in the Age of Robotics," *Management Accounting*, October 1984, p. 40; Schmarzback, Henry R., and Richard G. Vangermeersch, "Why We Should Account for the Fourth Cost of Manufacturing," *Management Accounting*, July 1983, p. 25; Dilts and Russell, op. cit.
8. Tanaka, Masayasu, "Cost Development of Cost Engineering in Japan," *Cost Accounting* (*Genkakeisan*), No. 278, 1984, p. 50.
9. Tanaka, Masayasu, "The Development of Cost Engineering in Japan," *Cost Accounting* (*Genkakeisan*), No. 278, 1984, p. 50.
10. Saito, Jun, "The Net Profit of ¥ 80 Million Earned by the Introduction of Target Cost," *Factory Management* (*Kojokanri*), December 1978, p. 20.
11. Suenaga, Shigeki, "Necessary Conditions for Cost Accounting," *Business Practice* (*Keieijutsumi*), March 1980, p. 20.
12. MITI, "Cost Management," *The Daily Industrial Newspaper* (*Nikkan Kogyo Shinbun*), 1969, pp. 126-209.
13. Gray, C.S., "Japan, Quality Control & Innovations — Total Quality Control in Japan," *Business Week*, July 20, 1981, pp. 23-24.
14. Monden, Y., "What Makes the Toyota Production System Really Tick?" *Industrial Engineering*, January 1981, p. 35.
15. Dearden, John, "The Case Against ROI Control," *Harvard Business Review*, May-June 1969, p. 124; Mauriel, John, and Robert N.

Anthony, "Misevaluation of Investment Center Performance," *Harvard Business Review*, March-April 1966, pp. 98-105; Reece, James S., and William R. Cool, "Measuring Investment Center Performance," *Harvard Business Review*, May-June 1978, pp. 29-30; Solomons, David, *Divisional Performance: Measurement and Control*, (New York: Financial Executive Research Foundation, 1965), p. 64.

16. Sakurai, M., L.M. Killough, and R.M. Brown, "Performance Measurement Techniques and Goal Setting: A Comparison of American and Japanese Practices," *Business Review of Senshu University (Senshu keieironshu)*, February 1985, p. 79.

17. Economic Planning Agency, *Survey on Searching Business Behavior*, Printing Office at Ministry of Finance, 1976.

# PART III

## Japanese Cost Accounting Practices and Standards

# 17

## Characteristics and Practical Applications of Japanese Cost Accounting Systems

*Takeo Yoshikawa, Professor of Accounting,*
*Yokohama National University*

The purpose of this chapter is to discuss the characteristics of cost accounting systems and their practical applications in Japan. The information is based mainly on the results of surveys and interviews in 1979[1] and 1984[2]. Although the Enterprise Management Association (EMA) has done several similar surveys,[3] there are some differences between them.

One difference is the size of the investigations and the number of companies surveyed. The EMA carried out its surveys mainly through its membership. The author's covered companies listed on the Tokyo Stock Exchange and 512 companies randomly picked from 1,024 possibilities. The main industries responding were food, chemical, iron and steel, pulp and paper, electrical equipment, machinery, shipbuilding, and transportation equipment.

We used 67 questions to describe the company, the purpose of cost accounting, accumulation of raw material, labor and other expenses, methods of allocating overhead cost, application of each cost accounting system, cost management for cost control and cost reduction, and the relationship between cost accounting and business decision making. One hundred and forty-six companies responded, a good response ratio as far as this type of survey is concerned. It is one of the largest questionnaires ever completed. The results should provide a basis for understanding cost accounting systems in Japan.

**Characteristics of Cost Accounting Systems in Japanese Industries.** Table 17.1, which combines results of the author's 1979 survey and the EMA's, reveals that many companies are taking advantage of electric data processing systems (EDPS) for cost accounting. In 1966, when 17.8 percent of Japanese industry used it, the popularity of EDPS was almost the same as that of the punch card system (PCS). Compared with EDPS, the adding machine (AM) was popular used by 76.9 percent of the companies. In 1971, however, EDPS use equalled that of the adding machine. In 1979, the percentage of EDPS users increased to 74.2 percent, the percentage of AM users decreased to 11.3 percent, and PCS users almost disappeared. In fact, the popularity of EDPS in cost accounting is directly proportional to the development of the computer.

| Method | 1966 | 1970 | 1971 | 1974 | 1979 |
|---|---|---|---|---|---|
| Adding Machines | 76.9% | 61.7% | 56.6% | 21.4% | 11.3% |
| Punch Card System | 16.4 | 5.2 | 2.6 | 1.0 | 2.6 |
| Electric Data Processing System | 17.8 | 40.1 | 55.3 | 73.3 | 74.2 |

**Table 17.1  A Comparison of Cost Accounting Methods**

EDPS is used mainly in the following cost management areas: cost control and cost reduction (33.8 percent), preparing financial statements (32.6 percent), budgeting (24.5 percent), and for business decision making (9.1 percent).[4] Three uses of EDPS in cost accounting are based on:

- A single-function software package.
- A multi-purpose software package.
- A database system.

According to companies surveyed, 31.5 percent conduct cost accounting with a single-function software package, while 48.3 percent use a software package with multiple functions. For effective management control and EDPS use, however, cost accounting on a database system has more to recommend it. Unfortunately, only 19.3 percent of the companies surveyed have adopted a database system for cost accounting.[5] Regardless of how inefficiently computer systems are used, it is almost impossible for Japanese companies to do cost accounting without EDPS.

According to the Japan Cost Accounting Standard(JCAS), there are five reasons to use cost accounting:

1. To set pricing and pricing policies.
2. To prepare financial statements.
3. To install cost management practices (including cost control and cost reduction).
4. To establish budgets and budgetary controls.
5. To make business plans and controls.

According to the survey, 44.5 percent of Japanese companies use cost accounting to attain cost management, 25.8 percent use it to prepare financial statements, and 13.5 percent use it for business planning and control. This order is, incidentally, the same as that for using EDPS for cost accounting. (See Table 17.2.)

Let's discuss the content of the cost accounting system in Japan. The cost of material acquired is calculated based on one of the following:

1. Invoice price.
2. Invoice price + casual acquiring expenses (including purchase commission, freight, insurance fee, and customs duties).
3. Invoice price + actual acquiring expenses + actual material handling expenses.
4. Invoice price + estimated acquiring expenses + estimated material handling expenses.

The most popular way to calculate the cost of material acquired is number 1 in the list: the invoice price used by 35.4 percent; the next is number 2, used by about 32.6 percent of all companies. In theory, number 3 might be the best way to calculate the cost of material acquired, and number 4 might be the most suitable way if you consider the economics of calculation. But the companies adopting number 3 are only 17 percent and only 13.6 percent adopt number 4.

To calculate the cost of material used, 61 percent use the weighted average method. FIFO (first in, first out) is applied by only 10.1 percent and LIFO (last in, first out) by only 2.5 percent.

|  | Food | Chem | Cera | Iron | Pulp | Elec | Mach | Ship | Total | % |
|---|---|---|---|---|---|---|---|---|---|---|
| Pricing | 2 |  |  |  |  | 6 | 3 |  | 11 | 7.0 |
| Financial Statement | 1 | 8 |  | 5 | 2 | 17 | 6 | 1 | 40 | 25.8 |
| Cost/Management | 3 | 11 | 2 | 7 | 6 | 20 | 10 | 10 | 69 | 44.5 |
| Budget/Control | 1 | 1 |  | 1 |  | 2 | 1 | 2 | 8 | 5.2 |
| Plan/Control | 1 | 5 | 2 | 1 | 1 | 6 | 2 | 3 | 21 | 13.5 |
| Others |  |  |  |  |  | 2 | 1 | 1 | 4 | 2.6 |
| No Answer |  | 1 |  | 1 |  |  |  |  | 2 | 1.3 |
| Total | 8 | 26 | 4 | 15 | 9 | 53 | 23 | 17 | 155 | 100.0 |

Food; food industry, Chem; chemical industry, Cera; ceramic industry, Iron; iron and steel industry, Pulp; pulp and paper industry, Elec; electrical machinery industry, Mach; machine industry, Ship; shipbuilding and transportation equipment industry.

Table 17.2  Japanese Interest in Cost Management

There are two distinct features regarding the calculation of labor cost. First, labor cost consists primarily of seven cost items: direct and indirect labor wages, salaries of factory office workers, miscellaneous wages and salaries (part-time and seasonal labor), overtime premium earnings and night shift bonuses, bonus payments and allowances (including dependent family member allowances, housing and commuting allowances), retirement allowances, and legal welfare expenses. Sometimes compensation for suspended work is included in labor costs.

The second feature is the form of payroll payments. In the case of factory office workers, 69.2 percent of the companies pay wages monthly, while 24.6 percent apply a combined monthly and daily wage system. There is no hourly or daily wage, or even a piecework pay system. This applies for both direct and indirect labor. For example, 46.9 percent of the companies adopt a monthly wage system, while the percentage of companies adopting a combined monthly and daily wage system is 40.4 percent. Only one company has adopted an hourly scale, and no company pays by piecework.

The fundamental wage system in Japan is monthly. Monthly wages make a big difference to the theoretical and practical calculation of wages. The last day of the monthly pay period seldom coincides with the last day of the fiscal period. The payroll register is closed on the 20th of the month and wages are paid on the 25th or the last day of the month. Therefore, if you follow the theoretical method of labor cost calculation, it is necessary to analyze the timecards at the end of the month for those labor costs incurred after the last monthly payroll date but not yet paid. In practice, 64.4 percent of surveyed companies admit the existence of unpaid wages. This is caused by the monthly wage system in Japan, and has few changes except for yearly salary increases. Therefore, even if there exists a periodical difference between the monthly pay period and the fiscal period, there is no need to calculate unpaid wages. The amount of monthly payments almost equals the amount of labor costs incurred, except during the month when the yearly increases are applied.

According to a U.S. cost accounting textbook,[6] product costs in the U.S. are classified into direct material, direct labor, and factory overhead. Product costs in Japan are classified into material costs, labor costs, and "other." Other costs consist of direct other costs and some overhead costs — and they have been increasing rapidly every year in Japan. As is well known, large Japanese companies receive a lot of support from their subcontractors; these subcontractors, in turn, receive support from other subcontractors. Take the example of electrical appliances or personal computers: 80 to 90 percent of the product unit is produced by subcontractors. The costs of subcontractors are called the "amount paid to subcontractors" and are classified as other costs. When the parent companies assemble parts and components produced by subcontractors, assembly is performed by robots. The costs of robots and other automated factory equipment are depreciation costs also applied to other costs. In the example of cost accounting computer software programs, most of the product costs are labor and other costs. The amount of other costs become high and thus important. So other costs are not other costs any more, and need to be given a new name.

The process of distributing, allocating, and absorbing overhead costs is the same in Japan and the United States: 58.2 percent of the companies use a direct distribution method, 22.6 percent use a step-ladder distribution method, and companies using other methods are less than 10 percent. When overhead costs are absorbed into the product cost, 41.2 percent of the companies absorb the overhead costs based on the hourly rate for direct labor. Only 16 percent, however, use the rate of volume of production. The reason why so many Japanese companies rely on an hourly direct rate for direct labor is because they want to use the cost allocation method for cost management, not for calculating the rational product unit cost. If the hourly rate is applied, cost centers will try to reduce the number of workers. And Japanese companies cannot lay off workers the way U.S. companies do. Because it is believed that the machine rate, or the rate of volume of production, cannot contribute to cost reduction, these rates are not applied more than the hourly rate to allocate costs.

Next, let's consider the use of cost accounting systems. The percentage of companies using a process cost accounting system is 61.5 percent, those using a job order cost accounting system is 32.7 percent, those using a lot cost system in process cost accounting system is 61.5 percent (37.8%/61.5%), those using a single process cost system is 25 percent (15.4%/61.5%), and those using a class cost system is about 13.5 percent (8.3%/61.5%).

Fifty-one companies use a job order cost system outside the company. Sixteen of them produce electrical machinery, 14 manufacture industrial machinery, and 14 are shipbuilding and transportation equipment companies. It is natural for big companies such as these to apply the job order cost system. Even they, however, produce marketable productsand operate large-scale production systems. One reason is simply the way of production. It was already mentioned that about 80 to 90 percent of the products are processed by subcontractors. Therefore, any processing, such as assembling and testing, done by the parent company is small. A second reason is that cost accounting by lot is simple — most companies are equipped with a computer-based production system, such as a material requirements planning (MRP) system, or something similar. It is reasonable that 32.7 percent use the job order cost system.

On the other hand, many companies producing electrical appliances, chemicals, heavy machinery, and iron and steel design and produce market-oriented products. They produce a diverse product line in small lots. Their production method and process cost accounting system, especially the lot cost accounting system, is popular. (See Table 17.3.)

Finally, there is a unique cost accounting system, called the non-cumulative (or non-pyramidal) method, developed by George Hillis Newlove.[7] About 20 companies surveyed use this method. A 1984 followup survey concerning the non-cumulative method revealed the following reasons for applying it:

- To calculate product costs, the non-cumulative method is much simpler to use than the cumulative method.
- The non-cumulative method can offer useful cost management information.
- By recognizing each process unit cost, it is possible to obtain basic data for predetermining costs per unit and the cost standard.[8]

*Japanese Cost Accounting for Cost Management.* When it comes to cost management in Japan, two subjects must be discussed. One is *cost control.* When applying the cost control concept, a standard cost is set up as a cost management goal by which the actual cost is controlled. The second subject for discussion is *cost reduction.* The standard cost itself is a target of cost management to be reduced by a cost accountant.

In the past, cost accountants controlled costs while production managers reduced them. After 1973, new business challenges arose

| Accounting Method | Food | Chem | Cera | Iron | Pulp | Elec | Mach | Ship | Total | % |
|---|---|---|---|---|---|---|---|---|---|---|
| Job Order Cost | 1 | 3 | | 2 | 1 | 16 | 14 | 14 | 51 | 32.7 |
| Process Cost | | | | | | | | | | |
| 1) Single/Process Cost | 1 | 6 | | 3 | 4 | 9 | 1 | | 24 | 15.4 |
| 2) Lot Cost | 3 | 14 | 2 | 6 | 3 | 23 | 6 | 2 | 59 | 37.8 |
| 3) Class Cost | 2 | 2 | 2 | 4 | | 2 | | 1 | 13 | 8.3 |
| Others | 2 | 3 | | 1 | 1 | 1 | 1 | | 9 | 5.8 |
| No Answer | | | | | | | | | 0 | 0 |
| Total | 9 | 28 | 4 | 16 | 9 | 51 | 22 | 17 | 156 | 100.0 |

Food: food industry, Chem: chemical industry, Cera: ceramic industry, Iron: iron and steel industry, Pulp: pulp and paper industry, Elec: electrical machinery industry, Mach: machine industry, Ship: shipbuilding and transportation equipment industry.

Table 17.3 Cost Accounting Systems

in areas such as oil consumption, technological innovations, a fluctuating exchange rate system, and trade friction. Now, cost accountants must deal with cost reduction as well as cost control.

We have to mention the relationship between cost accounting systems and cost control. Many product parts are designed as common parts to standardize production as much as possible. Therefore, we adopt a standard cost accounting system that includes MRP as part of the production management system.

***Classifying Costs with Cost Management Techniques.*** The quantity of raw material is managed by its method of purchase. Of companies purchasing raw materials, 53.4 percent make purchases based on the production schedule; 17.5 percent purchase after considering both the production schedule and market price. It is difficult to find a company that has adopted the two-bin system or EOQ model. Many companies that use the production scheduling method mainly apply MRP or the *kanban* and just-in-time system. Some have most of their raw materials supplied every two hours. Their total inventory, including raw materials, work in process, and finished products, equals one to one and a half days of production.

When discussing the price control techniques of raw materials, we can introduce the cost table approach. Prices of raw materials on the cost table are listed according to the purchasing cost standard or integrated engineering standard. The purchaser (vendee) and the supplier (vendor) assist each other when the cost table is formed at the framework and proposal, R&D, and production stages. The target cost at each stage is not just accumulated page cost, but the theoretically calculated or "should be" cost. The target cost is always greater than the actual cost so that the company can look forward to a higher minimum cost. When preparing the cost table, the company acquires new information related to the production technique and new raw material, in addition to devising new rational and strategic purchasing policies and making supplier comparisons. These cost table meetings also help inform everybody about standard costs.

Labor cost in Japan is relatively fixed. Wages and salaries are decided by the union and management, and generally change little during the production period. It is difficult, therefore, to find advantages in calculating a wage rate variance. On the other hand, it does help to calculate an efficiency variance because it tells us the state of worker efficiency. But direct labor figures recently have decreased as factories try to reduce their numbers by training workers to be multiskilled, regrouping different kinds of jobs, changing the concept of efficiency, introducing robots and automated machines, and applying the "principal-agent" model. The result is a decrease in direct labor costs and a decline in the value of calculating the efficiency variance.

The following are some examples of how to reduce the number of workers. Suppose we have three workers on job A and two workers on job B. To attain a 40-percent cost reduction, jobs A and B are combined to form a new job C, which is operated for several weeks by four workers. Once it is operating correctly, one worker is removed — resulting in the cost reduction. The value of having multiskilled workers in this instance is obvious.

Another example concerns a new concept of productivity. A factory producing 100 product units with 10 workers can increase its productivity by 25 percent in two ways. One is to have 10 workers produce 125 units. A second is to have 8 workers produce 100 units. Both approaches will attain a 25-percent productivity improvement, but the result differs completely from a cost management viewpoint. The first approach does not reduce labor costs, but rather increases the amount of inventory. The second approach, on the other hand, eliminates two workers without increasing inventory, although it does require a greater effort from management.

With the introduction of robots and factory automation systems, the number of production workers has decreased remarkably over the past few years. At the same time, cost control has carried over into other areas. An example is the case of a company that reduced its warehouse labor from 32 to 2 workers by introducing an automated warehousing management system. Some parent companies are assigning areas such as purchasing, control of raw materials, and labor intensive jobs to subcontractors, even if the work is located in the same factory. This is a typical use of the principal-agent model.

Two special cost variances are calculated under Japan's standard cost accounting system. One is the cost variance of the amount paid to subcontractors; another is unmatched cost variances. About 80 percent of one product is produced by subcontractors, so the amount paid to them is a large and important control target.

The life cycle of products and parts is short. Even in 1979, 55.1 percent of the companies using the standard cost accounting system changed standard costs twice a year. As product life cycles grow shorter and shorter, standard costs and the cost tables will have to change three or four times a year. The increasing amount of products produced from raw materials and parts not registered in the design engineering information system are making it difficult for the master material and master files to keep current with production speed. And the cost accountant cannot calculate real versus standard production costs without an up-to-date cost variance account.

Finally, some people feel that the standard cost accounting system is no longer useful for controlling costs. Shortened product life cycles make it difficult to properly maintain the standard costs. The use of factory automation (FA) or flexible manufacturing systems (FMS) makes it difficult to calculate a learning curve of labor costs. Therefore, the object of cost control at the production stage is to stabilize production quantities. Another reason is the development of EDPS. It is possible to calculate product costs quickly by computer in the real cost accounting system. In other words, the value of the standard cost accounting system is gradually decreasing. It is more useful to compare this month's actual costs with last month's. We have found, in fact, that cost control based on the actual cost accounting system is found mostly at companies who employ capable workers and utilize a competent management control system.

## Notes

1. Takeo Yoshikawa, "The Empirical Study of Cost Accounting in Japanese Corporations," *Keiei Jitsumu*, May 1979, pp. 2-32.
2. Takeo Yoshikawa, "Process Cost Accounting Systems Based on the Non-Cumulative Method," *Yokohama Keiei Kenkyu*, Yokohama National University, December 1984, pp. 67-96.
3. Surveys of Japanese cost accounting systems have been conducted several times by the EMA since 1959. The latest is its "Survey of Cost Accounting Systems of Japanese Companies," *Keiei Jitsumu*, February 1975, pp. 2-23.
4. Fumiyasu Takahashi, "Reconsidering Cost Accounting Standards Based on the Survey," Japan Cost Accounting Association, No. 281, May 1986, p. 113.
5. Ibid., p. 101.
6. C.T. Horngren, *Cost Accounting: A Managerial Emphasis*, 5th ed., (Englewood Cliffs, NJ: Prentice Hall, 1982), p. 30.
7. George Hillis Newlove, *Process Cost: Actual, Estimated, and Standard*, (1958), distributed by Hemphill Bookstore, Austin, TX, Chapter 5.
8. Takeo Yoshikawa, *op. cit.* (1984), p. 77.

# 18

## How Japanese Companies Allocate Corporate Costs

*Takeyuki Tani, School of Management, Kobe University*

According to the popular view of management accounting, corporate costs are not controllable for divisions and should not be considered part of the performance measurement of a divisional manager. Most Japanese and U.S. companies, however, are supposed to allocate corporate costs[1] and the discrepancy between theory and practice must be explained.

To identify when to allocate corporate costs and the reasons for allocating we have studied the allocation of corporate costs in Japanese divisional organizations.[2] This chapter, however, will report only the extent to which Japanese companies delegate each function (production, sales, research, administration, etc.) to their divisions and how they allocate corporate costs.

The study consists of four phases: (1) review of pertinent literature, (2) questionnaire survey, (3) in-depth personal interviews, and (4) analysis and observation. For the purpose of this chapter, the second phase is most important. The questionnaire was mailed in March 1985 to 560 mining and manufacturing companies with divisional managers. *The Personnel Directory 1984* categorized these Japanese companies as having sales of at least ¥50 million.

***Divisional Structure.*** Table 18.1 displays the frequency distribution of 1984 sales revenue of the respondents. Two hundred forty-two companies responded for a 43.21 percent response rate, although 26 companies answered that they did not have a divisional structure.

| Sales revenue (in ¥ billions) | Number | Percent |
|---|---|---|
| Under 10 | 21 | 9 |
| 10-70 | 94 | 41 |
| 70-130 | 34 | 15 |
| 130-190 | 22 | 9 |
| 190-250 | 11 | 5 |
| 250-310 | 13 | 6 |
| Over 310 | 36 | 15 |
| Total | 231 | 100 |

*Data for 11 firms were missing.

Table 18.1  Sales Revenue (1984 Sales Revenue for 231* Respondents)

The form of the divisional structure of the other 216 firms is presented in Table 18.2. This shows that divisionalization by product lines was popular in Japan. Each division in the typical divisional company had at least part of both production and sales functions. On the other hand, divisionalization by manufacturing/sales functions was rare.

| Divisionalization by | Number | Percent |
|---|---|---|
| Product Lines | 172 | 79 |
| Territories | 2 | 1 |
| Functions | 9 | 4 |
| Product Lines and Territories | 10 | 5 |
| Product Lines and Functions | 23 | 11 |
| Total | 216 | 100 |

Table 18.2  Form of Divisional Structure

*The Extent of Corporate Costs Allocation.* The first issue is the extent of corporate costs allocation in Japan. The respondents were asked (1) How much of each function was delegated to their divisions? (2) In case of imperfect delegation, did they allocate part or all corporate costs of each function to the divisions? and (3) Did they allocate costs according to a base of predetermined or actual amount?

The answers to questions 2 and 3 revealed that 85 percent, or 183 companies, were allocating costs. This does not mean that the remaining 32 firms did not allocate any corporate costs. Some allocated the costs of data processing and/or engineering at the corporate level without allocating the costs of functions such as accounting and personnel. Data processing and engineering functions and the direct cost of performing them are relatively easy to measure. Also, in the case of allocating indirect costs, a rationale can be adopted. Some companies allocated only these costs.

Allocating corporate costs is also practiced in U.S. companies. According to one study, 103 of 123 respondents (84 percent) allocated corporate costs for any purpose.[3] In this study, allocation purposes such as the performance measurement of a divisional manager, measurement of divisional profitability, and pricing decisions were not specified on the questionnaire. It was simply labeled "Performance Measurement in Divisional Organizations." Instead, respondents were asked whether or not they allocated corporate costs for all purposes. Table 18.3 summarizes the responses and shows that the same decision was generally applied to the treatment of corporate costs. At a glance, this differs from U.S. companies surveyed by Fremgen & Liao. According to their study, the extent of allocation for measuring a division manager's performance was higher than that for other purposes.[4] The respondents, in fact, mentioned that the main purpose of allocation is to measure the divisional manager's performance.

*Production Function.* A typical division in a Japanese company is fairly self-contained with respect to line functions. The respondents were asked in detail how they delegated each function to their divisions. The two questions asked were: (1) What percentage of manufacturing costs or costs of goods sold in a typical division are costs of production departments (cost centers) common to some divisions? and (2) What percentage of total manufacturing costs are the costs of goods transferred between divisions?

| | Number | Percent |
|---|---|---|
| Companywide Allocation | | |
| Same for Any Purpose | 150 | 88 |
| No Allocation for Some Purposes | 21 | 12 |
| No Response | 12 | — |
| **Total** | **183** | **100** |
| Discriminate Allocation | | |
| Same for Any Purpose | 29 | 94 |
| Allocating for Some Purposes | 2 | 6 |
| No Response | 1 | — |
| **Total** | **32** | **100** |

**Table 18.3 Allocation Differences by Purpose**

Subtracting the percentage from 100 reveals the independence (self-containment) of divisions with respect to the production function. The responses are presented in Table 18.4. One hundred percent independence signifies the absence of a common production department or goods transfer. First, the number of common production departments is small, which means a division's independence is high. Cases of high interdependence were found only in partial divisionalization. Second, internal transfer between divisions is practiced to take advantage of economies of scale. The percentage of internal transfer, however, is not high. Internal transfer, in fact, was sizable for cases of partial or functional divisionalization.

Allocating common production costs is the problem of transfer pricing. The 1985 questionnaire did not ask respondents about their method of transfer pricing.[5]

*Sales Function.* Respondents were asked what percentage of their total sales were that of the sales department common to some divisions. The indicator of divisional independence regarding the sales function was calculated by subtracting the percentage from 100. The responses presented in Table 18.5 show the high independence of a division. Low independence was found only in cases of functional or

| | With Regard to | | | |
|---|---|---|---|---|
| | Common Production Departments | | Internal Transfer between Divisions | |
| | Number | Percent | Number | Percent |
| Under 44% | 10 | 5 | 11 | 5 |
| 45-54% | 5 | 2 | 3 | 1 |
| 55-64% | 2 | 1 | 1 | 1 |
| 65-74% | 3 | 1 | 5 | 2 |
| 75-84% | 15 | 7 | 24 | 12 |
| 85-94% | 18 | 8 | 40 | 20 |
| 95-99% | 23 | 11 | 71 | 35 |
| 100% | 139 | 65 | 49 | 24 |
| No Response | 1 | — | 12 | — |
| **Total** | 216 | 100 | 216 | 100 |

**Table 18.4 Independence of Division — Production Function**

partial divisionalization. One hundred percent signifies no common sales department.

For the 65 companies with common sales departments, the respondents were asked (1) whether they allocated the common costs fully or partially; (2) when allocating, what bases for allocation were applied; and (3) whether they allocated the costs in predetermined or actual amounts. The responses are summarized in Tables 18.6, 18.7, and 18.8, respectively.

Table 18.7 reveals that cases of allocating costs on service performed has a slight edge. The cases contain (1) charging only direct costs, (2) charging direct costs separately and allocating indirect costs, (3) allocating both direct and indirect costs to sales, (4) applying transfer price, and (5) at least six firms allocating both direct and indirect costs on other bases including service performance. Correspondingly, allocating the actual or predetermined amounts with variances re-allocated was the most common practice (see Table 18.8).

*Research Function.* How independent is a division with respect to basic and applied research functions? Respondents were asked what percentage of total research costs were costs incurred in divisional

|  | Number | Percent |
|---|---|---|
| Under 15% | 17 | 8 |
| 15-29% | 5 | 2 |
| 30-44% | 4 | 2 |
| 45-59% | 3 | 1 |
| 60-74% | 6 | 3 |
| 75-90% | 9 | 4 |
| 90-99% | 18 | 9 |
| 100% | 151 | 71 |
| No Response | 3 | — |
| **Total** | 216 | 100 |

Table 18.5  Independence of Division — Sales Function

|  | Number | Percent |
|---|---|---|
| Full Allocation | 39 | 61 |
| Partial Allocation | 6 | 9 |
| No Allocation | 19 | 30 |
| No Response | 1 | — |
| **Total** | 65 | 100 |

Table 18.6  Allocating Costs of Common Sales Department

research facilities. Their responses are presented in Table 18.9. Independence of a division with respect to basic research is naturally low because it is not contained within a specific division. On the other hand, independence of a division with respect to applied research is relatively high.

Allocation practices for common research costs are summarized in Tables 18.10, 18.11, and 18.12. Notice in Table 18.10 that the percentage of full or partial allocation was lower, especially for basic research costs, than 85 percent of allocating in general. Three reasons for this were confirmed by the survey. The respondents were asked why they

| | Number | Percent |
|---|---|---|
| Charging only Direct Costs | 1 | 2 |
| Charging Direct Costs Separately and Allocating Indirect Costs Based on | | |
| Sales | 0 ⎤ | 0 ⎤ |
| Some Costs | 1 ⎬ 4 | 2 ⎬ 9 |
| Other Bases | 3 ⎦ | 7 ⎦ |
| Allocating Both Direct and Indirect Costs Based on | | |
| Sales | 9 ⎤ | 20 ⎤ |
| Some Costs | 5 ⎬ 28 | 11 ⎬ 61 |
| Other Bases | 14 ⎦ | 30 ⎦ |
| Negotiation Between Divisions and Sales Department | 1 | 2 |
| Transfer Pricing | 11 | 24 |
| Other Methods | 1 | 2 |
| **Total** | 46 | 100 |

Table 18.7  Bases for Allocating Costs of Common Sales Department

| Allocation | Number | Percent |
|---|---|---|
| Predetermined Amount | 13 | 30 |
| Predetermined Amount with Variances Reallocated | 7 ⎤ | 16 ⎤ |
| Actual Amount | 24 ⎬ 31 | 54 ⎬ 70 |
| No Response | 2 ⎦ | — |
| **Total** | 46 | 100 |

Table 18.8  Allocating Sales Department Costs in Predetermined or Actual Amounts

| | Basic Research | | Applied Research | |
|---|---|---|---|---|
| | Number | Percent | Number | Percent |
| 0% | 155 | 76 | 58 | 28 |
| 1-9% | 8 | 4 | 18 | 9 |
| 10-19% | 7 | 4 | 18 | 9 |
| 20-29% | 6 | 3 | 11 | 5 |
| 30-39% | 2 | 1 | 17 | 9 |
| 40-49% | 3 | 1 | 11 | 5 |
| 50-59% | 3 | 1 | 11 | 5 |
| Over 60% | 20 | 10 | 61 | 30 |
| No Response | 12 | — | 11 | — |
| Total | 216 | 100 | 216 | 100 |

Table 18.9  Independence of Division — Research Function

| | Basic Research | | Applied Research | |
|---|---|---|---|---|
| | Number | Percent | Number | Percent |
| Full Allocation | 106 | 51 | 115 | 55 |
| Partial Allocation | 29 | 14 | 33 | 16 |
| No Allocation | 73 | 35 | 60 | 29 |
| No Response | 8 | — | 8 | — |
| Total | 216 | 100 | 216 | 100 |

Table 18.10  Allocating Costs of a Common Research Department

did or did not allocate. Seven companies responded that they excluded basic research from allocating. Three said they did so because basic research had no short-term benefit for divisions. Instead they allocated only those costs that had some relation to divisional operations, thus eliminating conflict with regard to allocating.

| | Basic Research | | Applied Research | |
|---|---|---|---|---|
| | Number | Percent | Number | Percent |
| Charging Only Direct Costs | 4 | 3 | 9 | 6 |
| Charging Direct Costs Separately and Allocating Indirect Costs Based on | | | | |
| Sales | 7 ⎤ | 5 ⎤ | 8 ⎤ | 6 ⎤ |
| Some Costs | 3 ⎬ 28 | 2 ⎬ 21 | 3 ⎬ 33 | 2 ⎬ 23 |
| Other Bases | 18 ⎦ | 14 ⎦ | 22 ⎦ | 15 ⎦ |
| Allocating Both Direct and Indirect Costs Based on | | | | |
| Sales | 36 ⎤ | 27 ⎤ | 33 ⎤ | 23 ⎤ |
| Some Costs | 10 ⎬ 89 | 8 ⎬ 68 | 11 ⎬ 92 | 7 ⎬ 63 |
| Other Bases | 43 ⎦ | 33 ⎦ | 48 ⎦ | 33 ⎦ |
| Negotiation Between Divisions and Research Department | 4 | 3 | 3 | 2 |
| Other Methods | 7 | 5 | 8 | 6 |
| No Response | 3 | — | 3 | — |
| **Total** | 135 | 100 | 148 | 100 |

Table 18.11  Bases for Allocating Costs of a Common Research Department

| Allocating | Basic Research | | Applied Research | |
|---|---|---|---|---|
| | Number | Percent | Number | Percent |
| Predetermined Amount | 58 | 44 | 62 | 43 |
| Predetermined Amount with Variances Reallocated | 23 ⎤ | 18 ⎤ | 26 ⎤ | 18 ⎤ |
| | ⎬ 73 | ⎬ 56 | ⎬ 81 | ⎬ 57 |
| Actual Amount | 50 ⎦ | 38 ⎦ | 55 ⎦ | 39 ⎦ |
| No Response | 4 | — | 5 | — |
| **Total** | 135 | 100 | 148 | 100 |

Table 18.12  Allocating Research Costs in Predetermined or Actual Amounts

Similarly, one allocating firm stated that allocating research costs drew complaints from divisions that did not benefit from the research results. This belies the inefficiency of allocating research costs when large differences exist between divisions with regard to, for example, product life cycle and market share. To justify not allocating basic research costs, one company said that it disturbed strategic research planning because a division behaves according to short-term goals. This relates to the reason seven companies mentioned allocating in general. They claimed that allocating motivated a divisional manager to check the amounts allocated, thus helping to control corporate costs. This company probably took advantage of this control function except for basic research costs. Strategic planning was also practiced where a lower burden rate was applied for a new business.

Table 18.11 presents the allocation bases for research costs. It shows that the percentage of allocating based on the services performed was higher than other corporate costs.[6] For basic research, charging only direct costs, charging direct costs separately, at least eight companies allocating both direct and indirect costs that mentioned the use of service performed amount to at least 30 percent. For applied research, this amounts to 38 percent including 13 companies applying services performed for allocating both direct and indirect costs. Likewise, the number of companies allocating actual or predetermined amounts with re-allocated variances was slightly large.

**Administrative Functions.** Responses regarding the functions of purchasing and logistics and the extent of divisional independence and costs allocation prices are omitted from this chapter.

Independence of a division for the other corporate functions (especially administrative functions) are summarized in Table 18.13. Finance and the president's office are omitted because they are centralized in nature. The measure of independence is a percentage of costs incurred in functional offices of divisions to total functional costs.

As originally thought, divisional independence for administrative functions was low except for marketing and engineering. The latter functions are that of staff, but highly related to line functions of production and sales. This is why marketing and engineering, which are peculiar to divisional business, are delegated to a division. Data processing, accounting, and personnel were to some extent delegated to support divisional operations. The extent of allocating for

| | Accounting | Legal | Data Processing | Marketing | Public Relations | Personnel | Engineering |
|---|---|---|---|---|---|---|---|
| 0% | 106 (55) | 146 (78) | 90 (48) | 50 (27) | 121 (64) | 112 (58) | 47 (25) |
| 1-4% | 25 (13) | 24 (13) | 26 (14) | 20 (11) | 23 (12) | 28 (14) | 18 (9) |
| 5-9% | 8 (4) | 4 (2) | 4 (2) | 4 (2) | 6 (3) | 5 (2) | 11 (6) |
| 10-14% | 9 (5) | 2 (1) | 11 (6) | 4 (2) | 10 (5) | 4 (2) | 8 (4) |
| 15-19% | 2 (1) | 0 (0) | 4 (2) | 5 (3) | 0 (0) | 3 (2) | 3 (2) |
| 20-24% | 5 (3) | 5 (3) | 10 (5) | 2 (1) | 0 (0) | 4 (2) | 4 (2) |
| 25-29% | 2 (1) | 1 (0) | 1 (1) | 3 (1) | 1 (1) | 3 (2) | 1 (1) |
| Over 30% | 34 (18) | 6 (3) | 40 (22) | 98 (53) | 28 (15) | 34 (18) | 97 (51) |
| No Answer | 25 (—) | 28 (—) | 30 (—) | 30 (—) | 27 (—) | 23 (—) | 27 (—) |
| **Total** | 216(100) | 216(100) | 216(100) | 216(100) | 216(100) | 216(100) | 216(100) |

In parenthesis is percent.

**Table 18.13 Independence of Division — Administrative Functions**

each function is presented in Table 18.14. The percentage of at least partially allocating for data processing was slightly higher because service performed in this function is easier to measure. It is possible for a company to allocate only those costs, part of which are variable to services performed to some extent.

Table 18.15 summarizes the bases of allocating accounting and data processing at the corporate level. The comparison shows that the percentage of allocating based on service performed is higher for data processing than for accounting. One case of charging only direct costs, 12 cases of charging direct costs separately, and 18 companies applying service performed as other bases amount to 18 percent. In spite of the relative measurability of service performed, the percentage is much lower than that practiced by U.S. companies.[7]

Table 18.15 also states that the application of allocation bases other than sales and some costs was high. Bases for cost accounting are described in Table 18.16. First, we observe that the percentage of using multiple bases was high. Second, besides sales and capital employed, using the number of employees was popular for both single and multiple base users.

There are two reasons for using employees as an element of allocation bases. First, allocating corporate costs based on those resources allocated to a division should be fair and persuasive. This is also true for utilized capital. Second, using employees as a factor motivates a divisional manager to control the number of employees in his or her division. One accountant interviewed claimed that as motivation, however, this did not work well in a low-growth economic period when a firm has excessive employment. His company allocated corporate costs based on the capital utilized, which positively motivated the effective use of financial resources.

Finally, Table 18.17 presents the responses for accounting and data processing in which respondents allocated administrative costs in predetermined or actual amounts. Compared to the sales and research areas, the percentage of allocating a predetermined amount was slightly higher, especially for accounting, for two reasons. First, the difficulty of measuring service performed objectively for administrative costs hinders many companies from allocating an actual amount based on service performed.

Second, administrative costs generally are fixed in amount. By allocating the actual amount on actual bases for example, actual

| | Full Allocation | | Partial Allocation | | No Allocation | | No Response | Total |
|---|---|---|---|---|---|---|---|---|
| | Number | Percent | Number | Percent | Number | Percent | Number | Number |
| Finance | 134 | 65 | 40 | 19 | 34 | 16 | 8 | 216 |
| Accounting | 139 | 66 | 40 | 19 | 32 | 15 | 5 | 216 |
| Legal | 135 | 68 | 30 | 15 | 33 | 17 | 18 | 216 |
| Data Processing | 138 | 68 | 40 | 19 | 26 | 13 | 12 | 216 |
| Marketing | 125 | 67 | 32 | 17 | 29 | 16 | 30 | 216 |
| Public Relations | 132 | 65 | 40 | 19 | 32 | 16 | 12 | 216 |
| Personnel | 138 | 66 | 40 | 19 | 32 | 15 | 6 | 216 |
| President's Office | 136 | 65 | 40 | 19 | 34 | 16 | 6 | 216 |
| Engineering | 125 | 66 | 34 | 18 | 30 | 16 | 27 | 216 |

Table 18.14  Allocating Administrative Costs

|  | Accounting | | Data Processing | |
|---|---|---|---|---|
|  | Number | Percent | Number | Percent |
| Charging Only Direct Costs | 1 | 1 | 1 | 1 |
| Charging Direct Costs Separately and Allocating Indirect Costs Based on | | | | |
|   Sales | 1 ⎫ | 1 ⎫ | 2 ⎫ | 1 ⎫ |
|   Some Costs | 0 ⎬ 2 | 0 ⎬ 1 | 1 ⎬ 12 | 1 ⎬ 7 |
|   Other Bases | 1 ⎭ | 1 ⎭ | 9 ⎭ | 5 ⎭ |
| Allocating Both Direct and Indirect Costs Based on | | | | |
|   Sales | 53 ⎫ | 31 ⎫ | 47 ⎫ | 27 ⎫ |
|   Some Costs | 14 ⎬ 156 | 8 ⎬ 91 | 12 ⎬ 146 | 7 ⎬ 85 |
|   Other Bases | 89 ⎭ | 52 ⎭ | 87 ⎭ | 51 ⎭ |
| Negotiation Between Divisions and Corporate Department | 3 | 2 | 4 | 2 |
| Other Methods | 9 | 5 | 8 | 5 |
| No Response | 8 | — | 7 | — |
| **Total** | 179 | 100 | 178 | 100 |

**Table 18.15  Bases for Allocating Administrative Costs**

sales, a division's fixed administrative costs become variable costs. A division manager's decision may have a positive effect on the divisional contribution margin and therefore on corporate profit, but it may decrease a division's net profit because of increased allocation. This may motivate a division manager to take action inconsistent with corporate interest.[8] To avoid the problem, allocating a predetermined amount is often advocated in management accounting literature.[9] This method also removes uncontrollable factors from the measurement of a divisional manager's performance because a predetermined amount is applied for both actual and target performances. These practices were consistent with theory in this respect. More important, it was felt that the budget system worked more effectively for the groups allocating accounting costs by predetermined amounts (see Table 18.18).

**Single Base**

| | |
|---|---|
| Employees | 15 |
| Capital employed | 6 |
| Value added | 4 |
| Contribution margin | 2 |
| Service performed | 2 |
| Divisional capital pool | 1 |
| Marginal profit | 1 |

**Multiple Bases**

| | |
|---|---|
| Sales/employees | 5 |
| Sales/capital employed/employees | 5 |
| Capital employed/employees | 5 |
| Sales/employees/fixed assets | 2 |
| Capital employed/indirect costs | 2 |
| Sales/marginal profit | 1 |
| Sales/contribution margin | 1 |
| Sales/capital employed | 1 |
| Sales/capital employed/marginal profit/employees | 1 |
| Sales/capital employed/employees/equal amount | 1 |
| Sales/labor costs/fixed assets | 1 |
| Sales/gross margin/employees/gross fixed assets | 1 |
| Sales/indirect costs/employees | 1 |
| Sales/costs/employees/allocated capital charge | 1 |
| Sales/labor costs/employees/equal amount | 1 |
| Sales/gross profit/labor costs/entertainment expenses/service | 1 |
| Capital employed/value added/employees | 1 |
| Capital employed/gross profit/employees | 1 |
| Capital employed/marginal profit/employees | 1 |
| Capital employed/labor costs | 1 |
| Capital employed/number of managers | 1 |
| Employees/floor space | 1 |
| Employees/floor space/service | 1 |
| Value added/fixed costs | 1 |

**Others**

| | |
|---|---|
| Employees or floor space for different expense items | 1 |

**Table 18.16  Other Bases for Allocating Accounting Costs**

| Allocating | Accounting | | Data Processing | |
|---|---|---|---|---|
| | Number | Percent | Number | Percent |
| Predetermined Amount | 95 | 54 | 93 | 53 |
| Predetermined Amount with Variances Reallocated | 28 ⎫ | 16 ⎫ | 29 ⎫ | 17 ⎫ |
| | ⎬ 80 | ⎬ 46 | ⎬ 81 | ⎬ 47 |
| Actual Amount | 52 ⎭ | 30 ⎭ | 52 ⎭ | 30 ⎭ |
| No Answer | 4 | — | 4 | — |
| Total | 179 | 100 | 178 | 100 |

Table 18.17  Allocating Administrative Costs in Predetermined or Actual Amounts

| Allocating | Mean (Cases) |
|---|---|
| Predetermined Amount | 5.151 (93) |
| Predetermined Amount with Variances Reallocated | 5.000 (27) |
| Actual Amount | 4.633 (49) |
| Total Population | 4.976 (49) |

*Ranging from 1 to 7 with maximum value of 7.

Table 18.18  The Budget System's Effectiveness
as Perceived by the Accountant*

On the other hand, for costs in a sales department for which service performed is relatively measurable, allocating an actual or predetermined amount with variances re-allocated proved to have a positive effect on communication between divisions, and especially between divisions and accounting departments (see Table 18.19).

*Conclusion.* For allocating administrative costs, the practices of Japan's divisional companies are consistent with theory. Allocating predetermined costs, however, is not considered to be the theory's best solution. As was mentioned, allocation is generally denied in the

| Allocating | Between Divisions | Between Division and Accounting Department |
|---|---|---|
| | Mean (Cases)* | Mean (Cases) |
| Predetermined Amount | 4.000 (13) | 4.385 (13) |
| Predetermined Amount with Variances Reallocated | 4.857 (7) | 5.714 (7) |
| Actual Amount | 4.667 (24) | 5.167 (24) |
| Total Population | 4.500 (44) | 5.023 (44) |

*Ranging from 1 to 7 with maximum value of 7.

**Table 18.19  Effectiveness of Communication**

literature. The popularity of allocating in practice, however, is evidence that there must be some benefit neglected in the theory. Of course, it does bring with it some costs, for example, the cost of suboptimal decisions by divisional managers, so a costs/benefit analysis needs to be applied to the decisions about whether and how to allocate corporate costs.

As evidence of the necessity for such an analysis, let's examine why allocating actual amounts is more effective for costs in the sales department than for administrative costs. Although service performed is relatively measurable for a sales department, and therefore a portion of the costs vary according to the service performed, the costs are, to some extent, fixed. Allocating indirect costs based on service performed, therefore, may cause suboptimal decisions by a division manager. The cost of these suboptimal decisions, however, is supposedly lower than for administrative costs, which are largely fixed. Conversely, allocating an actual amount based on service performed is more effective in motivating a division manager to control service received. This cost/benefit analysis has prompted many firms to allocate costs of sales department in actual amounts. For administrative costs, however, the cost of a division manager's suboptimal decisions associated with allocating actual amounts outweighs the benefit. This may be why the practice of allocating administrative costs in predetermined amounts prevails.

## Notes

1. For practices in the U.S., see R.F. Vancil, *Decentralization: Managerial Ambiguity by Design* (Homewood, IL: Dow Jones-Irwin, 1979) and J.M. Fremgen and S.S. Liao, *The Allocation of Corporate Indirect Costs* (New York: National Association of Accountants, 1981).
2. The study was conducted in collaboration with T. Kobayashi, K. Mizoguchi and N. Ogura, "Investigation into the Allocation Practices of Corporate Costs" (in Japanese), *Kigyokaikei*, March/April 1986. For reasons to allocate such costs, see T. Tani, "Allocation of Corporate Costs in the Decentralization Organization" (in Japanese), *Kokumin keizai zasshi*, January 1986.
3. Fremgen and Liao, *op. cit.*, p. 33.
4. *Ibid.*, pp. 40-42.
5. For transfer pricing practices in Japan and its contingency theory, see, T. Tani's Fundamentals of Accounting for Performance in Divisional Organizations" (in Japanese) (Tokyo: Kunimotoshobo, 1983).
6. For U.S. practices, see Vancil, *op. cit.*, p. 112. The percentage of allocating research costs based on service performed (metered basis) is almost the same, but the percentage of negotiated allocation is much higher in the United States.
7. *Ibid.*, p. 112.
8. G.Shillinglaw, "Guide to Internal Profit Measurement," *Harvard Business Review*, March-April 1957, p. 86. D. Solomons, *Divisional Performance: Measurement and Control* (Homewood, IL: Richard D. Irwin, 1968), pp. 68, 73.
9. H.Bierman, Jr., and T.R. Dyckman, *Managerial Cost Accounting* (New York: Macmillan, 1971), p. 215; I.W. Keller, "The Return on Capital Concept," *NAA Bulletin*, March 1958, pp. 17-18; G. Shillinglaw, "Guide to Internal Profit Measurement", *op. cit.*, p. 86.; G. Shillinglaw, "Divisionalization, Decentralization and Return on Investment," *NAA Bulletin*, December 1959, pp. 29-30; G.Shillinglaw, "Problems in Divisional Profit Measurement," *NAA Bulletin*, March 1961, p. 86.

# 19

## Software Cost Accounting Mechanisms in Japan

*Michiharu Sakurai, Professor of Accounting,*
*Senshu University*
*Wallace J. Growney, Professor of Management*
*and Computer Science,*
*Susquehanna University*

In Japan, just as in the United States, preparation of computer software is an expensive, labor intensive process. Thus, controlling and accounting for software costs are pressing problems for Japanese management. Naturally, cost accounting methods attract attention as possible tools for raising the productivity of software development. The intent of this chapter is to describe cost accounting practices used by Japanese developers of computer software. Software may be produced in three types of companies: (1) companies called "software houses," (2) computer hardware manufacturers, and (3) diverse companies considered as "users." This chapter focuses on software houses; the other developers are mentioned only briefly. Data comes from three sources:

1. A 1986 mail survey of 175 software houses by the Cost Accounting Committee on Software sponsored by the Japan Information Service Industry Association (JISIA).

2. Interviews with 11 major software houses and two mainframe manufacturers.
3. Discussions at several seminars with high attendance by users.

*Use of Software Cost Accounting Systems in Japan.* In Japan, the information processing industry is defined as a service industry, and generally speaking, most service industries do not need a cost accounting system. Nevertheless, nearly 80 percent of Japanese software developers use some form of a cost accounting system. According to the results of the mail survey, 56.6 percent (99 of 175) of software houses regularly use a cost accounting system and 22.8 percent (40 of 175) use one when it is occasionally deemed necessary. Only 22.8 percent of software houses have no cost accounting system at all.

Software developers need to compute software cost for many reasons. The main purpose is cost control, as indicated by the fact that 33 percent (58 of 175) of software houses ranked cost control as the most important reason for having a software cost accounting system. Budgeting and pricing ranked second. Cost accounting for financial reporting reasons are not important to Japanese software developers.

Most Japanese software houses do report inventory in their financial statements. For example, 66 percent (65 of 98) of those that regularly use software cost accounting also report an inventory of software. A much more difficult consideration is how to compute the work in process cost of software. For the leading software houses, this is a major effort.

*Product Cost in Software Cost Accounting.* A rather definite measure of product cost is necessary to compute the inventory cost. The procedures for producing software are generally the same among all Japanese software developers, but the details differ among software houses, computer mainframe manufacturers, and the companies considered as users.

Although some software developers do include maintenance costs as part of software production cost, most developers exclude them. In Japan, contrary to the United States, more than 90 percent of software is "custom developed software" (JISIA, 1986); that is, not many software products are manufactured with the intent that they will be sold widely and possibly customized by the client. Rather, each job and client is considered unique, and software is customized specifically for the client. Maybe the Japanese are perfectionists who require that software fit their firm or situation exactly. Another major difference from the United States is that there are few Japanese software companies where coding and testing are regarded as part of the software production process. Rather, Japanese software houses focus primarily on systems analysis and design, and treat coding and testing as mechanical tasks that are either subcontracted out or relegated to part-time employees.

In this chapter, we divide software production into two distinct phases: development and maintenance. Although there are a few companies where cost accounting is applied only to the maintenance phase, its application to the software development phase is considered much more important. Thus, we concentrate almost exclusively on the software development phase. In its fullest sense, however, the software development phase may also include marketing and production activities. The relationships are shown in Figure 19.1.

Theoretically, costs incurred from marketing activities should be treated as period costs, and production costs should be treated as product costs. For example, market research is a marketing activity, so its cost is treated as a period cost. On the other hand, in most Japanese software houses, some systems analysis is performed before the proposal, and a more detailed systems analysis is done after the contract is won. One would expect costs for the systems analysis done before the proposal to be treated as a period cost. But over half of Japanese software houses treat this systems analysis cost as a product cost, unless the proposal fails, in which case they treat it as a period cost. Most likely, this dual treatment occurs because the process of systems analysis requires large amounts of work, time, and money.

*Characteristics of Software Cost Accounting at Three Production Stages.* The main production phase of software development is divided into three parts: (1) systems development, (2) data entry, and (3) operation. Although our primary focus is on systems development, Japanese software houses often operate as a service bureau also. So in some cases, we must include data entry and operation, and we outline the mechanics of these briefly. In addition, we will mention the cost accounting mechanisms and problems associated with software maintenance.

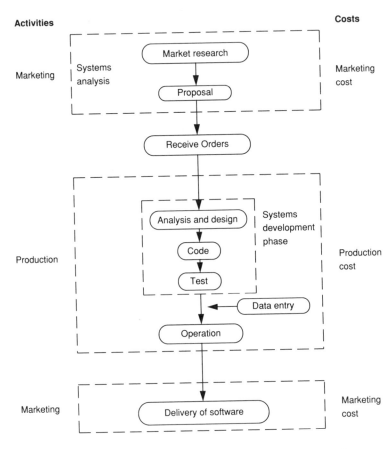

**Figure 19.1 Sample Software Development Cycle Showing Each Cost**

**Systems development costs.** As in the United States, systems development may be divided into four parts: analysis, design, coding, and testing. These can often be characterized as creative "brainwork," especially analysis and design. Since these efforts are similar to research and development, efficiency depends mostly on the relative abilities of the individual software engineers. The work is primarily labor intensive except for the testing phase which may require large amounts of computer time. Therefore, software cost accounting focuses on how to compute the cost of labor accurately, and on how to control it efficiently.

Computer time for testing can generally be recorded automatically by the computer and its cost is charged to a specific production order. When programmers compile code for a more general purpose, however, these machine costs are treated as an indirect cost and allocated throughout the software product line, based on the number of lines of code.

Which technique is more appropriate for software production, job order costing or process costing? Since both contract software and packaged software are produced in essentially the same way, a production order is generally issued in each case. Therefore, job order costing is considered best for systems development work; according to the mail survey, 66 percent (91 of 137) of software houses use this method.

**Data entry costs.** Data entry costs are measured by the accumulated time cards, which record time spent in this process. In the survey, 63 percent (42 of 67) of the companies use job order costing for data entry. Generally, direct costs for data entry consist of contract cost, labor cost, machine cost and material cost. When the amount of material is insignificant, however, it is treated as overhead. Costs for items or equipment used on several different projects, such as a computer or card sorter, are allocated as indirect costs on a working hours basis.

**Operation costs.** Operations costs are generally a function of computer time. Machine costs are based on the time the computer is used, and are charged to software products as a direct cost.

There are two distinct operations processes. One is an initialization operation for a software production order. The second is repetitive execution corresponding to routine service work, such as payroll processing. According to our survey, job order costing is more appropriate for the first, while process costing is appropriate for the latter.

**Maintenance costs.** Software development costs do not necessarily include or end with operations costs. Subsequent software revisions are usually necessary and this additional work is called "maintenance." In Japan, just as in the United States, it is estimated that the cost of maintenance is more than 60 percent of all software costs (OECD, 1985).

Whether software maintenance costs should be treated as capital or expenses is a matter of great importance when doing tax planning. As mentioned earlier, these costs are usually treated as period costs. Some companies, however, have implemented software cost accounting primarily for the purpose of cost control. An example is Melcon

Services, one of whose reports is shown in Table 19.1. This income statement by users reveals characteristics of a cost accounting system designed for software maintenance activities.

| Items | Data Center | User A | User B | User C |
|---|---|---|---|---|
| 1  Sales | | | | |
| 2     Direct Labor | | | | |
| 3     Parts Cost | | | | |
| 4     Direct Travel | | | | |
| 5     Direct Freight | | | | |
| 6     ... | | | | |
| 7 | | | | |
| 8          **Total** | | | | |
| 9  Maintenance/Sales (8/1) | | | | |
| 10  Contribution Margin | | | | |
| 11  Rate Contribution Margin | | | | |
| 12  Head Office Cost | | | | |
| 13  Total Cost | | | | |
| 14  Margin (1 — 13) | | | | |
| 15  Return on Sales (14/1) | | | | |

**Table 19.1  Income Statement by Users (Maintenance Phase)**

In the preceding section, we have outlined software cost accounting in the order of its production steps. We now return to our main focus, systems development.

*Procedure for Software Cost Accounting.* For the systems development phase of software production, cost accounting steps are similar to those used by hardware manufacturers: (1) accounting for the cost of material, labor, and overhead; (2) departmental cost accounting; and (3) product cost accounting. For hardware production, total absorption cost accounting is not as important for financial accounting purposes because administrative and marketing costs do not contribute to the product and its cost. But for custom-developed software, total absorption cost accounting is important for pricing and profitability analysis. Although the steps are the same for both hardware and software production, the details of these procedures differ.

**Cost accounting by cost items.** Natural classifications of cost, such as material, labor, and overhead, form the main differences between hardware and software cost accounting procedures. *Material Cost.* Compared to hardware production, software development involves only small amounts of material costs (paper, disks, and so forth). These are more like supplies, and are immaterial in dollar value relative to the total software development cost. Though Japan's Information Service Industry accounting guidelines include these items as material cost, 43 percent (54 of 132) of software houses treat them as overhead. One is CSK, one of the largest public software houses in Japan. Its production cost report is shown in Table 19.2.

| Cost Items | Fiscal Year | The 16th From Sept 21, 1983 To Sept 20, 1984 | | The 17th From Sept 21, 1984 To Sept 20, 1985 | | Difference |
|---|---|---|---|---|---|---|
| | | Amount | Percent | Amount | Percent | Amount |
| 1  Labor Cost | | 10,775,642 | 83.4 | 12,789,121 | 80.3 | 2,013,478 |
| 2  Contract Expense | | 955,279 | 7.4 | 1,777,213 | 11.2 | 821,934 |
| 3  Overhead | | 1,189,398 | 9.2 | 1,352,732 | 8.5 | 163,334 |
|    Computer Rental | | (129,215) | | (80,299) | | |
|    Depreciation | | (118,861) | | (100,904) | | |
|    Welfare Expense | | (143,211) | | (219,464) | | |
|    Travel Expense | | (235,262) | | (315,091) | | |
|    Rent | | (285,991) | | (295,283) | | |
|    Miscellaneous | | (276,859) | | (341,689) | | |
| Total Cost | | 12,920,320 | 100.0% | 15,919,067 | 100.0% | 2,998,747 |

**Table 19.2  Sample CSK Production Cost Report**

*Labor cost.* Labor costs include salary, fringe benefits, bonuses, and allowances for employee retirement benefits. On average, labor cost as a percentage of sales is high, 38.03 percent for 422 typical software houses during 1984 (IPPA, 1986). In addition, since contracting expense (19.96 percent of sales in 1984) is mainly labor, the cost of labor rises to almost 60 percent (38.03 + 19.96) of sales. Thus, it is important for software companies to install and refine a sophisticated labor cost accounting system. For cost control to be effective, it is necessary to divide labor costs into direct and indirect.

In typical Japanese software houses, bonus amounts are relatively steady each year. Semiannual bonuses each equal to between three and six months pay, depending on business conditions. Direct labor costs usually include not only payroll expenses but also a monthly allowance for these bonuses. Since many Japanese software companies are quite small, their directors often engage in software development work. The bonus to directors is treated as a labor cost item.

In practice, software development requires many hours of meeting time. If a meeting is called for a particular project, then the time can be included in direct labor hours for the project. On the other hand, if the meeting is mostly about general affairs, these labor costs must be allocated to projects as indirect costs.

*Overhead.* In a software house, there are other large computer related costs, such as machine rental, depreciation, hardware maintenance, and communication charges. These overhead costs should be carefully monitored and controlled, and clearly separated and allocated to projects. To have a precise picture of software costs, it is important not to group overhead costs together.

**Departmental cost accounting.** Classifying and accumulating product costs into departments is the second step of production cost accounting. Unlike hardware companies, only 75 percent (98 of 131) of software houses have implemented some forms of departmental cost accounting; 22 percent (29 of 131) have no departmental cost accounting system at all. (See Figure 19.2.)

It may appear that fewer software houses use departmental cost accounting because of their relatively small size. When asked, however, only a few companies attribute this to their small size. Rather, they attribute it to the difficulties of enforcing departmental control when producing software. In software firms, the cost departments are separated into producing departments and service departments. Service departments are further subdivided into service management and marketing management departments. Department names differ from company to company. Table 19.3 shows typical ones, and you can see that they are quite different from those encountered in hardware firms.

**(A)** No Departmental Cost Accounting (29 Companies)

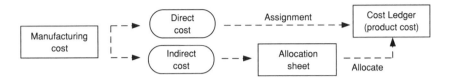

**(B)** Departmental Cost Accounting of Only Indirect Cost (5 Companies)

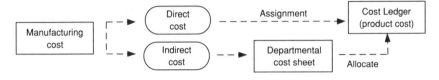

**(C)** Departmental Cost Accounting of All Cost Items (93 Companies)

**(D)** Others (4 Companies)

**Figure 19.2 Various Kinds of Departmental Cost Accounting**

While the division of production and sales functions is quite clear for large hardware manufacturers, it is not so clear for the smaller software firms. For example, in a software house, the marketing management department may play a similar role to that of the shop management department for a hardware firm. Also, it is often combined with the general management function of the head office. Thus, it is a matter of accounting policy whether one should treat the cost of that marketing management department as product cost or period cost. One thing is clear, however: the software industry is growing rapidly in Japan and, as competition among software houses becomes more intense, departmental cost accounting will become more vital.

**Product cost accounting.** The third step is product cost accounting, which determines a unit cost from the total product cost, and is

| Producing Departments Function | Title of Department |
|---|---|
| Programming | Development department, systems development department, engineering development department |
| Computer Processing | Computation office, information processing, computation department, computation center |
| Data Preparation | Card punch department, tape punch department |
| Dispatch of Sales Force | Personnel dispatch department, engineering service department |

| Service Departments Function | Title of Department |
|---|---|
| Service Management | Education department, planning department, R & D department, QC department, distribution department, data management department, systems management department, TSS management department, systems research center, software management department, etc. |
| Marketing Management | Sales planning department, sales department, marketing department, sales promotion department, machine sales department, general administration, accounting department, personnel department, etc. |

**Table 19.3  Typical Department Titles in a Software House**

especially relevant for pricing and inventory evaluation. Product cost accounting may use either job order or process costing. The latter simplifies the procedures and because of this, 13 percent (18 of 137) of software houses use it for systems development cost accounting.

The content of a software product is, in some ways, invisible. It is therefore difficult to determine a work in process cost for software by process costing. Thus, job order costing is thought to be the most appropriate and effective method for measurement and control of software development costs.

A production order is required for job order costing, and many types of job orders are used in the Japanese software houses. Generally, it contains a job number, customer name, job name, task outline, schedule, number of ordered goods, and estimated labor hours and machine hours. As the work proceeds, direct costs are charged and indirect costs are allocated for each product. We will briefly outline each.

*Labor costs.* Direct labor cost is computed by multiplying direct labor hours times labor rate. A timecard is used for recording labor hours. It shows the operator's name, department, job number, operation, start, finish, and elapsed time for each job. These are essentially the same for hardware cost accounting.

What type of labor rate should be used: a rate for each individual, an historical rate, or a predetermined average rate for the department? An individual rate is computed from monthly historical averages, which takes considerable time and effort. It is different for each worker, even if two or more workers perform the same job. Thus, it is unreasonable to use individual historical rates for inventory evaluation or for comparing efficiency of production orders.

Since most software houses rank their engineers into several grades based on educational background, experience, years of service, or working area, it is easy to classify an engineer into one of several classes. All in all, it seems appropriate to use a predetermined average labor rate for each class of software developer or for the kind of job being done. However, there is a significant exception: like the United States, Japan has quite a few new venture-type software houses with high staff turnover or frequent changes in the kinds of jobs they do. In such a company, a predetermined labor rate may not be the best method because of the large variance between it and the historical cost. This is particularly true if they use an average rate as the predetermined labor rate.

For systems development workers, such as a manager or a general secretary, the labor cost is treated as an indirect cost and allocated to products on a labor hour basis.

*Contract expenses.* There are two types of contract expenses: (1) payment for consignment or subcontracted work, and (2) payment for employees who are dispatched from other companies. Usually, these costs are treated as direct costs and charged to each job.

At this point, we must indicate that, for the most part, software is developed in one of two ways in Japan. First, many of the larger hardware firms have created subsidiaries and other affiliated companies especially for this purpose. These subsidiaries supply software at a relatively low labor cost...and highly specialized skill and consignment production is the norm. The contract expense is similar to purchase of low-price parts or partly finished goods to save labor costs for the parent company. Its cost should be charged to the appropriate job. One exception, however, is when, say, a key-to-tape device is consigned by other companies. Then its cost is treated as an indirect cost because such a device is likely to be used on several different jobs.

A second method of software production that has emerged over the last 10 to 15 years is dispatching software house engineers to other companies to develop software for the recipient company. One such software house is CSK. With about 4,200 employees, more than half are sent out. Contract cost for the dispatched employees becomes a labor cost for the recipients and an operation timecard is used to record the labor hours that each software engineer spends on each production order.

Incidentally as the software industry grows in Japan, more and more people will experience this continual switching of work locations. It may become somewhat of a social problem, for this location switching will threaten the software engineer's identity as, say, a CSK employee. This is notably significant in Japan where a worker's employer becomes church, family, and the core of existence.

*Machine rental cost.* Machine rental costs are computed by multiplying machine time by machine rate. This computed cost is charged to a product or production order in accordance with machine hours. Normally, machine time is measured by the computer's operating system each time a job is run; however, a machine rate is computed by dividing the total (usually fixed) machine rental cost and its related expense by the total time the machine is run. When this total machine time changes from one month to another, the machine rate changes correspondingly, and so does its cost to the user. Much to the dismay of managers who pay for computer processing, this means that the same job may cost different amounts from one month to the next. Therefore, it is desirable to use a predetermined machine rate to avert this difficulty.

*Purchase cost.* The purchase cost of a database management system or other software package necessary for developing a particular software product is charged to its production order. INTEK, one of three public software houses in Japan, includes this cost as a direct material cost; CSK treats it as a direct expense. On the other hand, the purchase cost of more general software packages to be used for developing a variety of products should be treated as a period cost, as might be done with supplies, for example. Or it may be treated as a capital expense and depreciated over time.

*Other costs.* Depreciation of machines, rental of real estate, and property tax are allocated across the product line. Materials such as printer paper are charged to a particular production order in some firms, but treated as general supplies in others. Indirect materials such as tape and magnetic disks are allocated to the products. Although traveling expenses can be easily identified with a particular software product, it is considered useless to measure it on a project basis. Therefore, travel expense is usually treated as overhead. Other direct expenses are charged to the appropriate production order, and other indirect costs are likely to be allocated across several products.

*Allocating overhead.* All indirect costs must be allocated. Direct labor hours or direct labor costs are usually handled on an allocation basis in Japanese software houses. According to the mail survey, 63 percent (77 of 122) of software houses use either direct labor hours (36 percent) or direct labor cost (27 percent). Like cost accounting, in hardware companies' over 70 percent of software houses use historical data to determine the cost, although a predetermined allocation method is preferable. A predetermined rate and actual cost are usually computed as follows:

(Step #1)
$$\text{Predetermined rate} = \frac{\text{predetermined overhead}}{\text{predetermined number of hours or cost}}$$

(Step #2)
$$\text{Actual cost} = \frac{\text{predetermined rate}}{\times \text{ actual number of allocations}}$$

When a predetermined allocation method is used, it is believed that overhead costs should be allocated to particular departments rather than to the development process as a whole. The kind of work differs from department to department; thus, for cost control purposes, it is appropriate to allocate overhead costs on a departmental basis.

*Cost ledger.* Finally, a cost ledger is prepared as a means of accumulating the cost of each product. Although many kinds of cost ledgers are used in Japanese software houses, the one shown in Table 19.4 is the one that the JISIA recommends.

Job number _____     Customer name _____

Start date _____     Completion date _____

| Direct Cost | | | | Indirect Cost | | | |
|---|---|---|---|---|---|---|---|
| Labor | Contract | Machine | Other | Items | Basis | Rate | Amounts |
| | | | | | | | |

| Previous process cost | | Total | |
|---|---|---|---|
| | | Labor Costs<br>Contract Cost<br>Machine Cost<br>Other Costs<br>Subtotal | |
| | | Overhead | |
| | | Total | |

**Table 19.4  Cost Ledger**

*Total Absorption Cost Accounting.* The total cost of software is computed by adding the selling and administrative costs to the product cost. For software developers, the total cost data is especially useful for pricing and management control. Therefore, total absorption cost accounting cannot be ignored. Of 130 software houses, 82 percent compute total cost either regularly (51 percent) or when it is deemed necessary (31 percent).

Figure 19.1 showed the scope of marketing costs. From that figure, the reader may think it is easy to distinguish the marketing costs from the production costs. This is not true, however, for software houses where many marketing management functions are mixed in with the production activities. On the other hand, it is not hard to distinguish between general administrative functions and production activities. The corporate offices of Japanese software houses are typically separate from the production and marketing locations.

In addition to its necessity for cost control (37 percent of 148 firms), total cost accounting is necessary for profitability control (32 percent) and pricing (19 percent). A developer's profitability measurement must include the cost of administrative and marketing activities, as well as the cost of the systems development.

**Conclusion.** In this chapter, we have outlined the software cost accounting practices of Japanese software developers. Although the basic workings are the same, there are some special characteristics in the mechanics of software cost accounting that distinguish it from normal manufacturing.

The discussion was confined to the mechanics of software cost accounting, and did not touch on other cost control problems such as standard costing, project cost estimating, work in process control, or total quality control as they are typically practiced by the software developers in Japan. We expect to write papers on these and other software related topics.

### References

1. JISIA, *White Paper of Information Service Industry for 1986*, edited by MITI, (Japan Information Service Industry Association, 1986), p. 88. (According to the survey, software production was 5.3 percent of the industry for 1982, 6.6 percent for 1983, and 8.3 percent for 1984.)
2. IPPA, *Report of Empirical Research in Information Processing Industry for 1984*, Information Processing Promoting Association (*jouhou shori shinko tigyo kyokai*), January 1986, p. 48.
3. OECD, *Software: An Emerging Industry*, (Paris: 1985), p. 35.
4. Sakurai, Michiharu. "The Mechanism of Software Cost Accounting Practices," *Industrial Management* (*sangyokeiri*), Japan Industrial Management and Accounting Institute, 1986, Vol. 46, No. 1, pp. 113-125.
5. Sakurai, Michiharu. "Principles of Software Cost Accounting," *Current Topics of Cost Accounting*, (Japan Accounting Association, 1986), pp. 115-126.
6. Sakurai, Michiharu. "Software Cost Control," *Industrial Management* (*sangyokeiri*), 1986, Vol. 46, No. 1, pp. 11-21.

# 20

## Rebuilding a Cost Accounting System from a Service Cost Standpoint: The Case of Mitsubishi Kasei

*Yoshikazu Miyabe, Director, Mitsubishi Kasei*

Mitsubishi Kasei's old cost system was established 30 years ago. It was based on calculating the total cost of each product via actual cost by allocating all costs to each product. This method was adopted because:

1. The company needed a precise cost system. Recognizing individual product costs was indispensable when determining the selling price of each product and attaining maximum profit.
2. The company wished to prevent any misjudgment that might arise using multiple decision-making data from a dual system of financial and managerial accounting.
3. At that time, computerization was in its infancy and even single-purpose computations required much time and effort.

The cost system based on individual products was useful for comparing total costs with selling prices. Because it included many allocated factors, however, it did not explicitly attribute responsibility to those persons in charge of cost management. It also could not present enough information for costs saving. This system was rigid. Being unable to fully utilize the computer's capacity, the allocation system heavily burdened the computing process as new computer programs were introduced.

The company then adopted a dual financial and managerial accounting system using a standard cost system. The chemical industry, however, differs greatly from machining or assembly industries, and it was difficult to determine standard costs correctly. Cost variance was too large and tended to cause inaccurate performance forecasting. We therefore had to abandon the standard cost system. When the actual cost system was adopted, we tried to simplify the allocation method, but the result had limited effect on the process of product diversification.

***Background of the New System.*** With the remarkable changes in the business environment during the last few decades, the cost system has come to require revisions. In the first place, a remarkable transition of product mix has emerged in the chemical industry. There is greater emphasis on providing products in small quantities and in more variety than on mass-producing commodities such as petrochemicals. Under the circumstances, the cost of service functions (which used to be supplementary functions) has become an important factor in the cost system.

Second, when cost saving centering around the control of production quantities and streamlining operations by reducing fixed costs are required, it has become necessary to clarify exactly where the responsibilities for cost should lie.

Third, as computer systems have been added and revised one after another, most employees, unless they were computer experts, were unable to understand the total system. Countermeasures became necessary.

Technological innovations in computer systems made high-speed, large-capacity computation possible. Data communication systems emerged. Due to this technological progress, the time needed for cost calculation today is remarkably shorter. Also, the development of a database system made the cost system usable for multiple purposes.

The new system was designed for the following:

1. *Thorough management of responsibility cost:* Costs at every stage of management are clearly identified by an accurate grasp of each cost at the place it occurs. This allows explicit attribution of responsibility. For this reason, cost departments as cost management units were reviewed and modified accordingly.

2. *Controlling cost by objectives:* The old management policy centered around cost factors was restructured as a system to make cost control by objectives possible.

3. *Introduction of the "service" concept:* As a means of control by objectives, the concept of service cost was introduced to correspond to the shift of product mix toward functional products. Emphasis was also placed on the cost analysis of non-manufacturing departments.

4. *Review of evaluating costs by individual product:* Cost control should be based on the aggregate cost of each cost department as a responsible unit. In this context, the cost of individual products is used only for reference and figures by allocation can be estimated. This information is necessary for improving profitability. The new system is able to present this data.

5. *Simplified and multi-purpose computation system:* The new computation system was simplified so that time would not be wasted maintaining computer programs. All costs are grouped into (1) raw materials/energy (variable cost) and (2) factor cost (fixed cost). Using this classification, the (1) cost table of responsibility costing unit by cost department, (2) cost table by individual product, and (3) aggregate cost control by objective became possible by applying a combination of basic data. Such a multi-purpose cost system is practical only with an advanced database system. (See Figure 20.1.)

6. *Shortening computation time:* By virtue of the large capacity computers and data communication networks, computation time was shortened. We can now determine monthly profit and loss by the fifth day of the following month. The shortened computation time made the dual system of financial and managerial accounting meaningless.

***Structure of the Cost Computing System.*** **Product cost.** Departing from the traditional cost control method of classifying costs into variable costs, fixed costs and overhead, the "service" concept was extracted from the traditional method of cost control and costs are classified as follows:

- *Raw materials and energy cost:* Amount of raw materials and energy consumed.
- *Direct value-adding cost:* Direct fixed costs of processing/manufacturing departments, excluding allocations from other departments.
- *Service cost:* This cost occurs at plants, sales and distribution/marketing departments, and head offices. It excludes direct processing/manufacturing costs (raw material and energy cost plus direct value-adding costs), interest and future cost inclusive of R&D.
- *Interest cost:* It is simply "interest payable − interest receivable = fund procurement cost."
- *Future cost:* It is cost spent today for future (see Figure 20.2).

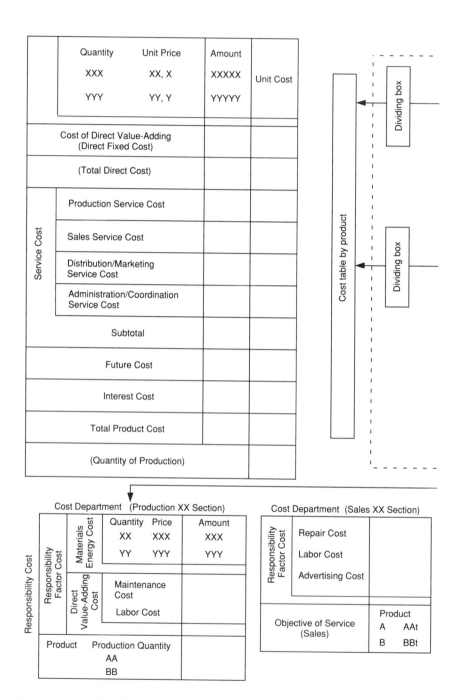

**Figure 20.1 The New Multi-Purpose Cost System**

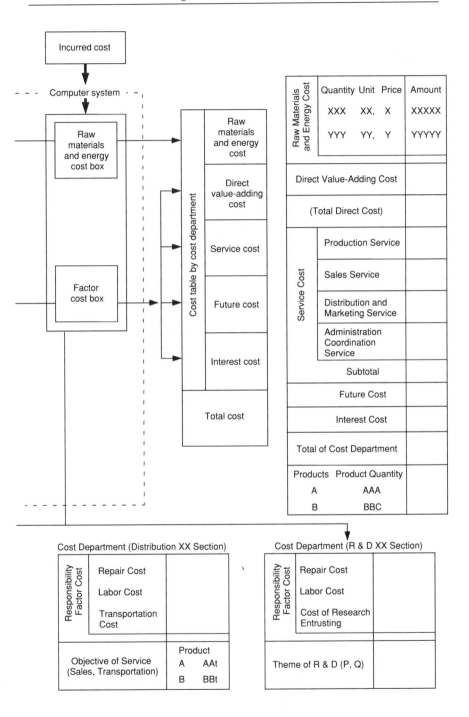

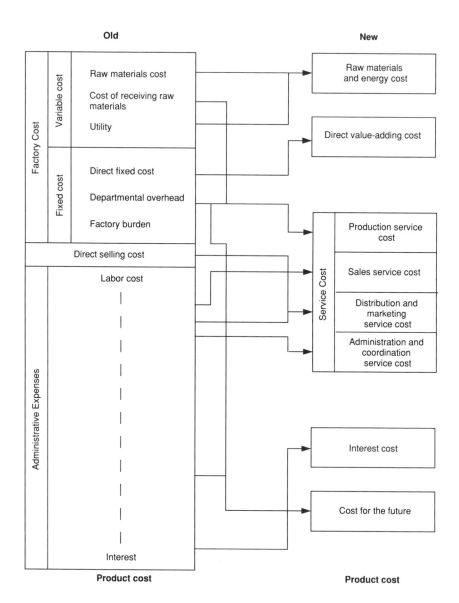

**Figure 20.2  Cost Classification**

**Classifying service cost.** Service cost is a rearrangement, with an objective, of traditional cost control measures based on the cost factor. It can be classified into (1) services in direct and indirect departments, or (2) service at various stages of corporate activities such as production and distribution.

Service cost combines these two views. *Production service cost* covers direct costs of the factory and the indirect costs of its administrator. *Sales service cost* covers direct costs such as business and technical service activities, market development and advertising, and distribution costs. Indirect costs are administrative and on-line sales costs. (See Table 20.1.) *Distribution and marketing service cost* covers the direct costs of transportation and warehouse storage and indirect costs of delivery. (See Table 20.2.) *Administration and coordination service cost* occurs at the company's head office in the areas of general administration, personnel accounting, purchasing, patent, auditing, management planning, and subsidiary and affiliate company administration.

**Establishing Target Cost and Cost Saving.** It is an enterprise's everlasting goal to increase its capacity for yielding profits. When business circumstances are severe, as seen when the exchange rate fluctuates, the company should establish a target cost and clear measures for the changing business environment. Generally, there are five ways to establish target cost:

1. Voluntary establishment by each cost management unit.
2. Across-the-board cost reduction at certain percentages.

| | Kind of Service | Breakdown of Cost |
|---|---|---|
| **Direct** | Business and technical service activity | Cost related to business departments and branch offices |
| | Market development, advertising and public relations | Cost of market development<br>Cost of advertising and public relations<br>Cost of free sample |
| | Functions of trading company and distributor | Handling commission<br>Sales commission |
| **Indirect** | Business administration | Cost related to administration and control of business departments and branch offices |
| | Administrative work | Sales accounting, credit control, etc. |
| | Sales on-line | Cost of system |

**Table 20.1  Sales Service Cost**

| | Kind of Service | Breakdown of Cost |
|---|---|---|
| **Direct** | Transportation | Facilities for tank truck, truck, and transportation expenses |
| | Loading, shipment | Loading expense for shipment, product storage (warehouse, stock point) Materials for repackaging Export expenses |
| | Insurance | Transportation coverage |
| **Indirect** | Delivery work | Cost related to delivery work |
| | Administration and coordination | Expenses related to production, sales, and distribution/marketing |

**Table 20.2  Distribution/Marketing Cost**

3. Calculation of cost backward from the required profit or target cost ratio.
4. An experience curve.
5. A prior index or government forecast, pharmaceutical price regulation, the foreign exchange rate, and so forth (see Table 20.3).

Each of these five methods has advantages and disadvantages, as shown in Table 20.3.

At Mitsubishi Kasei, the method of establishing target costs, as shown in Figure 20.3, is being studied. In practice, the person responsible for profit and loss is responsible for reducing the target cost. Final responsibility is attributed to the general manager of each business department. To save each cost component, the person responsible for the component(s) (the production department's plant manager, for example) tries to reduce costs under the authority of the business department's general manager. For support, the accounting department provides cost saving data. A business department establishes an action plan (see Table 20.4) and allots the targeted improvement amount to each responsible unit of the department. The improvement amount is the amount necessary to achieve the target cost.

| Method | Utility Value | Question | Scope of Application |
|---|---|---|---|
| Voluntary set up by cost control unit | Stimulates the sense of participation | Vulnerable to personal character of planner | |
| Across-the-board reduction | Simple and easy to understand | Relationship between life cycle and potential extent of reduction is disregarded | Effective in the early stage |
| Cost calculated backward from required profit | Easy to persuade from the standpoint of profit control | Index is needed to establish sales price | |
| Experience curve | Easy to persuade as an empirical rule | High tolerance for monopoly product and products in early stages | Has a large utility value as reference index |
| Prior index | Imperative if the index is the price determining factor | Few prior indices are available | Applicable for pharmaceutical and international merchandise |

Table 20.3 Methods to Establish Target Cost

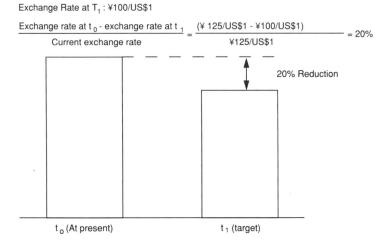

Exchange Rate at $T_1$ : ¥100/US$1

$$\frac{\text{Exchange rate at } t_0 - \text{exchange rate at } t_1}{\text{Current exchange rate}} = \frac{(¥125/US\$1 - ¥100/US\$1)}{¥125/US\$1} = 20\%$$

20% Reduction

$t_0$ (At present)          $t_1$ (target)

**Example 1: International Products**

Price is subject to periodic reduction at a certain rate to be specified officially by the government.

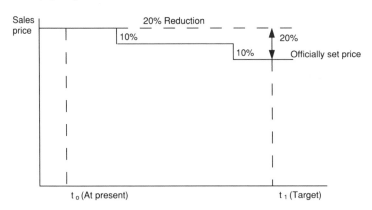

Sales price

20% Reduction

10%

10%

20%

Officially set price

$t_0$ (At present)          $t_1$ (Target)

**Example 2: Pharmaceuticals**

**Figure 20.3  Target Cost Studies at Mitsubishi Kasei**

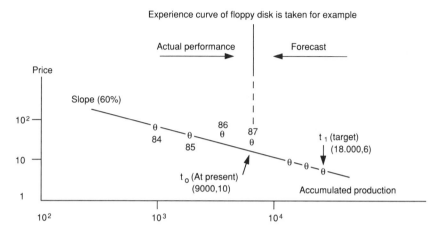

Experience curve of floppy disk is taken for example

Example 3: Other Products

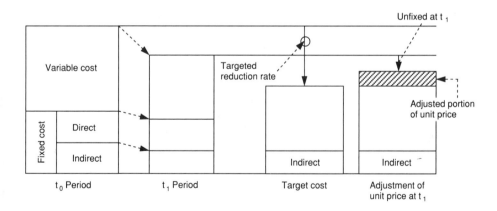

| Responsible Unit → Cost Item ↓ | Responsibility Cost — Plant — Production Department — Raw Materials and Energy Cost | Direct Value-Adding Cost | Total | Production Service Cost | Head Office — Branch Offices — Sales Service Cost | Distribution Service Cost | Research — Future Cost | Interest | Total | Administrative and Coordinating Service Cost | Total Cost |
|---|---|---|---|---|---|---|---|---|---|---|---|
| Basic Cost | | | | | | | | | | | |
| Target Cost | | | | | | | | | | | |
| Amount of Targeted Improvement | | | $a_1$ | $a_2$ | | | | | Ⓐ | Ⓑ | Ⓒ |

Table 20.4  Action Plan

Each responsible unit establishes an action program (see Table 20.5) for the achievement of the allotted target. If a unit is unable to establish an adequate action program, the unit will review the circumstances at the closing date of a period and set up additional action programs as needed. As to the savings in administration service costs not attributable to the business department, the relevant administration departments establish action programs for cost savings corresponding to the targeted amount of improvement.

Should the target not be fully achieved, business departments do not have to bear the cost reduction burden. The unachieved portion is held by the relevant administration department for immediate review of necessary countermeasures. (See Figure 20.4.)

**Dynamic Corporate Strategic Model.** Our current interest is to establish a dynamic corporate strategic model. There are new developments in portfolio planning and system studies, such as strategic issue management, to keep up with the unpredictability of the business

| Responsible Unit | | Counter-measure | Amount of Improvement | Time of Execution | Amount of Facilities Investment | Labor ± |
|---|---|---|---|---|---|---|
| Plant | Production Department | | | | | |
| | | | $a_1$ | | | |
| | Others | | | | | |
| | | | $a_2$ | | | |
| | | | $a_1 + a_2$ | | | |
| | | | | | | |
| Targeted Amount of Improvement | | | Ⓐ | | | |

**Table 20.5  Action Program**

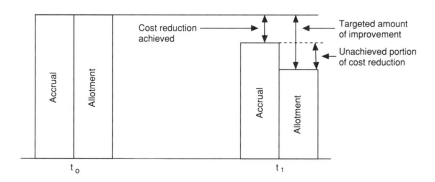

**Figure 20.4  Unachieved Versus Targeted Amounts**

environment. Yet it seems that the academic circle has not presented corporate strategic models for contemporary business environments where numerous rapid changes occur. Our concept of a dynamic corporate strategic model, though still in its early stages, is presented in Figure 20.5.

Over 10 years ago, we conceived of a prototype for a multi-stage multi-project maximum profit model using the mixed integer L/P as an algorithm. Now we wish to introduce portfolio planning as a standard for project selection corresponding to today's multiple corporate objectives, keeping the following points in mind:

1. A dimension related to the time factor of a strategy should be considered through the introduction of a product or business's life cycle, including the disposal cost of facilities.
2. While traditional portfolio models may pay attention only to the marketplace, the resource question should be reviewed as well.
3. Not only a company's internal growth, but its external growth should also be made possible. In this context, fund management as a separate area should be included in the scope of business activity.

Since portfolio planning does not fully cover financial decision-making as a factor, we intend to make up for such drawbacks by combining it with a corporate finance model. Financial strategies such as selecting finance sources and hedging function should be introduced into the model.

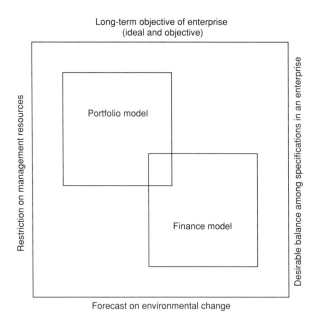

**Figure 20.5 Concept of Dynamic Corporate Strategic Model**

# 21

## Cost Management Problems in Multikind, Low- or Medium-Volume Production

*Shinichi Inoue, Faculty of Economics, Kagawa University*

This chapter reviews the trend of flexible manufacturing systems (FMS); multikind and low- or medium-volume production; and major problems of cost management in manufacturing companies in Japan.[1] Industries that frequently use FMS are mainly assembly industries such as shipbuilding, transportation equipment, and electrical appliances. Companies that frequently employ multikind, low-volume or multikind, medium-volume production systems are also mainly assembly industries. They have much in common with small-lot production systems. Multikind, low-volume production systems are used in industries such as ceramics, stone and clay, iron and steel, food and drink, electrical appliances, textile related, transportation equipment, and fabricated metals.

The main problem in cost management in those industries has been shifting from cost control of the production process to the management of product planning or cost planning. For example, purchase management of raw materials and rationalizing design using CAD/CAM, cost planning and cost estimation, quality control (mainly total quality control, or TQC), and just-in-time (JIT) have become important issues. Cost management techniques based on production management methods such as JIT, TQC, value engineering

343

(VE), value analysis (VA), and industrial engineering (IE) are becoming more essential than accounting methods such as standard costing. They emphasize not only cost management through management accounting but also through production management, and are aimed at complete, companywide cost management.

It has often been pointed out that the production methods of manufacturing companies were greatly influenced in the 1970s and 1980s by technological innovation, increased competition, and market diversification. Following the oil crises of 1973 and 1979, many companies were forced to choose multikind, low- or medium-volume production systems to meet diversifying consumer needs. And while it can be assumed that each company adopted appropriate methods for its own cost management, until now there has been no survey based research. In this chapter, we intend to verify (1) the shift to multikind and low- or medium-volume production, and (2) its influence on the cost management of Japanese manufacturing companies based on our mail surveys.

We will first explain the outline of our surveys, conducted by mail in 1982 and 1983. All manufacturing companies listed in the Tokyo Stock Exchange were investigated. The response rate ($\times$ 100) was 69.3 percent (623/899) in 1982 and 72.5 percent (655/908) in 1983. Here we use and analyze the results.[2]

***The Shift to Flexible Manufacturing Systems.*** Flexible manufacturing systems (FMS) have become popular among Japanese manufacturing companies.[3] Based on our 1983 survey, the ratio of FMS introduction in manufacturing companies is summarized as follows. Overall, the ratio of companies introducing FMS is 8 percent (simple mean). When we calculated the weighted mean by scale, the ratio of companies becomes 44 percent and the ratio of factories 18 percent. These figures show that larger rather than smaller companies tended to use FMS more frequently. This is verified when we note the weighted mean by scale: the introduction of FMS by company is 16 percent (scale I), 26 percent (II), 24 percent (III), and 55 percent (IV).[4] This shows more than half the companies of scale IV have introduced FMS and more than 20 percent of the factories have introduced it. FMS is introduced mainly among manufacturers of transportation equipment, electrical appliances, ships, and precision instruments. Next come iron and steel, fabric and apparel, and machinery. Everyone wants to have flexibility of production to meet the market's increasing diversification.

The shift of factories to FMS tends to be similar to that of companies by industry.

***The Shift to Multikind, Low- or Medium-Volume Production.***[5] Production methods depend mainly on the manufacturing activities of the companies, and production management is basically constrained by production methods. There are many ways to classify production methods. We will divide them here into three categories to reveal the shift to multikind and low- or medium-volume production:

*Production method #1 — by industry type:*

- Assembly production, i.e., auto industry.
- Mechanical process production, i.e., metal industry.
- Chemical process production, i.e., oil refinery industry.
- Other productions.

*Production method #2 — by product type and volume:*

- Multikind and low-volume production.
- Multikind and medium-volume production.
- Small-kind and mass-production.

*Production method #3 — by process management:*

- Single-unit production.
- Small-lot production.
- Large-lot production.
- Mass-production.

All three production methods relate directly to manufacturing activities. Above all, classification based on industry type is the most fundamental because it supposes a certain combination of raw materials, manufacturing processes (production lines), production facilities, and so on. This basic combination is not easily chosen or changed by management decision making, even if each company has often made various kinds of technological innovations in its continuing manufacturing activities. This sort of combination has a rather stable and fundamental character for various kinds of business activities. Compared to the technical character of the industry, the product type and volume and process management are dynamic and floating factors, dependent on the environment of the company and industry, even if the company continues certain specific business activities. These production methods have greater variability.

We will first examine the manufacturing activities from the standpoint of industry type because this is a basic and stable aspect less influenced by management decision making. Later, we will analyze them from the aspect of process management and the type and volume of products that have been influenced by management decision making. From this analysis, we will draw a map of low- or medium-volume variety productions by industry, scale, and production methods.

*Production method #1* by industry type is summarized as follows. In overall manufacturing companies, the number of assembly companies is the largest, followed by chemical process production and mechanical process production. Specifically, the results are assembly production, 40.8 percent; mechanical process, 17.9 percent; chemical process, 26.5 percent; other, 9 percent. We can say that Japan's structure of manufacturing industries centers chiefly on assembly production, chemical process production, and mechanical process production, in that order.

When we examine the facts industrywide, it becomes clear that the industries with a high percentage of assembly production are fabricated metals, 70.6 percent; machinery, 78.9 percent; electrical appliances, 80 percent; transportation equipment, 84.6 percent; precision instruments, 88.5 percent; and shipbuilding, 100 percent. These industries belong mainly to the assembly industry. Those industries with a high percentage of mechanical process production are textile related industries, 50 percent; publishing and printing, 33.3 percent; nonferrous metals, 53.6 percent; and iron and steel, 84.6 percent. The following industries have a high percentage of chemical process production: foods and drink, 47.9 percent; pulp and paper, 70 percent; chemicals, 74.5 percent; oil refinery and coal products, 77.8 percent; and ceramics, stone, and clay, 46.2 percent.

*Production method #2* classified by the type and volume of products directly reflects consumer needs and the diversified market. The ratio of low-volume, variety production is 38.5 percent; varied medium-volume production is 33.7 percent. This shows that over 70 percent of the companies are faced with adopting variety production. We can see that multikind, low- or medium-volume production is becoming the norm in Japan.

Analyzing production method #2 separately, we find that industries using multikind, low-volume production are precision instruments, 53.8 percent; publishing and printing, 66.7 percent; machinery, 66.7 percent; and shipbuilding, 83.1 percent. These industries are required to shift to low-volume, variety production. We find medium-volume, variety production in ceramics, stone, and clay, 38.5 percent; iron and steel, 38.5 percent; food and drink, 39.6 percent; electrical appliances, 43.2 percent; textile-related industries, 45.5 percent; transportation equipment, 48.1 percent; and fabricated metals, 52.9 percent. In the past, they all thought they could supply consumer demands by mass-producing goods. Today, they find themselves changing.

*Production method #3* considers process management. Our survey shows that in companies overall, 16.6 percent adopt a single-unit production system, 51.7 percent adopt small-lot production, 9.5 percent adopt large-lot production, and 13.7 percent employ mass production. We find that single-unit and small-lot production together account for nearly 70 percent of the variety production industry. We also find the shift to multikind, low- or medium-volume production spreading to all industries. The industries intensifying the shift toward small-lot production are transportation equipment, 71.1 percent; precision instruments, 69.2 percent; textile related industries, 63.6 percent; nonferrous metals, 61.6 percent; fabric and apparel, 60 percent; fabricated metals, 58.8 percent; electrical appliances, 56.8 percent; and iron and steel, 53.9 percent. Most belong to assembly or consumer related industries, such as fashion.

To emphasize the shift to multikind production, we will add a scale analysis. Analyzing companies by scale, we find that 19.6 percent belong to scale I, 47.4 percent (or nearly half the companies) to scale II, 16.6 percent to scale III, and 16.4 percent to scale IV.

When analyzed by industry type, the ratio of companies in assembly production is 47.9 percent in scale I, 41.7 percent in scale II, 34.7 percent in scale III, and 36 percent in scale IV. This indicates that the percentage of assembly industry becomes comparatively larger in small-scale industries. The ratio of companies in chemical processing increases as the scale grows larger: 16.8 percent in scale I, 29.6 percent in scale II, 34.7 percent in scale III, and 38 percent in scale IV. Mechanical processing companies show no difference by scale. The larger the scale, the smaller the ratio of low-volume, variety production when classified by type and volume of products: 47.9 percent in scale I, 20 percent in scale IV.

Next, judging from our classification by scale, the shift to small-lot production becomes clear. Overall, the ratio of small-lot production is 51.7 percent. The ratio of small-lot production is 60.5 percent in scale I, 54.2 percent in scale II, 47.5 percent in scale III, and 38 percent in scale IV. This shows a decrease in small-lot production as the scale increases. The ratio of varied low-volume production varies from 47.9 percent in scale I to 20 percent in scale IV. This is the reverse of low-variety, large-volume production. In medium-volume variety production, however, the ratio is around 34 percent with little variance by scale.

Finally, the cross-section analysis among production methods shows the following. In assembly production, multikind, low-volume production is the main production system and multikind, medium-volume production follows. In chemical process production, the shift is opposite that of the assembly industry. In other words, low-variety, large-volume production is more common in chemical process production. Mechanical process production occupies a middle position. This reflects industry's technical nature and shows that the assembly industry (1) is the first to respond to changing market needs and (2) can easily adopt FMS for the multikind, small-lot production it requires. Next comes the mechanical process industry. The chemical process industry, which is thought to have little relation to multikind production, has limited influence, especially on a smaller scale. There are difficulties, however, in adopting multikind or small-lot production due to the nature of the industry.

*Survey Results.* Having reviewed the shift to FMS and low- or medium-volume variety production in Japanese manufacturing companies, especially in the assembly industries, we will now analyze its impact on cost management and the major problems. We will look at it from two angles: (1) the viewpoint of the cost elements regarded by each company as important to cost management, and (2) the kinds of problems regarded by each company as important to cost management. First let's look at the important cost elements for cost management in each company.

The most important elements are: (1) direct raw material cost, (2) direct labor cost, (3) expenses from outside suppliers, (4) indirect labor cost, (5) utility cost, (6) depreciation, (7) selling expenses, (8) indirect raw material cost, (9) other factory expenses, and (10) general administrative expenses. This order is closely connected to the manufacturing cost ratio. In other words, the greater the ratio, the more important the cost element becomes. When we compare these results with the 1960 survey, the first and second were the same.[6] The ratio of direct labor cost is nearly 60 percent, which is decidedly large. Many companies ranked it first. As to the second-ranked direct labor cost, it shares 12 percent of the manufacturing cost — so the results are understandable. Among the other elements, however, expenses from outside suppliers ranked third in our survey — larger companies, especially assembly oriented, often advise and help subcontractors form outside supplier groups to maintain a continuous and timely supply of parts or partially finished products in small lot sizes. They work together to meet the production needs of the parent or assembly company through just-in-time or zero-inventory systems.

Examination by industry indicates that direct raw material cost ranks first in importance in cost management except for publishing and printing, oil refinery, and coal products. Direct labor cost is the second most important element, except for pulp and paper.

Expenses from outside suppliers are considerable in publishing and printing; the ratio of expenses from outside suppliers to manufacturing cost is 42 percent, an extremely large figure. It should be the leading element. Assembly industries put great emphasis on expenses from outside suppliers, for example, 3.06 percent in machinery, 2.88 percent in precision instruments, 2.59 in fabricated metals, 2.5 percent in shipbuilding, 2.4 percent in fabric and apparel, 2.15 percent in electrical appliances, and 1.77 percent in textile related industries. In those industries, expenses from outside suppliers rank third and have a high percentage of assembly production. Other industries (1.62 percent in nonferrous metals, 1.49 percent in iron and steel) have a high ratio of mechanical process production. This is connected to the high percentage of expenses from outside suppliers to manufacturing cost in the assembly industry.

These results are also proved by noting that the importance of expenses from outside suppliers at 2.57 percent ranks third in assembly production, at 1.40 percent ranks fourth in mechanical process production, and ranks below fifth in chemical process production. Analyzed from another angle, it is clear that expenses from outside suppliers are important because they rank third in single-unit, in low- and medium-volume variety production, and in small-lot production.

As with the cost of outside suppliers, indirect labor cost is also valued, ranking fourth in industries having a high percentage of assembly production (such as fabricated metals, machinery, electrical appliances, transportation equipment, precision instruments, and shipbuilding).

Those industries that consume more utility power naturally have a high percentage of utilities cost in their manufacturing cost. For example, pulp and paper, oil refinery, and coal products rank it second; iron and steel, and nonferrous metals rank it third; and food and drink, and textile related industries rank it fourth. In those industries, the ratio of utilities cost to manufacturing cost is relatively high. Its management is important, especially following the two oil crises.

Depreciation cost management is important — it is ranked fourth by fabric and apparel, and publishing and printing, and fifth by pulp and paper, electrical appliances, transportation equipment, and precision instruments. This is especially true for those companies introducing a high percentage of new equipment, such as FMS and numerically controlled (NC) machine tools.

Let's add one more analysis using scales and production methods: scale IV weighs the management of utilities cost higher (it ranks third) than other scales.

As mentioned above, production method #1 is distinguished by the fact that managing expenses from outside suppliers ranks third in assembly production, utilities cost ranks third in chemical process production, and mechanical process production becomes a mixture of both production systems. In production method #2, low- and medium-volume variety production put the cost elements in the same order. The distinguishing characteristic in our survey is that the percentage of expenses from outside suppliers is high in low-volume variety production.

In production method #3, expenses from outside suppliers rank third in small-lot and single-unit production, and fourth in large-lot production.

***Major Problems in Cost Management.*** In overall manufacturing companies, the order of importance is: (1) purchase management of raw materials, (2) improving yield rate, (3) maintaining a high operating rate, (4) quality control, (5) shortage of labor time, (6) replacing equipment, (7) reducing factory expenses, (8) rationalizing design, (9) rationalizing combined production processes, and (10) inventory control. Comparing these results with the 1960 survey, we find that at that time the rankings were: (1) replacing equipment (50 percent), (2) maintaining a high operating rate (41.9 percent), (3) improving the yield rate (36.9 percent), (4) purchase management of raw materials (31.9 percent), and (5) reducing factory expenses (25.6 percent).[7]

The primary problem of cost management in overall manufacturing companies is, first, the importance of managing the purchase of raw materials: deciding the kind of raw materials to use for a product and how to supply them — whether to provide them internally or order them from outside suppliers. It also concerns the problems of product planning, significant now because the percentage of raw materials as well as rationalizing design are factors in product and cost planning. For these purposes, cost targets are planned to be controlled by each division through value analysis (VA), value engineering (VE), and industrial engineering (IE).

A second problem relates to improving the yield rate and maintaining a high operating rate. This result is the same obtained by the 1960 survey [high operating rate (41.9 percent), and improving yield rate (36.9 percent)]. Improving the yield rate involves the cost of raw materials. A high operating rate involves decreasing the fixed cost per product unit. Once an investment is made in equipment, its cost becomes fixed and requires retrieval as quickly as possible to avoid the risk of technological innovation. Both items are regarded as important in both surveys.

Third, quality control ranked fourth, and is therefore considered significant. Here, quality control is understood to mean total quality control (TQC). It is regarded as important in improving not only the quality of products, but also the morale of workers in the overall production process through small-group activities called QC circles. This plays an important role in Japanese production management.

The next problem is the shortage of labor time and rationalizing the combined production processes. These are related to control of the production process and emphasis on cost management through production management control.

A fifth problem is inventory control. Japanese manufacturing companies are keen to reduce not only the inventory of finished products, but also those of raw materials and work in process. Their aim is stockless production through the JIT's kanban method. This is how the Japanese control inventory.

Finally, the investment problem of replacing or adding to machines or equipment ranked first in the 1960 survey, but only sixth in ours. This means that cost reduction through capital budgeting was the main problem in the 1960s. Capital investment in machines and equipment had been a key factor for cost reduction, but after 1975 most companies that could adopt multikind, low- or medium-volume production had already introduced FMS or other machine tools. For those companies, especially assembly oriented, other factors in production management have become more important.[8]

At this stage of the discussion, we will talk about the main shift to cost management by industry and production methods in multikind, low- or medium-volume production to clarify the shift in all companies. Purchase management of raw materials is a serious factor in the following industries: textile related industries and precision instruments rank it first; and electrical appliances, transportation equipment, and shipbuilding rank it second. This shift coincides with the ranking (first) in assembly production. This is also supported by the fact that expenses from outside suppliers vary from 9 to 18 percent of manufacturing cost in fabricated metals, machinery, electrical appliances, transportation equipment, precision instruments, and shipbuilding.

Second, rationalizing design ranks first in cost planning. It ranks eighth in overall manufacturing companies. In assembly production, it ranks second next to managing the purchase of raw materials. Electrical appliances rank it first, machinery and precision instruments rank it second, and transportation equipment and shipbuilding rank it third. This fact supports the explanation of the manager of a certain major electrical company who said that product cost is largely decided in the early stages of product planning and design. From this angle, life-cycle costing now becomes important.

Third, improving the yield rate ranks first in importance in chemical process and mechanical process production.

Fourth, a high operating rate is important in chemical process production (84.6 percent) and mechanical process production (87.4 percent), because the percentage of those productions is much lower than in assembly production (96.3 percent).[9]

Fifth, cost control is the most important because it encompasses production process management, the shortage of labor time, and quality control. The shortage of labor time ranks second in low-volume variety production; it ranks third in assembly, single-unit, and small-lot production.

*Conclusion.* In the previous sections of this chapter, we surveyed the shift toward FMS, multikind and low- or medium-volume production systems, and their impact on cost management in Japanese manufacturing companies. Only through this analysis can we understand that this shift has occurred primarily in the assembly industries, and that major problems in cost management in those industries relate to product and cost planning. Their aim is complete, companywide cost reduction not only through management accounting, but also through production management.

We have reviewed only a few aspects of the major problems of cost management. We need to continue studying multikind, low- or medium-volume production and its impact on cost management in countries such as the United States and Great Britain. We can then understand cost management problems in Japan's manufacturing companies in an international context. For that purpose, we need the cooperation of managers and scholars in those countries.

### Notes

1. Multikind and low- or medium-volume production are production systems that produce various kinds of products in small or medium production quantities (lot or batch sizes). In this chapter, we sometimes use *variety production* in the context of multikind production.
2. A scale using Roman numerals to classify companies is as follows:

   Scale (capital stocks) ($1 = ¥ 240)
   I from $2,083 to $4,166
   II from $4,167 to $20,832
   III from $20,833 to $41,666
   IV more than $41,667

3. FMS is a production system that combines NC machine tools, machining centers (MC), automatic conveyors (conveyor belts, robots, etc.), and computers. Its goal is the flexible use of machines, and a variety of products or parts are produced on a single production line.
4. See note #2 about scales.
5. Based on our 1982 survey.
6. See Kigyo Keiei Kyoukai (1960).

7. See Kigyo Keiei Kyoukai (1960). The percentages in parentheses equal the number of companies that regard the item important divided by the number of responding companies × 100.
8. See H.Seto (1981).
9. These percentages are the simple mean of the operations ratio in each production.

### References

1. Kigyo Keiei Kyoukai (The Business Administration Society), *Jittai bunseki genka kanri* (Survey on Cost Management), (Tokyo: Chuuou Keizai Sha, 1960).
2. Seto, H., "Seisan Kikan to Seisan Kanri (Production Period and Production Management)," in *Kigyou kanri no kihon mondai* (Basic Problems in Enterprise Administration), (Tokyo: Chikura Syobou, 1980).

# 22

## Problems with Japanese Cost Accounting Standards

*Yoshihiro Hirabayashi, School of Commerce,*
*Osaka City University*

Business cost accounting is done today not only for inventory evaluation and income determination, but also for furnishing data that is necessary for business planning as well as for product pricing and cost control. Japanese cost accounting standards have been established as working rules to consolidate these diverse purposes and to institute cost accounting. Generally accepted conventions of cost accounting have been summarized and codified into standards of procedure (the Cost Accounting Standards, published by the Enterprise Accounting Council of the Ministry of Finance in 1962) that enterprises must follow as their practices for cost accounting, regardless of their varied standpoints. Whereas business accounting principles are the general and basic accounting standards concerned with business accounting, Cost Accounting Standards are more concrete standards specifically concerned with cost. These two standards are therefore fundamentally related, the latter being a part of the former, or the latter being a supplement to the former.In other words, the Cost Accounting Standards form a part of the business accounting principles. Therefore each enterprise should follow the Cost Accounting Standards, as well as the business accounting principles in Japan.

At least the Ministry of Finance wishes that all enterprises take the Cost Accounting Standards into consideration. There are no penal regulations, however, for a violation of the Standards.

Enactment of the cost accounting standards in Japan goes back to the Manufacturing Cost Accounting Semi-Principles in 1937, and are similar to the *Grundplan des Selbstkostenrechnung* published by the Department of Economic Rationality in Germany. They were mostly for the purpose of information and were devoid of any legal obligations. With the rapid change in the wartime situation and for the purpose of delivery pricing military supplies, the "Outlines of Cost Accounting in the Army" were enacted by the army in 1939, and the "Semi-Principles of Cost Accounting in the Navy" was enacted by the navy in 1940. These were subsequently enforced in munitions factories. Since different standards of cost accounting had been enacted separately, the Cost Accounting Regulations were later enacted with the provision that every practice of cost accounting be in accordance with the cost accounting prescribed in it. The Outline of Industrial Cost Accounting was published by the Planning Board in 1942 as a concrete explanation of cost accounting for the Cost Accounting Regulations.

The new Cost Accounting Standards are not mere modifications of the two semi-principles and outlines. With economic stabilization after the war, the purpose of business cost accounting became diversified, and there arose a demand for certain accounting standards that could adapt to constant and continuous use and that would be applicable to any purpose of accounting. Thus, after ten or more years of discussion starting in 1950, the new Cost Accounting Standards were published to meet these demands.

The Cost Accounting Standards consist of five chapters. Chapter 1 states the purpose of cost accounting and its general standards. Chapter 2 specifically deals with elementary costs accounting, departmental cost accounting, and product cost accounting. Chapter 3 deals with accounting of standard cost, and Chapter 4 describes the calculation and analysis of variance from actual cost when cost is calculated with planned cost or standard cost. Chapter 5 concludes with account processing of cost variance, as described in the previous chapter. These are the main characteristics of the Cost Accounting Standards (hereinafter referred to as the Standards).

Although conventional cost accounting has been highly regarded for so-called financial accounting purposes, the Standards also make much of managerial accounting purposes, adjusted to accomplish the varied purposes of cost accounting at the same time. Second, the Standards prescribe cost accounting as a system where varied cost accounting purposes are fundamentally connected to the accounting system as a simultaneous achievement of different cost accounting goals. In other words, temporary and occasional cost accounting, which is irrelevant to the accounting system, is excluded from the scope of the Standards because it is an exception to the system itself. Third, the Standards describe standard cost accounting that is useful for cost and budgetary control purposes, as well as actual cost accounting, which is new to Japanese cost accounting standards. Fourth, the Standards describe the essential qualities of cost, emphasizing relevance to managerial purposes and normalcy. Fifth, the Standards consider direct costing thought; that is, the Standards approve direct cost accounting only in cases of a process cost system, provided the adjustment is made at the end of the settlement term. As a system, however, direct cost accounting is not approved because adjustment is always made at the end of the settlement term.

There is an increasing tendency toward revision of the Standards.[1] The issue of revising the Standards is one of the more urgent problems of accounting in Japan, especially with regard to cost accounting theory. A request for reconsideration of the Standards was submitted to the Ministry of Finance by the Japan Association of Cost Accounting in December 1976. As Okamoto summarizes, revision of the Standards has become an urgent issue because:

1. Revisions in the Commercial Law, the Tax Law and Business Accounting Principles.
2. Defects existing in the current Standards.
3. The development of cost accounting theory and its practice.[2]

Therefore, the revision of the Standards has become a major assignment following the revision in 1974 of the Business Accounting Principles. Various problems already existed when the Standards were enacted in November 1962, and have worsened in connection with number 3. The various aspects of revising the Standards will be discussed, and a variety of notable views and opinions will be given. The trend toward revision of the Standards is inevitable.

We think it is essential to review the problems of the Standards to fully understand these trends before revision starts.

It is difficult, however, to present and discuss here all the problems of the Standards that improvement. For this reason, only a few problems are treated here. These are the relationship between the Standards and the Business Accounting Principles, which was, so to speak, a direct result of the revision of the Principles; characteristic qualities of the Standards that are critical in reviewing the problems of the Standards since enactment; and, finally, the relationship between problems in the Standards and future trends in cost accounting.

### Relation Between the Standards and the Business Accounting Principles.

As is well known, an inseparable relation between the Standards and Business Accounting Principles (hereinafter the Principles) remained until revision of the Principles in 1974. But there arose some inconsistency or discrepancy between the Principles and the Standards when the revision of the Principles, aiming at consolidation with the accounting regulations of commercial law, were published in August that year. The Standards were neither reviewed nor revised when the new principles were published. Some temporal remedy was taken by deleting the words *Cost Accounting Standards*, which were shown in the notes on the Principles before revision, and inserting the words *appropriate cost accounting standards*.

Though some temporal remedies have been taken, it is apparent that the "Cost Accounting Standards" of the former principles are not identical to "appropriate cost accounting standards" because the word *appropriate* is added and the words *cost accounting standards* are not capitalized. Thus it is possible to interpret this to mean that there is no need to conform to the Standards in the case of a discrepancy between the two for cost accounting. The former consistency between the Principles and the Standards has been lost and, what is worse, the Standards will be ignored because of this. It is natural that there is such insistence about immediate review of the Standards and that necessary revisions be made. It is also natural to discuss why the capitalized expression *Cost Accounting Standards* is no longer used in the notes of the current Principles. Moroi says, "The notes after revision assume appropriate cost accounting standards as they ought to be, on the premise that it is dubious that the current Standards are no longer appropriate as they are now."[3] If there are questions about the appropriateness of the current Standards, they should be reviewed promptly before revision, or the inconsistency or discrepancy between the Principles and the Standards will remain. It is inevitable that this will increase the general feeling of unreliability about the Standards and, in this context, it is clear that revision is an urgent issue. In spite of the urgency, it is difficult to say that consistency will be easily achieved, although small modifications remain an urgent matter.

*The Basic Nature of the Standards.* The natural starting point for review of the Standards is how to view or define their nature. Many economists have expressed their opinions on the nature of the Standards. We present first the suggestions and views of Adachi, followed by a summary and analysis of the opinions on the nature of the Standards by Mizoguchi and Sakurai and, finally, an analysis by Ito.

It is impossible, according to Adachi, to discuss new standards and ignore the present Standards, but there are six possibilities for any new Standards to exist, and these are described as:

1. Establish cost accounting standards in the narrowest sense for the purpose of assisting the preparation of financial statements for external reporting.
2. Preserve practically all the current Standards.
3. Cover cost accounting in a broad sense, or the whole of ordinary cost accounting that is directly or indirectly connected to financial accounting institutes.
4. Set up managerial cost accounting standards, inclusive of extraordinary and/or ordinary cost accounting and cost analysis, besides a system of cost accounting in a broad sense.
5. Establish managerial cost accounting standards that will adjust and supplement the current Standards from the comprehensive viewpoint of managerial cost accounting or of cost accounting.
6. Establish managerial cost accounting standards from an original viewpoint, independent of the current Standards.[4]

To be precise, if the current Standards are to be revised, they should be revised in the area of managerial cost accounting standards as much as possible. If this is not possible, the establishment of cost accounting standards in the narrowest sense for external reporting should meet at least appropriate cost accounting standards that the Business Accounting Principles require.[5]

Mizoguchi groups the many analyses on the nature of the Standards roughly into two.[6] One group thinks that the current Standards have a more financial accounting standards nature, or the Standards are characterized as part of the Principles. This is close to what Adachi calls "cost accounting standards in the narrowest sense." The other group does not regard the Standards as only financial standards, but thinks that they have a management purpose. They include managerial accounting standards and are not limited to rules of actual cost accounting, but are related to financial statements for external report.

Sakurai groups the analyses on the basic nature of the Standards into the following three areas:

1. The Standards should be cost accounting standards that are useful mostly for financial accounting purposes to supplement the Principles.
2. The Standards should be cost accounting standards oriented mostly toward managerial purposes, and not confined by the Principles.
3. The Standards should be cost accounting standards that meet both the purposes of financial accounting and managerial accounting.[7]

Sakurai says, "As we can see, there seems to be a slowly growing trend toward providing the basic nature of the Standards from the standpoint of [number 3] in Japan. So far as this trend goes, it seems that the prospective revised Standards will not be much different from the current Standards in their basic form. However, what is important in this case, is that the former should not merely follow the latter but that the revised Standards should cover all ordinary cost accounting connected directly or indirectly with financial accounting systems so as to exercise managerial functions more effectively, this is where differences in the revision of the Standards will be found. The most significant points for the revision of the Standards."[8]

Ito says that one problem when reconsidering the Standards is that they have not become working rules. He wonders why, as long as consideration is limited to cost accounting for business administration and business decision making.[9] Two reasons are given. One is that the Standards are strongly characterized as part of the Principles. "To be more precise, the Standards have been strongly required, from the beginning, to function as cost accounting standards which could meet financial accounting needs."[10]

The other reason is that cost accounting for financial accounting, and cost accounting for business administration and/or business decision making, have aspects that are sometimes in conflict. They are, therefore, "... secondary because these cost accountings, which may be in a sense, heterogeneous, have been forced to be covered by the same standards. Their imperfection as Working Rules for other work became apparent due to their basic nature. To cover cost accounting for financial accounting and cost accounting for managerial accounting using the same standards may be possible on a more abstract level, but it is not easy at the level of Working Rules".

Ito's analysis is noteworthy, and it is natural that the two reasons he gives highlights the cost accounting standards as financial accounting standards. However, we are not trying to establish new cost accounting standards. We should not overlook the fact that the current Standards exist, whatever their appropriateness. Therefore, reconsideration of the Standards should be confined to the current Standards, whether we like it or not. What is needed, rather, is more effort to eliminate the various contradictions and defects that exist, and this conflict concerning revision of the Standards can be explained as a result of such an effort. Therefore, we must be ready for a long process of revision. We may disregard the length of time, though, when we remember how long it took to establish the current Standards themselves.

Frankly speaking, this author wishes to consider highly the current Standards because they treat the issue of cost accounting as a system, and they summarize generally accepted conventions of business cost accounting in Japan as working rules. In this context, it would be appropriate to reconsider the Standards. Of course, as mentioned, it is difficult to believe that a perfect revision of the Standards will be completed in a short time; a phased revision seems more realistic. The Draft of Cost Accounting Standards, which had been presented unofficially as material for discussion before the enactment of the current Standards, could be reexamined now to retain the keynotes of the Draft. After all, this draft, "Needless to say, efforts were made to connect and adjust them to financial accounting, was characterized as pointed out before, by also aiming at and trying for as far as possible the accomplishment of a synthetic adjustment under predominance of managerial accounting thought in contrast to financial accounting."[11]

In addition, research into the actual conditions previously quoted gives results concerning the directions for the revision as shown in Table 22.1. Revision by preserving the nature of the current standards in its scope is supported by the majority.[12]

Unnecessary to revise  . . . . . . 108 (34.6%)
Necessary to revise . . . . . . . . 204 (65.4%)

| | | |
|---|---|---|
| **a.** | To clarify their position as a part of Business Accounting Principles and establish cost accounting standards useful only for the purpose of financial accounting (financial accounting standards) | 25 (12.3%) |
| **b.** | To be free from Business Accounting Principles and establish cost accounting standards useful only for the purpose of business administration (managerial accounting standards) | 7 (3.4%) |

**Table 22.1  Directions for the Revision of the Cost Accounting Standards**

*Revision of the Standard.* As pointed out by many analysts, the current Standards have many content problems. Therefore, it will be necessary to consider each of these problems when the Standards are revised. Consideration is limited here to only a few: "Purposes of Cost Accounting" (Standard 1), "Essential Qualities of Cost" (Standard 3), "Direct Costing" (Standard 30), and "Costs Reports." The last two are not clearly provided for in the current Standards, but must be included in the Standards to keep pace with development in cost accounting theories and practices.

There are objections about the five purposes in Standard 1 the current Standards. There are criticisms about the interrelationship of the five purposes, especially between 4) Budgeting and budgetary control purposes and 5) Basic planning purposes. For example, Mizoguchi criticizes that project planning and period planning are mixed in with the purposes of 4) because the Standards divide business planning into administrative business planning and basic planning. To resolve this mixture, Mizoguchi proposes to divide business planning into period planning and project planning, with period planning and budgetary control included in the purposes of 4) and project planning included in the purposes of 5).[13] He thinks it would be desirable to have only three purposes for cost accounting: (1) financial statement preparation, (2) cost control, and (3) business planning. Four areas could be created by dividing number 3 into period and project planning.[14] Mizoguchi's criticism and proposals about the Standards seem to be supported by people in general. This author does not have any objection concerning these points.

It is widely known, however, that critical opinions have been expressed one after another on this issue of purpose since the enactment of the Standards. For example, Kubota says, "Though it is true that areas in current cost accounting functions for the purpose of pricing are limited and the amount is small, it is just as important for the General Standards for Preparation of Financial Statements as regards quality. Nevertheless, any general standards useful to pricing are not found in these Cost Accounting Standards. So long as we stand in the position that cost accounting standards are specifically characterized by what function they have in adjusting the accounting profit of external parties concerned, we regret that there is nothing to cover this."[15] He further criticizes the fact that the problem of purpose 2) has remained unsettled.

This is surely a proper criticism, and the pricing purpose, which had not been included originally in the Draft, is said to have been entered at the final stage of compilation. Kurosawa explains the reason once more by saying, "It seems to have been included because there was a very strong need for it, especially for the Defense Agency and other procurement agencies who wished to establish working rules for cost accounting as specific semistandards based on it. This is not the only reason why it was included but it was done because the need was highly valued.[16]

There is much argument on the "Essential Qualities of Cost." Many opinions are given on the provision in 3), "Cost is related to business purposes...." Analyses by two critics are given here. Amano, evaluating 3) as an excellent provision and one step forward, says, "Though it is not clear why 'in principle' has been added at the end of that section..., now that the quality of cost in financial expenses is denied, it lacks consistency to allow any exceptions."[17]

Opposing this, Kobayashi says, "The description is very strange. Why is the business purpose limited to the production and sale of goods? Why isn't it deemed as acquisition of profit? In the scope of the business purpose as profit acquisition, both production and sales are in the intermediate process as means, and in this sense, both purchasing and financial affairs are in the same dimension. Then, why is it that only production and sales are the processes related to the business purpose?"[18] He also says, "Some of the expenses for financial activities are surely included in general administration expenses. Only interest expenses, discounts, amortization of bond premiums and other special financial expenses are included in the non-cost items. It is very strange that financial activities are explained as a non-business process or irrelevant to business purposes. It seems sufficient only to include these special expenses related to financial affairs under non-cost items."

Thus, differences in understanding whether the business process should be explained as a process of production and sales activities, or a process of financial activities that should be included, derives from the different answers to the question of whether financial expenses are included in cost. This is the very issue under discussion.

Regarding the provisions of "Essential qualities of cost" in the current Standards, however, it must be noted that the confining phrase of "In the cost accounting system" is added at the top. The noncost quality of financial expense is possible only "in the cost accounting system." Without this confining phrase, it is possible for financial expenses to be included in the cost. At the time of decision about a substitute draft, it will be possible to include interest payable in the imputed cost to compare costs in the substitute.

When we consider, purely theoretically, what the cost is, what interest is payable but, needless to say, not just cost, cost is a process of creating new values through the intermediation of productive labor in the production process. Led by labor, the machinery and materials as the means and object of labor are consumed productively. Therefore, expenses generated in the sales and general administration departments cannot be included in the cost, except for certain special areas such as transportation and storage. From a purely theoretical point of view, this author is doubtful of the explanation in the Standards that "cost is the economic value consumed in connection with sales."

There is the question now whether or not social costs can be included in the cost for an enterprise. Surely it is possible in the scope of the provisions in "Essential Qualities of Cost" because part of social cost is recognized as cost. In the case of a revision in the Standards, however, much more discussion concerning social cost will be necessary, and it will be necessary to clarify the cost quality in social cost by narrowing the discussion on its possibility of internalization as cost or expense. Yamagata says, "As regards the Standards, it is necessary to specify them as a concept of cost in that only cost generated for supplying production 'without a negative influence on society' defines cost. That is, if the confining condition is phrased as 'without negative influence on society' is not newly included in the concept of cost, it will be impossible to recognize social cost."[19]

There is the argument on the inclusion of "Direct Costing" in the Standards. Most opinion, however, supports the systematization of direct costing. This seems to be largely influenced by the fact that direct costing has been discussed almost at length now. It is widely used by many enterprises and fast becoming an accepted accounting practice.

In a recent survey on conditions, the cost accounting method used for the preparation of financial statements was selected from these four: actual absorption costing, standard absorption costing, actual direct costing, and standard direct costing. The total results of all industries polled are:[20]

| | |
|---|---|
| Actual absorption costing | 163 (47.1%) |
| Standard absorption costing | 85 (24.9%) |
| Actual direct costing | 48 (13.9%) |
| Standard direct costing | 44 (12.7%) |

Even though there is a difference between actual costing and standard costing, a total of 92 enterprises have adopted direct costing for preparation of financial statements. This exceeds the total of 85 enterprises adopting standard absorption costing. It is important, therefore, how direct costing is positioned in a revision of the Standards.

Of course, some analysts say that it will be difficult to approve direct costing as a system. Moroi says, "As a noteworthy request from a business administration viewpoint, there is the opinion that direct costing should be accepted as a system. Although the provisions of the current Standards concerning direct costing are not always appropriate as they now stand, it is difficult to promote direct costing as a system. If ever direct costing is approved as a cost accounting system, the Standards may provide, in accordance with the provisions of the actual costing system and standard costing system, that the direct costing system is cost accounting where variable costs of a product are calculated and the result is included in the major book of financial accounting, and calculations of product cost and financial accounting are fundamentally connected by means of variable cost but, is such a provision acceptable from the viewpoint of financial accounting? Will such a provision be acceptable from the beginning as regards business accounting, commercial law and the tax law? We cannot but say that there is almost no hope of favorable answers to these questions. If these provisions were accepted, fixed costs would be excluded from the elements of cost of inventory assets but such accounting does not seem to have reached the stage of social and international approval."[21]

Following are some interpretations of the term *seidoka* (systematization) that widen its meaning and content. For instance, Cost Accounting Standards Special Committee interprets this *seido* as "system" in its "Studies of Cost Accounting Standards": Cost accounting system means cost accounting which is made ordinarily and repeatedly, following certain procedures of calculation...and in this line of meaning, the possibilities are forms in which:

1. Direct costing is ordinarily adopted and the results of costing are adjusted by absorption costing at the end of the fiscal year.
2. Direct costing is ordinarily adopted and at the end of the fiscal year, absorption costing is made for external reporting based on annual data, separately from direct costing.
3. Direct costing and absorption costing are made dually every month.[22]

It is doubtful, however, if such a wide interpretation of "system" can be accepted.

As we have seen, to include direct costing as a system in the Standards, there are diverse problems to be solved. We may say, however, that we have reached a basic agreement that "It is necessary to move the explanation on direct costing from Standard 30 to somewhere else and to make it clear that the introduction of direct costing is possible, regardless of the type of costing"[23] because, after all, systematization is inevitable for direct costing which is the embodiment of variable cost, so long as cost is variable by the nature.

Last, we consider the issue of "Cost Reports." Although this was specified to some extent in the Draft, the specification has been deleted except for some points in the current Standards. In connection with disclosures and the issue of enactment of the Freedom of Information Act, disclosure of costs will profit but never harm enterprises as long as they fulfill their social responsibilities. Of course, it is undeniable that there are a variety of restrictions, and it is obvious that disclosing overall costs without any reservation is an illusion in the present economic system. On the other hand, absolute refusal concerning cost disclosure would be contrary to present trends. Cost should be disclosed as much as possible — after full discussion. Including cost disclosures in the Standards would provide a process for this. For reference, the chapter consists of 50 (the significance of cost reporting), 51 (a statement of manufacturing costs), 52 (a description of cost variance in income statement) and, 53 (the cost report as an internal report). There is no problem with 53. As for the so-called external report in 50 to 52, there are no problems because cost disclosures with that amount of detail are required by other accounting laws. Therefore, no objections will be raised against the renewal and enactment of the chapter on Cost Reporting. Progress will be made if the renewal becomes a positive declaration. An appropriate form of cost disclosure will be considered on the basis of this.

**Conclusion.** Some issues related to the Standards have been mentioned and commented upon, but the author has not presented any of his own proposals. The intention here is to classify the contents of argument, present the materials for discussion in the future, and to assist international understanding of the Standards in Japan.

### Notes

1. From recent research, opinions on revision of the Standards are: unnecessary to revise — 34.6 percent, necessary to revise — 65.4 percent. Fumiyasu Takahashi, "Reconsideration of the Cost Accounting Standards," *Cost Accounting* (1986), No. 281 p. 114.
2. Kiyoshi Okamoto, ed., *Study of the Cost Accounting Standards* (Kunimoto Shobo, 1981), p. 20.
3. Katsunasuke Moroi, "Review of the Cost Accounting Standards," *Business Accounting*, (1977), Vol. 29, No. 2, p. 22.
4. Kazuo Adachi, "Directors for Revision of the Cost Accounting Standards," *Business Accounting*, (1977), Vol. 29, No.2, pp. 33-34.
5. *Ibid.*, p. 38.
6. Kazuo Mizoguchi, "On the Argument Concerning the Cost Accounting Standards (1)," *Accounting*, (1978), Vol. 114, No. 4, pp. 1-8.
7. Michiharu Sakurai, "Trends in the Academy for the Revision of the Cost Accounting Standards," *Senshu Collected Treatises of Business Administration*, (1979), No. 28, p. 60.
8. *Ibid.*, p. 61.

9. Hiroshi Ito, "Reconsideration of the Costs Accounting Standards, (1)," *Cost Accounting* (1978), No. 220, p. 32.

10. *Ibid.*, p. 33.

11. Atsuo Tsuji, *Study of Managerial Accounting* (Dobunkan, 1977), p. 44.

12. Takashashi, *op. cit.*, p. 114.

13. Kazuo Mizoguchi, *Modern Cost Accounting* (Kunimoto Shobo, 1978), p. 46.

14. Kazuo Mizoguchi, *The Latest Lectures on Cost Accounting* (Chuo keizai sha, 1979), pp. 20-22.

15. Otojiro Kubota, "The Nature of Cost Accounting," (1963), Vol. 83, No. 1, p. 45.

16. Discussion, "A Study of the Cost Accounting Standards," *Industrial Accounting* (1962), Vol. 2, No. 12, p. 173.

17. Yoshinori Amano, "Concept of Costs in a Cost Accounting System," *Business Accounting* (1963), Vol. 15, No. 1, p. 69.

18. Yasuo Kobayashi, "Questions on the Cost Accounting Standard," *Industrial Accounting* (1963), Vol. 23, No. 1, p. 77.

19. Okamoto, *op. cit.*, p. 70.

20. Takahashi, *op. cit.*, p. 96.

21. Moroi, *op. cit.*, p. 26.

22. Okamoto, *op. cit.*, p. 127.

23. Kaichiro Banba, "Issues To Be Considered in the Cost Accounting Standards," *Business Accounting* (1977), Vol. 29, No. 2, p. 9.

# 23

## Physical Distribution Cost Accounting Standards Set by Japan's Ministry of Transport

*Osamu Nishizawa, School of Commerce, Waseda University*

Japan's Ministry of Transport established "The Uniform Standard of Physical Distribution Cost Accounting" in March 1977. Having participated on the committee preparing the Standard, the author will discuss physical distribution cost accounting, centering around the Standard.

Physical distribution (PD) cost for manufacturers refers to the economic value consumed in PD related to manufacturing and marketing activities of a certain manufacturer. From this definition, PD cost prescribed in the Standard is known to have the following characteristics.

*It is a business PD cost for a private shipper.* The Standard deals with PD cost for individual businesses, namely, business PD cost. Business PD cost breaks down to PD cost for private shippers and that for public PD operators. The PD cost that the Standard stipulates is that for manufacturers.

*It is a PD cost on a business activity basis.* Some manufacturing companies are undertaking functions of wholesalers or retailers, and vice versa. The use of the PD cost concept on a business entity basis, therefore, may lead to a considerable difference in the amount of PD cost for businesses belonging to the same industrial sector, depending on the extent of sharing and plurality of their business activities. For this reason, the Standard has adopted a concept on an activity basis instead of a business entity basis.

*PD cost paid by other companies is included.* PD cost is not always consumed directly by a company. In some cases, the company bears the PD cost paid by its suppliers or customers. PD cost consumed directly is "PD cost paid by own company" and PD cost borne indirectly is "PD cost paid by other companies." It is necessary to recognize and compute both of them as business PD cost. Otherwise, an identical PD activity may bring about differences in the amount of business PD cost, depending on who primarily bears the cost.

*It is an economic value to be consumed.* PD cost is essentially consumption of an economic value. An economic value is a representation in terms of monetary value of goods and services consumed. The amount of money consumed to carry out PD activities is PD cost, which may also be called PD expenses, but it is essentially different from PD expenditures or PD assets.

**Classifying and computing PD cost.** The Standard prescribes that the processes of PD cost accounting are purchase, intracompany, marketing, goods-returning, and disposal process (excluding production process). Interpreted as a flow, PD is classified into the following seven processes:

1. Purchasing
2. Production
3. Intracompany
4. Marketing
5. Recovery
6. Goods-returning
7. Disposal

**Basic patterns of PD cost accounting.** The Standard prescribes that PD cost accounting shall be conducted by PD processes, cost elements, and PD functions. When necessary, classification and totaling by business segments is also carried out to prepare managerial data.

*PD cost accounting by PD processes.* PD cost is classified as PD cost in purchase, intracompany, marketing, recovery, goods-returning, and disposal process. The required amount of money for each of them is totaled.

*PD cost accounting by cost elements.* PD cost is classified into material, personnel, utility, and maintenance costs, and general and special burdens. The required amount is totaled.

*PD cost accounting by PD functions.* Classification of PD cost on a function basis is packaging, transportation, warehousing, and handling cost. The required amount of money is totaled.

*PD cost accounting by business segments.* PD cost is classified by organizations, productions, territories, customers, etc. The required amount is totaled.

*PD cost accounting by operation level.* PD cost is divided into fixed and variable cost. The required amount is computed.

*PD cost accounting by controllability.* PD cost is divided into controllable and uncontrollable cost, and the required amount is computed.

**Classifications of PD Cost.** As already stated, PD cost in a broad sense may be classified on a PD process basis into categories — that is, PD cost in purchase, production, intracompany, marketing, recovery, goods-returning, and disposal processes. Here is a supplementary explanation of the definitions given in the Standard.

**Classification by PD processes.** *PD cost in the purchasing process* is, for manufacturers, the cost involved in the completion of delivery of raw materials or packaging materials purchased from suppliers. Such PD cost includes transportation, warehousing, and handling costs for receipts, which are, in financial accounting, added to raw material costs, packaging material costs, and prices of purchased goods as external subcosts, and presented as a lump sum in financial statements. It is impossible, therefore, to infer from financial accounting where these PD costs in purchase process come from.

*PD cost in the production process* is the cost of processing and finishing of raw materials into final products. As PD cost in production process constitutes a part of production cost, it is not included in the PD cost discussed in the Standard.

*PD cost in the company process* is, for manufacturers, the cost of packing finished products for transport and confirming sales to customers. Confirmation of sales here means conclusion of a regular sales contract. PD cost in intracompany processes for manufacturers includes packaging cost at factories (i.e., transport packaging cost), transportation cost from factories to branch offices (including sales offices and distribution centers), and handling and warehousing cost at branch offices.

*PD cost in the marketing process* is the cost of complete shipment and delivery of products or goods. For manufacturers, the PD cost includes costs for packaging, shipping, and delivery at their branch offices.

*PD cost in the recovery process* is the one incurred by manufacturers for recovery of used containers from customers for reuse. The cost includes repurchase or transportation cost, but not washing or reproduction cost. The Standard, therefore, treats PD cost in recovery process as a PD cost in purchase process.

*PD cost in returned goods process*, for manufacturers, is the cost involved in PD incidental to returns of unsold products or goods, including costs for inspection, assortment, transportation, warehousing, and handling.

*PD cost in disposal process* is the cost of recovering and disposing of products, goods, containers, and materials for packaging or transportation. It includes costs for transport, storage, and handling, but not disposal itself or antipollution measures.

Each PD cost in marketing, recovery, goods-returning, and disposal process is added to sales and general administrative cost in financial accounting. Only a small amount of such PD cost is stated in independent items, such as freight paid.

**Classification by Cost Elements.** Classification of PD cost by cost elements is one based on accrual of costs in financial accounting. As stated earlier, PD cost paid by the company itself is the cost that company consumed directly, while PD cost paid by other companies is consumed indirectly.

The Standard gives no particular definition of PD cost paid by a company itself, but merely classifies it into private versus public PD cost. In the case when PD operation is entrusted to an outside PD undertaker or a subsidiary engaged in PD, the charge is public PD cost. The cost required for operating PD for itself is private PD cost, which breaks down to the following five costs:

1. *Material costs:* The costs involved in the consumption of materials.
2. *Personnel costs:* The costs involved in hiring a labor force.
3. *Utility costs:* The rates for services provided by public utilities.
4. *Maintenance costs:* The costs involved in utilization, operation, and maintenance of PD facilities.
5. *Burdens:* Private PD cost other than those listed.

What is noteworthy here is *burdens*. The classification of "special burdens" is one of the features of the Standard. Special burdens refer to PD cost that is computed on a different basis than financial accounting. More specifically, they refer to depreciation expenses and internal interest. From the standpoint of PD management, it is necessary to adopt a management accounting method that is different from the financial accounting method for both these expenses. To show this fact clearly, the Standard separates these expenses from general burdens and calls them "special burdens."

**PD Cost Classification by Functions.** Classification by PD functions breaks down PD cost on the basis of function for which PD cost is incurred. It aims at managing PD cost by functions and by divisions of responsibility, and also aims at making accounting by business segments, such as by-products, more accurate.

As mentioned before, PD cost refers to the economic value consumed to physically distribute objects that consist of tangible materials and information. The economic value required for distributing tangible materials is material distribution cost, while the economic value required for distributing intangible information is information distribution cost. PD cost has been conventionally taken as material distribution cost, but more comprehensive understanding of PD cost, including information distribution cost, is necessary. Material distribution cost includes the following five items.

1. *Packaging cost* refers to transport packaging cost. Commercial packaging cost is excluded from it. There has been widespread misunderstanding so far that all packaging cost is PD cost. In fact, commercial-packaging cost is part of production cost, and is not included in PD cost. It should be noted that transport packaging costs only are included in PD cost.
2. *Transportation cost* is the cost required for transferring products from one place to another, with the goal of creating utility of places. The cost is divided into (1) public transportation costs and (2) private transportation costs. While conditions of public transportation costs are readily known — the costs are stated independently in financial statements — private transportation costs are dispersed in several statement items, making their conditions difficult to indicate unless cost accounting for private transportation is conducted.
3. *Warehousing cost* is the cost of storing, or warehousing, products for a certain period of time, with the aim of creating utility of time. Warehousing cost is classified into (1) public warehousing costs and (2) private warehousing costs. Public warehousing costs are

stated independently in financial statements, in items like storage charges paid, warehousing fees, or custody fees, which makes conditions of the costs readily comprehensible. On the contrary, private warehousing costs are dispersed to several items of financial statements. This makes it impossible to grasp the conditions of the costs unless a cost accounting for a private warehouse is conducted, as is the case with transportation cost.

4. *Handling cost* is the cost of transferring products in the course of packaging, transportation, warehousing, and production in the distribution process. The two methods used to treat this cost are (1) lump-sum statements and (2) dispersed statements. Although opinion is divided on which method should be used, the Standard chooses the lump-sum statement.

5. *Production cost* in the distribution process is the cost of increasing PD efficiency in a material distribution process. In a broad sense, there are three categories in this cost: (1) production costs for manufacturing, (2) production costs for sales, and (3) production costs for PD. Among those, production costs for manufacturing and sales are included in production cost and marketing cost, respectively, so that production costs for PD alone are counted in PD cost. Two classes other than material distribution cost are:

   • *Information distribution cost:* Cost of dealing with and conveying information about material distribution. It can be classified into three areas: (a) stock-control costs, (b) order-filling costs, and (c) customer service costs.

   • *PD management cost:* Cost of planning, coordination, and control of PD. It is broken down into PD management cost (a) in the field and (b) in the home office.

**Classifying PD Cost by Managerial Objectives.** Classification by managerial objectives is required for planning and controlling PD. Since the Standard restricts itself to PD cost accounting aimed at performance appraisal, it does not take into account special cost aimed at decision making.

For the purpose of policy making, planning, or cost management of PD or sales, the already mentioned PD cost classifications are not always sufficient. Classification of PD cost by business segments in which PD is functioning is also required. They can be classified by:

• Department
• Product
• Territory
• Customer
• Other

To compute PD cost based on these classifications, the cost is divided into *direct* and *indirect* PD costs.

This is a classification needed for planning and control of PD, which classifies PD cost by its variability according to fluctuations of PD operation level. PD operation level here is the degree to which a particular PD system is utilized. In other words, it is a scale to measure the extent of PD activities, and is represented in terms of quantity, such as the number of articles, tonnage, cubic meters, working hours, etc., or in monetary terms.

When PD operation level is determined individually for functions such as packaging, transportation, warehousing, and handling, separate quantitative scales may be employed. On the other hand, when PD operation level of overall PD function is to be determined, a unified quantitative or monetary scale is required. On an operation level basis, PD cost is classified as *fixed* and *variable* PD costs.

Classification by managerial controllability is also essential from the standpoint of PD management. PD cost is divided into *controllable* and *uncontrollable* PD costs.

**PD Cost Accounting by Cost Elements.** PD cost accounting by cost elements is a procedure in which PD cost consumed in one PD cost accounting period (a month or a quarter) is classified by cost elements, as already discussed. In principle, the accountant uses the PD Cost Accounting Sheet by process and cost element. Here, required costs in each cost element are totaled by PD processes — purchase, intra-company, marketing, goods-returning, and disposal. Among those cost elements, computation of private PD cost (excluding burdens) is conducted as described in the next section. Unless otherwise stated, procedures of computation are based on the Cost Accounting Standards prepared by the Financial Accounting Deliberation Council of the Ministry of Finance.

**Computing Private PD Cost.** *Material costs.* Having been divided into direct and indirect material costs, material costs are computed separately. Direct material costs whose consumption volume are measurable are computed by multiplying consumption volumes by consumption prices. Indirect material costs and the direct material costs whose consumption volumes are difficult to determine are computed using the inventory method: the amount of inventories at the beginning of the period are added to the period's amount received, and ending inventories are deducted from the total.

*Personnel costs.* Personnel costs are divided into direct and indirect personnel costs and worked out separately. The *direct* personnel costs whose working hours or working volume is measurable are computed by multiplying working hours or volume by the wage rate. *Indirect* personnel costs — the direct personnel costs whose working hours or volume is immeasurable — are worked out by adding the period's unpaid amount to the period's paid amount and subtracting the prepaid amount.

*Utility costs.* In principle, utility costs such as electricity, gas, and water are computed by multiplying the metered consumption volume during a proper cost accounting period by their unit rates.

*Maintenance costs.* Maintenance costs, such as repairing expenses, consumable materials expenses, taxes and public fees, rents, and insurance charges, are computed from the amount of money spent during a cost accounting period. The amount is determined by adding accrued expenses to paid expenses and subtracting prepaid expenses from the total.

*General burdens.* General burdens are computed from an amount spent during a cost accounting period. The amount is determined by adding accrued expenses to paid expenses and deducting prepaid expenses from the total.

**Computing special burdens.** Two major items of special burdens, depreciation expenses and internal interests, are computed differently from the financial accounting method. Depreciation expenses are computed by the straight line method based on acquisition cost, useful life, and zero residual value. Internal interests are calculated by multiplying the appraised value of fixed assets for use in the PD department and the book value of inventory assets by a fixed rate.

In financial accounting, the depreciation period is determined by legal useful life, residual value is 10 per cent of acquisition cost, and the declining balance method is used. The Standard, however, employs the actual useful life and the straight line method, reducing residual value to zero.

As for internal interests, computation of interest in financial accounting is the amount of interest-bearing liabilities (loans payable, notes discounted, bonds, etc.) that is computed according to a borrowing period and the public rate of interest. The Standard prescribes, however, that the criteria for computing interest are the assessed tax value of fixed assets and the book value of inventory assets. Interests are computed according to their amounts on hand at the end of the period and the internal rate of interest.

**Computing other costs.** PD costs other than private PD cost are computed as public PD costs and PD costs paid by other companies. Public PD cost is computed from a payment amount in a cost accounting period. PD cost paid by other companies is a unique feature of the Standard. PD cost paid by other companies in the *purchasing process* is computed by multiplying the quantity of or the number of cases of purchases by estimated unit cost. PD cost paid by other companies in the *marketing process* is computed by multiplying the quantity or the number of cases of sales by estimated unit cost.

**PD Cost Accounting by Function.** PD cost accounting by functions is a procedure to classify by PD functions the PD cost consumed during a PD cost accounting period, as already mentioned, and total them.

*Material distribution cost.* To raise the cost management level, material costs, personnel costs, utility costs, maintenance costs, general burdens, and special burdens that fall under private PD cost, and public PD cost are computed by functions — that is, material distribution (packaging, transportation, warehousing, handling, production in distribution process), information distribution, and PD management — and also by processes — that is, purchasing (including recovery), intracompany, marketing, goods-returning, and disposal.

*Information distribution cost.* Since information distribution cost is difficult in many cases to compute by functions or by processes, lump-sum computation will do.

*PD management cost.* The case is similar to information distribution cost: lump-sum computation will do.

**Cost Accounting by Management Objectives.** In principle, PD cost classified by business systems is computed by product and by territory.

*PD cost accounting by products.* Material distribution cost by products is calculated by breaking it down into packaging cost, transportation cost, warehousing cost, handling cost and production cost in marketing process. To do this, a unit to total PD cost, or a cost unit, is fixed first. A cost unit may be decided on several bases, such as kind, brand, group, specification, shape, etc., of products. The cost unit from the standpoint of PD cost management is selected from among these. Material distribution cost is then divided into direct and indirect cost in relation in the classification cost unit (product A, B, or C).

Direct cost is charged directly to a proper product, while indirect cost is allocated among related products, and both are totaled.

*PD cost accounting by territories.* Material distribution cost by territories is computed and broken down to packaging cost, transportation cost, warehousing cost, handling cost, and production cost in marketing process. First, a cost unit is chosen from among the choices of business district, city, distance of transportation, location of customers, etc. Material distribution cost is then divided into direct or indirect cost in relation to the cost unit chosen (territory A, B, or C). Charge or allocation of cost is carried out like accounting by products.

*PD cost accounting by other cost units* is conducted using similar methods.

# PART IV

## The Organizational Aspect of Management Accounting in Japan

# 24

## The Organization of Management Accounting Functions in Japanese Corporations

*Katsuyasu Kato, Professor of Management*
*Yoshitaro Harasawa, Professor of Organization Theory*
*Yoshikaza Toyoshima, Professor of Management Accounting*
*Kazumasa Kikuchi, Professor of Accounting*
*Tadashi Kuriyama, Professor of Economic Statistics*
*All Faculty of Economics, Tohoku University*

The management accounting organization of Japanese corporations has been strongly influenced by U.S. controllership since World War II. The Industrial Rationalization Council of the Ministry of International Trade and Industry (MITI) submitted two reports to MITI in 1950 and 1953 on reforms of the organization of accounting functions.[1] MITI attempted to introduce U.S. control to Japanese corporations in response to the proposals of the council's reports.

According to the organization chart shown in the 1950 report, the controller and finance departments are under the authority of the executive committee (*johmukai*). The controller department oversees budgeting, accounting, statistics, and audit. The finance department oversees credit and collection, investments, accounts payable, and funds sections. This is similar to the organization charts of the controller and treasurer departments shown in Horngren's text, so we call it Horngren's controller/treasurer model.[2]

U.S. controllership was originally introduced to facilitate the modernization of Japanese management; concentrate the controller's functions such as general accounting, budget preparation, and internal auditing in the accounting department; and, at the same time, to separate the finance function from the controller's functions. Despite MITI's efforts, however, U.S. controllership has never been established in Japanese corporations. In recent years, many Japanese corporations tended to disperse the functions already named to departments (not sections) such as the accounting department, control department, planning department, corporate planning staff under the president's control, the audit department, and others.

Little systematic empirical analysis, however, has been done on the management accounting organization in Japanese corporations. It is unclear how — and for what reasons — Japanese corporations distribute the controller's functions among departments. Recently the increasing importance of long-range planning has led corporations to respond effectively to the market and technology environment. Therefore, when trying to present a faithful picture of the management accounting organization in Japanese corporations, we need to include long-and middle-range planning needs, in addition to general accounting, budget preparation, budgetary control, internal auditing, and finance functions.

We sent questionnaires to 420 random samples of 1,264 corporations (financial, insurance, and service industries excluded) listed on the Tokyo Stock Exchange as of October 1981. Two hundred and fifty-four companies replied.

The theme of this chapter is to describe and evaluate the realities of management accounting organization in Japanese corporations. On the basis of our survey, we shall identify the important types of Japanese management accounting organization by how the six functions are dispersed among departments. We shall then explain the dispersion of management accounting functions, based on results of another discriminating analysis,[3] and examine how they function by interviewing some typical corporations. Finally, we shall point out and evaluate the features of Japan's management accounting organization.

### Types of Organizations in Terms of Their Dispersion of Management Accounting Functions.
Our survey assigns six functions to the management accounting function:

1. General accounting.
2. Budget preparation.
3. Budgetary control.
4. Internal auditing.
5. Long- and middle-range planning.
6. Finance.

Among the 252 corporations participating in this study, only 170 have all six functions. It is not proper to classify simultaneously corporations having all six functions with those lacking some (called "developing organizations). We have analyzed only corporations having all six, leaving the remainder for future analysis.

In classifying organizations in terms of their dispersion of management accounting functions, we have separated corporations where each management accounting function is allotted to a department from those where a function is allotted to more than one department. We have called the former "Group I" and the latter "Group II." With this classification, the distribution of departments to which the management accounting functions are allotted is shown in Table 24.1. Comparing Group I and Group II, we recognize a significant difference: the former possesses a larger ratio of research and development (R & D) expense to total sales, and a larger fluctuation in the ratio of ordinary income to total assets in the five years. In this chapter, we have analyzed only those corporations belonging to Group I.

| Number of Departments | Group I | Group II | Total |
|---|---|---|---|
| 1 | 12 | — | 12 |
| 2 | 32 | 15 | 47 |
| 3 | 32 | 21 | 53 |
| 4 | 21 | 21 | 42 |
| 5 | 1 | 10 | 11 |
| 6 up | 0 | 5 | 55 |
| Total | 98 | 72 | 170 |

Table 24.1 Number of Departments in Groups I and II

**Type classification by number of departments.** 1. *One-department-concentration type.* Those 12 corporations where all six management accounting functions are allotted to a unique department can be called "one-department-concentration" type. This type differs from Horngren's controller/treasurer model because the finance function is also allocated to the same department.

2. *Two-department-dispersion type.* How the six management accounting functions are allocated to two departments is shown in Table 24.2. In these cases, (1) "independent long- and middle-range planning" type and "independent internal auditing" type are relatively numerous, while (2) the "independent finance" types are few.

3. *Three-department-dispersion type.* Let's consider the 32 corporations that allot the six management accounting functions to three departments. The dispersion of the functions is shown in part 2 of Table 24.2. Of the three-department-dispersion types, 15 are of "independent long- and middle-range planning" type, and 23 are of "independent internal auditing" type. Both types are relatively numerous, as in the case of the two-department-dispersion corporations, but the fact that there are as many as 11 "independent finance" types makes this category quite different from the two-department-dispersion category.

4. *Four-department-dispersion type.* The dispersion of the functions in these 21 corporations is shown in Table 24.3. The most frequently appearing type is the one where internal auditing and long- and middle-range planning or finance is independent from other functions. On the other hand, functions most frequently associated are general accounting and budgeting, and the second most frequently associated is the combination of budgeting and long- and middle-range planning. The least frequently associated are general accounting and finance.

5. *Five-department-dispersion type.* Only one corporation is a five-department-dispersion type. Budget preparation and budgetary control are together in the same department with the other functions allotted to separate departments.

**Frequently appearing types.** In this section, we analyze the dispersion of the six management accounting functions in 98 corporations having all six functions and, in addition, belonging to Group I. In conclusion, we will pick up the most frequently appearing dispersion types as described in Table 24.3. This implies that when Japanese

**(1) Two-Department Type**

| | Functions | | | | | | Number of Corporations |
|---|---|---|---|---|---|---|---|
| | [1] | [2] | [3] | [4] | [5] | [6] | |
| | ○ | × | × | × | × | ○ | 4 |
| | ○ | × | × | ○ | × | ○ | 2 |
| | ○ | ○ | × | × | × | ○ | 1 |
| | ○ | ○ | ○ | × | × | ○ | 4 |
| | ○ | ○ | ○ | × | ○ | ○ | 6 |
| | ○ | ○ | ○ | ○ | × | ○ | 11 |
| | ○ | ○ | ○ | ○ | ○ | × | 4 |
| **Total** | | | | | | | 32 |

**(2) Three-Department Type**

| | Functions | | | | | | Number of Corporations |
|---|---|---|---|---|---|---|---|
| | [1] | [2] | [3] | [4] | [5] | [6] | |
| | ○ | ○ | ○ | ○ | × | ☆ | 5 |
| | ○ | ○ | ○ | × | ○ | ☆ | 2 |
| | ○ | ○ | ○ | × | × | ☆ | 1 |
| | ○ | ○ | ○ | × | ☆ | ○ | 10 |
| | ○ | × | × | × | × | ☆ | 3 |
| | ○ | × | × | ☆ | × | ○ | 11 |
| **Total** | | | | | | | 32 |

**(3) Four-Department Type**

| | Functions | | | | | | Number of Corporations |
|---|---|---|---|---|---|---|---|
| | [1] | [2] | [3] | [4] | [5] | [6] | |
| | ○ | ○ | ○ | × | ● | ☆ | 12 |
| | ○ | ● | ● | × | ● | ☆ | 7 |
| | ○ | ● | ● | × | ☆ | ○ | 2 |
| **Total** | | | | | | | 21 |

The management accounting functions are denoted as follows:

[1] = general accounting     [4] = internal auditing
[2] = budget preparation     [5] = long/middle planning
[3] = budgetary control      [6] = finance function

The same symbol implies that the corresponding function is allotted to the same department.

**Table 24.2 Dispersion of the Management Accounting Functions**

| Type | Function | | | | | | Number of Corporations | Notes |
| --- | --- | --- | --- | --- | --- | --- | --- | --- |
| | [1] | [2] | [3] | [4] | [5] | [6] | | |
| I | O | O | O | O | O | O | 12 | One-department-concentration type |
| II-1 | O | O | O | X | O | O | 6 | Independent International Auditing Type |
| II-2 | O | O | O | O | X | O | 11 | Independent Long/Middle-Range Planning Type |
| II-3 | O | X | X | X | X | O | 4 | Joint General Accounting and Finance Type |
| II-4 | O | O | O | X | X | O | 4 | Joint International Auditing and Long/Middle-Range Planning Type |
| II-5 | O | O | O | O | O | X | 4 | Independent Finance Type |
| III-1 | O | X | X | ● | X | O | 11 | Joint General Accounting and Finance Type (A) |
| III-2 | O | O | O | X | ● | O | 10 | Joint General Accounting and Finance Type (B) |
| III-3 | O | O | O | O | X | ☆ | 5 | Independent Finance and Long/Middle-Range Planning Type |
| IV-1 | O | X | X | ● | X | ☆ | 7 | Joint Budgeting and Long/Middle Range Planning Type |
| IV-2 | O | O | O | X | ● | ☆ | 12 | Joint General Accounting and Budgeting Type |

Table 24.3  Frequently Appearing Types of Dispersion

corporations allot the management accounting functions to more than one department, they first make the long- and middle-range planning and internal auditing independent from other functions, while finance is separated later from other functions. As a result, the "independent finance" type shown in Horngren's controller/treasurer model occurs less frequently in Japanese corporations.

1. *Type I corporations.* Corporations in this category come from the primary, secondary, and tertiary industries. In the case of secondary industries, we can observe this type only in steel and machinery. This category of corporation typically includes those with fewer employees and no subsidiaries. In other words, most belong to the second section of the Tokyo Stock Exchange. These smaller corporations do not need to differentiate management accounting functions among departments. Divisionalization is a little lower than Group I corporations. The increasing sales rate almost equals the average of Group I, but the ratio of income to net equity and to total capital are low, and fluctuate greatly. We can characterize these corporations as having "unstable performance and low growth rate."

2. *Type II-1 corporations.* Corporations belonging to this category can be found in the secondary industries, (with the exception of the construction industry), most of which are listed in the second section of the Tokyo Stock Exchange. Their capital stock, total assets, and number of employees are almost half of those corporations belonging to type II-2, and their annual sales are limited to about 70 percent of the latter.

The number of corporations possessing subsidiaries and those that are divisionalized are least in this type. Due to their smaller size, they are experiencing more rapidly increasing sales rates and higher ratios of income to net equity and to total capital as compared to Group I. They suffer, however, from greater fluctuations in sales — but this lack of stability has not affected their rapid growth rate.

3. *Type II-2 corporations.* Corporations (especially machinery and electrical manufacturing) of this type can be found in the secondary industries, except construction. Their capital stock and total assets are much less than Group I's average. They have fewer employees than type III and type IV corporations and annual sales are small. While these corporations are small in size, a greater number of them have subsidiaries and are divisionalized than the type II-1 corporations. On the other hand, they are similar to type II-1 corporations

because they have a more rapidly increasing growth rate and larger fluctuations in sales.

4. *Type II-3 corporations.* This type of corporation is frequently seen in the chemical and machinery industries (secondary industries) and in the land transportation industry (tertiary industry). They are among the smallest corporations, much smaller than that of type 1, and none are divisionalized or diversified. They are the most unstable corporations with the largest fluctuations in normal income.

5. *Type II-4 corporations.* To this category belong corporations such as construction, glass and ceramic, and electrical manufacturing industries (secondary industries) and the trading and commerce industries (tertiary industries). They are among the largest of the type II corporations, and all are listed in the first section of the Tokyo Stock Exchange; however, they are less divisionalized and diversified. They are the most stable corporations with the smallest fluctuations in their sales rates.

6. *Type II-5 corporations.* This type of corporation can be found in food, glass and ceramic, and electrical manufacturing industries (secondary) and in real estate companies (tertiary). They are larger than the average type II and are all listed in the first section of the Tokyo Stock Exchange. They are divisionalized, like an average type II corporation, but are less diversified. Despite small increases in the sales rate, they are stable corporations with small fluctuations.

7. *Type III-1 corporations.* This type of corporation is found in all industries, but primarily the secondary industries. Since their capital stock, total assets, number of employees, and annual sales are lower than type III-2, we may characterize these corporations as "midsize." Note that most of them, however, have subsidiaries. They are divisionalized at a higher rate and continue to be diversified. They can be described as stable-growth corporations, with an increasing rate of sales that is not as high as type III-2, but higher than the average of Group I. Their fluctuations in rate of sales are far smaller than those of type III-2.

At Kawasaki Heavy Industry, the merit of the planning department taking charge of short-range and long/middle-range planning simultaneously is that the planning functions are centralized. Although long-range plans are made independently of short-range plans, the short-range plans can be drawn up in the context of the long-range plan.

8. *Type III-2 corporations*. This type of corporation can be seen in all industries, but mostly in electric power and gas. The averages of their capital stock, total assets, number of employees, and annual sales are second only to Type IV-2, but many more are listed in the second section of the Tokyo Stock Exchange than corporations belonging to Group I. The number of corporations having subsidiaries and adopting a divisionalized system almost equals the average of Group I. Because the average increasing sales rate is the largest and the number of fluctuations is only a little larger than Group I's average, they can be characterized as corporations with a high growth rate.

9. *Type III-3 corporations*. All corporations of this type are secondary — textile, pulp, paper, chemical, and steel. Their size and the degree of divisionalization/ diversification put them between type III-1 and type III-2, but only a few are listed in the first section of the Tokyo Stock Exchange. Fluctuations in their increasing rate of sales and normal income are the smallest, and they are the most stable corporations.

10. *Type IV-1 corporations*. This type of corporation can be seen in the steel and electric machinery industries (secondary) and in trading and sea transportation industries (tertiary). Their capital stock is small (slightly larger than type III-1) and they have few employees. Their total assets are lower than Group I's average, and annual sales are the second largest next to type IV-2. All corporations are listed in the first section of the Tokyo Stock Exchange, and all have subsidiaries. The degree of divisionalization is a little lower than the average of Group I.

On the other hand, the increasing sales rate is small, like type IV-2, but fluctuation is larger than Group I's average. Although the ratio of income to net equity is high, its ratio to total assets is low. Fluctuations are small because of the large amount of total assets.

11. *Type IV-2 corporations*. This type of corporation can be seen in all industries, but mostly in secondary and a few in tertiary. All are listed in the first section of the Tokyo Stock Exchange (like type IV-1) and have subsidiaries. Familiar Japanese corporations such as Hitachi, Nippon Electric, and Nippon Steel are included in this category. The averages of their capital stock, total assets, number of employees, and annual sales are all overwhelmingly large. Those that are not divisionalized are slightly larger in number than those that are, but it seems that diversification has progressed overall. Although the increasing sales rate, and the ratio of income to net equity

and to total assets are all lower than Group I's average, their fluctuations are smaller. They can be regarded as mature, stable corporations.

At Nippon Electric, organizational dispersion by divisionalization has differentiated the accounting functions, thereby separating departments such as finance and EDP. As a result, each division has its own planning department, and many of the controller functions of the accounting department have been transferred to the planning departments.

***Determining Factors of Types of Departmental Dispersion.***  We have tried in another paper to analyze what factors influence the departmental dispersion of management accounting functions in Japanese corporations through discriminant analysis. Dependent variables are like those listed in Table 24.3; independent variables are the environmental and strategic factors measured in the scales listed in Table 24.4. The selection of measures was based on the following assumptions:

1. Corporation size can be measured by the logarithm of annual total sales and the number of employees as of April 1, 1981. The bigger the scale, the more complex the corporation.
2. Environmental uncertainty in the case of corporations qualified for the Tokyo Stock Exchange can be categorized by type: competitive and stable. This uncertainty can be measured by assessing the degree of competitiveness.
3. While technological competitiveness can be measured by averaging the past 5 years' ratios of research and development cost to annual total sales, market competitiveness can be measured by the ratios of advertising cost to total annual sales. The bigger these averages, the more competitive the corporation.
4. Instability of performance can be measured by the standard deviations of the ratios of normal income to total annual sales and to total assets in the past 5 years. The larger these deviations, the greater the instability.
5. Degree of diversification can be measured by averaging the ratios of main product sales to total sales for the past 5 years. The smaller the average, the more diversified the corporation.
6. Degree of decentralization can be measured by adding point digits assigned as follows: 1 point to the wholly divisionalized, 2 points to the partly divisionalized, and 3 points to the nondivisionalized corporations. The smaller the sum, the more centralized the corporation.

As mentioned in the previous section, the distinguishing feature of the management accounting organization in Japanese corporations, when compared with Horngren's controller/treasurer model,

| | | Measurement Scales |
|---|---|---|
| Environmental Factors | Size of corporation | Number of employees (logarithm)<br>Annual total sales (logarithm) |
| | Uncertainty of market | Ratio of advertising to sales (average of 5 years) |
| | Uncertainty of technology | Ratio of R & D to sales (average of 5 years) |
| | Instability of performance | Annual increasing rate of sales (standard deviation)<br>Ratio of normal income to total assets (standard deviation) |
| Strategic Factors | Diversification | Ratio of main product sales to total sales (average of 5 years) |
| | Decentralization | Degree of divisionalization |

**Table 24.4  Independent Variables Explaining the Differences Between Types**

is that department dispersion can be observed. We can see that the functions of long- and middle-range planning and internal auditing tend to be allotted to independent departments; the separation of the finance function follows.

We have already done discriminant analysis in another paper to find out what factors determine:

- The number of departments in charge of management accounting functions.
- Departmental dispersion of the internal auditing function.
- Departmental dispersion of the long- and middle-range planning function.
- Departmental dispersion of the finance function.

We will explain how the typical types of management accounting organizations, taken from the 11 types classified earlier, work in reality, based on the major findings of our analysis and personal interviews.

**Factors increasing the number of departments.** The factor that plays the most important role in increasing the number of departments participating in the management accounting functions is the scale of the corporation. This reflects the fact that, in general, the number of management departments is influenced by the size of the corporation.

The next most important factors are diversification and technological competitiveness. When this survey was conducted, the Japanese economy had overcome the first oil crisis and had started growing through diversification.[4] Diversification made corporate scales larger, resulting in an increase in the number of departments.

Other factors that increase departments are market competitiveness and stability of performance. Big businesses in Japan are usually groups of corporations that have subsidiaries. Any control they have over the environment comes through the exchange of information and addition of subsidiaries.[5] This is why the stable rate of return was possible, despite environmental factors such as technological and market competitiveness. The stability, working as a kind of slack factor to management organization, has resulted in an increasing number of departments and an ensuing dispersion of management functions to them.

**Factors separating internal auditing from others.** As shown in Table 24.2, the ratio of corporations of the "independent internal auditing" type to the total (6/32, 23/32, 21/21) changes as the number of departments increases. This shows that scale is the most important factor for making the internal auditing function independent.

Our survey shows that the internal auditing function in Japanese corporations tends to be independent as an "internal auditing department under the immediate control of top management": those under the president, 21 percent; under senior executive and director, 18 percent; under executive and director, 26 percent; and under vice president and director, 12 percent. This tendency may mean that top management has absolute power, but our interviews show that only a few auditing departments have independent staff and their auditing authority is not always strong. For example, in a large heavy industry corporation and a construction company, the auditing department is concurrently in charge of the internal auditing function. In Japanese corporations, strict internal control is not preferred. Rather "portable shrine management," or "groupism" that attaches importance to harmony, works also in the field of management accounting.[6]

In an interview at a large automobile manufacturer, we were told internal auditing is conducted in a friendly, participatory, friction-free manner. At a large construction corporation, we were told internal auditing is limited in its ability to criticize other departments because people felt it inappropriate to be too severe on fellow colleagues.

In our discriminant analysis, we divided the sample corporations into two groups, those of independent internal auditing type and others, and we applied the discriminant analysis to the two-department-dispersion type and three-department dispersion type corporations. According to the analysis, the most important factor for departmental independence of internal auditing is the introduction of a division system in the case of two-department-dispersion type corporations. In the case of three-department-dispersion type corporations, the most important factors are corporation size and environmental uncertainty due to market competitiveness. On the other hand, our interviews show that divisionalization was, in many corporations, a matter of the departmental independence of internal auditing.

**Factors separating long- and middle-range planning from others.** According to Table 24.2, the ratio of corporations of the independent long- and middle-range planning type to the total (11/32, 15/32, 14/21) changes as the number of departments increases; however, this increasing ratio is not as large as that of internal auditing. The result is that departmental independence of this function depends mainly on market and strategic factors rather than corporation size. Our analysis, like that applied to internal auditing, found that the following factors define the departmental dispersion of management accounting functions:

1. Advancing diversification/decentralization and stable market environment, in addition to corporation size in the case of two-department-dispersion type corporations.
2. Stable performance and technological environments in the case of three-department-dispersion type corporations.
3. Uncertain technological environment but stable performance in the case of four-department-dispersion type corporations.

According to our analysis, the necessity of long- and middle-range planning increases as the control of resources and schedule becomes more crucial in diversified and divisionalized corporations. This function is attainable when market and technological environments are stable and, therefore, long-range forecasting is relatively easy.

In our interviews at an oil and a construction company, managers of the numerical control (NC) department told us that they had stopped long-range planning when long-range forecasting had become almost impossible because of the oil crisis. An electrical manufacturing company, we were told, had recently dropped the word "plan" because sales forecasting had become too uncertain. Instead, the term *prospective order* was used.

**Factors separating finance functions from others.** As shown in Table 24.2, the ratio of corporations of independent finance type to the total (4/32, 11/32, 19/21) increases rapidly as the number of department increases. We can say that an increase in size is the main factor in separating the finance function, and the separation occurs in relatively large-size corporations. It should be noted that divisionalization is related to the separation of the finance function. When we asked division managers what was the most important index for which they assume responsibility, 66.4 percent said the amount of income. The least important was ROI (9.7 percent). Concerning their authority over capital investment decisions within the division, only 1.8 percent of divisions decide for themselves, while 29.2 percent made the decision but needed approval from headquarters; 39.8 percent said the division and headquarters discuss these issues together; 13.3 percent said the division decides under a headquarters framework; and 14.2 percent simply said "headquarters decides." This means that division authority over the finance function is weak in Japanese corporations. On the contrary, the finance function of headquarters to provide funds for the divisions is strengthened as divisionalization increases.

In our interviews, most of the managers of finance departments in independent finance type corporations told us that, so far, the duty of finance departments in Japanese corporations was mainly to borrow money as smoothly as possible from banks. It was only recently that their core duty became the investment of surplus money. For instance, a large automobile company and a construction company recently added a new department to manage their investments. After the first oil crisis, profitable investment of surplus money is indispensable for Japanese corporations to maintain the stable normal income.

Since the capital market has grown rapidly, Japanese corporations gradually shifted financing away from traditional indirect financing (borrowing from banks) methods to direct financing (from capital market), and diversified their methods of financing. This is another reason for the independence of the finance function.

*Conclusion.* We have analyzed management accounting organization in 98 Japanese corporations, all of which have six management accounting functions not shared by two or more departments. We present here some concluding remarks based on the facts found so far.

The nature of management accounting organization in Japanese corporations can be found in the structure of the *keiribu* or accounting department. If we classify the types of management accounting organization according to (1) whether or not the finance function is separate from the *keiribu* and (2) to what extent management accounting functions other than general accounting are concentrated in the *keiribu*, then the 11 representative types of management accounting organization can be classified into four categories (see Table 24.5).

1. As shown in Table 24.5, types I, II-1, II-2, II-4, and III-2 belong to the category of Strong Keiribu, where the accounting department is in charge of finance as well as most of the other management accounting functions. The percentage of corporations belonging to this category is about 50 percent, while the percentage of those belonging to the category of Semistrong Keiribu is comparatively low (18 percent).

| | Finance Function | | Total |
|---|---|---|---|
| | **Non-Separate Type** | **Separate Type** | |
| **Concentrate Type** | Type I(12)<br>Type II-1(6)<br>Type II-2(11)<br>Type II-4(4)<br>Type III-2(10)<br>("Strong Keiribu": 50%) | Type II-5(4)<br>Type III-3(5)<br>Type IV-2(12)<br><br>("Well-balanced": 24%) | 74% |
| **Diversified Type** | Type II-3(4)<br>Type III-1(11)<br>("Semistrong Keiribu": 18%) | Type IV-1(7)<br>("Weak Keiribu": 8%) | 26% |
| **Total** | 68% | 32% | 100% |

**Table 24.5  Four Categories of Accounting Departments (Keiribu)**

As for the categories of finance-separate type, the Well-Balanced Keiribu, to which types II-3, III-3, and IV-2 belong, is about 24 percent. It is larger than that of the dispersed type, the Weak Keiribu, to which type IV-1 belong.

Thus, we can observe many cases where management accounting functions are concentrated in the accounting department, even if finance is allotted to other departments. This implies that accounting departments are powerful in Japanese corporations.

2. As mentioned earlier, the larger the size of the corporation, the more the management accounting functions are dispersed to many departments. Such dispersal is done mainly by separating functions such as internal auditing and long/middle-range planning from the accounting department. Such dispersal may be aimed at strengthening the check system by making an independent auditing department, and at separating the routine and non-routine planning functions by allotting the long- and middle-range planning functions to a department other than keiribu. The dispersal does not necessarily result in the weakening of the accounting departments' power.

3. The well-balanced type, in which most management accounting functions are concentrated in the accounting department while finance is allotted to another department, is distinctly American in character. In many cases, internal auditing and long- and middle-range planning functions are independent. This type of management accounting organization is called a well-balanced organization in this context.

Among these well-balanced corporations, types II-5, III-3, and IV-2 have the same organization as the typical controller system. It should be noted that corporations such as Hitachi, Nippon Electric, and Nippon Steel belong to this category. As a whole, however, the number of such corporations is relatively so small that we can say the U.S.-style controller system is not firmly established in Japanese corporations.

4. To understand the nature of management accounting organization in Japanese corporations, another important point must be considered. Influential members of the board of directors also serve concurrently as the president, executive vice president, and so on. As a result, the structure of top management becomes concentrated, which differs from an organization with board members who are not part of top management. In the former, most of the corporation's power lies with the president.

In Japanese corporations, the top management function is essentially carried out by the executive committee (*johmukai*), composed of senior members of the officer-directors. The relationship between such an executive committee and the management accounting organization is important. In general, the power of the immediate superior to the accounting department seems strong among top executives. Remember that most management accounting functions are concentrated in the keiribu of many corporations.

In cases where planning and control functions are concentrated in the accounting department, short-range profit control will be its top priority. But when the long- and middle-range planning functions are separated from this department, and the top manager is a different senior officer-director than the senior member of the accounting department (especially in type IV-2), the short-range and long-range profit control functions will be well-balanced because the checks-and-balances mechanism will work among top management.

## Notes

1. MITI Industrial Rationalization Council, *The Manual of Procedures for Implementation of Internal Control* (in Japanese) (1950), and *The Outline of Internal Control in Business Firms* (in Japanese) (1953).
2. Horngren, Charles T., *Cost Accounting: A Managerial Emphasis*, 5th ed. New York: Prentice-Hall, pp. 10-12.
3. Kato, K., et al., "Departmental Dispersal of Management Accounting Functions in Major Japanese Corporations: A Discriminant Analysis for Detecting Determinant Factors" (in Japanese). In Sakata and Moriwaki (eds.), *Essays on the Anniversary of Professor Kazuo Takamatsu's Sixtieth Birthday*, Tokyo: Dobunkan Publishing Company, 1988.
4. This conclusion is derived from materials such as: (a) Yoshihara, Sakuma, Itami, and Kagono, *Diversification Strategies of Japanese Corporations* (in Japanese), Nihon Keizai Shimbunsha, 1981, Chapter 2; (b) Business Behaviors Section, MITI Bureau of Industrial Policy, *New Indices of Managerial Power: Trial Business Evaluations by Qualitative Factors* (in Japanese), Printing Office, Ministry of Finance, 1982, Chapter 4; (c) Kagono, Nonaka, Sakakibara, and Okumura, *Comparative Study of Business Management in Japanese and American Corporations* (in Japanese), Nihon Keizai Shimbunsha, 1983, Chapter 5.
5. The following materials are referred to: (a) Yoshino, Y., *Japanese Marketing System: Adaptation and Innovation*, Tokyo: Diamond Publishing Co., 1976, Chapter 3; (b) Shimizu, R., *Growth of Corporations* (in Japanese), Chuo-Keizaisha Co., 1984, Chapter 1; (c) Gotoh, N., "Corporate Groups in Japan" (in Japanese), *Business Review*, Institute of Business Research, Hitotsubashi University, 1983, Vol. 30, No. 3/4.
6. In the interests of management, clear distinctions are not made in employees' qualifications, roles, salaries, and so on. Instead, importance is given to the harmonious behavior of the group. This is a distinctive feature of Japanese management.

# 25

## Corporate Strategies and Divisionalized Management Control at Matsushita

*Tamio Fushimi, School of Business Administration,*
*Keio University*

It is commonly understood that most electric industrial organizations in Japan have adopted the divisionalized management system originally invented by some pioneer companies in the United States in the 1920s. It has spread nationwide during some ten years after that. After World War II, especially after the early 1960s, large diversified enterprises in Japan successively adopted this management system. That was partly because the Ministry of International Trade recommended this system, expecting to use the growing industrial enterprises as a base for the developing Japanese economy.

Matsushita Electric Industrial Co., Ltd, is one of the leading companies that has adopted the system. Its historical background goes back further than other Japanese companies: Matsushita's divisionalized system was launched in 1933, two years before the company was incorporated as a joint-stock company. It is said that Mr. Konosuke Matsushita, the founder of the company, had a firm management philosophy from the beginning, that is: "There should be an optimal scale of business for a manager to be able to control it effectively by himself" and "As a company grows and expands into new business areas, it is wise to give the person appointed to manage the new area the authority necessary to manage all operations — from production through sales." This simple philosophy of the founder has always been the foundation of the company's management style, except for the period during World War II, when the company was forced to run munitions factories. This management system, with the help of the various subsystems created by many cooperative people supporting Matsushita is said to have been the driving force behind the company's successful expansion during the period of high growth in the Japanese economy.

Although Matsushita's accounting and control systems were developed by the Matsushita group itself, corporate management and its staff have been paying continuous attention to the systems of the excellent U.S. companies. The company's senior executive officer in charge of accounting and control said in an interview that they were paying constant attention to the management accounting systems of General Electric Company (GE) because it is an excellent model to learn from. In the early 1970s, however, GE encountered the difficult situations when their management control system, which had been regarded as being well designed, was hindering the development of its corporate strategies, and they had to restructure its control systems. What interests us the most is that Matsushita encountered the same kind of strategic problems as GE did in the latter half of the decade.

This chapter presents a case study about how Matsushita's corporate management tried to solve their strategic problems, as compared with GE's case. Taking a look at its management accounting system, we analyze the essential points of their trial.

**GE's Problem.** According to the Harvard Business School case, "General Electric Company (B)" (written by R.F. Vancil), GE's problems were in the form of sudden underliquidation, which came as something of a surprise. GE's critical situation in 1973 was that the amount of net interest expense that corporate management charged to the operating components (approximately 130 product departments) was only about 55 percent of the amount that should have been paid to the outside. The following points were cited about the direct causes:

- The prime rate skyrocketed and far exceeded the imputed rate of interest charged to each component.
- There were many cases when corporate management was forced to "forgive" the cumulative investment in product lines, which were

abandoned for the relief of the product departments that had failed in new products or in new businesses, discharging the corresponding interest.

This was not GE's only problem, however; it was just a visible peak on an iceberg. The point is that the management accounting system that they had believed to be almost perfect was actually hindering the development of companywide strategies. One of the critical problems was that the investment center system that GE had adopted could not meet the expectation of corporate management. Mr. Smith, who was the president at that time said, "The way of allocating corporate resources should be biased in favor of our high-growth, high-potential, newer businesses even if that means a reduction in the resources available for our mature businesses that are growing more slowly."

GE's corporate management found that a solution would not be reached until they cast aside their traditional accounting control system. The means of solving the dilemma was the restructuring of organization and the development of new programming techniques. The strategic business unit (SBU) and the product portfolio management (PPM) are two well-known examples of the new concepts and techniques introduced then.

The approach adopted by GE was regarded as one of the typical examples of innovative management control of a decentralized organization. We believe that Matsushita's top managers must have known that, but they took, at least superficially, a different approach, as we show in the next section.

*A Brief Survey of Matsushita's Decentralized Organization.* Matsushita Electric has long been known as a leading home appliance manufacturer in Japan, gaining the top market share in many areas of home appliances. According to the 1983 annual report on a consolidated basis, its net sales were almost ¥4 trillion, the net income before taxes was about ¥500 billion, and it had 125,000 employees.

In the same year, Matsushita Electric, the chief corporation of the group, had 36 operational divisions. The organization had been simplified compared to its structure of ten years before, when there were 56 division general managers who reported to one of 17 group executives. Each divisions was a self-supporting unit with its own "internal capital." In the consolidated financial statements, more than 80 affiliated companies were included. There were approximately 145 divisions within the group, out of which 114 were manufacturing divisions.

**Organizational structure and responsibility accounting.** The organizational structure in 1983 for Matsushita's business activities is summarized in Figure 25.1. The distribution channels for the domestic market could be divided roughly into three: home appliances, housing equipment, and specialty products. There was also a fourth channel through which various products were exported overseas. Moreover, many products were manufactured and marketed by overseas subsidiaries.

Every division of Matsushita Electric had been operating as if it had been an independent corporation. When a new division was installed, corporate management provided the division with the initial capital funds for acquiring the net assets, which were defined as the sum of the standard working capital fixed assets (plant and equipment) less reserves for retirement allowances, and so on. The initial amount of the net assets invested by corporate management was credited to the balance sheet of the division as an "internal capital." (See Figure 25.2.)

It had been the established policy of top management to make each division financially independent. The division manager was expected to cover the investment in the additional working capital and fixed assets with its cash earnings, the sum of the residual income, and the depreciation of fixed assets. There were rare cases when corporate management provided funds to a division in the form of "internal capital increases." Decisions about a division's investment policies were left to the division manager's discretion, as long as they could be financed with its accumulated net cash flow.

When a division operated without borrowing from the corporate treasurer's office, the before-tax net income of the division was determined as operating income less the imputed interest cost for the internal capital. The residual income (RI) of the division was defined as the before-tax net income less the charge for taxes and dividends. (In 1983, the charge was 60 percent of the before-tax net income.) The residual income was added to retained earnings on the division's balance sheet.

Divisions that were recently installed and had prospects of growing sometimes had investment amounts larger than their cash earnings.

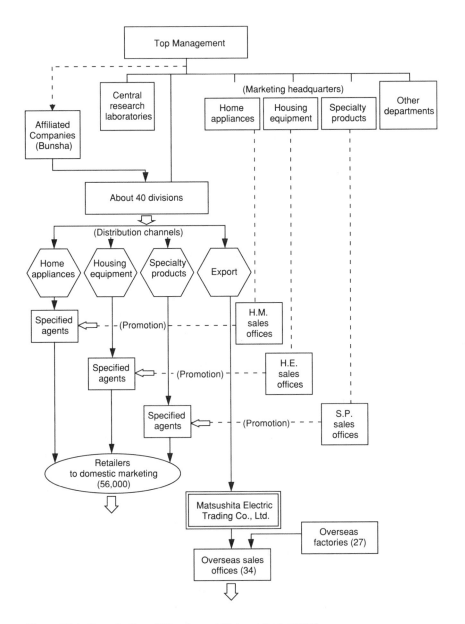

**Figure 25.1 Organizational Structure at Matsushita (ca1983)**

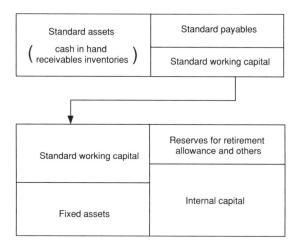

**Figure 25.2 A Matsushita Division's Balance Sheet**

The general managers of these divisions had to borrow money from the corporate treasurer's office, which was nicknamed "Matsushita Bank," to fill the deficit in cash flow. The division managers were never allowed to borrow money from outside banks.

When a division's accumulated cash flow was not sufficient for its necessary investment and the division manager wanted to borrow money from the corporate treasurer's office, the treasurer and the staff examined the details of the request, just like an outside banker would do. When the request was granted, the treasurer's office charged a certain rate of interest that was a little higher than commercial bank interest rates.

On the other hand, some divisions carrying mature products would receive cash earnings in excess of investment. If a division had a surplus net cash flow, the surplus would be first appropriated for repayment of loans from the treasurer's office. If a division had no more loans outstanding and still had a surplus, it would deposit it in the treasurer's office.

In the late 1970s, the majority of the home appliance divisions had surplus cash flows. For example, the radio division, TV division, and others with a long operating history had accumulated an earned surplus nearly 10 to 12 times their "internal capital." There were often large amounts of "deposits in their corporate accounts," as illustrated

in Figure 25.3. And, as the general managers of these divisions actually profited from these corporate deposits, in all likelihood, they
were well satisfied with their positions.

| Standard working capital | Reserves |
|---|---|
| | Internal capital |
| Fixed assets | |
| | Earned surplus |
| Deposits in the corporate account | |

**Figure 25.3 The Balance Sheet of a Division in a Mature Business Area
at Matsushita**

As for the accounting system for evaluating the profitability of
each division, Matsushita had almost the same system as GE had: residual income (RI) was used as the basic measure of profitability. In
addition to the annual reporting system, the company had a system
called monthly accounting settlement. Monthly financial reports
were comprised of the income statement, balance sheet, and the
summary of cash flows. (See Monden, [1985], Chapter 3.)

The controller and his staff at the corporate office examined and
followed up on the monthly and annual performance as compared
with the budgeted plan. The division manager should have reviewed
the division's performance as compared with the original budget,
making his own observations about the performance and comment-
ing on issues to be improved.

The recent trend is to make operating income (before adding the
interest income from the deposits in corporate account), sales

amount, and market share a set of basic criteria. To compare the profitability of divisions, the ratio of operating income to sales was applied as the most important measure.

**Problems in the 1970s.** This brief survey would suggest that the top management of Matsushita Electric, two-thirds of whose business in the 1970s was related to home appliances, must have had the same awareness of the crisis as GE's former president Smith had. In 1977, Konosuke Matsushita, the founder of the company, who had been regarded as the company's ruler after he resigned as chairman of the board, created a sensation when he appointed Toshihiko Yamashita president. Yamashita was just a low ranking director on the board. This kind of appointment was unusual in any Japanese company. Around that time Matsushita began transforming itself from strictly home appliances to an all-round manufacturer of electric and electronic-related products.

From the viewpoint of management control, the innovative processes of Yamashita and the corporate executives supporting him had three important aspects:

1. To change management's awareness: all management — from top managers to operational managers — should know about the crisis and the necessity of shifting their business territories and reemphasizing their productivity.
2. To restructure the divisionalized organization: modify the organizational philosophy, reshuffle personnel, and consolidate or merge divisions.
3. To improve the accounting and financial control: for example, nullify divisions' corporate accounts and corresponding earned surplus.

The following is our observation of each of these three aspects.

*All Managers Have an Awareness of the Crisis.* Since taking over the position of president, Yamashita appealed repeatedly to the members of the management committee (almost all the general managers of divisions, sales offices, and major affiliated companies in the group), and made his appeals known outside the company, that the corporation needed innovative management. One of his most famous speeches was given at a New Year conference held January 1984. To the nearly 7,000 executives and managers there, he said:

> One of our most urgent problems is directing more energy to our newer specialty products, especially the information-related products

with a higher growth rate than the more mature products such as home appliances. We must meet the needs of the times.

He also spoke about his goals: increase the sales volume of the specialty products 20 percent annually for the next three years and increase the ratio of their sales in the overall sales of the group from 31 to 39 percent in that same period. The specialty products included electronic components such as semiconductors, information-related devices, and other industrial products.

Business journalists reported that the president showed his readiness to carry the burden himself and cut off management's retreat by publicizing the numerical targets. The announcement of Yamashita's strategic turnabout was described as closely related to the "Action-61" campaign, which covered a three-and-a-half year period from mid-1983 to the end of 1986. One of its major goals was to turn the Matsushita group by 1986 from a home appliances manufacturer to an all-round manufacturer of electric- and electronic-related products.

Many tales were reportedly told within the company to explain why the "Action-61" plan had to be pursued. One was:

> Almost 30 years ago, in 1956, Matsushita's annual sales were about half Hitachi's. In 1973, however, Matsushita overtook Hitachi. Many thought this was because Hitachi failed to adjust itself to the times by still adhering to heavy industrial products. Matsushita, meanwhile, gained market share in home appliances, a rapid growth area in those years. Similarly, NEC's current sales are about half Matsushita's, but NEC occupies a large portion of the computer area. If Matsushita fails to take action in time, within ten years it will be overtaken by NEC.

*Restructuring the Divisionalized Organization.* The characteristics of Matsushita's divisionalized organization were described as:

- The underlying philosophy of its divisionalized system was a "one product for one division" principle, letting the division specialize in each product area. This enabled a quick and flexible response to the market, as well as efficient production.
- The division general manager was given full authority for managing division activities, and he was obliged to bear the responsibility of keeping a satisfactory level of profitability as the top executive of a financially independent organization having "internal capital." As a result of keeping this management style, Matsushita's managers became the most profitability-minded in the industry.

**A review of the divisionalized system.** Matsushita's division-alized system was considered to be most suitable for the home appliances industry, which had been diversifying and growing during the period of Japan's rapid economic growth. Competitiveness emerging from this growth and responsibility in the accounting system induced them to develop new products and new technology, and to produce the products efficiently.

In the 1970s, however, when the Japanese economy entered a period of low growth, many home appliance manufacturers entered a mature period. At that time, Matsushita's corporate management found various problems in its divisionalized system. Here are some comments made by business journalists:

> Difficulties frequently arose where cooperation was poor between divisions dealing with multifunctional products such as radiocassettes and other "system products." Specialization and division of labor had been overly promoted, and the exchange or transfer of personnel across divisions became difficult. Division general managers often rejected the transfer of competent personnel under them. This resulted in stagnation.

Soon after becoming president in 1977, Yamashita said he would focus on "reactivating the organization" and "bringing up human resources" to make management more aggressive and to strengthen the competitiveness and profitability of the company. A brief chronology follows:

- In 1977, Yamashita appointed himself head of the central research laboratory, showing that Matsushita was fully aware of the importance of developing new technologies.
- The same year, the general planning offices were consolidated into the corporate planning department, drawing attention to the importance of having corporate-level strategies. The department general managers started to report directly to the president in 1980.
- In 1978, Yamashita abolished the "business group" organization and four executive vice presidents in charge of these business groups were released. All divisions were placed under the president's direct supervision.
- In the same year, Yamashita announced the modification of Matsushita's organizational policy and started promoting interdivisional personnel rotation.
- In 1979, Yamashita began restructuring the organization of domestic marketing.

- In 1982, he nullified the divisional corporate account system and its corresponding earned surplus. He said this drastic measure alone would reactivate the divisionalized organization.
- In 1983, he announced and started the companywide "Action- 61" plan.
- In 1984, Yamashita began merging and reorganizing the divisions, and restructuring the business groups.

**The radio and tape recorder divisions: a case of competition in the same territory.** The first part of the division reshuffle occurred in December 1984, when the radio and tape recorder divisions were merged to form the general audio division.

As mentioned in the previous section, Matsushita's divisionalized system had been organized on the basis of "one product for one division." Respect for division autonomy had prevailed throughout the organization. Many employees had worked for a certain division since it had started and would continue there until they retired. This organizational policy was effective while Japan's economy was in its high growth period and demand for products such as radios, TVs, washing machines, refrigerators, stereos, and so on was high. It allowed the company to gain high market shares in various product areas. As the economy's rapid growth slowed down, however, market diversification and technological compounding increased. A series of multifunctional products appeared — and many proved successful. Under such circumstances, corporate management found it necessary to reexamine its policy of "one product for one division."

A typical case was the competition for the radiocassette market within the radio and tape recorder divisions. Radiocassettes, called *radikase,* were regarded by the recorder division manager as a "radio with a tape recorder." The competition between these two divisions was considered greater than that between Matsushita and its competing manufacturers. To put an end to the competition, corporate management decided to merge the two divisions. There were three aims:

1. To eliminate the vain competition in the same market segment and conduct more efficient marketing activities.
2. To reduce costs substantially by improving the efficiency of the production processes. The tape recorder division, which had thoroughly integrated its parts production system, would be merged into the radio division, which was assembling purchased parts.
3. To shift human and engineering resources to new and growing areas. (This point was considered the most important point of all.)

**Structuring other business groups.** Triggered by the first successful consolidation, the company successively restructured its divisionalized organizations. The following are the major examples.

The new "motor division" was born out of the electric gears and the precision motor divisions. The major goal of this merger was to meet diversified demands for microprecision motors in promising new areas such as factory automation and office automation.

The business units of two TV divisions were reshuffled and the new TV division and visual equipment division were born. The new TV division would deal with the usual color and monochrome televisions; the visual equipment division would be in charge of CRT, CATV, video disk, laser disk, and so on. The latter's sales were expected to grow much faster than the former's for many years.

The divisions of electric oven, electric ricecooker, and rotisserie equipment were merged into a new electric cooking appliances division. The merger was part of a plan to enter new business areas such as electronics products for use in the home.

Along with restructuring these divisions, Matsushita also restructured the organizations of the marketing departments.

**Nullifying the Division Corporate Accounts.** In November 1982, Yamashita notified all division managers of the decision to write off most of their corporate account deposits (the accumulated surplus of net cash flow) and their earned surplus corresponding to the deposits. It was a complete surprise to the division managers. The total amount of these deposits from the divisions' balance sheets was almost ¥200 billion. This reduced the former balance of the corporate account by an average of 8 percent. According to a senior executive officer in charge of accounting and control, the major aims of this measure were:

1. To do something about the large amount of money that had accumulated in many divisions. For example, in the case of long-established divisions with mature product lines such as home appliances, the interest accrued from their deposits in corporate accounts sometimes exceeded the amount of their operating incomes.

2. To reactivate the productivity of divisions. "If the interest from your deposits amounted to as much as your operating income, you would not try as hard to increase your productivity," said the officer. "You would avoid risks such as developing new products."

Although the impact of these drastic measures differed according to division, it was true that most divisions faced more stringent financial situations than before. These measures seemed revolutionary to outsiders, but most Matsushita managers reportedly demonstrated a cooperative attitude toward the plan, believing it necessary to do anything to help the company. The radio division's chief accountant said, for example:

> Our division and others with a long operating history had large deposits in the corporate account. Therefore the nullification had considerable impact — but it was not severe. The profitability of the division has already been evaluated through operating income before adding the interest from the deposits... Before the divisions were merged, nullification measures had already begun, eliminating discussions about which division would gain most from the merger. Also, the new policy of crossdivisional personnel rotation had already gone into effect.

**Conclusion.** We have discussed what occurred at Matsushita during the decade with Yamashita as the company's driving force. We would like to make some additional observations.

The underlying philosophy of Matsushita's methods of solving its strategic management control problems seems to have been almost identical to the product/business portfolio management that GE developed. Yet, there also seems to be considerable differences in implementation between the two for attaining the strategic goals. We seldom heard the expression *product portfolio management* uttered by the top management of Matsushita during our research activities.

Our interpretation of this is that most U.S. corporations seem to regard each of their divisions as a component unit where *financial resources* are to be invested. Most Japanese corporations, including Matsushita, seem to regard a division as a component unit where *human resources* are invested. The top management of Japanese companies believes that the U.S. approach of product portfolio management, which aims at the effective allocation of financial resources, is not especially effective for solving management problems like those of Matsushita and GE.

Under the Japanese approach, with its principle of lifetime employment, the effective re-allocation of human resources is paramount for attaining the strategic goals already mentioned. Matsushita, as well as most other Japanese companies, operates from the standpoint of not expanding by purchasing growing businesses and not divesting itself of mature businesses.

Another aspect we would like to point out is that Matsushita has been called a "debt-free company" in the sense that the interest paid to the bank and other creditors is less than the interest income from its investment in securities and other financial assets. According to some commentators, the revolutionary measure of nullifying the division's corporate account was taken to take money from divisions in mature business areas and to reinvest it in more promising business units. But, in our opinion, this is not true. There was no need for management to void the deposits, because each division's accumulated cash flow was deposited in the corporate treasurer's office anyway. What worried corporate management was that they no longer had their investment in the home appliances area, with a few exceptions, such as the videocassette recorder. Therefore, by restructuring the divisionalized organization, they were promoting new business units in which to pour their capital resources.

Matsushita Electric did not re-allocate financial resources, rather it re-allocated human resources, which involves deliberate preparation over a period of time. That explains why Matsushita took a decade or more to solve the same kind of strategic management problems GE had.

### References

1. Anthony, R.N. Case: *General Electric Company (A)*. Harvard Business School.
2. Anthony, R.N., J. Dearden, and N.M. Bedford. (1984). *Management Control Systems*, 5th ed., Richard D. Irwin.
3. Fushimi, T. Case: *Matsushita Electric Industrial Co., Ltd.: Divisionalized Management Control*. Keio Business School.
4. Hino, S. (1982). *Matsushita keiri daigaku no hon*. Matsushita Accounting College.
5. Majima, H. (1978), *Matsushita denki no jigyobusei*. Divisionalized System of Matsushita.
6. Monden, Y. (1985). "Japanese Management Control Systems," in Y. Monden, R. Shibakawa, S. Takayanagi, and T. Nagao (eds.), *Innovations in Management: The Japanese Corporation*. Atlanta: IE & Management Press.
7. Nishizawa, O. (1981). *Koshueki no gendoryoku: Matsushita denki no jigyoubusei kaikei* (Motive Power for Big Profit: Divisional Accounting Systems at Matsushita), Part 102. *Diamond Harvard Business*.
8. Vancil, R.F. Case: *General Electric Company (B)*. Harvard Business School.
9. Yamaichi Securities Co., Ltd. (1981). *Matsushita denki no kenyu* (Research in Matsushita). Toyo-Keizai Shinposha.

# 26

## Characteristics of Performance Control Systems in Japanese Corporations

*Yasuhiro Monden, Institute of Socio-Economic Planning, University of Tsukuba*

An organization's performance control system, or management control system, is the system through which top management controls the decision making of middle management. Although there are many different types of performance control systems, the most important in Japan are the budget system, management by objectives, and the merit rating system. This chapter will examine the criteria to be used when designing these systems, the model for each type, and correlations between them. Characteristics of management control systems in Japanese corporations will be examined, with a focus on management by objectives.

*Criteria for Designing a Management Control System.* What criteria can be used when remodeling a management control system? The framework developed in the United States has two aspects: (1) a cost benefit analysis or alternative system, and (2) an analysis of each system's motivational effects.[1] A cost benefit analysis compares the cost and benefits of each system and indicates the one that produces the largest net effect. This criterion may seem obvious, but since convenience is often overemphasized, cost is not always given sufficient consideration. Analysis or the motivational effects of each system has two goals: (1) to secure goal agreement and (2) to promote managerial effort. Securing goal agreement means uniting personal and organizational goals. This includes making the goals of middle managers harmonious with those of senior managers. Promoting managerial effort means encouraging employees to work toward the organization's goal. Securing goal agreement does not necessarily guarantee subgoals that are in harmony with the organization's goals. Top management should plan a system that invites each manager to regard the company's subgoals as personal goals.

Let's look at the budget system. Division managers, for example, accept the profit budget of their own division, treating the measure of its performance as data for their own evaluation. In this way, the profit budget becomes a measure to secure goal agreement. From a motivational viewpoint, it is an important subsystem of the management control system. For the budget to be accepted by subordinate managers, however, other methods may be necessary. Management by objectives (MOB) plays an important role here. While the budget is based on data, the MOB goals are agreed upon by top and middle management. In this sense, management by objectives may be called a system that triggers an organization to meet its budget.[2]

It is important to adopt a system that has a favorable influence on effort and performance from the viewpoint of management control system planning. To better understand the criterion of "promoting effort," the expectancy theory regarding motivation is useful.[3] In expectancy theory, managers tend to have two kinds of expectations: effort-performance expectation and performance-reward expectation. Effort-performance (E-P) expectation is the expectation that a certain amount of effort will result in a certain level of performance. Performance-reward (P-R) expectation is the expectation of a certain reward when a certain level of performance is attained. Reward refers not only to a promotion, salary increase, or bonus, but also to the inner feeling of accomplishment and satisfaction. With both these expectations in mind, managers are motivated to invest effort for reward. Figure 26.1 shows this relationship.

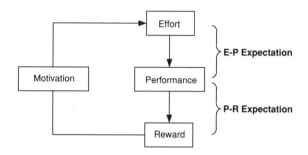

**Figure 26.1  Effort-Performance and Performance-Reward Expectations**

Because managers concentrate effort in areas where their performances are measured in E-P expectation, selecting standards for performance evaluation becomes important. In a budget system, determining the budget or standard level is crucial. In management by objectives, the method of evaluating objectives is important.

Since managers concentrate their efforts on areas where their performance influences their own reward in the case of P-R expectation, selecting a reward or incentive system is paramount. This falls under planning the merit system, which involves both ability and performance appraisals. More companies, however, are beginning to adopt results over performance evaluation as a management goal.[4]

The case of Tokyo Shibaura Denki Ltd. ("T company") will serve as an example of management by objectives involving both the traditional budget control and merit rating system within the framework of the management control system. We will first highlight the Japanese characteristics of management by objectives.

***Characteristics of Japan's Management by Objectives.*** Management by objectives (MOB) originated in the United States. Because of the strong individualistic U.S. tendency in business, MOB's applicability is apparently restricted to an individual manager level. In Japan, however, MOB is characteristically carried out with the cooperation of all the workers as well as their managers in an area.[5] We therefore call the U.S. version the "individualist type" and Japan's version the "group type." Some characteristics that seem typically Japanese will be extracted from the case of T company.

T company's management accounting system is fairly advanced. The company adopted the organizational system of profit centers run by operational divisions fully equipped to perform long- or middle-term profit planning and short-term budgetary control. The aim of this system is profit management. Rather than limiting participation to top management, it is necessary to involve workers at operational levels in the profit management system. MOB is a means to this end; it is a way to accomplish the objectives of the organization.

Combining individual desires or objectives with organizational objectives is also a motivational factor in MOB. The word motivation seems to refer mainly to monetary rewards in the United States. Inner rewards such as job satisfaction or a feeling of accomplishment are given greater importance in Japan. Monetary rewards are not discouraged; it is simply felt that inner motivation should come first.

One reason that the Japanese system of management is characterized as the group type is because of the tendency to break work areas into smaller units. Smaller units composed of six to eight people allow personal relationships to form among members. Organizational theory in the West is based on opposition between an organization and its individual members. In the Japanese business world, small groups are emphasized. These groups are supposed to help motivate both the organization and the individuals.

In allocating work, measures are used to make tasks interesting and to avoid excessive division of duties so that one person can plan, initiate, and see a project to its completion. This is called *job enrichment*. Another unique Japanese characteristic is the career development program (CDP). CDP is aimed at developing human abilities, and presupposes the lifetime employment system. Looking ahead approximately ten years, management develops a program that encourages a person's specialty. Accordingly, a job program approximately three years long is planned and revised yearly. As a result, MOB in Japan includes both individual development objectives and primary business objectives. A typical CDP card is shown in Table 26.1.

When a Japanese management control system is characterized as a group type, it should be noted that the system of communication within a work area is important. Communication in an organization is often limited to meetings among top management. In the West, it sometimes includes union representatives. Workers are informed of decisions without having participated in the decision-making process. If decisions are made by all members of a company, however, the probability of putting them into practice is higher. Group decisions are considered superior to individual decisions with respect to decision implementation in the T company. Because of this, meetings with attendance by all members are encouraged. Everyone related to an issue should attend the meeting, and the amount of information should be equal between managers and workers. Prior to making a decision, all members discuss the issue on an equal footing. When it is time to decide, the managers take responsibility for making the decision.

Before establishing objectives, a meeting attended by all members is held to discuss any problems, such as those in a division's business plan for the coming year or in a work area's budget for the next period. Such problems are singled out and categorized, and then middle managers determine the general objectives of their own divisions in counsel with top management. Next, they inform their managers of the scope of the requested items and general objectives, and then let their subordinates plan the details themselves. Based on these detailed objectives, objective cards are made and finalized by the managers and their subordinates. A general meeting is then held to present the objectives. (See Table 26.2 and Figure 26.2.)

When it is time to evaluate results, workers first evaluate themselves. Afterward, they hold a meeting with their supervisors. When they reach an agreement, the supervisors' evaluations are determined and written on the objective card. A meeting is then scheduled to present the results. Finally, the evaluation is utilized as reference data for merit ratings. Since objectives are established cooperatively with the participation of the entire work area, the phenomenon of cooperation by all participants is bound to be created at the stages of establishing, performing, and evaluating objectives even if an objective belongs to an individual.

| | | CDP card | | | | |
|---|---|---|---|---|---|---|
| Date of plan | Position at time of plan | CDP plan | | | | |
| | | 1st year | 2nd year | 3rd year | 4th year | 5th year |
| 1975 Nov. | Department of X<br><br>In charge of X | | Magnetron examination experiment | The same as left negative pole design | The same as left positive pole design | |
| 1976 Nov. | The same as above | | | The same as above | The same as above | Magnetron department of output design |
| 1977 Nov. | The same as above | | | | The same as above | The same as above |
| | | | | | | |

From Toshiba (ed.), *Monkuhyo kanri no shinko*, pp. 58-59

**Table 26.1 An Example of the CDP Card**

| | Name | | | | | |
|---|---|---|---|---|---|---|
| | | | | | | Development program (from the time of joining the company to 10 years after) |
| 6th year | 7th year | 8th year | 9th year | 10th year | | |
| | | | | | | |
| | | | | | | Magnetron general engineer |
| Magnetron magnetism design | | | | | | |
| | | | | | | |

| Nth term of the year | | | | Objective card |
|---|---|---|---|---|
| Field | Weight (from which) | Objectives (what) | Standards of Accomplishment (how much) | Policies for accomplishment (how) |
| Business Objectives | 30 | Drafting the plan of the system modification | 10/1 Present to a meeting of top management | Primary focus is on the issue of revising the divisionalized system |
| | 25 | Promotion of the facsimile network plan | The first term: Tokyo-Osaka | To compose a project team with the operational division |
| | 20 | Transfer of stock affairs to dealers | Complete the transfer by the end of the term | Total transfer Transfer of volunteer |
| | 15 | Revising rules on division duties | A trial will be made at the operational branch in Osaka | Establishing a revision committee whose primary concern is performance fields |
| | 10 | Rationalizing the service section | 15% personnel reduction | Concentrate on passenger cars and telephone |
| Self-improvement and development objectives | 50 | Dispatching staff section members to foreign law schools | Mr. Aoyama | Replacements must be graduates of next year's group |
| | 50 | Conducting study meetings concerning environmental relations | Once every other month | Lectures by specialists Discussion |
| | | | | |
| The process is midterm follow-up | Modification of objectives: None<br><br>State of progress: lack of efforts by the business division revision committee study meetings concerning environmental relations not yet held<br><br>Advisory item: contact between staff section and service section was encouraged | | | First term objectives |

From Toshiba (ed.), *Ibid.*, pp. 179-180

**Table 26.2  An Example of the Administration Department's Objective Card**

| | | Individuals | Groups | Section chief of the administration department | |
|---|---|---|---|---|---|
| Schedule (deadline) | | Contracting parties (with whom) | | Result evaluation (what is the result?) | |
| | | | | Self-evaluation | Evaluating supervisors |
| Research  Drafting  Presentation to top meeting ◄──►◄──►◄──► | | Top group | | A Ⓑ C  Research was insufficient | A Ⓑ C  Submitted data was insufficient |
| Establishing the  Preparation  Construction master schedule ◄──►◄──►◄──► | | Telecommunication operation division | | Ⓐ B C  Success | Ⓐ B C  Although successful, cost exceeded budget by 20% |
| Drafting  Negotiation  Preparation  Execution ◄──►◄──►◄──►◄──► | | X Trust Inc. | | Ⓐ B C  Finished successfully | Ⓐ B C  You did a good job |
| Research  Drafting a  Discussion  Execution meeting  tentative  and revision plan ◄──►◄──►◄──►◄──► | | Operational branch in Osaka | | A B Ⓒ  Unsatisfactory because of poor results | A B Ⓒ  Use this time's experience to redo it |
| Drafting  Negotiation  Execution ◄──►◄──►◄──► | | | | A Ⓑ C  Reduce personnel by 10% | A Ⓑ C  Fortunately, there was no trouble |
| Leave Japan  Matriculation ◄──►◄──► | | The education section | | Ⓐ B C  Everything proceeded according to the plan | Ⓐ B C  The vacancy needs to be filled until next spring. |
| Execution  Execution  Execution ◄──► ◄──► ◄──► | | The group outside the company | | A B Ⓒ  It was held only once due to difficulties in getting lecturers | A B Ⓒ |
| | | | | A B C | A B C |
| | Notes | | | | |

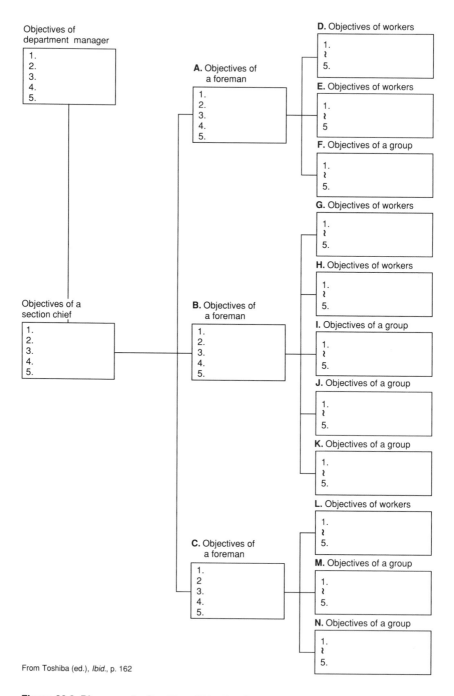

**Figure 26.2  Diagram of a One-Year Objective System**

## Notes

1. Horngren, C.T., *Cost Accounting: A Managerial Emphasis*, 5th ed. New York: Prentice-Hall, 1982.
2. Tokyo Shibaura Denki (ed.). *Mokuhyo kanri no shinko* (Establishing Roots of Management by Objectives). Aoba Shuppan, 1977, p. 33. While the budget is applied to the entire work area, the objectives are given to each individual. The budget expresses work in terms of money or volume. MOB involves the methods to attain it. Often, the budget offers the lowest degree of expected performance, while the objectives decide how much money will be given to a work area based on its efforts.
3. Lawler III, E.E. *Pay and Organizational Effectiveness: A Psychological View*. New York: McGraw-Hill, 1971. [Adachi, Hashio (trans.), *Kyoyo to sohiki koritsu* (Salary and Organizational Efficiency). Tokyo: Diamond Publ., 1972, pp. 150-155.]
4. Nihon Norisu Kyokai (ed.). *Saishin jinji koko to hyoka sisutem jisureishu* (Collected Examples of Current Merit Rating and Evaluation Systems). Nichino, 1983, p. 345. Although ability is evaluated when considering a promotion or raise in salary (i.e., "pay according to ability"), for bonuses, it is appropriate to stress the contribution of results to performance.
5. Examples of T company are drawn from the following books: Tokyo Shibaura Denki, (ed.). *Mokuhyo kanri jissen manual* (A Practical Manual of Management by Objectives) (revised). Sangyo Norisu University, 1972; Tokyo Shibaura Denki (ed.). *Mokuhyo kanri no shinko*.

   For the characteristics of the Japanese system of management by objectives, this paper is indebted to: Asao, Ko. "Mokuhyokanri no konnichiteki igi" ("The Present Significance of Management by Objectives"), in Nihon Keiei Gakkai (ed.), *Sangyo gijutsu no shintenkai to keikeikanri no kadai* (Development of New Industrial Technology and Management Themes). Chikura, 1983, pp. 208-214.

# 27

## Personnel Evaluation and Incentive Systems in Japanese Corporations

*Satoru Takayanagi, Institute of Socio-Economic Planning, University of Tsukuba*

In Japanese firms, there have been almost no differences in wage and promotion grades among employees having the same number of years of experience. Still fundamentally low in Japan, wages, bonuses, and promotions are determined by age and years of experience. In other words, Japanese corporations are still based on the so-called Japanese management system, consisting of lifetime employment and seniority. Without an objective and rational institutional incentive system, however, employees will not work hard in a modern society. In recent years, progressive firms have been making deliberate efforts to move gradually toward an incentive system that emphasizes performance and ability. To give incentives to individual employees, a corporation must evaluate each personally. Thus, the formal appraisal system is being introduced in Japan. This chapter will discuss incentive systems and formal appraisal systems in Japanese corporations.

***Japanese Incentive Systems.*** Japanese companies offer mainly two kinds of incentives to employees. One is pecuniary (wages and bonuses) and the other is promotion. In recent years, Japanese corporations have tried to manage their employees in such a way as to make them work as efficiently as possible. To attain this efficiency, it is necessary for the company to introduce a rational incentive system. Japanese corporations are still using the so-called Japanese management system, with lifetime employment and seniority system. Traditional Japanese incentive systems are based on broad social considerations and personal qualifications, such as age and education, rather than on the basis of the work performed or the employee's ability. Recently, many firms have tried to introduce a system that emphasizes performance and competence. So today's incentive systems in Japanese corporations are based both on the traditional seniority system and on job performance and ability. Generally, a corporate employee's salary level is determined by years of experience and education, but about 10 to 30 percent is determined by the employee's performance and ability.

**Salary and bonuses.** Japanese wages are determined primarily by seniority. An older employee gets a higher wage, even if his or her ability or performance level is low. Recently, however, Japanese companies have introduced an efficiency wage, or wage by job classification. According to government statistics, 13.8 percent of Japanese companies in 1980 determined employee wages solely by job classification and ability, 80.6 percent determined wages by both job classification and seniority, and only 5.6 percent determined wages solely by seniority.

The typical Japanese firm raises an employee's salary not only by considering years of experience and education, but also by performance and ability (real contribution and expected ability to contribute to the firm). On average, the best employee can get a 20-percent raise in salary compared to an average employee. The worst employee can get a 20-percent decrease in salary compared to an average employee. It means that if an average employee receives a 4-percent raise, then the best employee will get a 4.8-percent raise and the worst employee will get a 3.2-percent raise. The percentage increase or decrease is computed the same way for bonuses.

If an employee's salary is based on contribution to the firm, these methods of wage determination are curious. One wonders if the difference in salary between the best and worst employees is too small to be an incentive. But the Japanese believe that this 20-percent difference is enough incentive. A productive Japanese will feel appreciated by the firm and will expect future promotion.

**Promotion system.** In Japanese corporations, promotion is a more important incentive than salary and bonus. Almost all Japanese workers and officers work hard toward promotion to higher ranking jobs such as *kacho* (section head) and *bucho* (department head). Promotion guarantees, of course, higher salary and larger bonuses. So if employees want higher salaries, they must be promoted to higher ranking job.

As already mentioned, promotion is fundamentally based still on years of service and education, and on performance and ability. Employees who perform well and can be expected to perform a higher ranking job will be promoted, but in a certain limited traditional range. Even the best employee can be promoted to a higher position only two or three years earlier than the average employee.

To put the traditional promotion system in proper perspective, we shall introduce the traditional reward system as described by Yoshino. University education has been an important prerequisite for career advancement, and opportunities for those without college degrees have consequently been extremely limited. Within a given level of education, career advancement has been based on seniority. This is particularly true for the first ten to 15 years of an employee's career. In fact, seniority has been so rigidly observed that promotions to certain lower level managerial positions have been determined by the year of the employee's graduation from college, which, of course, corresponds to the year of entry into the firm. Prospective employees are carefully chosen from among the graduates of leading universities. In this sense, a minimum competence level is necessary for initial entry; however, individual differences in competence and ability within this group are ignored, at least for the initial phase of the individual's career. Essentially, everyone within the same category in terms of years of service and education level is treated the same. Thus, the entire personnel management program, including the reward system, in Japanese corporations is designed on a collective rather than on an individual basis.

The strong emphasis on seniority for promotion has meant that career advancement in Japan, although highly predictable, is extremely slow. There is some variance, but the general rule is that an employee must be with the company for at least eight to ten years before being promoted to the rank of subsection chief. It takes another several years before an employee is ready to become the chief of a section — the first managerial position of any significance. Fifteen to

20 years of seniority are required before an employee is promoted to the position of deputy of department head, the highest middle management status. Only managers in their early fifties are considered for top management positions.

But even in this rigid, seniority-based reward system, competence or ability is not totally ignored. Formal differentiation gradually becomes apparent after ten to 15 years of service, or at about the time the executive is considered for the position of section chief. Those who are extremely competent may advance to this position a year or two sooner than the normal rate, and they are likely to be put in charge of key sections. Although competence and performance become progressively important as one moves higher in the managerial hierarchy, these qualifications are always considered within the overriding seniority framework. There is a minimum acceptable age for every position, and even the most competent are not promoted before they reach the prescribed minimum age level. (See M. Y. Yoshino, [1968]. *Japan's Managerial System: Traditional and Innovation*. Cambridge, MA: MIT Press, pp. 236-237.)

Job rank in the corporation reflects social status. A corporate superior has a higher social status than a subordinate. *Bucho* has a higher status than *kacho*. *Kacho* has a higher status than a rank-and-file employee. White collar workers have a higher status than blue collar workers. An employee's family is also influenced by this corporate/social ranking.

**Characteristics of incentives in Japan.** Generally, nonmonetary incentives such as social status or fame are more important than monetary incentives. Even small relative differences are important for a Japanese employee, who expects results from incentives in the long run. In the short run, there are no or only small differences among employees, especially among young employees. But these small differences will make a large differences in the long run.

Fundamentally the Japanese want to be equal, even if there are large differences in ability and performance. The Japanese seniority system (lifetime employment and wage determination by years of service and rank) fit in with Japanese ideas of equality. The Japanese want to be equal, especially within the corporation. If an employee is not treated equally, he or she feels isolated from the other members. To keep employee loyalty to the corporation, the corporation must make each employee feel equal within the work group.

But to be efficient, we need to have an incentive system. A feeling of inequality sometimes makes people idle. When there is no difference in wage and promotion between competent and idle workers, a competent worker could become lazy. A Japanese business corporation seeks to increase efficiency and introduce effective incentive systems even in this atmosphere of equality Japanese society.

*Personal Evaluation.* To give incentives personally, it is necessary to evaluate employees individually. A personnel evaluation system must be established. In Japan, employees are evaluated by their corporations for decisions about promotions, job changes, pay raises and bonuses, and so on. In many corporations, these evaluations are done once a year and the results are used for many purposes, but in other corporations, different evaluations are done once or twice a year, each for different purposes.

**Personnel evaluation for raising salary and bonus.** 1. *Appraisal term and evaluator.* Generally speaking, personnel evaluations for raising salary are done twice a year (90 percent), and for deciding bonuses once a year (90 percent). Evaluators' are primary (a direct superior) and secondary superior (or a manager of personal department).

2. *Methods of evaluation.* In Japan, a corporation evaluates employees mostly by relative order, but an evaluations by absolute score are increasing. In 1983, out of 156 corporations, 50 used absolute scores. The most surprising fact is that the firms using the absolute evaluation method show better performance than the firms using relative evaluations. The average profit rate of the firms using absolute evaluations is higher.

What are the important items covered in an appraisal? Table 27.2 shows the results of our survey.

Employees in marketing or production are evaluated by performance. Marketing activity results directly reflect sales amounts, market

| | Absolute Evaluation | Relative Evaluation |
|---|---|---|
| Bonus | 6.23% | 4.64% |
| Raise in salary | 5.76% | 4.63% |

Profitability is gross profit divided by equity capital.

**Table 27.1  Evaluation and Profitability Methods**

| Job | Item | Bonus | Raise in Salary |
|-----|------|-------|-----------------|
| Plan, control | Goal attainment | 46.7% | 22.2% |
|  | Ability to perform job | 13.3 | 37.6 |
| Marketing | Sales amount | 73.0 | 61.2 |
|  | Market share | 17.0 | 30.2 |
|  | Profitability | 55.5 | 46.5 |
| Production | Production amount | 43.9 | 36.8 |
|  | Cost reduction | 78.9 | 66.9 |
|  | Shortening of production period | 31.7 | 28.1 |
|  | Quality control | 64.2 | 58.8 |

**Table 27.2 Survey Results**

share, and profitability. Production activity results reflect product amounts, cost reduction, and shortening of production period.

Firms using sales or product amounts as important evaluation items show low performance (low profitability and low growth rate). On the other hand, firms using shortening of production period as an important evaluation item show high performance (high profitability and high growth rate). From this fact, to attain efficiency in Japan, firms must not evaluate employees by sales amounts or production, but by shortening of production period, and so on. (See Table 27.3.)

**Personnel evaluation for promotion.** Evaluations are done in almost all corporations (89 percent) once a year. One of the most important functions of the personnel department is to coordinate and check personnel data.

1. *Method of personnel appraisal.* The percentage of firms using self-appraisal is about 10 percent. The percentage using absolute evaluation is 50 percent (71 out of 143), and this percentage is higher in the case of bonus and salary than in promotion. Performance of the company using absolute appraisals is higher than those using relative appraisals.

   Evaluation items that Japanese firms think are important for promotion are ability to perform job and ability to manage subordinates well. Other items such as expert knowledge, manner of performing job, and ability to plan are also considered. In short, the most important appraisal item is not real performance, but the

| | | Use | Do Not Use |
|---|---|---|---|
| Sales amount in marketing department | Profitability | 4.18% | 5.91% |
| | Growth rate | 119.38 | 128.45 |
| Production amount in production department | Profitability | 4.60 | 5.89 |
| | Growth rate | 116.86 | 126.93 |
| Shortening of production period in production department | Profitability | 7.18 | 4.76 |
| | Growth rate | 128.52 | 121.30 |

**Table 27.3 Performance Differences Between Firms Using or Not Using the Following Items When Evaluating Employees for Salary Raises**

expected ability to perform job and manage subordinates well. For promotion, important evaluation criteria include:

| | |
|---|---|
| Ability to perform job | 92.7% |
| Ability to manage subordinates | 80.8 |
| Results of performance | 68.2 |
| Expert knowledge | 48.3 |
| Ability to plan | 45.0 |
| Manner of performing job | 41.1 |
| Years of service | 39.7 |
| Examination for promotion | 18.5 |

**Table 27.4 Important Evaluation Criteria**

2. *Examination for promotion.* Some firms in Japan (24 percent) have examinations for promotion. In these firms, examinations are necessary requirements for promotion. Qualifications for taking the examination is usually the superior's recommendation. The examination consists mainly of an interview, writing an essay, and other written examinations about professional subjects.

**Job Rotation and Promotion.** In Japan, promotion means changing to a new, higher ranking job. So job rotation is seen by employees as a step to promotion. Job rotation for one employee (in the case of an officer) occurs on average every five years. For example, an employee rotated to the position of *kacho* will rotate to another job after five years of service. The job rotation interval is shorter (an average of four years) in large corporations (over 5,000 employees) than in smaller corporations (under 1,000 employees) — an average of six years. (See Table 27.4 on previous page.)

| | Company Size | | | |
| --- | --- | --- | --- | --- |
| | Small | Medium | Large | Average |
| General staff | 6.16 | 5.26 | 4.09 | 5.17 |
| Marketing | 6.10 | 5.00 | 3.91 | 4.97 |
| Production | 6.27 | 4.87 | 4.28 | 5.50 |
| Research | 7.59 | 6.12 | 5.19 | 6.22 |

**Table 27.5  Average Number of Years a Manager Stays in the Same Post in Japan**

Note in Table 27.6 that corporations with a job rotation interval near average show clearly higher performance (high profitability and growth rate) than those with a shorter or longer job rotation interval.

| | | Rotation Interval | | | |
| --- | --- | --- | --- | --- | --- |
| | | Short | Mid | Long | Average |
| General staff | Profitability | 4.7% | 5.8% | 5.7% | 5.4% |
| | Growth rate | 127.6 | 126.7 | 118.0 | 124.8 |
| Marketing | Profitability | 4.7 | 6.8 | 4.1 | 5.3 |
| | Growth rate | 125.4 | 129.0 | 116.5 | 124.8 |
| Production | Profitability | 5.5 | 4.5 | 6.4 | 5.3 |
| | Growth rate | 126.7 | 125.6 | 118.1 | 124.5 |
| Research | Profitability | 3.3 | 5.3 | 6.7 | 5.4 |
| | Growth rate | 121.7 | 129.4 | 123.3 | 125.4 |

(Data shown are taken from our survey about Japanese personnel appraisal system, 1984.)

**Table 27.6  Rotation Interval and Corporate Performance**

# 28

# Internal Auditing in Japan: A Survey

*Shigeo Aoki, School of Business, Asia University*
*Michiharu Sakurai, School of Business, Senshu University*

This chapter highlights the present state of internal auditing in Japan based on "The Statement of Responsibilities of Internal Auditing" and the 1985 survey on internal auditing in Japan. This was the sixth survey following the 1982 survey conducted by the Internal Auditors Association of Japan. These kinds of surveys have been conducted every three years since 1961. Dr. Aoki was the chairman.

The Institute of Internal Auditors (IIA), with headquarters in the United States, first issued "The Statement of Responsibilities of Internal Auditing" in 1947. It was later revised several times. The 1981 revision states the nature, objective, and scope of the internal auditor.

Internal auditing is an independent appraisal activity established within an organization as a service to the organization. It is a control that examines and evaluates the adequacy and effectiveness of other controls.

The objective of internal auditing is to assist members of the organization in the effective discharge of their responsibilities. To this end, internal auditing furnishes them with analyses, appraisals, recommendations, counsel, and information concerning the activities reviewed. The audit objective includes promoting effective control at a reasonable cost.

The scope of internal auditing encompasses the examination and evaluation of the adequacy and effectiveness of the organization's system of internal control and the quality of performance in carrying out assigned responsibilities. The scope of internal auditing includes:

• Reviewing the reliability and integrity of financial and operating information and the means used to identify, measure, classify, and report such information.
• Reviewing the systems established to ensure compliance with those policies, plans, procedures, laws, and regulations that could have a significant impact on operations and reports, and determining whether or not the organization is in compliance.
• Reviewing the means of safeguarding assets and, as appropriate, verifying the existence of such assets.
• Appraising the economy and efficiency with which resources are employed.
• Reviewing operations or programs to ascertain whether results are consistent with established objectives and goals and whether the operations or programs are carried out as planned.

This statement of responsibility is completely understood and practiced in Japan.

**The Survey Results and Our Comments.** The 1985 survey for internal auditors in Japan received 421 responses. Over the years, the response rate shows a steady increase:

| | |
|---|---|
| 1970 survey | 157 companies |
| 1973 survey | 160 companies |
| 1976 survey | 208 companies |
| 1979 survey | 280 companies |
| 1982 survey | 361 companies |
| 1985 survey | 421 companies |

There were 18 types of industries represented and the results were close to those in similar categories in the Tokyo stock market. The manufacturing sector represented 57 percent of the responses, with 252 companies participating. A comparison with previous surveys follows:

| Types of Industry | 1979 | 1982 | 1985 |
|---|---|---|---|
| Manufacturing | 175 (62.5%) | 206 (57%) | 252 (57%) |
| Non-manufacturing | 105 (37.5%) | 155 (43%) | 179 (43%) |

The majority of responding companies had a large number of employees and sizable capital stock:

| Number of Employees | Number of companies and Percentage of respondents | |
|---|---|---|
| Less than 1,000 | 89 | 21.9% |
| 1,000-3,000 | 135 | 33.2 |
| 3,001-5,000 | 61 | 15.0 |
| 5,001-10,000 | 55 | 13.5 |
| Over 10,000 | 66 | 16.2 |

| Size of capital stock | Number of companies and Percentage of respondents | |
|---|---|---|
| Under ¥ 10 million | 57 | 14.5% |
| ¥ 11-50 million | 126 | 32.1 |
| ¥ 51-100 million | 58 | 14.8 |
| ¥ 101-500 million | 114 | 29.1 |
| Over ¥ 501 million | 37 | 9.4 |

**Organization.** Internal auditors in Japanese companies operate in one of two ways:

1. The internal auditor may either (a) belong to an independent department (see Figure 28.1) or (b) become part of an already established department with equal rank compared to other departments (see Figure 28.2).
2. The internal auditor may report to upper management in the form of (a) the chairman, president, or vice president; or (b) the statutory auditor. (See Figure 28.3.)

The survey definitely shows the second type as most prevalent, and the trend continuing to grow:

| To whom does the internal auditor report? | Number of companies and Percentage of respondents | |
|---|---|---|
| (1) Equal standing with other departments | 148 | 35.1% |
| (a) An independent department | 99 | 23.5 |
| (b) A regular department | 49 | 11.6 |
| (2) Reports to upper management | 273 | 64.9 |
| (a) Chairman, president, vice president | 252 | 60.0 |
| (b) Statutory auditor | 21 | 4.9 |

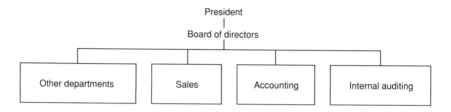

**Figure 28.1 Internal Auditing as an Independent Department**

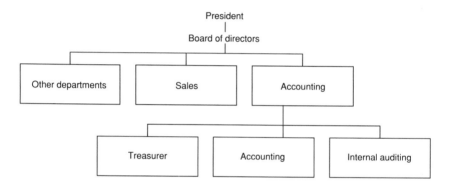

**Figure 28.2 Internal Auditing as Part of an Established Department**

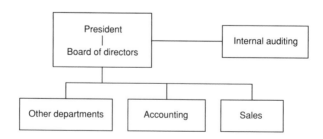

**Figure 28.3 Internal Auditing Reporting to Upper Management**

This trend may be due to:

1. The internal auditor reports to upper management.
2. The operational auditor covers the main scope of internal auditing.
3. Internal auditing is growing in independence and stature.

*How many internal auditors are there per company?* The number of internal auditors differs from company to company, especially according to size (capital stock) and type of industry (for example, banking and insurance), but has no relation to the number of employees. The following shows the average number of internal auditors in major industries.

| Industry | Average Number of Internal Auditors | | |
|---|---|---|---|
| | 1-6 | 7-15 | 16 + |
| Chemical | 27 | 1 | 0 |
| Bank & insurance | 11 | 13 | 16 |
| Iron & metal | 19 | 7 | 1 |
| Gas & electric | 3 | 7 | 1 |
| Commerce | 43 | 9 | 6 |
| Transportation | 3 | 6 | 2 |
| Construction | 31 | 5 | 0 |

*What was the internal auditor's former experience?* The following results are from the 1979 survey. Since internal auditing developed out of accounting or financial auditing, it is only natural that most internal auditors started in accounting departments. Today, with the scope of internal auditing extending to operations auditing, many internal auditors come from various functional departments.

| | Percentage of Companies Surveyed |
|---|---|
| Accounting | 86.1% |
| Marketing | 51.9 |
| Labor | 35.1 |
| Research & development | 24.0 |
| General management | 26.9 |
| Purchasing | 22.6 |
| Production | 14.9 |
| EDP | 11.5 |
| New employee | 5.8 |
| Other | 5.8 |

**Internal audit program.** The most important function of the audit program is to determine what theme should be put into effect and how. The survey showed the following results:

*How is the audit theme determined?*

|  | Number of Companies and | Percentage of Respondents |
|---|---|---|
| Internal auditor decides | 154 | 36.6% |
| Upper management suggests | 64 | 15.2 |
| Internal auditor decides theme at upper management's request | 262 | 62.2 |
| Internal auditor decides from proposals of operating departments | 34 | 8.1 |

*Where did the ideas come from?* In the case of Japanese management, discussing issues with other departments is much more important than analyzing one's own department:

|  | Number of Companies and | Percentage of Respondents |
|---|---|---|
| Upper management | 220 | 52.3% |
| Operating department | 194 | 46.1 |
| Auditing department or working paper | 187 | 44.4 |
| Management data | 79 | 18.8 |
| Records | 58 | 13.8 |
| Conferences | 53 | 12.6 |
| Previous managers | 40 | 9.5 |
| Process charts | 25 | 5.9 |
| Other companies | 19 | 4.5 |
| Rumor | 16 | 3.8 |

*What time period does the audit program cover?* The audit program covers about the same length of time as the accounting period. For many Japanese companies, this is still 6 months.

|  | Number of Companies and | Percentage of Respondents |
|---|---|---|
| 1 year | 311 | 84.0% |
| 6 months | 50 | 13.5 |
| Individual audit program | 9 | 2.5 |

*Who gives final approval to the audit program?* The results of the survey show that internal auditors are becoming an integral part of the management team. They are usually consulted when upper management decides the audit program, and thereby receive more recognition.

|  | Number of Companies and Percentage of Respondents | |
| --- | --- | --- |
| President | 242 | 64.7% |
| Executive in charge of audit department | 51 | 13.6 |
| Executive committee | 36 | 9.6 |
| Head of audit department | 29 | 7.4 |
| Others | 16 | 4.7 |

**Internal auditing methods.** Before beginning an audit, the head of internal auditing usually notifies the department involved.

|  | Number of Companies and Percentage of Respondents | |
| --- | --- | --- |
| Head of internal auditing notifies the head of department to be audited | 335 | 80.7% |
| Person in charge of audit notifies the department | 42 | 10.1 |
| President notifies the department | 31 | 7.5 |
| Others | 7 | 1.7 |

*Who gathers and analyzes the necessary data during the audit?* In most cases, the internal auditing department gathers and analyzes data, but many companies do it with the help of the department audited.

|  | Number of Companies and Percentage of Respondents | |
| --- | --- | --- |
| Internal auditing department | 245 | 59.9% |
| Audited department | 10 | 1.2 |
| Combination of the two | 162 | 38.9 |

*Is a checklist used?* In the United States, a checklist may be a necessity. In Japan, there is much discussion about its merit and demerits. When the checklist is used properly, it is advantageous. In fact, the number of companies using a checklist is increasing. Of the companies surveyed, for example, the increase was from 54 percent in 1982 to 56.8 percent in 1985. In the industry category, banking and insurance (38 companies, 95 percent) and electrical appliance (26 companies, 70.2 percent) were the leading users.

**Reports.** Internal auditors generally meet with the management of the audited department to discuss findings and recommendations before submitting the final report:

|  | Number of Companies and | Percentage of Respondents |
|---|---|---|
| Yes | 358 | 85.1% |
| No | 63 | 14.9 |

"The Statement of Responsibilities of Internal Auditing" says the following about independence:

> Internal auditors should be independent of the activities they audit in order to work freely and objectively. This independence allows internal auditors to render the impartial judgments essential to a good audit and is achievable through organizational status and objectivity.
>
> Organizational status should be sufficient to assure (1) a broad range of audit coverage, and (2) adequate consideration of and effective action on audit findings and recommendations.
>
> Objectivity requires that internal auditors have an independent mental attitude and an honest belief in their product. Drafting procedures, designing, installing, and operating systems are not audit functions. Such activities are presumed to impair audit objectivity.

We believe that discussion of the findings and recommendations is essential for effective internal auditing. Concerning the independence of internal auditing, we surveyed the following questions:

*Does the report include suggestions for corrective procedures?* Although such suggestions are not essential in an audit report, they usually contain them:

|  | Number of Companies and | Percentage of Respondents |
|---|---|---|
| Yes | 187 | 44.4% |
| Yes, when necessary | 210 | 49.9 |
| No | 24 | 5.7 |

*When must the report be submitted?* Reports must be timely. This is the main principle of internal reporting and, in the case of internal auditing, is imperative. Our survey found:

|  | Number of Companies and | Percentage of Respondents |
|---|---|---|
| Within 6 days | 115 | 28.3% |
| Within 2 weeks | 162 | 39.9 |
| Within 1 month | 104 | 25.6 |
| Over 1 month | 25 | 6.2 |

*To which senior executives is the report distributed?* In most cases, the report is distributed to the president or chairman of the board.

|  | *Number of Companies and*<br>*Percentage of Respondents* | |
|---|---|---|
| To the president or chairman of the board | 160 | 76.9% |
| To the executive officer in charge of<br>the internal audit | 21 | 10.1 |
| To the board of directors | 18 | 8.7 |
| Other | 9 | 4.3 |

*Are the managers of the unit audited given a copy of the report?*

|  | *Number of Companies and*<br>*Percentage of Respondents* | |
|---|---|---|
| Yes | 322 | 76.5% |
| Yes, when necessary | 65 | 15.3 |
| No | 34 | 8.2 |

*To whom are audit reports sent?* Audit reports are usually sent to the president, and in some companies, to executives or statutory auditors:

|  | *Number of Companies and*<br>*Percentage of Respondents* | |
|---|---|---|
| President | 313 | 74.4% |
| Upper management | 46 | 10.9 |
| Administrators of internal audits | 87 | 20.7 |
| Statutory auditors | 71 | 16.9 |

*Are followups conducted?* Following the release of an audit report, followup or corrective action taken by the audited department should be confirmed. This survey indicated the following:

|  | *Number of Companies and*<br>*Percentage of Respondents* | |
|---|---|---|
| Yes | 204 | 98.1% |
| No | 4 | 1.9 |

*How long are audit reports held?* Most companies do not hold audit reports for a specific length of time. Others, however, hold them for over 10 years.

|  | *Number of Companies and*<br>*Percentage of Respondents* | |
|---|---|---|
| Undecided | 88 | 42.3% |
| Forever | 39 | 18.8 |
| 10 years and over | 43 | 20.7 |
| Up to 9 years | 35 | 16.8 |

**Management audit.** In Japan, many internal auditors wish to have greater recognition for themselves and their position. Some want management to expand the scope of the internal audit. For this reason, they actively promote management audits, which go beyond the usual operations audit. Following is the 1979 survey of the opinions of internal auditors.

*Do you think management and operations audits differ from each other?* Most internal auditors believe they are not the same. About one-third of the internal auditors, however, believe they are identical:

|  | Number of Companies and Percentage of Respondents | |
| --- | --- | --- |
| Yes | 103 | 69.7% |
| No | 45 | 30.3 |

*How does the management audit differ from the operations audit?* There are differences of opinion on the concept of the management audit.

|  | Number of Companies and Percentage of Respondents | |
| --- | --- | --- |
| Includes an audit of upper management's planning and policy | 67 | 65.0% |
| Should be a systematic, general approach | 59 | 57.8 |
| Uses scientific audit techniques | 4 | 3.9 |
| Requires creative thinking on the auditor's part | 5 | 4.0 |

*What is the scope of an audit on upper management's planning and policy?*

|  | Number of Companies and Percentage of Respondents | |
| --- | --- | --- |
| To confirm the execution of planning and policy | 39 | 58.2% |
| To offer suggestions | 25 | 37.2 |
| To evaluate the adequacy of planning and policy | 25 | 37.3 |

**Cooperation with the CPA audit.** In Japan, a SEC audit by a certified public accountant (CPA) has been compulsory since 1951. Financial statement audits from 1951 to 1956 were imperfect, considering the present-day situation. Progress was made during this time, however, as companies developed internal control systems. In this part of the survey, we considered the relationship and cooperation between internal auditing and the CPA audit. Both internal and external auditing have their functions, but it has been recognized in the past that internal auditing activities influence the extent of the CPA audit program. This has brought a reduction in the time and scope of the public accountant's activities. The 1986 survey showed, however, that cooperation between internal and external auditing is not strong:

|  | Number of Companies and Percentage of Respondents | |
|---|---|---|
| Yes | 136 | 34.1% |
| No | 262 | 65.9 |

*Are copies of internal audit reports sent to the CPA?*

|  | Number of Companies and Percentage of Respondents | |
|---|---|---|
| Yes | 25 | 6.1% |
| Yes, when the CPA requests them | 90 | 22.3 |
| No | 289 | 71.6 |

The reason for this lack of cooperation may be due to the internal auditor's emphasis on the operations audit and the CPA's emphasis on completeness.

**Auditing the information systems.** Recent developments in the field of information processing have brought about the necessity of auditing information systems. Although a majority of the large Japanese companies use highly sophisticated computers, the development of the information systems audit is inferior to the American standard.

*What department enforces the audit of information systems?*

|  | Number of Companies and Percentage of Respondents | |
|---|---|---|
| Internal audit department | 106 | 25.3% |
| Other departments | 8 | 1.9 |
| Internal audit department cooperating with other departments | 25 | 5.9 |
| No audit at present | 282 | 66.9 |

*Does your company have a special staff for information systems audits?*

Number of Companies and
Percentage of Respondents

| | | |
|---|---|---|
| Yes | 24 | 22.6% |
| Under consideration | 11 | 10.7 |
| No | 71 | 66.7 |

*What is the main purpose of the information systems audit?*

Number of Companies and
Percentage of Respondents

| | | |
|---|---|---|
| Safety | 76 | 54.7% |
| Reliability | 88 | 64.0 |
| Effectiveness | 79 | 56.8 |

*What is the main coverage of the information systems audit?*

Number of Companies and
Percentage of Respondents

| | | |
|---|---|---|
| Maintenance control of the data file | 86 | 61.9% |
| Utilization of output data | 85 | 61.1 |
| Internal control of system itself | 77 | 55.4 |
| Input control | 73 | 52.5 |
| EDP systems security | 73 | 52.5 |
| Equipment maintenance | 68 | 48.9 |
| Output control | 61 | 43.9 |
| Organization of the systems department | 58 | 41.7 |
| Systems planning, design, and development | 55 | 39.7 |
| On-line controls | 44 | 31.7 |
| Cost control of systems department | 44 | 31.7 |
| Microcomputer | 9 | 6.5 |

**The relationship between internal and statutory auditors.** The auditing systems in Japanese companies are more complicated than those of the United States. Public companies have the following audits:

1. CPA audit according to SEC rules.
2. Audit according to the Commercial Law (statutory auditor is one of the officers of the company). This audit consists of an accounting and an operational audit. When the company's paid-in capital is over ¥500 million, a CPA audit by Commercial Law is also required.
3. Internal audit.

Japanese companies have problems coordinating these three audits. Before the Commercial Law was revised in 1974, its statutory audit was only a formality, except in a few companies. At present, however, many companies are trying to activate the Commercial Law's statutory audit. Because the three audits have different aims, as much duplication as possible should be eliminated.

*How do statutory auditors organize their staff?*

| | Number of Companies and Percentage of Respondents | |
|---|---|---|
| Full-time staff | 107 | 25.4% |
| Some internal auditors assist | 65 | 15.4 |
| All internal auditors assist | 57 | 13.6 |
| No staff | 192 | 45.6 |

*Do statutory auditors have an auditor's manual for their own use?*

| | Number of Companies and Percentage of Respondents | |
|---|---|---|
| Yes | 276 | 65.6% |
| Under consideration | 34 | 8.1 |
| No | 111 | 26.3 |

*What is the scope of the statutory auditor's operation?*

| | Number of Companies and Percentage of Respondents | |
|---|---|---|
| Accounting, operations, and subsidiary and affiliated company audits | 260 | 65.0% |
| Accounting and operations audits | 112 | 28.0 |
| Operations audit only | 16 | 4.0 |
| Accounting audit only | 12 | 3.0 |

*Is there cooperation between statutory and internal auditors?*

| | Number of Companies and Percentage of Respondents | |
|---|---|---|
| Yes | 147 | 36.1% |
| No | 261 | 63.9 |

The results indicate that duplication exists among statutory auditors, CPAs, and internal auditors.

**Conclusion.** Internal auditing practices in Japan are progressing. The organization in Japan that promotes internal auditing is the Tokyo Chapter of the Institute of Internal Auditors (IIA-Japan). It has been active in installing and developing internal auditing in this country. Several problems, however, must be overcome:

1. Improvement of the internal auditor's abilities.
2. Expansion of the operations audit into a management audit.
3. Promotion of the information systems audit.
4. Cooperation among the internal auditors, CPAs, and statutory auditors.

We believe that internal auditing in Japan will improve greatly when these problems are solved.

# PART V

## Other Topics

# 29

# Applying Quantitative Methods to Cost and Management Accounting Practices: A U.S.–Japanese Comparison*

*Yutaka Kato, School of Management, Kobe University*

A large amount of research concerning the application of quantitative methods, including those of management science and statistical analysis, to cost and management accounting decisions has been conducted in the past 30 years. Between the late 1960s and early 1970s, the so-called user decision-model approach was dominant both in the United States and Japan.[1] Most researchers devoted their efforts to developing more efficient and effective quantitative models to improve management planning and control activities. Nevertheless, this approach has had little influence on today's accounting research.

* The Japan Industrial Management and Accounting Institute (Sangyo-Keiri Kyoukai) provided research support for the U.S. research; Japan's Ministry of Education for the Japanese research. The U.S. research was conducted while the author was a Fulbright Scholar at the School of Business Administration, University of North Carolina at Chapel Hill. E. Blocher, R.L. Brummet, Chee W. Chow, R.S. Kaplan, and M.W. Maher made constructive comments on the questionnaire. An earlier draft of this chapter was reviewed by participants in management accounting workshops at Kobe University in Japan.

One possible explanation for the decreasing research output via the user decision-model approach is that other disciplines, such as *the information economics studies* and/or *the agency theory* applications, in cost and management accounting studies have been emerging rapidly in recent years.[2] Another possible explanation for the limited impact of the user decision-model approach is that there may be few remaining applicable problems or topics of quantitative methods to research. Does a decreasing level of research output directly lead to the applicability of the user decision-model approach? Has this approach had little impact on the business decision?

It is a well-known criticism from advocates of the information evaluation approach that the user decision-model articles do not consider costs and benefits of decision models explicitly.[3] It is true that most of the research done according to this approach has neglected crucial problems in practice. We have developed many decision models without explicitly examining whether they are worth applying to real business problems. Costly models that require nonexistent data and/or that are based on tight statistical and mathematical assumptions never satisfied will not work.

Against these assertions, we think the user decision-model approach still has potential and will generate fruitful outcomes. But it is necessary to know whether research based on this approach is worth executing. We seldom know what kind of cost and management accounting decisions are suitable for quantitative applications. If we could know the real business problems, there would be great possibility in pursuing this approach as one of the accounting research methods. We must recognize the accountants' perceptions for quantitative methods. We also have to know the extent that quantitative methods are used.

Although a number of studies have investigated the use of quantitative methods in industry, few provide an in-depth analysis.[4] We really know little of what has been done in practice concerning cost and management accounting activities, especially when it comes to the application of quantitative methods.

The research presented here provides a comprehensive analysis of quantitative method application in current business practice both in Japan and the United States.[5] Research results are also supported empirically. Analyses featuring these two characteristics are few. Therefore, we believe this chapter will provide an opportunity to know the current cost and management accounting practices in both countries. From this study, we can also obtain information to assess the applicability of the user decision-model approach.

*Research Methodology.* Research methodology is almost identical between the Japanese and U.S. studies. Therefore, the results from both groups are quite similar. Summary of two research outlines is provided in Table 29.1.

Analytical readings of the studies based on the user decision-model approach and the comprehensive examination of contemporary cost and management accounting textbooks were conducted to write questions included in questionnaires.[6] After several revisions, the questionnaires were printed in final form.[7]

|  | Japan | United States |
|---|---|---|
| Population | 629 companies listed with Tokyo Security Exchange (first section) as of November 20, 1985 | Fortune 500 companies (1984) |
| Supporting Organization of the Study | Management Accounting Workshop (Graduate School of Business Administration, Kobe University) | Center for Accounting and Auditing Research (University of North Carolina at Chapel Hill) |
| Date of Questionnaire | November 25, 1985 | May 15, 1984 |
| Deadline for Reply | January 20, 1986 | July 19, 1984 |
| Title of Person to Whom Questionnaire Was Addressed | Accounting Executives | Accounting Executives |
| Anonymity of Respondent | Not considered | Considered |
| Contents of Research Packet | Questionnaire  Prestamped envelope  Letter of research  request | Questionnaire  Prestamped envelope  Letter of research  request  Return post card |

**Table 29.1 Summary of Research Outlines**

The questionnaire used in the United States is ten pages long and has 47 questions. The Japanese questionnaire is 14 pages long with 66 questions. It includes all the questions contained in the U.S. version. Questions are categorized as follows: costing systems and cost classification, CVP analysis, standard cost system, cost allocation (service department costs, joint and by-product costs, and overhead), variance investigation decisions, capital budgeting, decision support systems, general questions on quantitative methods, and demographic information of companies and respondents. Questions appearing in the Japanese questionnaire only focused on microcomputers, organizational factors, and so on.

|  |  | Maximum | Minimum | Average |
|---|---|---|---|---|
| Sales ($, thousands) | Japan | 42,429,466 | 57,593 | 1,984,800 |
|  | U.S. | 40,180,000 | 520,180 | 3,682,562 |
| Total Assets ($, thousands) | Japan | 24,060,000 | 68,000 | 1,934,000 |
|  | U.S. | 37,243,000 | 86,585 | 3,052,307 |
| Number of Employees | Japan | 80,084 | 191 | 6,637 |
|  | U.S. | 369,545 | 818 | 33,956 |

* $1.00 = ¥ 150

**Table 29.2  Summary Information of Respondents in Japan and the United States**

Each accounting executive was sent a research packet including an individually addressed cover letter explaining the research project.[8] The mailing resulted in 125 replies out of 500 in the U.S. (25 percent) and 168 out of 629 in Japan (26.7 percent). Of these, 103 usable completed questionnaires (20.6 percent) were received in the United States and all replies in Japan were usable. Tables 29.2 and 29.3 show summary information about respondents. The chi-square goodness-of-fit test of the sample distribution to the population distribution were conducted. We could observe a minor bias in the samples toward the larger companies in scale measures, but there were no statistically significant differences in terms of the several scale measures (sales, total assets, and number of employees) and among industry group.

Therefore, we could infer from our samples what has been occurring in Japanese and U.S. companies. No additional attempt to increase the sample was made because the samples seemed to distribute well.

### Quantitative Methods in Cost and Management Accounting Activities.

To what extent are the largest Japanese and U.S. companies utilizing quantitative methods in cost and management accounting activities? Research results appeared in Table 29.4.

We treat companies that score 2 or less on the seven-point Likert scale as the no/little users for each technique, between 3 and 5 as the moderate users, and 6 or more as the extensive users. Adoption rate of each method was measured by the ratio of number of companies that score 4 or more on the Likert scale to the whole. Even though we count the adoption rate of each technique conservatively, the adoption rates in the U.S. companies are high except for waiting lines (queuing theory): 55.9 percent for simulation, 2 percent for waiting lines (queuing theory), 69.9 percent for forecasting techniques, 38.2 percent for probabilities and decision theory, 61.8 percent for statistical analysis (CPM and PERT), 65.7 percent for inventory models, 35.6 percent for linear programming, 22.5 percent for mathematical programming (other than linear programming), and 31.4 percent input-output analysis. The reason for the low adoption rate for waiting lines may be its lesser applicability to cost and management accounting activities. They are applied mainly to production management, operation management, or some other fields.

Reviewing Table 29.4, it can be easily found that the U.S. firms are the heavier users of quantitative methods than the Japanese counterparts. In both countries, we found a tendency toward quantitative methods. Among the various quantitative methods, simulation, forecasting techniques, statistical analysis, and inventory models are the relatively more widely used techniques in both countries.

Strong correlation between the extent of current use and the degree of satisfaction for each method was observed in both countries.[9] This indicates that the more extensively a technique is utilized, the higher the satisfaction with its use.

*Future Use.* Are there any tendencies to adopt quantitative methods more extensively in the future? We observed a strong correlation between the extent of current use and the extent of future use for each technique in both countries. The Wilcoxon's signed rank test

| SIC Code | Industrial Group | Japan | | United States | |
|---|---|---|---|---|---|
| | | Number of Companies | Number of Respondents | Number of Companies | Number of Respondents |
| 10 | Metal Mining | 7 | 1 | 10 | 1 |
| 20 | Food and Related Products | 52 | 14 | 68 | 11 |
| 21 | Tobacco Manufacturers | — | — | 3 | 2 |
| 22 | Textile Mill Products | 42 } | 11 } | 10 | 1 |
| 23 | Apparel and Other Finished Products | | | 12 | 2 |
| 24 | Lumber and Wood Products | | | 10 | 2 |
| 25 | Furniture and Fixtures | 18 } | 5 } | 1 | 1 |
| 26 | Paper and Related Products | | | 19 | 3 |
| 27 | Printing, Publishing, and Products | | | 19 | 2 |
| — | Medicines and Medical Equipment | 44 | 15 | — | — |
| 28 | Chemical and Allied Products | 69 | 24 | 72 | 15 |
| 29 | Petroleum Refining and Related Industries | 10 | 0 | 36 | 5 |
| 30 | Rubber and Miscellaneous Products | 8 | 2 | 11 | 3 |

|  | Industry | | | | |
| --- | --- | --- | --- | --- | --- |
| 31 | Leather and Leather Products | — | — | 1 | 0 |
| 32 | Stone, Clay, Glass, and Concrete Products | 32 | 5 | 16 | 1 |
| 33 | Primary Metal Industries | 36 | 11 | 26 | 11 |
| 34 | Fabricated Metal Products | 42 | 5 | 21 | 5 |
| 35 | Machinery | 82 | 26 | 38 | 9 |
| 36 | Electrical and Electronic Machinery and Equipment | 99 | 25 | 65 | 13 |
| 37 | Transportation Equipment | 47 | 13 | 41 | 10 |
| 38 | Measuring and Controlling Instruments | 16 | 6 | 16 | 4 |
| 39 | Miscellaneous Manufacturing | 25 | 5 | 5 | 1 |
|  | Unknown | — | — | — | 1 |
|  | **Total** | 629 | 168 | 500 | 103 |
|  | **Percentage** |  | (26.7%) |  | (20.6%) |

**Table 29.3 Number of Respondents by Industry**

| Quantitative Method | No/Little Users | Moderate Users | Extensive Users | Adoption Rate* | |
|---|---|---|---|---|---|
| Simulation | 29 | 60 | 13 | 55.9% | U.S. |
| | 79 | 74 | 13 | 47.4% | Japan |
| Waiting Lines | 90 | 10 | 1 | 2.0 | U.S. |
| | 154 | 2 | 0 | 0.0 | Japan |
| Forecasting Technique | 18 | 64 | 20 | 69.9 | U.S. |
| | 62 | 80 | 14 | 50.6 | Japan |
| Probability/ Decision Theory | 53 | 45 | 4 | 38.2 | U.S. |
| | 135 | 20 | 1 | 9.6 | Japan |
| Statistical Analysis | 24 | 55 | 23 | 61.8 | U.S. |
| | 85 | 57 | 14 | 36.5 | Japan |
| Network Analysis | 45 | 47 | 10 | 46.8 | U.S. |
| | 136 | 19 | 1 | 6.4 | Japan |
| Inventory Models | 17 | 62 | 23 | 65.7 | U.S. |
| | 102 | 46 | 8 | 28.8 | Japan |
| Linear Programming | 51 | 43 | 7 | 35.6 | U.S. |
| | 133 | 22 | 1 | 10.3 | Japan |
| Mathematical Programming | 64 | 33 | 5 | 22.5 | U.S. |
| | 141 | 15 | 0 | 5.1 | Japan |
| Input/Output Analysis | 57 | 37 | 8 | 31.4 | U.S. |
| | 119 | 33 | 4 | 19.9 | Japan |

Adoption rate = $\dfrac{\text{number of companies scoring 4 or more on the Likert scale}}{\text{number of valid responses}}$

**Table 29.4  Adoption Rate of Each Technique**

was conducted to ensure whether there were any differences between the degree of current use and future use for each method. We could find no statistically significant difference for each method in Japan and the United States. This suggests that companies in both countries want to stay at the same position concerning the extent of future use. The current heavy users will use those methods extensively, but the seldom users indicate a lesser tendency to use those techniques in the future.

**Some Characteristics of Extensive Users.** We would like to discuss the influence of the organizational scale factors on the use of quantitative methods in the U.S. firms. Sales and total assets were chosen. Based on the Mann-Whitney U test, only statistical analysis and input/output analysis were the techniques used extensively by the large-scale companies.[10] Concerning the other eight techniques, we could not find any statistically significant differences among companies. Research conducted earlier suggests that larger companies prefer to use most of the quantitative method extensively, but we could not find such tendencies from our research.

**Top Management Support.** Earlier research suggests that the degree of top management support for modeling was a factor that could influence the use of quantitative methods. The companies that scored 5 or more on the Likert scale for the top management support measure were denoted as the high support group, and 4 or less as the low support group. Between these two groups, we found three techniques (statistical analysis, probabilities and decision theory, and inventory model) were used extensively.[11] But in terms of the other seven techniques, we could not find statistical differences. This result was *not* identical to the previous studies.

The adoption rate, the influence of scale measures, and the top management support variable may indicate that the U.S. companies stay at the mature phase of applying the quantitative method to cost and management activities. In other words, there is little possibility that the more extensive techniques will be used in U.S. firms. On the contrary, Japanese firms seem to be at the "diffusion stage" of use, but there may be little possibility of enlarging the application of other quantitative methods.

**Use of Purpose-of-Use-Specified Quantitative Models.** Kaplan (1977) surveyed the quantitative model applications to cost and management accounting activities. He commented on whether each of the applications were worth executing based on little empirical evidence. This part of the research will supplement Kaplan's attempt. The topics surveyed are cost estimating, CVP analysis under uncertainty, CVP analysis for multiple products, several cost allocation problems (including service department cost allocation, joint and/or by-product cost allocation, and overhead allocation), variance investigation decisions, incremental cash flow analysis, and capital budgeting. The research results are summarized in Table 29.5.

The U.S. firms are also heavier users of quantitative methods than the Japanese firms (excluding simulation for cash flow analysis). Roughly, the topics for which quantitative techniques have a relatively high adoption rate in both countries are incremental cash flow

| | | Adoption rate (%) | |
| | | | |
| Topics | Techniques | Japan | United States |
|---|---|---|---|
| Cost Classification | Linear Regression | 4.6 | 23.1 |
| | Multiple Regression | 4.6 | 15.4 |
| CVP Analysis | Probability/ Decision Theory | 17.9 | 39.7 |
| | Mathematical Programming | 21.4 | 25.0 |
| Service Department Cost Allocation | Matrix Algebra | 8.3 | 7.9 |
| Joint Cost Allocation | Mathematical Programming | 0.0 | 2.2 |
| | Game Theory | 0.0 | 0.0 |
| Overhead Allocation | Mathematical Programming | 1.2 | 1.0 |
| Variance Investigation Decision | Bayes Theorem | 0.0 | 2.0 |
| | Regression | 2.3 | 2.0 |
| | Control Chart | 5.4 | 15.8 |
| Cash Flow Analysis | Probability | 12.5 | 40.4 |
| | Simulation | 59.4 | 10.5 |
| Capital Budgeting | Mathematical Programming | 3.7 | 18.0 |

**Table 29.5 Quantitative Model Applications to Cost/Management Accounting Activities: Comparative Results**

analysis, capital budgeting, cost estimating, and CVP analysis. On the other hand, cost allocation and variance investigation decisions are the topics over which quantitative methods have a minor influence. Topics belonging to the first category seem to be directly related to management accounting activities. Therefore, it may be possible to conclude that techniques related mainly to management accounting activities have a higher percentage of use.

On the contrary, topics closely related to product costing (excluding cost estimating, from which we can get various suggestive information for management accounting decisions) seem to be less attractive from the managers' standpoint. Companies may suspect that any changes in their product costing procedures would be unfavorable from the cost benefit perspective.

Research results so far tell us that our efforts to develop quantitative models for management accounting activities seem to have some impact on the practice, especially in the U.S. Based on the research findings, we will reach a different conclusion from Kaplan's assertion.

***Decision Support and Quantitative Methods.*** Decision support systems (DSS) are an interactive computer-based information system that helps decision makers utilize data and models to solve ill-structured problems.[12] Therefore, quantitative methods are part of DSS. Early DSS was developed from scratch; programmers built models using FORTRAN and/or PL/I, even COBOL. Most later DSS was built around the DSS generator and is a "package" of related hardware and software that provides a set of capabilities to build the applications (we will call the DSS application the specific DSS) quickly and easily.

**User profiles of decision support systems.** There are two types of DSS generators. One is the large-scale financial planning system (DSS generator, hereafter) that is used interactively through terminals connecting to the mainframe computers. The other is the spreadsheet financial planning system (spreadsheet, hereafter) that was developed mainly for microcomputers.

At first, the extent of use of both systems in the largest Japanese and U.S. firms was examined. The results are presented in Table 29.6. Obviously, spreadsheets are widely used in practice for cost and management accounting decisions. Though DSS generators have already taken root in the United States, they are not fully utilized in Japan. Interview researchers of some 30 Japanese firms tell us that most of them are planning to adopt DSS generators in the near future. The Japanese nonusers have a great interest in the DSS generators of the next generation. Moreover, the degree of satisfaction with the DSS generators is high in both countries. From these findings, we can conclude that the demand for the information systems that support business decision making is extremely high. These two types of DSS could also be utilized for financial accounting activities (including accounting data processing), but their main targets seem to be the management planning and control activities, especially in the case of the DSS generator.

| | | In Use | No Use |
|---|---|---|---|
| DSS generator | Japan | 11 (6.5%) | 157 (93.5%) |
| | U.S. | 46 (45.1%) | 56 (54.9%) |
| Spreadsheet | Japan | 107 (63.7%) | 61 (36.3%) |
| | U.S. | 97 (94.2%) | 6 (5.8%) |

**Table 29.6  Extent of DSS Use**

Applying spreadsheet to cost and management accounting decisions is a common phenomenon in today's business world, and the adoption rate of the DSS generators in Japanese firms is low. Therefore, we will focus on the DSS generator in the U.S. firms.

There were statistically significant differences in scale measures — sales, total assets, and number of employees — between the DSS generator users and the nonusers.[13] Growing in scale will lead to the increasing complexity of the firm's decision environment. As contingency theorists of the organization and DSS researchers described, organizational environment complexity will increase the information processing load of the firm and the number of ill-structured decisions.[14] We suspect that heavy information processing loads and the need for solving ill-structured decisions are major factors in adopting DSS generators.

The chi-square tests revealed that companies adopting process costing systems for product costing and producing joint products and/or by-products have a higher adoption rate of the DSS generator. Tables 29.7 and 29.8 summarize these findings, which may suggest that the DSS generators are widely used in the "process" industries. To prove this, the chi-square test was executed. Table 29.9 reveals that our inference was right. There may be three reasons why DSS generators are widely used among the process industries:

1. Process industries are usually large in scale. Therefore, the ad hoc decisions, such as capital budgeting decisions, become critical in terms of the amount to invest. In such cases, decision makers usually want to obtain varied information for the decision support.
2. By means of the automated manufacturing systems and the use of MS/OR techniques, most process industries have already stored a large amount of data in their databases. These industries need exert a minimum of effort to prepare various data for DSS.
3. Most of the manufacturing process has already been automated in the process industries. Therefore, work efficiency is a high priority.

The next step will be to study the effectiveness of the variance decisions in the organization. We know process industries have some characteristics that make the introduction of DDS easy. It does not necessarily mean, though, that DSS is not suitable for other industries. Rather, DSS is applicable to all kinds of industries.

**Main factors for introducing the DSS generator.** Table 29.10 contains information on the influential factors for adopting the DSS

| | DSS Generator | | |
|---|---|---|---|
| Costing Method | Users | Nonusers | Total |
| Job order | 4 | 18 | 22 |
| Process | 28 | 20 | 48 |
| Operation | 10 | 10 | 20 |
| Others | 4 | 8 | 12 |
| Total | 46 | 56 | 102 |

* Chi-square = 10.698, d.f. 3, significant at .05 level.

**Table 29.7  Costing Methods Versus DSS Generator**

|  | DSS Generator | | |
| --- | --- | --- | --- |
|  | Users | Nonusers | Total |
| Have Joint Products/ By-products | 26 | 20 | 46 |
| Have No Joint Products/ By-products | 20 | 36 | 56 |
| Total | 46 | 56 | 102 |

Chi-square = 4.416, d.f. 1, significant at .05 level.

**Table 29.8  Joint Products/By-Products and DSS Generator**

|  | DSS Generator | | |
| --- | --- | --- | --- |
|  | Users | Nonusers | Total |
| Process Industry | 24 | 11 | 35 |
| Other | 22 | 45 | 67 |
| Total | 46 | 56 | 102 |

Chi-square = 10.443, d.f. 1, significant at .01 level.

**Table 29.9  Industry Group Versus DSS Generator**

generator. In general, the internal examination (staff advice and one's own judgment) will lead to the final decision to adopt the DSS generator. It is natural that the final decision is made after evaluating the possible alternatives. Advice from external parties, for example, accounting firms and/or consulting firms, plays a less influential role. As we can predict, however, external parties as information providers have a certain influence in the evaluation process of choosing a DSS generator. Current users of DSS generators indicate that advice from consulting firms does play a role in evaluating the DSS generator alternatives.[15]

| | DSS Generator | | | Spreadsheet |
|---|---|---|---|---|
| | Whole | Users | Nonusers | |
| Own Judgment | 4.97 | 4.84 | 5.05 | 5.21 |
| Staff Advice | 5.42 | 5.39 | 5.26 | 5.47 |
| Advice from Accounting Firms | 2.47 | 2.64 | 2.33 | 2.18 |
| Advice from Consulting Firms | 2.60 | 2.98 | 2.16 | 2.05 |

Figures are mean values of respondents.

**Table 29.10 Influential Factors for Adopting DSS**

**Usefulness of DSS.** DSS tends to be aimed at the less well-structured, underspecified problems that upper-level managers typically face. The Mann-Whitney U tests were executed to discover whether DSS has this characteristic. The users of the DSS generator realize that it contributes to the improvement of "management control" and "strategic planning" activities.[16] It is obvious that the current users of the DSS generator evaluate its ability for semistructured situations, which are common mostly in management control and strategic planning activities. The philosophy of the DSS has become a common body of knowledge not only in academia, but also in practice. There were no statistically significant differences, in terms of the usefulness of the DSS generator to "operational control" activities, between the current DSS generator users and the nonusers. Users of both types of DSS thought that the DSS generator would contribute more to management control and strategic planning than operational control.[17] In addition, they perceived that the DSS generator would contribute more to strategic planning activities than the spreadsheet.[18] They may think of the DSS generator as a better decision support tool than the spreadsheet for these activities, most of which consist of ill-structured decisions. Users of the spreadsheet only thought it would be more useful for operational control activities than for management control or strategic planning decisions.

From these findings, we can infer that the U.S. firms properly use the DSS generator for semistructured situations and the spreadsheet for well-structured decisions. Although, the U.S. firms use DSS both ad hoc and in an institutional way, user cases indicate that Japanese firms prefer to use the DSS generator for formal planning devices.[19]

**Relationship of DSS and quantitative methods.** In this section, we will discuss the relationship between DSS generator use and utilization of quantitative methods. The Mann-Whitney U tests revealed that probabilities and/or decision theory, forecasting, and mathematical programming were the techniques that the DSS generator users prefer.[20] Most DSS generators have the model base, which contains a library of quantitative models, and the model base management systems (MBMS), which enables decision makers to utilize the model base fully for decision support.[21]

One of the most frequently used functions of DSS is the "what-if" analysis. For example, what if one change is made in the model, what impact will it have on the whole model? Forecasting techniques and probabilities and/or decision theory are essential to the "what-if" analysis. It is quite easy for novice computer users to conduct a series of "what-if" analyses with DSS. This may be why DSS generator users favor these techniques so much more compared to the nonusers.

What about mathematical programming? With the DSS generator, it is not too difficult to conduct the "goal-seeking" analysis via the goal programming and multiperiod model building combined with the dynamic programming techniques. "Goal seeking" is the opposite operation of the "what-if." For example, what would one variable need to be if we want the target variable to have a certain value?

In addition, as previously mentioned, the DSS generator is widely used among the "process" industries that have been using OR/MS techniques, especially the mathematical programming (including linear programming) techniques for production planning and job scheduling. The reasons discussed may explain the use of mathematical programming techniques by DSS generator users.

**Factors influencing the future use of quantitative methods.** In the questionnaires, a question about the extent of the influence of five factors, (1) continuing education for managers, (2) management involvement in the modeling process, (3) quantitative education in college, (4) improvement in available large-scale financial planning systems (DSS), and (5) simplicity and ease of use of the model, on the future use of the quantitative methods was inserted. The results are summarized in Table 29.11.

| | Little Influence | Moderate Influence | Extensive Influence |
|---|---|---|---|
| Continuing Education for Managers | 9 | 70 | 23 |
| Management Involvement in the Modeling Process | 8 | 70 | 24 |
| Quantitative Education in College | 14 | 63 | 25 |
| Improvements in Available Large-Scale Financial Planning Systems (DSS) | 20 | 57 | 25 |
| Simplicity and Ease of Use of Model | 6 | 34 | 62 |

**Table 29.11  Influential Factors for Adopting Quantitative Methods**

Each factor, especially "simplicity and ease of use of model," was perceived as important. Again, the analysis of the DSS generator users versus nonusers was examined. The results were somewhat interesting. The users perceived that improvement in available DSS generators and quantitative education in college would play an active role in the future use of quantitative methods.[22] In the United States, the DSS generator users apply output information from the quantitative models more extensively and have a greater interest in future DSS generators, compared to the nonusers.[23] These facts indicate that the DSS generator users realize the importance of the quantitative methods for improving the cost and management accounting activities in efficient and effective ways. In other words, the nonusers may not realize the potential of either the DSS generator or the quantitative methods in the United States. DSS generator users in Japan do not indicate a particularly high degree of satisfaction with the current DSS generators.

In terms of "quantitative education in college," we may assume that it is not necessary for managers to know the exact algorithms of the quantitative methods. Although there is much criticism of the curriculum that overemphasizes the quantitative-oriented education in undergraduate schools, users of the DSS generator suspect that college education will play an essential role in this subject. This belief also implies that the quantitative methods are important in the DSS generator.

**Perceived Benefits of and Barriers to Applying Quantitative Methods to Cost/Management Accounting Activities.** Each respondent was asked to evaluate the perceived benefits of applying quantitative methods to cost/ management accounting activities with the seven-point Likert scale. The results are shown in Table 29.12. We do not find any particularly different level of perception among the five benefits. Most respondents think the quantitative methods will contribute most to "rational and consistent decision making," but "direct payoffs" are not expected as much.

|  | Little Contribution | Moderate Contribution | Extensive Contribution |
|---|---|---|---|
| Rational and Consistent Decision-Making | 11 | 71 | 20 |
| Timely Decision-Making | 21 | 67 | 14 |
| Correct Decision-Making | 15 | 71 | 12 |
| In-Depth Understanding for Management Planning and Control Processes | 20 | 67 | 14 |
| Direct Payoffs (Such as Sales Increase or Cost Reduction) | 23 | 69 | 10 |

**Table 29.12 Perceived Benefits of Quantitative Methods**

The DSS generator users, as compared to the nonusers, perceived that quantitative methods would contribute to "rational and consistent decision making" and "correct decision making."[24] It is needless to explain these findings. We hypothesized that the DSS generator users would give a high evaluation to the quantitative methods for "timely decision making," but such a tendency was not found from the analysis.

**Perceived barriers.** There are many barriers to the use of quantitative methods. In this section, we will examine whether different perceptions exist between U.S. and Japanese firms. In the questionnaires, 17 perceived barriers appeared. Respondents were asked to rank these barriers from one (the weakest barrier) to seven (the strongest barrier). Results appear in Table 29.13.

We would like to summarize the results of the factor analysis before discussing the perceptions of barriers in both countries. Table 29.14 contains the summary information of the factor analysis of the perceived barriers to applying quantitative methods to cost/management accounting activities.[25] Quite different perceptions of the barriers exist between Japanese and U.S. firms. U.S. firms think that barriers in Factors 1 and 2 are crucial. Compared with the Japanese firms, BARR1 and BARR3 were the ones that the U.S. firms perceived as difficult to clear, based on the chi-square tests. On the contrary, Japanese firms perceived BARR 5, 7, 8, 9, 13, 15, and 17 as the hardest barriers to overcome.

We would like to interpret these results with the consideration that the U.S. firms are heavier users of quantitative methods compared to their Japanese counterparts. It is likely that the U.S. firms have encountered various obstacles to constructing or implementing quantitative methods to cost/management decisions. Therefore, Factor 2 (difficulty of getting data for models) is the crucial barrier to overcome for firms that have a lot of experience applying quantitative methods to management decisions. On the contrary, Japanese firms think Factor 1 (managers' time constraints and lack of knowledge of quantitative methods) and Factor 4 (low level of management involvement in the modeling process) are hard to overcome. This means that most Japanese firms are still at the starting point for applying quantitative methods. Japanese firms do not consider Factor 1 so crucial. This may come from poor experience with modeling. The prerequisites of applying quantitative methods may not have been established in most Japanese firms. Another possible interpretation is that most Japanese firms know they will encounter these difficult situations before constructing models. In this case, they do not want to construct quantitative models that will generate additional management problems or poor performance.

Let us examine how U.S. respondents using the DSS generator perceive the barriers to applying quantitative methods to cost/

| Variable name | Content | Ranking * | |
|---|---|---|---|
| | | Japan | U.S. |
| BARR1 | Unrealistic assumptions of the model | 14 | 4 |
| BARR2 | Required data are difficult to quantify | 9 | 2 |
| BARR3 | Required data are not available | 15 | 7 |
| BARR4 | High costs of acquiring the required data for the model | 6 | 6 |
| BARR5 | High costs of developing and running models | 3 | 9 |
| BARR6 | Benefits of using models are not clearly understood by managers | 4 | 1 |
| BARR7 | Insufficient time for managers to examine the use of the model | 1 | 3 |
| BARR8 | Lack of knowledge of quantitative models by management accounting personnel | 2 | 8 |
| BARR9 | Models require use of computer, and managers are unwilling or unable to use computer for decision making | 11 | 16 |
| BARR10 | Key management personnel do not encourage use of models | 12 | 12 |
| BARR11 | Management distrusts the use of quantitative models | 17 | 14 |
| BARR12 | Management is successful without using quantitative models | 5 | 5 |
| BARR13 | Recent college graduates with quantitative training have not yet attained position of influence | 10 | 17 |
| BARR14 | Necessary information for managers is not available from quantitative models | 16 | 10 |
| BARR15 | Lack of proper reporting systems or channels to communicate output information to top management | 7 | 15 |
| BARR16 | Difficulties in understanding output information from models | 13 | 11 |
| BARR17 | Users of output information have little involvement or influence in the modeling process | 8 | 13 |

* Ranking was computed based on the mean values.

**Table 29.13 Perceived Barriers to Adopting Quantitative Methods**

| Factor 1 | Managers' time constraints and lack of knowledge of quantitative methods | |
|---|---|---|
| | BARR 6 | .58 |
| | BARR 7 | .70 |
| | BARR 8 | .61 |
| | BARR 9 | .64 |
| Factor 2 | Difficulty of getting data for models | |
| | BARR 1 | .48 |
| | BARR 2 | .75 |
| | BARR 3 | .71 |
| | BARR 4 | .71 |
| Factor 3 | Managers' unwillingness to use models | |
| | BARR 10 | .59 |
| | BARR 11 | .63 |
| | BARR 12 | .58 |
| Factor 4 | Low level of management involvement in the modeling process | |
| | BARR 15 | .56 |
| | BARR 16 | .66 |
| | BARR 17 | .69 |

Figures are factor loadings of variables to each of the factors.

**Table 29.14 Factor Analysis Output**

management activities. They note that 3 of 17 perceived barriers to applying quantitative methods are not so critical, compared to the nonusers' perceptions. These three barriers are unrealistic assumptions of the model, benefits of using models are not clearly understood by managers, and necessary information for managers is not available from quantitative models.[26] The ranking of the 17 perceived barriers were measures by mean values from the most difficult (ranked one) to the easiest (ranked seventeen) to overcome. The three barriers not so critical to U.S. DSS generator users ranked 4, 1, and 10, respectively. Although they are highly ranked barriers to overcome, the DSS generator users think they are moderate compared to the nonusers' perception. These findings are not surprising. Once DSS generators have been introduced, companies would make every effort to develop the specific DSS to pinpoint their crucial problems. After repeated trial and error, they would hit upon one of the more satisfactory models with the DSS generator. Companies that have workable models do not mind the three perceived barriers as much as the nonusers do.

*Conclusion.* This chapter tried to explore the state of the art in quantitative methods in cost and management accounting activities in the largest Japanese and U.S. firms. We can observe many insightful facts. There are quite different perceptions of the quantitative methods between Japan and the United States. More research will be needed to explore why those different perceptions exist between the two countries. To continue this type of research, we have to investigate the real-world problems. We might say that the gaps between cost and management accounting research and practices are obvious. The gaps must be filled in from both sides.

### Notes

1. Concerning the terminology *user decision-model approach,* see Horngren (1975) and Demski and Feltham (1976). Demski and Feltham (1976) describe the progress of management accounting as the historical communication approach, the user decision-model approach, and the information evaluation approach.
2. Demski and Kreps (1982) reviewed agency theory and information economics studies, as well as the user decision-model research.
3. Demski and Feltham (1976; pp. 7-8) reviewed agency theory and information economics studies, as well as the user decision-model research.
4. Chow and Adams (1982) reviewed the previous research. Among the articles they reviewed, only Vatter (1967) and Kiani Aslani (1977-1978) give us some insight.
5. This chapter presents only part of the research results. Anyone interested in other findings can request the author to send working papers. All are written in Japanese.
6. References especially useful for these tasks are Demski and Kreps (1982), Dopuch, Birneberg, and Demski (1982), Horngren (1982), Kaplan (1977) and (1982), and Maher (1982).
7. If a reader would like a questionnaire packet, please write the author and specify the Japanese or English version.

8. The priority for addressing the questionnaires to the accounting executives was (1) Vice President-Controller (or Comptroller), (2) Controller (or Comptroller), (3) Vice President (other than Controller), (4) Chief Executive Officer, (5) Treasurer. Standard & Poor's Register of Corporations, Directors, and Executives: Vol. 1, Corporations, 1984 (for the U.S. research) and Diamond's Register (Kaisha Shokuinnroku) of 1985 (for the Japanese research) were used for compiling the mailing list.

9. The Spearman rank correlation coefficients Rho were significant for each of the techniques at .01 level, one-tailed test. Statistical outputs are eliminated because of limited writing space.

10. We distinguish large-scale companies and small-scale companies by the Fortune 500's median values of sales and total assets. The more companies grow in scale, the more complex the organizations will be. Organizational complexity makes it difficult to grasp the input-output relationships of the firm. Therefore, input/output analysis may be preferred by the large-scale companies. The Mann-Whitney statistics follow:

|  | Sales | Total Assets |
|---|---|---|
| 1. Input/Output Analysis | 1.711* | 2.738** |
| 2. Statistical Methods | 1.547*** | 1.477*** |

---

* Significant at .05 level, one-tailed test.
** Significant at .01 level, one-tailed test.
*** Significant at .10 level, one-tailed test.

11. The Mann-Whitney statistics were 3.376 for statistical methods, 2.144 for probabilities/decision theory, and 1.970 for inventory models. They were statistically significant at the .001, .05, and .05 levels, one-tailed test, respectively.

12. Sprague and Carlson (1982).

13. The Mann-Whitney statistics are 1.8777, 3.0737, and 1.8964 for sales, total assets, and number of employees, respectively. Total assets is significant at the .01 level, and the others are significant at the .05 level, one-tailed test.

14. See Lawrence and Lorsch (1967). Keen and Scott Morton (1978, p. 7) indicate that environmental uncertainty would make an impact on the effectiveness of decisions rather than the efficiency.

15. The Mann-Whitney statistic is -2.3469, significant at the .01 level, one-tailed test. This means that current users of the DSS generator think that advice from consulting firms is relatively important in the evaluation process of the DSS generator, as compared to the nonuser's perception. Current users may learn by experience the importance of advice from consulting firms, at the introductory stage of using the DSS generator. This is consistent with the fact

that vendors often introduce users to a consulting firm to ensure best use of the DSS generator and, on a request basis, to assist the development of a specific DSS to be used on that system.

16. See Anthony (1965) for "strategic planning," "management control," and "operational control." The Mann-Whitney statistics are 2.1680 for management control and 3.5915 for strategic planning. Both are statistically significant at the .01 level, one-tailed test.

17. Wilcoxon's T statistics were 174.5 (number of ranks = 31) between operational control and strategic planning and 63.5 (number of ranks = 24) between management control and operational control. The first was statistically significant at .10 level and the latter at .01 level, one-tailed test.

18. The Wilcoxon's T statistic was 117 (number of ranks = 29) and statistically significant at .05 level, one-tailed test.

19. Concerning the difference between the "ad hoc" DSS and "institutional" DSS, see Donovan and Madnick (1977).

20. The Mann-Whitney statistics for probabilities and/or decision theory, forecasting techniques, and mathematical programming were 2.5573, 2.0501, and 1.6836, respectively. Probabilities and/or decision theory is statistically significant at the .01 level, the others are significant at the .05 level, one-tailed test.

21. The general functions of the model base management systems are model generation, model restructuring, model updating, and report generation-inquiry. See Sprague and Carlson (1982, pp. 262-263).

22. The former was significant at the .05 level (1.7979) and the latter at the .10 level (1.6355), by the one-tailed Mann-Whitney U tests.

23. The former was significant at the .01 level (4.4510) and the latter at the .05 level (2.2094), by the one-tailed Mann-Whitney U tests.

24. Both were significant at the .10 level (U = 1.3416 and U = 1.2842), by the one-tailed Mann-Whitney U tests.

25. To extract factors, the iterated principal factor analysis using squared multiple correlations for the prior communality was performed. The varimax rotation was applied to the four extracted factors.

26. The Mann-Whitney statistics were -1.8124, -1.6829, and -0.7113, respectively. Each of them was significant at the .05 level, one-tailed test.

### References

1. Anthony, R.N. (1965). *Planning and Control Systems: A Framework for Analysis.* Cambridge, MA: Harvard University, Graduate School of Business Administration.

2. Chow, C.W., and G.L. Adams. (1982). "Quantitative Techniques in Management Accounting: The Relation Between Classroom Teaching and Real-World Applications," *Collegiate News & Views,* Vol. 35, No. 35 no. 3, pp. 7-12.

3. Demski, J.S., and G.A. Feltham. (1976). *Cost Determination: A Conceptual Approach.* Iowa State University Press.
4. Demski, J.S., and D.M. Kreps. (1982). "Models in Managerial Accounting," *Journal of Accounting Research.* Vol. 20 suppl.
5. Donovan, J.J., and S.E. Madnick. (1977). "Institutional and Ad Hoc DSS and Their Effective Use," *Data Base.* Vol. 8, No. 3, pp. 79-88.
6. Dopuch, N., J.G. Birnberg, and J.S. Demski. (1982). *Cost Accounting: Accounting Data for Management's Decisions,* 3rd ed. New York: Harcourt Jovanovich.
7. Horngren, C.T. (1975). "Management Accounting: Where Are We?" *Management Accounting and Control: Proceedings of the Robert Beyer Symposium on Management Accounting and Control.* Madison: University of Wisconsin.
8. _____ . (1982). *Cost Accounting: A Managerial Emphasis,* 5th ed. New York: Prentice-Hall.
9. Kaplan, R.S. (1977). "Application of Quantitative Methods in Management Accounting: A State of the Art Survey." *Management Accounting: A State of the Art.* Madison: Robert Beyer Lecture Series, University of Wisconsin.
10. _____ . (1982). *Advanced Management Accounting,* New York: Prentice-Hall.
11. Keen, P.G., and M. Scott Morton. (1978). *Decision Support Systems: An Organizational Perspective.* Boston: Addison-Wesley.
12. Kiani-Asklani, R. (1977-1978). "Do Corporate Controllers Use Quantitative Tools Currently Taught in Managerial Accounting?" *The Accounting Journal,* pp. 278-294.
13. Lawrence, P.R., and J.W. Lorsch. (1967). *Organizational and Environment.* Cambridge, MA: Division of Research, Harvard Business School.
14. Maher, M.W. (1982). "Management Accounting Literature: Past, Present, and Future." Unpublished, University of Michigan.
15. Sprague, R.H., and E.D. Carlson, *Building Effective Decision Support Systems.* New York: Prentice-Hall.
16. Vatter. (1967). "Operations Research in American Companies," *The Accounting Review,* pp. 721-730.

# 30

## The Relationship Between Environment and Budgeting Systems in Japanese Corporations

*Hiromitsu Kojima, Department of Economics,*
*Hokkaido University*

Today, the environment surrounding corporations is increasingly mobile and unstable. Corporations are required to adapt quickly to changing conditions. They set up various kinds of management systems in their efforts to be responsive. Budgeting systems, among other management systems, are especially important because they determine and implement plans about utilization of management resources in relation to the environment.

The budgeting systems of many corporations have the following problems: (1) authority does not lie with the responsibilities, (2) rational and scientific budgeting is difficult, (3) there is not enough participation and cooperation between top management and the work-site segment in budgeting, and (4) inflexible budgets have been implemented. Consequently, many suggestions have been made for overcoming these problems: contingency planning, zero-base budgeting, and the planning-programming-budgeting system (PPBS), to name a few. (PPBS refers to the whole system covering strategic planning, long-range planning, and yearly budgeting.) But these suggestions have remained suggestions — they have not been implemented by corporations. There has not been enough recognition of the fact that a rational, improved, more desirable budgeting system must match the environmental setting and organizational characteristics of an individual corporation. To make effective suggestions for the rationalization and improvement of budgeting systems, it is necessary to determine how budgeting systems are implemented by their corporations in relation to these two factors.

It must be admitted that there have been sufficient empirical analyses of budgeting systems from such a standpoint. Most studies in the past were either general surveys on the mechanics of budget preparation, or case studies of individual budgeting systems. Few studies have dealt with a systematic and empirical analysis of budgeting systems in relation to their environmental settings (Bruns and Waterhouse, 1975; Hayes, 1977; Swieringa and Moncur, 1972). This chapter attempts a systematic and empirical analysis of budgeting systems in the corporation's environmental setting to fill the gap between general surveys and case studies.

*Hypothesis and Method of Analysis.* The conventional contingency theory concentrated on typifying the relationship between task environment and organizational characteristics. It gives only fragmentary answers to the question of why the effectiveness of the organization increases when there is a certain relationship between these factors. The information-processing model first presented a clear explanation in answer to this question: "As uncertainty in the immediate task environment increases, so does the need for increased amounts of information, and thus the need for increased information-processing capacity; the organization will be more effective when there is a match between the information-processing requirements and information processing capacity of the organization." The validity of the information processing model has recently been recognized by a number of studies, and is receiving a great deal of attention (Duncan, 1972; Galbraith, 1977; Lawrence and Lorsch, 1967; Lorsche and Morse, 1974; Nadler et al., 1979; Nonaka, 1972; Tushman and Nadler, 1978). In this chapter, the relationship between the environmental setting and the budgeting system was analyzed according to the information-processing model. Figure 30.1 shows the theoretical framework for analyzing the relationship between environmental setting and the budgeting system. Following is a brief explanation of the theoretical framework.

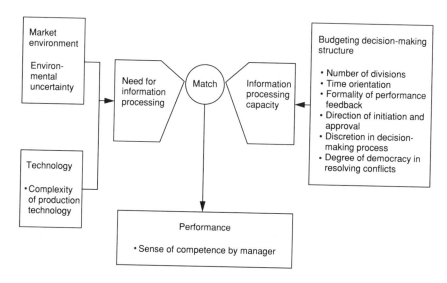

**Figure 30.1 Theoretical Framework**

In this analysis, market environment and technology were regarded as task environment. To cope with the need for information processing associated with increased environmental uncertainty, organizations exercise budgeting decision-making structures (structure and behavior of the budgeting system). The information-processing capacity of the organization is determined by the budgeting decision-making structure. Performance is a function of the match between the need for information processing and the information-processing capacity.

Next, operationalization was attempted on the concepts composing the theoretical framework: market environment, technology, budgeting decision-making structure, and performance. The process of operationalization of a concept consists of choice of dimension(s), choice of indicator(s) for each dimension chosen, and choice of the measuring instruments(s) for each indicator chosen (see Table 30.1). We will elaborate on the operationalization of the concept of performance.

A budgeting system is a system for management. Therefore, evaluation of any budgeting system must be made in relation to the overall management performance. The overall management performance is affected not only by the budgeting decision-making structure, but also by various other factors. Therefore, it is impossible

| Concept | Dimension | Indicators for Dimension | Measuring Instruments for Indicator |
|---|---|---|---|
| Market environment | Environmental uncertainty | Level of environmental uncertainty | Stability and potential of demand<br>Market share and influencing power of corporation<br>Intensity of competition in product market<br>Predictability about competitor's actions |
| Technology | Complexity of production technology | Complexity of production system | Woodward's 6-step scale |
|  | Number of divisions | Number of products | Standard merchandise classification list |
|  |  | Number of autonomous divisions | Number of autonomous divisions/annual sales (in 10 billion yen) |
| Budgeting decision-making structure | Time orientation | Long or short term planning? | Degree of organization of long-range planning<br>Integrity of contents of long-range plans |
|  | Formality of performance feedback | Formal or flexible performance feedback concerning budget? | Degree of formality in performance feedback for budget |

| | | | |
|---|---|---|---|
| Budgeting decision-making structure, cont'd. | Direction of initiation and approval | Bottom-up or top-down preparation of budget guidelines? | Direction of flow of budget guideline preparation<br>Degree of specificity of budget guidelines |
| | | Level of budget initiation in organizational hierarchy | Where decision-making items concerning budget are initiated |
| | Discretion in decision-making process | Personal or mechanical budget review? | Degree of participation by budget department in sales budget review |
| | Degree of democracy in resolving conflicts | Democratic or despotic resolution of conflicts in budget committee? | Degree of cooperation between budget department and divisions<br>Degree of democracy in resolving conflicts in budget committee |
| Performance | Sense of competence by manager | Strong or weak sense of competence by manager in budgeting system? | Confidence of members of division about achieving budget target<br>Confidence of division manager about achieving budget target<br>Level of mental pressure on division manager in budgeting system |

**Table 30.1 Summary of Operationalization of Concepts**

to separate the contribution of the budgeting decision-making structure from overall management performance, to measure and analyze it alone. In this chapter, therefore, "strong or weak sense of competence by manager in budgeting system" has been employed as the performance indicator. "Sense of competence by manager" is the degree of confidence felt by a manager in the budgeting system; this means the extent to which individuals gain psychological gratification from successfully mastering the world around them (Lorsch and Morse, 1974). Based on these considerations, the following hypothesis was presented.

> *Hypothesis:* An effective budgeting system shows the following five characteristics concerning its structure and behavior as environmental variety (uncertainty of market environment and complexity of production technology) increases:
>
> 1. Plans are set from the viewpoint of shorter terms.
> 2. Performance feedback becomes more flexible.
> 3. Direction of initiation and approval is likely to be bottom-up in a greater number of cases.
> 4. There is greater discretion in decision making.
> 5. Conflicts are resolved through a more democratic method.

Ten manufacturing companies were chosen as subjects for this study, and the survey took place in 1975. (See Table 30.2.) The data were collected by means of questionnaires and interviews with budget managers and division managers. Answers to the questionnaires were converted to numerical values, using a five-point bipolar scale.

*Analysis and Discussion of Results.* The extent of environmental variety was measured by the method, using the ranking of environmental uncertainty and the ranking of complexity of production technology (see Figure 30.2). The extent of environmental variety was expressed as the square root of the sum of the squares of the ranks (the rank of environmental uncertainty and the rank of complexity of production technology), i.e., distance from the origin (radius of concentric circles). The bigger the radius of the circle on which the organization is located, the more its environmental variety; the smaller the radius, the less the variety.

As shown in Figure 30.2, the shoe company was discovered to have the greatest environmental variety, followed by the newspaper,

|  | Power Company | Bakery | Food Company | Shoe Company | Chemical Company |
|---|---|---|---|---|---|
| Year Established | 1951 | 1919 | 1957 | 1921 | 1912 |
| Capital (¥ billion) | 217 | .63 | 1.4 | .018 | 2.13 |
| Sales (¥ billion) | 63.6 | 28.5 | 33.2 | 3.7 | 21.3 |
| Number of Employees | 17,900 | 3,402 | 1,800 | 500 | 1,540 |
| Main Products | Electric power (rates) | Bread, pastries, ice cream | Tomato ketchup, sauces, natural juices | Men's shoes | Building materials, chemicals, electronic circuits |

**Table 30.2A  Summary of Subject Organizations**

|  | Special Steel Company | Electric Appliance Company | Vehicle Company | Newspaper Company | Ceramics Company |
|---|---|---|---|---|---|
| Year Established | 1950 | 1949 | 1896 | 1942 | 1904 |
| Capital (¥ billion) | 12.5 | 7.3 | 4.1 | .3 | 4.16 |
| Sales (¥ billion) | 160 | 200 | 53.2 | 37.3 | 30.2 |
| Number of Employees | 9,200 | 19,500 | 4,300 | 4,015 | 4,000 |
| Main Products | Special steel materials, steel goods, industrial furnaces, cast steel | Electric equipment for automobiles | Trains, iron structures, industrial machine, plants | Daily and monthly magazines, irregular publication | Ceramics, whetstones, electronic parts, environmental tools |

**Table 30.2B**

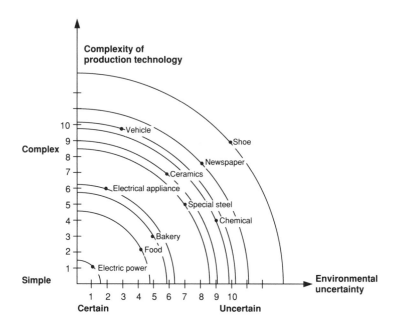

**Figure 30.2 Environmental Variety of Subject Organizations**

vehicle, chemical, ceramics, special steel, electric appliance, bakery, and food companies, in that order. The power company was discovered to have the least environmental variety.

The ten subject companies were divided into two groups according to the level of the sense of competence; the top five in one group, and the bottom five in another. The top five were the shoe, power, newspaper, bakery, and food companies. The bottom five were the vehicle, electrical appliance, ceramics, chemical, and special steel companies. In each group, seven rank correlation coefficients were obtained between the variable of environmental variety (one variable) and the variables of budgeting decision-making structure (seven variables).

The results in Table 30.3 show that six rank correlation coefficients of the top five group were larger than then the corresponding correlation coefficients of the bottom five group. This indicates that the degree of match between environmental variety and budgeting decision-making structure is related to performance. The hypothesis of this study, therefore, has been generally supported.

Let's examine the results of the top five groups shown in Table 30.3. The ranking in the second column, "Environmental Variety," completely coincides with the ranking in the third column, "Number of Divisions," and the rank correlation coefficient is 1. This means that the greater the environmental variety, the greater the number of divisions.

The rank correlation coefficient between the fourth column, "Time Orientation," and Environmental Variety" is 0.65. This means that the organization with a more unstable environment cannot have a long-range viewpoint, and does not set long-range plans. On the other hand, the organization with a more stable environment is setting long-range plans covering several years and using projects allocated in the first year of its long-range plan for budgeting. This supports the hypothesis: "Under an effective budgeting system, plans are set from the viewpoint of shorter terms as environmental variety increases."

The rank correlation coefficient between the fifth column, "Formality of Performance Feedback," and "Environmental Variety" is as high as 0.90. This result supports the hypothesis: "Under an effective budgeting system, performance feedback becomes more flexible as environmental variety increases."

Through analysis of the overall organizational structure, Lorsch (1965) has presented a theory that "less structured organizations are more effective when their tasks have a higher level of uncertainty and changeability; more structuralized organizations are more effective when the certainty of the task is high." The results of our study support Lorsch's theory.

The rank correlation coefficient between the fifth column, "Direction of Initiation and Approval (I)," and "Environmental Variety" is a moderate 0.50. This result indicates that the preparation process of budget guidelines may be determined by factors other than environmental variety.

The rank correlation coefficient between the seventh column, "Direction of Initiation and Approval (II)," and "Environmental Variety" is as high as 0.90. This result supports the hypothesis: "Under an effective budgeting system, direction of initiation and approval is likely to be bottom-up in a greater number of cases as environmental variety increases."

The rank correlation coefficient between the eighth column, "Discretion in Decision-making Process," and "Environmental Variety"

**Table 30.3A** Match between Environmental Variety and Budgeting Decision-Making Structure: (A) Top Five Group with Stronger Sense of Competence and (B) Bottom Five Group with Weaker Sense of Competence

| Organization | Environmental Variety | Number of Divisions | Time Orientation | Formality of Performance Feedback | Direction of Initiation and Approval (I)** | Direction of Initiation and Approval (II)*** | Discretion in Decision-Making Process | Degree of Democracy in Resolving Conflicts |
|---|---|---|---|---|---|---|---|---|
| Shoe | 181 (1)* | 2.70 (1)* | 4.0 (1)* | 7.0 (1) | 4.5 (1)* | 5.3 (1)* | 8.00 (1)* | 8.50 (1)* |
| Newspaper | 128 (2) | 0.80 (2) | 7.0 (3) | 6.0 (2) | 2.5 (4) | 4.7 (2) | 5.35 (4) | 7.97 (2) |
| Bakery | 34 (3) | 0.32 (3) | 6.0 (2) | 6.0 (2) | 3.5 (2) | 3.8 (3) | 7.17 (2) | 7.10 (3) |
| Food | 20 (4) | 10.22 (4) | 7.0 (3) | 4.0 (4) | 1.5 (5) | 3.0 (5) | 6.39 (3) | 6.75 (4) |
| Power | 2 (5) | 0.16 (5) | 7.0 (3) | 4.0 (4) | 3.0 (3) | 3.1 (4) | 5.30 (5) | 5.80 (5) |
| Spearman Rank Correlation Coefficient | 1.00 | 1.00 | 0.65 | 0.90 | 0.50 | 0.90 | 0.70 | 1.00 |

**Table 30.3B**

| Organization | Environmental Variety | Number of Divisions | Time Orientation | Formality of Performance Feedback | Direction of Initiation and Approval (I)** | Direction of Initiation and Approval (II)*** | Discretion in Decision-Making Process | Degree of Democracy in Resolving Conflicts |
|---|---|---|---|---|---|---|---|---|
| Vehicle | 109 (1) | 1.04 (3) | 4.0 (1) | 6.0 (3) | 3.0 (3)* | 3.9 (5) | 4.75 (5) | 8.03 (2) |
| Chemicals | 97 (2) | 1.07 (2) | 6.0 (2) | 6.0 (3) | 4.0 (1) | 4.0 (4) | 5.89 (3) | 6.78 (5) |
| Ceramics | 85 (3) | 1.72 (1) | 8.0 (1) | 8.0 (1) | 2.0 (4) | 5.7 (2) | 6.06 (2) | 8.11 (1) |
| Steel | 74 (4) | 0.25 (5) | 6.0 (2) | 7.0 (2) | 4.0 (1) | 4.4 (3) | 6.46 (1) | 6.86 (4) |
| Electric Appliances | 40 (5) | 0.58 (4) | 8.0 (4) | 6.0 (3) | 2.0 (4) | 6.0 (1) | 4.80 (4) | 7.77 (3) |
| Spearman Rank Correlation Coefficient | 0.30 | 0.50 | 0.70 | 0.20 | 0.30 | -0.90 | -0.30 | 0.10 |

* Parenthesized figures indicate ranking of each indicator within the group.
** Indicator: Bottom-up or top-down preparation of budget guidelines.
*** Indicator: Level of budget initiation in organizational hierarchy.

is as high as 0.70. This result can be interpreted as indicating that more discretion is given to divisions directly related to sales in organizations with a more unstable market environment among other environmental factors. In other words, the more stable the corporation's market environment, the more structured the planning procedures and the higher the reliance on objective data in decision making.

The ranking in the ninth column, "Degree of Democracy in Resolving Conflict," completely coincides with the ranking of "Environmental Variety." This result indicates that, in organizations with a complex technological environment, top management does not exercise its authority over coordination of units at the lower level. Coordination among lower-level units is made democratically. Such democratic coordination is likely to give a stronger sense of competence to managers.

*Conclusion.* The results of this empirical study concerning relationships among market environment, technology, budgeting decision-making structure, and sense of competence by the manager have proven that the degree of match between environmental variety and the budgeting decision-making structure is related to a sense of competence. These results provide the following useful guideline for designing a budgeting system that is optimal for adapting to the environment; that is, when the degree of match between the environment and budgeting decision-making structure decreases as a result of changes in the environment, performance can be improved by increasing the degree of match with changes in the budgeting decision-making structure.

### References

1. Bruns, W.J., and J.H. Waterhouse. (1975). "Budgetary Control and Organizational Structure." *Journal of Accounting Research*, 13: 177-203.
2. Duncan, R.B. (1972). "Characteristics of Organizational Environments and Perceived Environmental Uncertainty," *Administrative Science Quarterly*, 17: 313-327.
3. Galbraith, J. (1977). *Organization Design*. Reading, MA: Addison-Wesley.
4. Hayes, D.C. (1977). "The Contingency Theory of Managerial Accounting." *The Accounting Review*, 52: 22-39.
5. Kojima, H. (1982). *Kigyokankyo to kanrishisutemu* (Environment and Management Systems). (Written in Japanese.) Tokyo: Chuokeizaisha.

6. Lawrence, P.R., and J.W. Lorsch. (1967). *Organization and Environment*. Boston: Research Division, Harvard Business School.
7. Lorsch, J.W. (1965). *Product Innovation and Organization*. London: Macmillan.
8. Lorsch, J.W., and J.J. Morse. (1974). *Organizations and Their Members*. New York: Harper and Row.
9. Nadler, D.A., J.R. Hackman, and E.E. Lawler III. (1979). *Making Organizational Behavior*. Boston: Little, Brown.
10. Nonaka, I. (1972). *Organization and Market: Exploratory Study of Centralization Versus Decentralization*, Ph.D. dissertation, Graduate School of Business Administration, University of California, Berkeley.
11. Swieringa, R.J., and R.H. Moncur. (1972). "The Relationship Between Managers' Budget-Oriented Behavior and Selected Attitude, Position, Size and Performance Measures," *Empirical Research in Accounting: Selected Studies*, 194-205.
12. Thompson, J.D. (1967). *Organizations in Action*. New York: McGraw-Hill.
13. Tushman, M., and D.A. Nadler. (1978). "Information Processing As an Integrating Concept in Organizational Design," *Academy of Management Review*, 3: 613-624.
14. Woodward, J. (1965). *Industrial Organization: Theory and Practice*. London: Oxford University Press.

# 31

## Financial Characteristics of Japanese Corporations

*Rinya Shibakawa, Institute of Socio-Economic Planning, University of Tsukuba*

It is a commonly known fact that Japanese firms had a strong tendency to be dependent on short-term debt. For instance, the debt/equity ratio, which was 35 percent in overall industries, was 302 percent in manufacturing industries in 1967. This means debt amounted to more than three times equity. The main reason for such a debt increase lies in the fact that companies endeavored to reduce costs through equipment modernization in an effort to improve production efficiency. They also tried to modernize production processes by introducing advanced techniques from foreign countries like the United States. Textile, chemical, steel, and shipbuilding companies made remarkable progress using this method.

Competition between lending institutions, accompanied by an increasing number of bank branches countrywide, is the second reason. By expanding the branch network, banks could absorb and accumulate funds from customers and actively lend monies to companies. There is no denying, therefore, that the competition among banks for deposits and lending resulted in the increasing debt/equity ratios in the industrial environment.

When a company's sales growth ratio and the industry as a whole maintain high levels, most companies suffer from a shortage of funds. With unavailable cash to remedy such conditions and with acutely short internal funds, companies inevitably had to depend on external funds. The debt was mostly short-term, and the issuance of bonds was negligible because the bond market structure was not flexible enough to use its funds for capital expenditures. This made the financial relationship between commercial banks and companies still stronger.

To illustrate this fact, let's look at the financial connection within the same group (*keiretsu*). City banks concentrated funding to these *keiretsu*. The bond among the same *keiretsu* — such as Mitsubishi or Sumitomo, the old financial trusts — is strong. They received financing privileges from the city banks. It is true, however, that companies belonging to the same *keiretsu* may receive financing from other *keiretsu* banks. Also, the percentage of total funds obtained from the main bank are not always high. Companies try to keep their financing rates among correspondent banks equal. Of course, they enjoy preferential treatment from the main banks in terms of financing and borrowing conditions. Borrowing customs of Japanese companies from commercial banks will be explained.

First, if they rely only on their *keiretsu*, it is impossible to cover the tremendous demands of equipment expenditures. In addition, it is wise to stretch the network of mutual stock ownership among as many other industrial companies as possible. Second, although borrowers must bear the risk of fluctuating investment income, the banks also share this business risk. Their financing ratio from external sources is high, and secured loans are common forms of long-term financing.

In U.S. companies, the debt ratio is low, and plant and equipment are generally financed by retained earnings. They do not borrow beyond the level of their ability to bear the business risk. This restricts the quantity and modernization of equipment, and helps to explain why Japanese companies promote it more actively.

The existence and behavior of giant corporations have an insignificant influence on the Japanese economy. The 284 companies with capital stock of over ¥50 billion hold 37.88 percent of the total owners' capital. These giant corporations form company groups within the same groups. The most famous company groups are the Big Six: Mitsui, Sumitomo, Mitsubishi (which was the Zaibatsu prior to World War II), Fuyo (Fuji), Sanwa, and Daiichi Kangin. These groups strengthen their connections with one another through mutual stock ownership, presidents' meetings within groups, and financing fellow group members. (See Table 31.1.)

| Company Groups / Items | Holding Stock Ratio | Lending Ratio | Dispatching Officers Ratio |
|---|---|---|---|
| Mitsui | 16.3 | 18.3 | 4.1 |
| Mitsubishi | 26.1 | 24.9 | 13.1 |
| Sumitomo | 27.4 | 27.3 | 13.4 |
| Fuyo (Fuji) | 16.3 | 21.0 | 4.7 |
| Sanwa | 16.9 | 19.1 | 5.8 |
| Daiichi Kangin | 14.0 | 12.8 | 8.9 |

(Source) *Kigyo keiretsu soran* (1981), *Toyo Keizai Shinposha.*

**Table 31.1  The Six Big Company Groups**

| | 1979 | 1980 |
|---|---|---|
| Number of companies | 1732 | 1734 |
| Government and Local Government | 0.2 | 0.2 |
| Institutions | 69.4 | 70.5 |
| Financial Institutions | 38.8 | 38.8 |
| Banks and Bank Trusts | 19.5 | 19.2 |
| Life Insurance | 12.3 | 12.5 |
| Casualty Insurance | 4.9 | 4.9 |
| Security Finance Companies | 0.9 | 0.9 |
| Other Banks | 1.2 | 1.3 |
| Security Companies | 2.0 | 1.7 |
| Business Institutions | 26.1 | 26.0 |
| Foreign Institutions | 2.4 | 4.0 |
| Individuals, Others | 30.4 | 29.2 |
| Foreign Individuals | 0 | 0.1 |

(Source) *Nihon Keizai Shimbun,* July 17, 1981.

**Table 31.2  Holding Stock Ratios (Percent)**

The phenomenon of mutual stock ownership illustrates the management control characteristic of Japanese corporations. As shown in Figure 31.1, the ratio of individual stock holdings decreased rapidly after 1950, and institutional stockholders held almost 40 percent by 1980. Since the issue of stock results in greater mutual stockholding by *keiretsu*, it is easier for securities companies to accept the new issues, and they implicitly consent without intervention of partners' management. This shows that, in Japan, the management control has been established. This phenomenon of institutionalization in stockholders will conceivably prevent the takeover of Japanese companies by foreign companies or foreign nationals. The Japanese government and Japan's corporate management fear takeover by U.S. industry giants as a result of the liberalization of foreign capital. They therefore sought to hold one another's stock as a precaution.

**Stabilizing Capital Structure.** In their high-growth period, Japanese companies lacked capital and were forced to rely on debt capital. Financial institutions found they could earn a profit by lending money. In other words, there was a favorable return on investment (ROI) and an active economic environment. This is nothing more than an increase of growth ratio and market share in a high-growth period. It was likely that cash flow would increase along with the rising market share.

The relationship between ROI and debt financing is widely known as a leverage effect. An effect such as return on equity capital increases with the use of leverage. The return on equity is:

$$(1) \qquad q = r + (r - i)\, \frac{D}{S}$$

where

$q$ = return on equity
$r$ = ROI
$i$ = interest rate
$$\frac{D}{S} = \frac{\text{debt}}{\text{equity ratio}}$$

In this equation, if $i$ and $D/S$ are constant, then $r$ alone is variable. Therefore

$$(2) \qquad \tilde{q} = \tilde{r} + (\tilde{r} - i)\, \frac{D}{S}$$

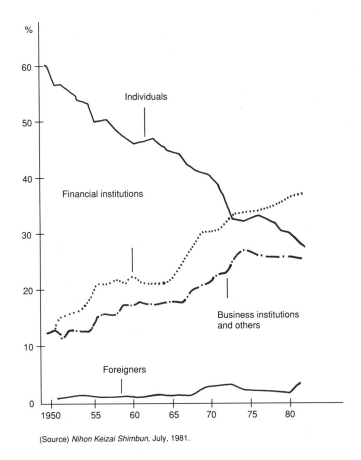

(Source) *Nihon Keizai Shimbun*, July, 1981.

**Figure 31.1 Trends of Holding Stock Ratio by Owners**

Assume that variable $\tilde{r}$ is distributed normally. We can show two parameters of this equation, the mean and standard deviation:

(3)
$$E\ (\tilde{q}) = E\ (\tilde{r}) + \{E\ (\tilde{r}) - i\}\ \frac{D}{S}$$

(4)
$$= E\ (\tilde{r})\ \{1 + \frac{D}{S}\} - i\ \frac{D}{S}$$

(5)
$$\text{Var}\ (\tilde{q}) = \{1 + \frac{D}{S}\}^2\ \sigma^2\ (\tilde{r})$$

or

$$\sigma\ (\tilde{q}) = \{1 + \frac{D}{S}\}\ \sigma\ (\tilde{r})$$

(6)
$$= \sigma\ (\tilde{r}) + \sigma\ (\tilde{r})\ \frac{D}{S}$$

In Equation 6, we can define $\sigma(\bar{r})$ as the business risk that relates to the volatility of earnings by investment decisions, and $\sigma(\bar{r})D/S$ as the financial risk that relates to the volatility of earnings by financing decisions. The former has something to do with fluctuations in business income and earnings before interest and taxes; the latter deals with net income fluctuations.

Let's examine the leverage effects using Equation 6:

(i)    If $r = i$,    $q = r$
(ii)   If $r > i$,    $q > r$
(iii)  If $r < i$,    $q < r$

In short, the return on equity equals ROI (i) since $r$ equals $i$; (ii) when ROI becomes larger than the interest rate, return on equity is greater than ROI; and (iii) is the reverse of (ii).

The assumption of a constant $D/S$ means that, if debt over equity is constant, then the interest rate (i) is also constant. If we relax this assumption, the ratio of debt to equity rises. If we assume a constant interest rate, then:

(i)    If $r = i$,    $q = r$
(ii)   If $r > i$,    more and more $q > r$
(iii)  If $r < i$,    more and more $q < r$

While the implication is fundamentally the same, differences lie in the use of leverages. For instance, in case (ii), if the return on total assets is greater than the interest rate, the return on equity is greater than ROI.

As is clear from the analysis, it is $r > i$ alone that allows leverage to work favorably on the companies concerned. They can then expand business by leverage. The behavior of Japanese companies in the high-growth period is an example. When there are favorable investment opportunities, as in Equation 6, business as well as financial risks do not serve as a source of anxiety. When ROI drops below the interest rate $r < i$), however, the existence of debt increases the possibility of default.

It may be safely said, therefore, that default means the same as $r < 1$. Thus, in a low-growth period, it is more likely that companies will suffer a loss in performance. They have to return to a balance of debt and decrease their amount of investment as much as possible. This means making risk [ $\sigma(r)D/S$ ] as small as possible, or risk decreases by increasing equity ($S$).

***Diversification of Financing Mix.*** The previous section considered the financial behavior of Japanese corporations during the stable growth period following the first oil crisis. There were two guiding principles of financial behavior: (1) the goal of sales growth, and (2) the rate of return on total assets (ROI). Sales growth was emphasized in times of high economic growth; ROI was effective in guiding capital efficiently and played an important role in creating internal funds. ROI increases greatly influenced not only the debt/equity ratio, but also leverage effects. Their relationship to each other must be considered along with the interest rate. ROI relates to the supply of funds created, just as sales growth relates to demand. If sales growth is overemphasized, the company risks a shortage of funds. When overly stressed, however, ROI results in excessive funds. Therefore, to normalize the balance between the supply and demand of funds, these two contradicting goals must be balanced. Only when this equilibrium is attained can companies become financially self-sufficient.

Donaldson (1984) states that to attain an equilibrium between total supply and demand of funds, they must be equal. Then the sales growth is greater than the goals of industry, and also the rate of investment growth equals the rate of sales growth. From this theorem, we can reach the following growth equation:

(7)     $g(S) = r [\text{RONA} + d (\text{RONA} - i)]$

where  $g(S)$ = companies' rate of sales growth

RONA = rate of return on set assets

[RONA = operating earnings $(1 - t)$

$$+ \quad \frac{iD (1 - t)}{\text{total assets} - \text{current debt}}]$$

$r$ = retention ratio

$d = \dfrac{\text{debt}}{\text{equity ratio}}$   $(D = \text{debt})$

$i$ = expected after-tax interest rate

$t$ = corporate tax rate

Now, in the case of $d = 0$, $r = 1$, companies with zero debt have a 100-percent retention ratio with a rate of sales growth equal to RONA. As shown in Figure 31.2, we can draw a 45-degree diagonal line because RONA equals the rate of sales growth. Self-sufficiency can be realized along this line. A point above the line reflects a shortage of funds, and a point below the line represents excess funds. In reality, however, companies have to coordinate their goals system, which means balancing the supply and demand of funds since there is little chance that the debt/equity ratio will be zero.

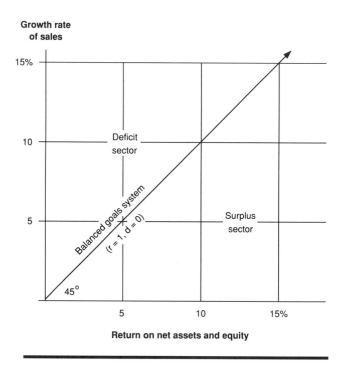

Note: r = earnings retension ratio
      d = debt/equity ratio
(Source) Donaldson (1), Figure 4.1, p. 68.

Figure 31.2  Self-Sustaining Goals System for a Company with Zero Debt and Zero Dividends

We will now discuss the financial behavior of Japanese corporations from the standpoint of a balanced goals system, with semiconductor industries in Japan as an example. The integrated circuit (IC) industries have a high skill level of adding value to products compared to the electronics, biotech, new materials industries called the ultra-modern techno-industry. The Japanese IC industries are managed as divisions of established companies, contrary to those in the

United States, which themselves specialize in these products. For example, the heavy electric divisions of Hitachi, Toshiba, and Mitsubishi electric companies could not increase sales in March 1984. Their respective electronics divisions, however, achieved rapid growth sustained by the demands for office automation equipment and semiconductors. In addition, sales of the semiconductor division equalled 12 percent of total sales, reflecting a rate of increase of this investment over its rate of sales increases. In this year, these companies actively pursued semiconductor equipment for all investments. For example, Hitachi spent ¥800 million of its total ¥1,800 million, and Toshiba ¥1,030 million of ¥1,505 million.

Let's look at the case of Hitachi. The period of analysis is from 1977 to 1983 (see Table 31.3), and the assumptions are:

1. We regard total sales as the sale of semiconductors because it is impossible to separate these two sales amounts, due to the dominance of semiconductor sales over other divisions.
2. We take debt equity ratio as being the long-term debt equity ratio.

In Figure 31.3, rate of sales growth, RONA, retention ratio, debt equity ratio, and after-tax interest rate are shown annually. We set the average of $r$ and $i$ as each target T, and the target of debt equity ratio $d$ is the average of 1981-1983 because this ratio is relatively stable during these years. Two solid and dotted lines are drawn, based on growth Equation 7. The solid line shows 66.62 percent in the target or retention ratio; the dotted line shows 55 percent. If we see the solid line as an equilibrium of self-sustaining goals, the company's total performance is included in the excess zone of the diagram, deviating significantly from the equilibrium line. The goals, therefore, must be corrected. The retention ratio was set at 55 percent levels, equal to other companies in the same industry. It is the dotted equilibrium line. As a result, Hitachi's performance reached the standard value ( ◇ mark) in zone II in the 1979-1980 period, but moved to zone I, the growth area, between 1981 and 1982. Shortage of funds had to be financed from external sources, which means deviating from the self-sustaining goals system.

Toshiba, in Figure 31.4, shows unstable movement in its rate of sales growth and RONA, especially from 1982 to 1983, but in 1982, it is regarded as moving toward zone II. For reference, in Figure 31.5 (see page 499), Mitsubishi entered the unsuccessful achievement

| Items / Company | Growth of Sales | | RONA | | Retention Rate | | Debt Equity Ratio | | Rate of Interest (*0.5) | |
|---|---|---|---|---|---|---|---|---|---|---|
| | H | T | H | T | H | T | H | T | H | T |
| **Year** | | | | | | | | | | |
| 1977 | 7.24% | 10.02% | 13.99% | 13.99% | 49.93% | 27.32% | 78.75% | 92.37% | 4.05% | 4.51% |
| 1978 | 8.70 | 16.88 | 15.28 | 17.81 | 57.80 | 39.95 | 70.86 | 75.40 | 3.71 | 4.10 |
| 1979 | 12.50 | 15.13 | 18.68 | 28.53 | 69.94 | 68.25 | 59.30 | 57.67 | 4.36 | 4.94 |
| 1980 | 14.66 | 8.40 | 19.23 | 26.32 | 69.62 | 64.71 | 53.60 | 54.73 | 5.21 | 5.94 |
| 1981 | 9.96 | 12.90 | 17.99 | 24.48 | 70.96 | 64.45 | 44.68 | 34.75 | 5.07 | 6.19 |
| 1982 | 8.99 | 1.48 | 17.49 | 19.49 | 73.54 | 62.05 | 42.70 | 36.93 | 4.81 | 5.69 |
| 1983 | 13.50 | 14.25 | 15.50 | 36.98 | 74.57 | 61.31 | 51.55 | 49.48 | 4.29 | 5.18 |
| **Average** | | | | | | | | | | |
| 1977-83 | 10.79% | 11.29% | 16.88% | 23.94% | 66.62% | 55.43% | 57.35% | 57.33% | 4.50% | 5.22% |
| 1981-83 | 10.81 | 9.54 | 16.99 | 26.98 | 73.02 | 62.60 | 46.31 | 40.39 | 4.72 | 5.69 |

(Note: H = Hitachi, T = Toshiba)

**Table 31.3 Annual Performance of Main Financial Ratios (1977-1983)**

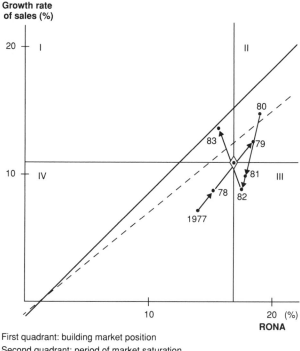

First quadrant: building market position
Second quadrant: period of market saturation
Third quadrant: harvesting period
Fourth quadrant: liquidating period

**Figure 31.3 Hitachi's Performance (1977-1983)**

zone II in 1981 and 1982, and again in 1983. This brought a decrease in RONA. Mitsubishi adopted the strategy that depended most on external funds, however, to accommodate its increasing growth rate. And Mitsubishi seems to be restricting itself to the self-sustaining goals system more than Hitachi and Toshiba.

In other words, we note that Hitachi and Toshiba chose the strategy of new product development, which needs internal and external funds and their diverse resources to cope with the ROI deterioration of saturated products. The tendency now is to regard funding the development of new technology and products as more important than merely raising ROI by reducing costs. Hitachi best exemplifies this strategy. Table 31.4 (see page 498) shows Toshiba and Hitachi's actual conditions of equipment financing right after the first oil crisis.

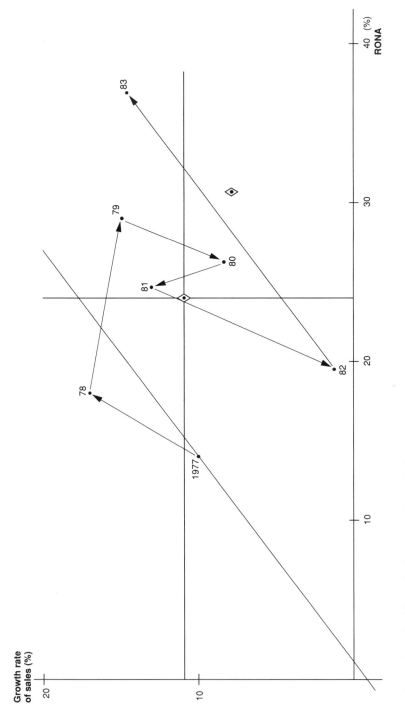

**Figure 31.4 Toshiba's Performance (1977-1983)**

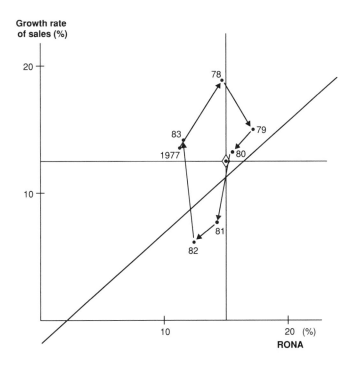

**Figure 31.5 Mitsubishi's Performance (1977-1983)**

Hitachi tried to drastically reduce its debt capital and increase its self-financing as compared to Toshiba, which arranged various financings. Hitachi, however, promoted internationalization of finance around 1979, when economic conditions were restored. Hitachi, which had not carried out financing in the international market until then, actively pushed its overseas business and financing. As the first step, it took the highest bond rating (AAA) in 1980 of two bond-rating agencies, Standard & Poors' (S&P) and Moodys, issued $150 million of convertible bonds in 1981, and accomplished ADR issues of stock on the New York Stock Exchange. The capital structures of semiconductor companies in Japan and the United States is shown in Table 31.5 (see page 502).

*Conclusion.* As bank borrowing was the most profitable means of financing, banks and companies created a closer relationship than usual. We find this in the phenomenon of a main bank system, financing within similar groups, and dispatching corporate officers.

| Methods of Financing | Names of Firms | | | |
|---|---|---|---|---|
| | Fuji Heavy Industries, Ltd. | Ebara Corporation | Toshiba Corporation | Hitachi Ltd. |
| Deferment of Equipment Construction/Reduction of the Size of the Firm | No | Yes | No | Yes (partial reduction of the size of the firm) |
| Methods of Equipment Financing | Debt capital and equity capital | Only equity capital since 1974 | Equity capital, debenture, and convertible debenture | Only equity capital since 1974 |
| Forms of Collateral | Factory foundation and others | Factory foundation, national loan, and stock collateral | Securities, collateral of a company's entire assets | Mortgage on factories |

| | | | | |
|---|---|---|---|---|
| Debenture Issue and Convertible Debenture Issue | Debenture in 1975/convertible debenture in 1973 | Convertible debenture in 1977 | Convertible debenture in 1973 and 1974 and debenture in 1974, 1975, and 1976 | Debenture in 1974, and convertible debenture in 1973 |
| Flotation of Foreign Bonds | Debenture on German Mark base | No | Convertible debenture on dollar base | No |
| Conditions on the Limit of Dividend | No | No | Yes (on an unsecured debenture) | No |
| Other Characteristics | Debts and repayment of long-term loans from correspondent banks in balance | No long-term loan/quickening repayment of debts | Making use of many short-term foreign exchange debts | Making use of many long-term foreign exchange loans/the amount of repayment of debts is conspicuous |

Table 31.4 Shifting Methods of Financing Long-Term Debt (October 1973-March 1979)

| | Internal Funds | Stocks | Bonds | Other Debts |
|---|---|---|---|---|
| (Japanese Industries) | | | | |
| Fujitsu | 44.6% | 10.5% | 11.9% | 33.0% |
| Hitachi | 45.6 | 14.8 | 5.4 | 34.2 |
| Mitsubishi Electric | 31.0 | 14.3 | 9.5 | 45.2 |
| (U.S. Industries) Average 1975-79 | 79.0% | 6.6% | 8.6% | 5.8% |

**Table 31.5  Main Capital Sources of Japanese and U.S. Semi-Conductor Industries**

When the companies entered the low-growth period after 1973, however, capital expenditures were controlled and the banks were mostly abandoned. But this does not mean that the top management of Japanese companies have the independence of their U.S. counterparts. We must take into account the existence of financing customs between banks and companies. This is called *karikae*, or debt renewal, which means that payments and borrowing are repeated regularly. Some debt balance always remains and full repayment is not expected at once. This equals the liquid reserve of off-balance sheets in some sense. Thus, financing debt not substantially different from equity and does exist in the financial behavior of large Japanese corporations.

Japanese management paid little attention to the price of stocks (formation) in the capital markets over long periods because the stock exchange in Japan developed slowly until 1970 and funds were issued in par value. An explicit relationship between stock prices and other financial goals does not exist. Since growth rate pressures are strong, demands for capital expenditures are great, and RONA is often sacrificed. We must trade off the growth rate of sales with RONA, and maintain a balance between the supply and demand of funds over time. Japanese companies reflect their owners, however, and this is the cause of their high stability of retention ratio. Managers naturally control only the debt/equity ratio. Because of this priority of growth rate, Japanese companies easily resort to debt capital, a phenomenon that appeared frequently in the high-growth periods. Once growth is stable, they can finance profitability from external sources, controlling the growth rate and RONA, because of the increase of internal sources (earning rate and depreciation). This is the reason convertible bonds increase drastically abroad.

### References

1. Ando, Y. (1982). *Nihon niokeru kigyosyudan to kaisya shikai* (Company Groups in Japan and Corporate Control). Iwata, I., and Takahashi, S., eds., Otsuki Syoten.
2. Donaldson, G. (1984). *Managing Corporate Wealth: The Operation of a Comprehensive Financial Goals System*, Praeger.
3. Itami, H. (1982). *Nihonteki keireiron o koete — kigyo keieiryoku no hikaku* (Beyond the Theory of Japanese Management: Comparison of Management Power of Japanese and U.S. Companies). Toyo Eizai Shinposha.
4. Kobayashi, J. (1985). *Kaigai shikin chotatsu* (Overseas Financing). Yuhikaku.
5. Shimura, Y. (1984). *IC sangyo no shintenkai* (New Development of IC Industry in Japan). Diamond Publishing.

# 32

## The Dividend Policy of Japanese Corporations

*Yasuhiro Yonezawa, Institute of Socio-Economic Planning,
University of Tsukuba*

The purpose of this chapter is to explain the dividend policy of
Japanese corporations from the theoretical and empirical points of
view. The Japanese dividend policy is explained best by the *permanent
profit hypothesis*; that is, corporations pay out as dividends a certain
proportion of their permanent profits. In the case of asymmetrical information between management and investors about future profits,
the dividend works as a signal of inside information concerning future profits. Then, dividend policy becomes a more simple matter.

Miller and Modigliani (hereafter M.M.) argued that corporate
dividend policy itself does not make sense in determining its stock
price. In one assumption of the M.M. model, however, if a perfect information structure is replaced by an *asymmetrical information structure*
between investors and corporate managers, this proposition cannot
be established.

Let's consider, for instance, that some financial variables (or policy) reveal the important corporate activity or decisions known only
to insiders (management). If investors can estimate such inside information by watching these financial variables, the variables become
relevant to stock price and are said to have information content. Our
purpose is to pick up the *dividend per share* of Japanese corporations as

such a financial variable and make the information content of dividends clear from the theoretical and empirical points of view to analyze the economic mechanism of Japanese corporate dividend policy.

First, we will set up our theoretical model of dividend policy under the asymmetrical information structure. By this, we mean that permanent corporate profits — calculated by inside information in our model — determine the current dividend payout. Therefore, the dividend has the information content of permanent corporate profit. We will then test this hypothesis with data from Japanese corporations.

Our empirical test does not reject this hypothesis. The stable movement of dividend is also explained by this hypothesis because changes in permanent profits are more stable than fluctuations in the actual profits. We do not need ad hoc explanations like Lintner's partial adjustment hypothesis; partial adjustment of dividend to the target one.

The information content of dividend policy has been studied in two ways. One is a signaling approach (Bhattacharya, 1979); another is an accounting information approach (Pettit, 1972; Watts, 1973). The former starts the theory by assuming that a dividend has some information content, then discusses a sufficient condition under which a signaling equilibrium exists. The latter discusses empirically the information content of an actual dividend without any theoretical background.

There are two excellent exceptions. Miller and Rock (1985) discuss the microfoundation of the information content of dividend policies comprehensively, referring to the effects of investment decision. Since they are usually discussed only in the restrictive (for example, two-period) model, however, it is difficult to test them empirically. Although Nakamura and Nakamura's (1985) approach is more similar to our theory, they still rely on Lintner's (1956) partial adjustment hypothesis.

Thus, these approaches have some weak points in describing the actual Japanese dividend policy. Our main purpose is to present a dividend policy in a dynamic framework with information content, and to show that this hypothetical dividend policy corresponds fairly well to the actual Japanese dividend policy.

***Japanese Dividend Policy.*** The dividend policy of Japanese corporations consists of two steps. First, through financial policies, management plans to detrend a stream of expected after-tax net profit per share $x_t$ (hereafter simply called profit). As a result, a stream of expected profit becomes trendless, although it may jump or move cyclically, as shown in Figure 32.1. So they must increase the number of shares when $x_t$ is growing.

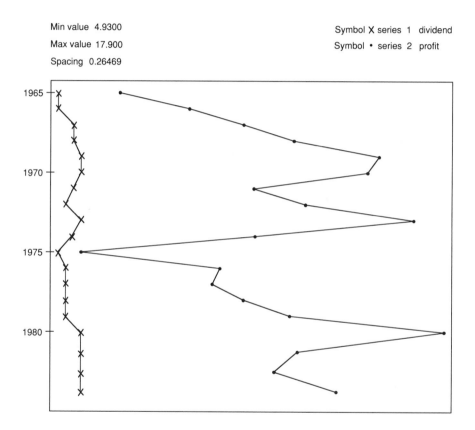

Min value  4.9300

Max value  17.900

Spacing  0.26469

Symbol X series  1  dividend

Symbol •  series  2  profit

**Figure 32.1  Fluctuation of Dividends and Profits in All Industries**

They have taken the following two alternative financial methods to increase the number of shares:

1. Formerly, they detrended $x_t$ by allotting new shares at their face value, which is ¥50 in the standard case and much lower than the market value. This financial policy has two functions: (a) to finance the funds needed and (b) to increase the number of shares. This policy has recently been replaced by the policy of issuing shares at the market value.

2. They recently detrended $xt$ by the stock dividend (free distribution). It corresponds to a stock split in the United States. This policy's only function is to increase the number of shares.

Since these two methods can increase share quantity without diluting stockholders' rights, they can adjust the number of shares properly.

Second, managers compute the permanent after-tax net profit per share (permanent profit) at time $t$, $xpt$ with inside information. Permanent profit can be defined as the constant profit with the same present value as the actual expected profit stream.[1] Thus, with the expected profit stream and discount rate, management can calculate permanent profit, which may be regarded by management as the normal profit. For example, if management regards an increase of actual profit as transitory, the calculated permanent profit is much more stable than that of actual profit. Since this permanent profit can be obtained with management's inside information about expected future profits, corporate outsiders, such as investors, cannot see these permanent profits directly. Then management decides the dividend payout per share (or simply, dividend) $dt$ as follows:

$$(1) \qquad d_t = kx_{pt} \qquad 0 \le k \le 1$$

where $k$ is a constant payout ratio. Since the dividend is linked to permanent not current profit, it fluctuates slowly.

**Dynamic Behavior of Dividends.** With the dividend policy composed of these two steps, the dynamic behavior of dividends can be formulated approximately using the following equation, under the rational expectations of managers about future expected profits:[2]

$$(2) \qquad d_{t+1} = \theta d_t + e_{t+1}$$

$$E\left(\frac{e_{t+1}}{d_t}\right) = 0$$

where the value of $\theta$ must be nearly 1. So it is like the *random walk*, which implies that in forecasting $dt + 1$, $dt$ is the sufficient statistic. In other words, $dt$ summarizes all the information available at time $t$, so $et + 1$ is the unpredictable error. It is important that Equation 2 be achieved under whatever complicated moving pattern of profits satisfies the trendless condition. This is our fundamental equation of dividend policy.

*Information Content.* In the case of asymmetrical information between management and investors, the dividend policy already discussed plays an important economic role because investor information is bound to be inferior to that of management. They can know only permanent profits with uncertainty. It is useful for investors to calculate their demand prices for stock.[3] If it becomes available to every investor, the stock market becomes more efficient.

As far as Japanese dividend policy is concerned, if investors know the levels of each corporation's $k$, each of $xpt$ can be known to them by $dt/k$. In other words, $dt$ has information content of $xpt$ under this asymmetric information structure and influences the share price as follows:

$$d_{t+1} > 0 \, d_t \longrightarrow \text{good news}$$
$$d_{t+1} < 0 \, d_t \longrightarrow \text{bad news}$$
$$d_{t+1} = 0 \, d_t \longrightarrow \text{no news}$$

Good news corresponds to an increase in the current permanent profit. Every investor can perceive that management gets good news about the expected future profits. On the other hand, bad news corresponds to a decrease in the permanent profit.

*Empirical Analysis.* In the United States, management pays special attention to the "dividend-payout ratio" (dividend/profit) and tries to maintain it at a certain level for a long time. On the other hand, Japanese management makes much of the "dividend ratio" (dividend/face value of a stock) and manages to maintain it at a certain level. We can support these well-known facts with data. In the Japanese financial system, the face value of a stock is ¥50 and the profit fluctuates between ¥8 and ¥18, dividend stays around ¥5. In fact, dividends of Japanese corporations have been stable. But as already described, dividend payout has not been independent of profit. For instance, when profit increased in 1973, dividend increased also. In the following section, we will test our dividend hypothesis (Equation 2) with 33 industrial groups using the 1965-1983 annual data.

**Empirical results.** The estimated results of Equation 2 are shown in Table 32.1. Except for some industries such as electrical appliances, marine products, and sea transportation, the estimated value of $\Theta$ is close to 1. Almost all industries have the property of

$E(et + 1/\ dt) = 0$, but some industries, such as credit and leasing, trucking, and sea transportation, do not.[4] Table 32.1 also shows the tendency of profits: $a = 1$ implies trendless, $a < 1$ implies increasing, and $a > 1$ implies decreasing.[5] Except for textile products, petroleum, iron and steel, metal products, marine products, air transportation, and electric services, all of which have $a < 1$, estimated $a$ are close to 1. We find that estimated $\Theta$ are close to 1, even for these dull industries. Thus, we can reject our random walk hypothesis in only some industries.

**Discussion.** Under our assumption, we can estimate a dividend payout ratio for each industry.[6] (See Table 32.1.) The estimated $k$ of all industry is 33 percent. Those of iron and steel, marine products, railroad transportation, and electric services are relatively high. On the other hand, electrical appliances, motor vehicles, other manufacturing, credit and leasing, sea transportation, and communications are relatively low. In general, relatively high growth industries, for example electrical appliances, motor vehicles, other manufacturing, credit and leasing, sea transportation, and communications have low $k$. The reverse is true for textile products, iron and steel, metal products, marine products, air transportation, and electric services. By reducing dividend payout ratios, such industries can reach a sufficient volume of retained earnings for high investment ratios.

**The Lintner hypothesis.** We must now refer to the famous Lintner hypothesis on dividend policy, which we took up as an alternative hypothesis. Lintner formulated the following dividend hypothesis to explain the dividend payout policy of U.S. corporations:

$$(3)\quad D_t - D_{t-1} = c\,[D_t^* - D_{t-1}]\quad 0 \le c \le 1$$

In this setting, it is important to confirm that actual dividend $D_t$ does not convey any information to investors. $D_t$ is determined by $X_t$ and $D_t - 1$, but investors can observe $X_t$ and $D_t - 1$ directly. Therefore, there is no information content on dividends.

Why does management delay the adjustment of dividends? Is there a reasonable cause? Unlike investment behavior, adjustment

---

\* $D_t$ is the target total dividend payout at time $t$, and is determined by $k_0 + k_1 X_t$. $X_t$ is profit (not per share) at time $t$. This equation shows the partial adjustment process of actual dividend $D_t$ from the previous dividend $D_t - 1$ to the target; $D_t$; $c$ is the adjustment parameter.

| Industry Type | ∅ | p* | a | k |
|---|---|---|---|---|
| All | 1.008 | −0.084 | 1.03 | 0.33 |
| Food | 1.008 | −0.302 | 1.03 | 0.30 |
| Textile Products | 0.975 | 0.114 | 0.86 | 0.72 |
| Paper and Pulp | 1.015 | −0.036 | 0.97 | 0.40 |
| Chemicals | 0.979 | 0.291 | 1.04 | 0.30 |
| Drugs | 1.003 | −0.064 | 1.00 | 0.30 |
| Petroleum | 1.017 | −0.164 | 0.13 | −** |
| Rubber | 1.014 | −0.025 | 0.99 | 0.30 |
| Clay and Grass Products | 1.009 | 0.168 | 1.01 | 0.38 |
| Iron and Steel | 1.000 | −0.162 | 0.81 | 0.91 |
| Metal Products | 0.984 | 0.025 | 0.89 | 0.66 |
| Machinery | 1.011 | 0.414 | 1.01 | 0.35 |
| Electrical Equipment | 1.035 | 0.173 | 1.05 | 0.20 |
| Shipbuilding | 0.989 | −0.095 | 1.01 | 0.50 |
| Motor Vehicles | 1.024 | 0.400 | 1.00 | 0.25 |
| Transportation Equipment | 1.013 | 0.136 | 0.93 | 0.41 |
| Precision Instruments | 1.036 | 0.077 | 0.99 | 0.32 |
| Other Manufacturing | 1.007 | 0.180 | 1.04 | 0.21 |
| Marine Products | 0.934 | −0.132 | 0.83 | 0.87 |
| Mining | 1.001 | −0.002 | 0.97 | 0.43 |
| Construction | 0.987 | 0.335 | 0.98 | 0.40 |
| Trade | 0.999 | −0.003 | 1.02 | 0.29 |
| Retail Stores | 1.009 | 0.288 | 1.00 | 0.36 |
| Credit and Leasing | 1.029 | −0.562 | 1.02 | 0.19 |
| Real Estate | 0.998 | −0.131 | 1.03 | 0.38 |
| Railroad Transport | 0.999 | −0.334 | 0.98 | 0.87 |
| Trucking | 1.000 | 0.436 | 1.01 | 0.50 |
| Sea Transport | 0.932 | 0.648 | 0.97 | 0.13 |
| Air Transport | 0.972 | −0.147 | 0.64 | 0.44 |
| Warehousing and Harbor | 1.001 | 0.061 | 1.01 | 0.39 |
| Communication | 1.000 | −0.432 | 1.02 | 0.15 |
| Electric Utilities | 0.997 | −0.399 | 0.89 | 0.95 |
| Gas Utilities | 0.992 | −0.170 | 0.95 | 0.77 |
| Services | 1.014 | −0.210 | 1.04 | 0.35 |

Estimated ∅ and a are all significant at 1% level.

Note    * Estimated first order serial correlation of et
       ** Since estimated a is too low, we cannot get an economically meaningful value of k.

**Table 32.1  Dynamic Behavior of Dividend and Dividend Payout Ratio**

of dividend payout usually needs no adjustment costs. In summary, the Lintner hypothesis lacks a rational explanation for this partial adjustment.

**Conclusion.** We have seen that Japanese corporations have information content about their corporate permanent profit. So at first, we set a dividend policy model with information content which we call the permanent profit hypothesis. Then we showed that the dividend must follow the random walk in the case of this hypothesis. This permanent profit hypothesis cannot be rejected by the Japanese panel data. In the previous studies, researchers tried to explain the Japanese dividend policy with the Lintner hypothesis, which cannot, however, explain the information content of dividend policy. So the permanent profit hypothesis is the important economic concept for Japanese dividend policy.

### Appendix

Management must make $x_t$ stable for a long time. What can be done to achieve this goal? Can management attain this goal without affecting other financial policy?

Assume a nonstochastic balanced corporate growth. Then the growth rate of debt and of stock quantity must follow the relationship

$\varphi$ * growth rate of debt + $(1 - \varphi)$ * growth rate of stock number

$= g$ to stabilize $x_t$

to stabilize $x_t$. Where w $= (r/R)b$, $R$ is the rate of total return on corporate capital stock, $r$ is the rate of interest, $b$ is the debt-capital ratio, and $g$ is the corporate growth rate. For any given $R$, $b$, $g$, and $r$, the relationship is drawn as $AA$ in Figure 32.2.

On the other hand, cash outflow from the corporation must equal the cash inflow to the corporation at every period. This budget constraint can be formulated as

$g + R_k = b$ * growth rate of debt +

$(1 - b)$ * growth rate of stock number $+ Z$

LSH is the cash outflow and RSH is the cash inflow per capital stock. Where

Where $Z = (1 - t)(R - rb)$, $t$

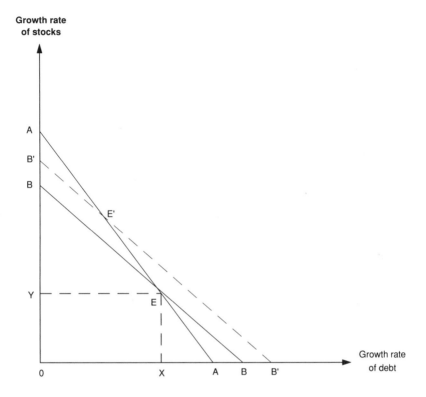

**Figure 32.2 Relationship of Financial Policies**

is the corporate tax rate. For any given $R$, $b$, $g$, and $r$, the relationship is drawn as $BB$ in Figure 32.2.

Even if $R$, $g$, and $r$ are given to a corporation, the corporation can get any financial target $\bar{b}$ and $\bar{k}$. These $\bar{b}$ and $\bar{k}$ can be attained by the financial policy that corresponds to $E$ in Figure 32.2; that is, the growth rate of debt $OX$ and the growth rate of total shares $OY$. Thus, under the Japanese dividend policy, managers can get any $k$ independent of $b$ using these financial policies.

Now, consider the case in which management will increase $k$. Then line $BB$ must shift to $B'B'$ and the equilibrium point must shift from $E$ to $E'$. So they must decrease the growth rate of debt and increase the growth rate of stock quantity.

## Notes

1. For the concept of permanent profit in the accounting theory, see Beaver (1981) references.
2. Permanent profit is calculated in the following way:

(i) $\quad x_{pt} = \dfrac{r}{1 + r} V_t$

(ii) $\quad V_t = \displaystyle\sum_{i=0}^{\infty} \dfrac{E\,[x_t + {}_i\,|\Omega_t]}{(1 + r)^i}$

Here, $r$ is the constant market interest rate. Management using the inside information available at time $t$; $\Omega_t$, expect the future profit as $E(x_t + {}_i/\,\Omega\, t)$; therefore $V_t$ is the present value of the stream of future profits.

With Equations 1 (i) and (ii), we get the following equation:

(iii) $\quad E\,(d_t + 1|\Omega_t] = krx_t + (1 + r)\,d_t$

If we assume that (1) value of $kr$ is small enough and (2) management and the market expect $d_t + 1$ *rationally* at time $t$, we can get Equation 2. Since we omit $x_t$ from the original equation, $\Theta$ need not be equal to $1 + r$.

3. In the competitive market, the expected rate of return on retained earnings must equal the market interest rate. With an ex-dividend stock price at time $t$, $P_t$ must be

$$P_t = \sum_{i=1}^{\infty} \dfrac{x_t + {}_i}{(1 + r)^i}$$

regardless of any dividend policy.

4. We can derive the following empirical results for the overall industry:

$$d_t = 1.080d_{t-1} - 0.007x_{t-1} - 0.038x_{t-2} + 0.013x_{t-3}$$
$$\;(10.29)\qquad (-0.022)\qquad (-1.35)\qquad (0.52)$$
$$R^2 = -0.076 \quad SEE = 0.277 \quad DW = 2.306$$

So $d_t$ is the sufficient statistic for $d_t + 1$.

5. $a$ of each industry is estimated value of the following equation:

$$x_{jt} = a_j x_{jt-1} + u_{jt}$$

$$\text{cov}\ (u_{jt},\ u_{jt-1}) = 0$$

6. In note 5, we can derive the following equation from Equation 1 (i) and (iii):

$$d_t = \left( \frac{(kr}{1 + r - a)} \right) x_t + u_t$$

By estimating this equation by O.L.S., we can get the estimated $k$ with any given $r$ and $a$. We set $r$ to be 0.15.

## References

1. Beaver, W. (1981). *Financial Reporting: An Accounting Revolution,* Prentice-Hall.
2. Bhattacharya, S. (1979). "Imperfect Information, Dividend Policy and 'The Bird in the Hand Fallacy'," *Bell Journal of Economics.*
3. Lintner, J. (1956). "Distribution of Incomes of Corporations Among Dividends, Retained Earnings and Taxes," *American Economic Review.*
4. Miller, M. and Modigliani, F. (1961). "Dividend Policy, Growth and the Valuation of Shares," *Journal of Business.*
5. Miller, M. and Rock, K. (1985). "Dividend Policy Under Asymmetric Information," *Journal of Finance.*
6. Nakamura, A., and Nakamura, M. (1985). "Rational Expectation and the Firm's Dividend Behavior," *Review of Economics and Statistics.*
7. Pettit, R. (1972). "Dividend Announcements, Security Performance and Capital Market Efficiency," *Journal of Finance.*
8. Ross, S. (1972). "The Determination of Financial Structure: The Incentive Signaling Approach," *Bell Journal of Economics.*
9. Watts, R. (1973). "Information Contents of Dividends," *Journal of Business.*

# 33

## Total Factor Productivity Analysis: Measuring the Impact of Privatization at Nippon Telegraph and Telephone Corporation

*Muneya Sato, School of Commerce,*
*Yokohama City University*

Under the strong leadership of the Japanese government and the cabinet of Nakasone, the privatization policy of Nippon Telegraph and Telephone Public Corporation (NTT) and Japan Tobacco Monopoly Public Corporation was applied. These two public corporations, previously operated under strong government control, were organized into new private companies in April 1985.

This privatization was possibly due to the large national financial deficits that had accumulated for many years. The *ad hoc* Public Administration Reform Council was established to solve this problem. The council's first decision was to reform these two financially sound public companies. Privatization of Japan National Railways Public Corporation, the greatest contributor to the public sector's deficits, was postponed until 1987. This chapter will discuss, from an accounting viewpoint, the economic effects NTT's privatization has brought.

When the second *ad hoc* Public Administration Reform Council published its third set of recommendations, it listed three purposes for reforming public corporations:

1. To free a company from governmental constraints and give it managerial autonomy through privatization.
2. To help a company become aware of its business performance and enhance the spirit of enterprise.
3. To improve a company's organizational effectiveness and promote its efficiency by destroying monopolistic principles and introducing market competition.[1]

Although only a year and a half have passed since NTT's privatization, we will investigate the degree to which the three purposes were attained. Purposes 1 and 2 were achieved successfully because the new Telecommunications Act was implemented smoothly and NTT's organizational reform executed without strong opposition. Various indicators concerning Purpose 3 point to a sharp rise in NTT's efficiency.

This research is difficult because of the many objectives of its organizational reform and the dimensions of its measurement. In addition, different conclusions reflect different points of view. In this chapter we will analyze the relationship between privatization and NTT's degree of efficiency in achieving it.

***Public Services and Efficiency.*** NTT has exclusively provided telecommunications services to users throughout Japan under government patronage. In other words, NTT's income was guaranteed, and was enough to hire a large labor force of over 320,000 workers in 1984. The questions of whether or not NTT service charges were based on cost, and whether or not costs of excess labor and wasted resources were included in those charges, were raised by people supporting the government's reform plan. The aim of the reform groups was to break up inefficient public services.

NTT was the first target chosen for reform. The government and administration reform committee's aim was to eliminate the gigantic deficits of all inefficient public sectors in Japan by breaking up and reforming such organizations.

Conflicts occurred between the diverse parties. For example, NTT's management and labor union conflicts emerged and were resolved. There are conflicts between NTT and (1) the Ministry of Post and Telecommunications (MPT) and (2) the new common carrier companies.[2] These conflicts emerged over differences about how to maintain the same monopolistic public services and still enhance efficiency through competition. In the end, NTT was granted managerial autonomy and received the government's privatization plan. This made NTT a private corporation, making the telecommunications market in Japan competitive, as in the United States and Great Britain.

***Accounting Measures of the Effects of Privatization.*** Enhancing efficiency was the most important goal of NTT's reform. How did NTT accomplish this difficult task? We have already said we cannot precisely measure the efficiency of privatization because of the wide scope of purposes. There are many criteria for measuring efficiency, and many indexes for each criterion. One set of criteria used is profit, sales, market share, growth, productivity, cost, and the labor-distribution ratio. Had we substituted profit or profitability for efficiency, reform would be unnecessary — NTT had been profitable for years. In this case, rather than choosing profit as a criterion, we chose social reform. We believed that enhancing organizational efficiency would make service charges less costly for users as well as produce business profits. Growth and profitability were two goals along with high quality and low cost services.

We chose productivity as a criterion of efficiency in this framework; specifically, total factor productivity (TFP). When large organizations experience major restructuring, decision variables change on different levels simultaneously. Profits, business volume, price, labor productivity, and the relationship between these variables also change. TFP analysis is suited to this situation because it can measure both level changes of different variables and the increase or decrease of the main objective variables (productivity, for example) resulting from privatization.

**Several accounting data.** Several accounting data concerning operating results and financial conditions of two periods will be used. Table 33.1 shows NTT's final profit and loss (P & L) statement as a public corporation.[3] Table 33.2 shows NTT's first P & L statement as a private corporation.[4]

We used the total productivity analysis to see how the privatization process affected revenue and the cost structure and the extent to which NTT's profitability and productivity were influenced. Comparing the two tables, we find that sales and revenue increased by ¥ 544 billion and operating expenses by ¥ 624 billion. We cannot know, however, why these changes occurred until we apply the accounting technique of variance analysis (or cost variance analysis).

Table 33.3 presents the differential revenue and cost data calculated using data from Tables 33.1 and 33.2. First, there were many

| | Billion Yen | Million U.S. Dollars |
|---|---|---|
| Sales and Revenue | ¥4,546 | $22,730 |
| Operating Expenses | 3,783 | 18,915 |
| Operating Income | 763 | 3,815 |
| Other Income | 127 | 635 |
| Other Expenses | 394 | 1,970 |
| Ordinary Income | 496 | 2,480 |
| Extraordinary Income | 83 | 415 |
| Extraordinary Charge | 251 | 1,255 |
| **Net Income** | ¥328 | $ 1,640 |

US $1 = ¥200

**Table 33.1  NTT's Final Profit and Loss Statement as a Public Corporation**

| | Billion Yen | Million U.S. Dollars |
|---|---|---|
| Sales and Revenue | ¥5,091 | $28,283 |
| Operating Expenses | 4,407 | 24,483 |
| Operating Income | 684 | 3,800 |
| Other Income | 43 | 239 |
| Other Expenses | 411 | 2,283 |
| Ordinary Income | 316 | 1,756 |
| Allowance for Tax | 176 | 978 |
| **Net Income After Tax** | ¥140 | $ 778 |

US $1 = ¥180

**Table 33.2  NTT's First Profit and Loss Statement as a Private Corporation**

changes in NTT's accounting procedures and disclosure system because of privatization. For example, nonoperating income and extraordinary income in Table 33.3 changed largely in content. The method to calculate depreciation cost was also altered. The privatized NTT now pays income tax (national and local), enterprise tax, stamp duty, and so on.

| | March 1985 | March 1986 | Differences |
|---|---|---|---|
| 1. Total Revenue | ¥4,756 | ¥5,134 | ¥378 |
| Sales | 4,546 | 5,091 | 545 |
| Non-Operating Income | 127 | 25 | − 102 |
| Extraordinary Income | 83 | 18 | − 65 |
| 2. Total Cost | ¥4,428 | ¥4,818 | ¥390 |
| Labor Cost | 1,556 | 1,744 | 188 |
| Material Cost | 704 | 778 | 74 |
| Capital Cost | 2,168 | 2,296 | 128 |
| Commission Fee | 140 | 130 | − 10 |
| Various Taxes | 63 | 132 | 69 |
| Interest Cost | 394 | 368 | − 26 |
| Depreciation Cost | 1,319 | 1,464 | 145 |
| Loss on Assets Abandoned | 252 | 189 | − 63 |
| Loss on Doubtful Account | — | 13 | 13 |
| 3. Profit Before Tax | ¥328 | ¥316 | ¥ − 12 |
| Income Tax | — | 176 | 176 |
| 4. Profit After Tax | ¥328 | ¥140 | ¥ − 188 |

Billion Yens

**Table 33.3 NTT's Differential Data Between the Two Periods**

Second, total cost in Table 33.3 is classified into three groups: labor, material, and real capital costs. This classification is similar to that of production factors in economic theory and is generally seen in public institutions in Japan. Of the three groups, capital costs is the most controversial. In accounting, it is regarded as the cost of services rendered other than labor and material services. All tax costs, commission fees, depreciation costs, interest costs, loss on doubtful accounts, and loss on abandoned equipment are treated as capital costs.

Seeing how NTT's revenues from the various telecommunications services changed through privatization will explain why the revenue structure was changed. Table 33.4 shows the segmented operating income statement in 1983 and 1984.[5] In 1985, NTT stopped disclosing segmented accounting reports by services. Sales data by services only are disclosed in the annual reports to stockholders and to the Ministry of Finance.

The operating revenue in 1985 reached ¥5,091,409 billion ($28.3 billion). Of this, ¥4,233,722 billion was from telephone services, ¥52.5 billion from telegraph services, ¥251.4 billion from leased circuit services, ¥153.3 billion from data communications facility services, ¥142.2 billion from sales of terminal equipment, and ¥258 from miscellaneous services and activities.

Table 33.5 shows NTT's five-year summary of operating income by services, an indication of what is occurring to the telecommunications market structure in Japan. The most important changes are (1) the sharp increase in revenues from data communication (DC) services, (2) the low growth rate of telephone income, and (3) the decline and fall of the telegram and telex.

***NTT's Total Factor Productivity (TFP) Analysis.*** Productivity analysis is widely used in corporate business management and the comparative efficiency analysis of both industrial sections and the international economy. We have used total factor productivity (TFP) concepts as criteria for assessing the efficiency of privatization of organizations. The concept was introduced into the economic research field by Solow (1957) in the 1960s, and was revised to the index numbers of productivity performance by Theil (1974) and others.

The basic purpose is to explain the productivity changes of three production factors, such as labor, material, and capital. Production and cost amounts by factor are measured separately and then totalled, excluding the individual price-change effects. The following equation is an example.[6]

$$(1) \quad \text{Total productivity ratio} = \frac{(P_1/P_0)}{(F_1/F_0) - 1}$$

or

$$\text{Total productivity ratio} = \frac{(\Sigma_i p_{i0} q_{i1} / \Sigma_i p_{i0} q_{i0})}{(\Sigma_j p_{j0} f_{j1} / \Sigma_j p_{j0} F_{j0} - 1}$$

where $p_1$ is the year's production (output) amount and $p_0$ is that of the previous year. $F_1$ is the year's total cost (input) and $F_0$ is that of the previous year. In the first equation, $p_1/p_0$ can be called the production growth rate and $F_1/F_0$, the cost growth rate. These growth rates are

| Division / Item | Telephone | Telegram | Telex | Leased Circuits Services | Data Communication | | |
|---|---|---|---|---|---|---|---|
| | | | | | Network Services | Facility Services | Total |
| **1984** | | | | | | | |
| Operating Revenue | (32) 4,226,070 | 37,173 | 17,683 | 107,261 | (14,842) 155,084 | 145,080 | 285,321 |
| Operating Expense | 3,697,336 | 152,983 | 27,895 | 71,742 | 99,809 | (14,874) 142,159 | 227,125 |
| Operating Profit | 528,734 | 115,811 | 10,213 | 35,519 | 55,275 | 2,921 | 58,196 |
| Rate of Margin | 87% | 412% | 158% | 67% | 64% | 98% | 80% |
| **1983** | | | | | | | |
| Operating Revenue | 4,089,212 | 38,682 | 20,982 | 103,127 | (14,164) 138,775 | 122,835 | 247,446 |
| Operating Expense | 3,514,517 | 162,574 | 28,073 | 64,949 | 84,858 | (14,164) 142,545 | 213,239 |
| Operating Profit | 574,695 | 123,892 | 7,091 | 38,178 | 53,916 | 19,710 | 34,206 |
| Rate of Margin | 86% | 420% | 134% | 63% | 61% | 116% | 86% |

(Million Yen)

**Table 33.4 NTT's Operating Profit and Loss Statement: Line of Business Report**

| Services \ Year | 1981 | 1982 | 1983 | 1984 | 1985 |
|---|---|---|---|---|---|
| Telephone | 3,639 | 3,807 | 3,984 | 4,112 | 4,234 |
| Telegram | 32 | 34 | 35 | 37 | 38 |
| Telex | 27 | 23 | 20 | 18 | 15 |
| Leased Circuit | 94 | 99 | 102 | 107 | 251 |
| D.C. Network | 97 | 108 | 115 | 136 | 153 |
| D.C. Facility | 93 | 108 | 121 | 139 | — |
| New Services | | | | | 400 |

(Billion Yen)

**Table 33.5 Five-Year Summary of Line of Business Data**

calculated by using the basic price (here, we use the previous year's) for measuring $p_1$ and $F_1$ to remove the price effects seen in the second equation.

**Accounting formulation of TFP.** An experiment that reformulates TFP into an accounting model used to evaluate corporate efficiency is the net income and productivity analysis (NIPA) developed by American Telephone and Telegraph Company (AT&T).[7] With this model, and with systematic calculations using the annual reports of two successive periods of other internal data, we can assess an organization's productivity measure and evaluate its allocation of resources policy. Because this cannot be fully described here, we will apply numerical NTT data to a slightly modified NIPA model. First, let's define the concept of TFP:

$$TFP = PCITR - (PCILC + PCIMC + PCIRCC)$$

where

PCITR = physical changes in total revenues
PCILC = physical changes in labor cost
PCIMC = physical changes in material costs
PCIRCC = physical changes in real capital costs

Concerning this definition, we must emphasize several points. Physical changes are changes in revenue or cost attributable to volume change, and these correspond to the price-effect excluding production or cost amounts shown in Equation 1. In other words, physical changes are equivalent to volume variances in cost accounting. We can easily calculate TFP by using variance analysis if the necessary data are available. Relevant data are P & L statements for two consecutive periods, such as those in Tables 33.1 and 33.2.

Second, to continue with this analysis, we must make assumptions in obtaining fluctuating data of price and quantity (physical) factors of production resources. In standard variance analysis, revenue or sales variance is usually divided into price and volume variances:

$$(2) \quad S_1 - S_0 = P_1 \times Q_1 - P_0 \times Q_0$$

$$= \underbrace{(P_1 - P_0) \times Q_1}_{\text{price variance}} + \underbrace{P_0 \times (Q_1 - Q_0)}_{\text{volume variance}}$$

where

$S_1$ = sales of this period
$S_0$ = sales of previous period
$P_1$ = price of this period
$P_0$ = price of previous period
$Q_1$ = sales volume of this period
$Q_0$ = sales volume of previous period

Another example of cost variance analysis is:

$$(3) \quad L_1 - L_0 = R_1 \times H_1 - R_0 \times H_0$$

$$= \underbrace{(R_1 - R_0) \times H_1}_{\substack{\text{labor rate} \\ \text{variance}}} + \underbrace{R_0 \times (H_1 - H_0)}_{\substack{\text{labor hour} \\ \text{(efficiency)} \\ \text{variance}}}$$

where

$L_1$ = labor cost of this period
$L_0$ = labor cost of previous period
$R_1$ = labor rate of this period
$R_0$ = labor rate of previous period
$H_1$ = labor hours of this period
$H_0$ = labor hours of previous period

To calculate TFP, we must separate volume or efficiency variances of revenue and costs from other variances. To do so, we must gather every measure of a corporation's price and volume factors, always difficult because these data are not usually disclosed in the annual report or ever made at all. Several assumptions are therefore made. For example, suppose total labor hours are unavailable. We are forced to choose the number of employees as a substitute.

Third, the most difficult measure to get is the relevant data for capital costs. In our framework, capital costs include not only interest costs, but miscellaneous costs other than labor and material costs. We again are forced to make an assumption about physical change in real capital costs.

If our assumptions are valid and reasonably obtained, we can easily calculate the organization's TFP. The equation of TFP using price variance terms could be:

(4) TFP + revenue price variances − cost price variances
= change in net profit

Equation 4 indicates the relationship between TFP and change in profit. Because of the existence of price variance, an increase in productivity does not always mean an increase in profit. In this way, we can estimate the enhancement of an organization's productivity using two successive financial statements. We can also relate increases in productivity to changes in profit.

**NTT's case.** The starting point of TFP analysis is differential data of an organization. (See Table 33.3.) First, we should ascertain that differences in revenues and costs between the two periods studied were calculated correctly. Next, we perform variance analysis using these differences by item. Of course, it is necessary to gather additional information. Table 33.6 shows NTT's TFP analysis summary sheet, which we will analyze briefly.

(1) First, TFP amounted to ¥510 billion in 1985. As stated in the first section of Table 33.6, this figure is calculated as follows:

(5) TFP = ¥545 billion − (−¥49 billion + ¥80 billion + ¥4 billion
= ¥510 billion

Sales volume variance is the same as sales variance. (We assume there was no price variance because there were no remarkable price fluctuations in telecommunications services).

(2) As in Table 33.3, the difference in labor cost is ¥188 billion, and this variance is divided into a labor cost volume variance of ¥49 billion and an increase in labor costs (rate variance) of ¥237 billion. The former labor variance accrued because of the sharp decline in the number (about 10,000) of employees. The latter (unfavorable) variance occurred because of large increases in the base rate of payroll and retirement pay.

| | 1985 |
|---|---|
| 1. Total factor productivity | 510 |
|     Sales volume variance | 545 |
|     Labor cost volume variance | −49 |
|     Material costs volume variance | 80 |
|     Real capital increase | 4 |
| 2. Sales price variance | 0 |
| 3. Real capital increase | 4 |
| 4. Increase in labor costs | 237 |
| 5. Change in material costs | −6 |
| 6. Change in various taxes | 69 |
| 7. Change in non-operating income | −102 |
| 8. Change in extraordinary income | −65 |
| 9. Change in commission fee | −10 |
| 10. Increase in depreciation cost | 145 |
| 11. Change in interest costs | −26 |
| 12. Change in doubtful account loss and other | 13 |
| 13. Change in loss on equipment abandoned | −63 |
| 14. Decrease in income before tax | −12 |

(Billion Yen)

**Table 33.6  NTT's TFP Analysis Summary Sheet**

(3) Material costs increased by ￥74 billion for the year, but purchase prices of telecommunications equipment and material gradually decreased because of the foreign currency exchange gain of ￥6 billion. We thus estimate a material cost volume variance of ￥80 billion. This figure decreased TFP by the same amounts, but this variance is inevitably accompanied by an increase in sales volume.

(4) Other costs increased by ￥124 billion, but it is difficult to discriminate between price and volume factors. We therefore use them as NIPA did. Volume variance of capital cost is calculated by multiplying profit-capital rate (2.911 percent, for this year) by the increase in real assets for the year. This is how the real capital increase of ￥4 billion in Table 33.6 is measured. Items 6 to 13 in the table are all price variances of capital costs.

(5) For nonoperating income, extraordinary income, depreciation cost, and loss on doubtful accounts, institutional changes (alterations of contents and exchange of accounts) occurred. An increase

or decrease in these accounts is not considered to be a result of change in productivity, and we treat these as price variances.

(6) To sum up, TFP in 1985 reached ¥510 billion, of which ¥363 billion is considered to be the result of privatization. NTT's six-year TFP summary and relevant data are shown in Table 33.7. TFP in 1985 reached ¥510 billion, almost 3.5 times larger than in 1984. We assume this includes the privatization effects and estimate it accordingly. As seen in Table 33.6, sales volume variance is ¥545 billion, a figure that would be smaller had privatization not been carried out. We can therefore estimate the normal (without privatization) sales variance by multiplying 1984 sales by the average sales increase rate. The average sales increase rate calculated for the past four years was approximately 1.04 percent. We arrive at normal sales amounts using this equation:

$$¥4,546 \text{ billion} \times 1.04\% = ¥4,728 \text{ billion}$$

Subtracting this from 1985 sales, we get ¥363 billion. These amounts may result from various sales promotion activities and the merchandising of new services, now possible in the new environment after deregulation.

| Year | 1980 | 1981 | 1982 | 1983 | 1984 | 1985 |
|---|---|---|---|---|---|---|
| TFP | 94.4 | 119.1 | 191.1 | 217.3 | 141.3 | 510.0 |
| Price Cut | * | * | | * | * | |
| Sales | 3,841 | 3,985 | 4,181 | 4,384 | 4,546 | 5,091 |

(Billion Yen)

**Table 33.7  The Change of NTT's TFP**

*Conclusion.* Tables 33.6 and 33.7 indicate several points concerning privatization:

- A new high in TFP was attained in the fiscal year ending March 1986.
- The increase in TFP of ¥510 billion was mostly offset by, or allocated to, the increase in labor costs (rise in payroll and retirement pay). In addition, it was offset by the increase in various taxes and the decrease in nonoperating and extraordinary income, resulting from the institutional change.
- The increase in depreciation cost also depends on the change in calculation method, and this is a minus factor in net income.

- Net income before taxes decreased by ¥12 billion. Net income after taxes decreased by ¥188 billion because of newly charged income tax payments.

Having been assigned several new burdens, from the productivity standpoint, NTT has performed surprisingly well in spite of these circumstances.

NTT's financial performance for the year after privatization was satisfactory. It is possible to attribute this to its aggressive strategy of seeking new business and selling newly developed services, enhancing labor productivity, and settling internal conflicts. The deregulation policy has made the Japanese telecommunications market free and competitive. The competition will be more severe, however, especially in leased circuit service, telephone service, and value-added network service. If overall demand for telecommunications services decreases, NTT cannot maintain its previous high performance. NTT's workers should strive to sell new services to more and more people. We believe the method of productivity analysis explained in this chapter will be useful for checking these trends.

## Notes

1. The Second *Ad Hoc* Public Administration Council, "The Third Recommendations to the Reform Plan for Public Administration System," July 1982. See also Ishikawa and Sato, (1986) and Sato (1985).
2. See Ishikawa and Sato (1986) for information about the various conflicts and the organizational behavior of many firms in relation to NTT's reform.
3. These 1984 data are from NTT's public relations department.
4. These are 1986 NTT figures.
5. This segmented reporting comes from NTT (1984). The statements were compiled by NTT's internal auditors for yearly submission to the Ministry of Posts and Telecommunications.
6. See Electricite de France (1980).
7. This model was developed by AT&T for assessing periodic business efficiency and planning purposes. For more detail, see Cahundry and Burnside (1980).

## References

1. Cahundry, A., and Burnside, M. (1980). "Net Income and Productivity Analysis (NIPA) As a Planning Model."
2. Denny, M., DeFontenay, A., and Werner, M. (1980). "Total Factory Productivity for Management."

3. Electricite de France. (1980). "Overall Factor Productivity (OFP) and EDF's Management." *Etudes Economiques Geuerates*.
4. Ishikawa, A., and Sato, M. (1986). "Human Factor Issues in Reorganizing NTT." *Human Factors in Organization Design and Management*. North-Holland, pp. 629-635.
5. NTT. (1984). "NTT's 1983 Auditor's Report."
6. NTT. (1986). "Annual Report 1986" (in English).
7. NTT Public Relations Department. (1985). "1984 News Release."
8. Sato, M. (1985). "The Cost Structure of Telecommunications Companies." *Journal of Public Utility Economics*, (The Japan Society of Public Utility Economics), Vol. 37, No. 2., pp. 1-30.
9. Solow, R.M. (1957). "Technical Change and the Aggregate Production Function." *Economics and Statistics Review*, Vol. 39, No. 3, pp. 312-320.
10. Theil, H. (1974). "A New Index Number Formula." *Economics and Statistics Review*, Vol. 50.

# About the Editors

*Yasuhiro Monden* is Professor of Cost and Management Accounting and Operations Management at the University of Tsukuba's Institute of Socio-Economic Planning, Tsukuba-shi, Japan. He currently serves as Dean of the Graduate Program of Management Sciences and Public Policy Studies at the university. He was a visiting professor at the State University of New York at Buffalo during the 1980-1981 school year.

Professor Monden has gained valuable practical knowledge and experience from his research and related activities in manufacturing industries. He has had the following books published in English: *Toyota Production System* (1983), *Innovations in Management: The Japanese Corporation* (1985), and *Applying Just-In-Time: The American/Japanese Experience* (1986). An additional five books on the JIT production system have been published in Japanese. He has written five books in Japanese on management accounting with basic research on transfer pricing and profit allocation and case studies on decision-support systems.

He is currently International Director of the Management Accounting Section of the American Accounting Association and an editorial board member of the AAA journal *Management Accounting Research*. He also serves as executive member and director of the board of the Japan Financial Analysis Association.

He was awarded the 1984 Nikkei Prize by the *Japan Economic Journal* and the 1977 Prize of the Japan Accounting Association.

*Michiharu Sakurai* is Professor of Accounting in the School of Business at Senshu University in Tokyo. He received his doctorate in accounting from Waseda University.

531

His published books include *Managerial Cost Accounting* (1979), *Study of U.S. Management Accounting Standards* (1982), *Cost Accounting* (1983), *Cost Accounting for Software* (1987), and *High Tech Accounting* (1988). He has published numerous articles in Japanese and American journals such as *Industrial Management, Diamond Harvard Business* (the Japanese version of the *Harvard Business Review*), *Kigyoukaikei* (Business Accounting), *Kaikei* (Accounting), and *Sangyoukeiri* (Industrial Accounting).

Professor Sakurai is active in the Japan Accounting Association and the Japan Cost Accounting Association. He received the 1979 Japan Accounting Association Award for Outstanding Contribution to Accounting Literature and the 1982 Japanese Certified Public Accounting Association Academic Award. He currently serves on numerous Japanese government and industrial committees related to the cost accounting of high tech, software, communications, and service industries. He was also a researcher and consultant to the CAM-I Cost Management Systems project.

# Index

533

# Also Available

Productivity Press publishes and distributes materials on continuous improvement in productivity, quality, customer service, and the creative involvement of all employees. Many of our products are direct source materials from Japan that have been translated into English for the first time and are available exclusively from Productivity. Supplemental products and services include newsletters, conferences, seminars, in-house training and consulting, audio-visual training programs, and industrial study missions. Call 1-800-274-9911 for our free book catalog.

## Quality Function Deployment
### Integrating Customer Requirements into Product Design
edited by Yoji Akao

More and more, companies are using quality function deployment, or QFD, to identify their customers' requirements, translate them into quantified quality characteristics and then build them into their products and services. This casebook introduces the concept of quality deployment as it has been applied in a variety of industries in Japan. The materials include numerous case studies illustrating QFD applications. Written by the creator of QFD, this book provides direct source material on Quality Function Deployment, one of the essential tools for world class manufacturing. It is a design approach based on the idea that quality is determined by the customer. Through methodology and case studies the book offers insight into how Japanese companies identify customer requirements and describes how to translate customer requirements into qualified quality characteristics, and how to build them into products and services.
ISBN 0-915299-41-0 / 400 pages / $75.00 / Order code QFD-BK

## Handbook of Quality Tools
### The Japanese Approach
edited by Tetsuichi Asaka and Kazuo Ozeki

The Japanese have stunned the world by their ability to produce top quality products at competitive prices. This comprehensive teaching manual, which includes the 7 traditional and 5 newer QC tools, explains each tool, why it's useful, and how to construct and use it. Information is presented in easy-to-grasp language, with step-by-step instructions, illustrations, and examples of each tool. A perfect training aid, as well as a hands-on reference book, for supervisors, foremen, and/or team leaders. Here's the best resource on the myriad Japanese quality tools changing the face of world manufacturing today. Accessible to everyone in your organization, dealing with both management and shop floor how-to's, you'll find it an indispensable tool in your quest for quality.
ISBN 0-915299-45-3 / 336 pages / $59.95 / Order code HQT-BK

Productivity Press, Inc., Dept. BK, P.O. Box 3007, Cambridge, MA 02140 1-800-274-9911

# JIT Factory Revolution
## A Pictorial Guide to Factory Design of the Future
*by Hiroyuki Hirano/JIT Management Library*

Here is the first-ever encyclopedic picture book of JIT. With 240 pages of photos, cartoons, and diagrams, this unprecedented behind-the-scenes look at actual production and assembly plants shows you exactly how JIT looks and functions. It shows you how to set up each area of a JIT plant and provides hundreds of useful ideas you can implement. If you've made the crucial decision to run production using JIT and want to show your employees what it's all about, this book is a must. The photographs, from Japanese production and assembly plants, provide vivid depictions of what work is like in a JIT environment. And the text, simple and easy to read, makes all the essentials crystal clear.
ISBN 0-915299-44-5 / 227 pages / $49.95 / Order code JITFAC-BK

# TQC for Accounting
## A New Role in Company-wide Improvement
*by Takashi Kanatsu*

TQC for accounting means more than streamlining office procedures or upgrading financial analyses. It requires, instead, a linking of the basics of marketing with the fundamentals of accounting through the medium of TCQ. This book is a guide for top and middle managers who wish to turn their companies around by redesigning the roles played by the accounting, sales, and marketing departments. The book's format offers detailed examinations of accounting TCQ in relation to a company's business plan, accounting department, and specific statistical methods. Its use will help to create the "awareness revolution" that is imperative in turning around a factory or any type of company. (Winter, 1991)
ISBN 0-915299-73-9 / 176 pages / $45.00 / Order code TQCA-BK

# 20 Keys to Workplace Improvement
*by Iwao Kobayashi*

This easy-to-read introduction to the "20 keys" system presents an integrated approach to assessing and improving your company's competitive level. The book focuses on systematic improvement through five levels of achievement in such primary areas as industrial housekeeping, small group activities, quick changeover techniques, equipment maintenance, and computerization. A scoring guide is included, along with information to help plan a strategy for your company's world class improvement effort.
ISBN 0-915299-61-5 / 264 pages / $34.95 / Order code 20KEYS-BK

**Productivity Press, Inc., Dept. BK, P.O. Box 3007, Cambridge, MA 02140 1-800-274-9911**

# Total Manufacturing Management
## Production Model for the 1990s
*by Giorgio Merli*

One of Italy's leading consultants discusses the implementation of Just-In-Time and related methods (including QFD and TPM) in Western corporations. The author does not approach JIT from a mechanistic orientation aimed simply at production efficiency. Rather, he discusses JIT from the perspective of industrial strategy and as an overall organizational model. Here's a sophisticated program for organizational reform that shows how JIT can be applied even in types of production that have often been neglected in the West, including custom work.
ISBN 0-915299-58-5 / 224 pages / $39.95 / Order code TMM- BK

# Management for Quality Improvement
## The 7 New QC Tools
*edited by Shigeru Mizuno*

Building on the traditional seven QC tools, these new tools were developed specifically for managers. They help in planning, troubleshooting, and communicating with maximum effectiveness at every stage of a quality improvement program. Just recently made available in the U.S., they are certain to advance quality improvement efforts for anyone involved in project management, quality assurance, MIS, or TQC.
ISBN 0-915299-29-1 / 324 pages / $59.95 / Order code 7QC-BK

# Achieving Total Quality Management
## A Program for Action
*by Michel Perigord*

This is an outstanding book on total quality management (TQM) — a compact guide to the concepts, methods, and techniques involved in achieving total quality. It shows you how to make TQM a company- wide strategy, not just in technical areas, but in marketing and administration as well. Written in an accessible, instructive style by top European quality expert, it is methodical, logical, and thorough. A historical outline and discussion of the quality-price relationship, is followed by an investigation of the five quality imperatives (conformity, prevention, excellence, measurement, and responsibility). Major methods and tools for total quality are spelled out and implementation strategies are reviewed.
ISBN 0-915299-60-7 / 384 pages / $39.95 / Order Code ACHTQM-BK

**Productivity Press, Inc., Dept. BK, P.O. Box 3007, Cambridge, MA 02140 1-800-274-9911**

# The Quality and Productivity Equation
## American Corporate Strategies for the 1990s
*Ross E. Robson (ed.)*

How well will your business succeed in the next decade? What challenges are in store, and how are you planning to meet them? Here's what over thirty of America's most forward-thinking business and academic leaders (including John Diebold, Malcolm Forbes, Donald Ephlin, Alan Magazine, and Wickham Skinner) are already thinking about and doing. Based on presentations made at Utah State University's College of Business "Partners in Business" seminars for 1989. Take advantage of their expertise to shape your own strategy.
ISBN 0-915299-71-2 / 558 pages / $29.95 / Order code QPE-BK

# A Revolution in Manufacturing
## The SMED System
*by Shigeo Shingo, translated by Andrew P. Dillon*

SMED (Single-Minute Exchange of Die), or quick changeover techniques, is the single most powerful tool for Just-In-Time production. Written by the industrial engineer who developed SMED for Toyota, the book contains hundreds of illustrations and photographs, as well as twelve chapter-length case studies. Here are the most complete and detailed instructions available anywhere for transforming a manufacturing environment to speed up production (Shingo's average setup time reduction is an astounding 98 percent) and make small-lot inventories feasible.
ISBN 0-915299-03-8 / 383 pages / $70.00 / Order code SMED-BK

# Variety Reduction Program (VRP)
## A Production Strategy for Product Diversification
*by Toshio Suzue and Akira Kohdate*

Here's the first book in English on a powerful way to increase manufacturing flexibility without increasing costs. How? By reducing the number of parts within each product type and by simplifying and standardizing parts between models. VRP is an integral feature of advanced manufacturing systems. This book is both an introduction to and a handbook for VRP implementation, featuring over 100 illustrations, for top manufacturing executives, middle managers, and R&D personnel.
ISBN 0-915299-32-1 / 164 pages / $59.95 / Order code VRP-BK

Productivity Press, Inc., Dept. BK, P.O. Box 3007, Cambridge, MA 02140 1-800-274-9911

# The Eternal Venture Spirit
## An Executive's Practical Philosophy
by *Kazuma Tateisi*

Like human health, organizational health depends on discovering the causes of symptoms that indicate an imbalance in the system. Tateisi, founder and CEO of Omron Industries, one of Japan's leading electronics companies, analyzes the signals of "big business disease" and how to respond to them so that technological innovation and entrepreneurial spirit can thrive as the organization grows and the market changes. An outstanding book on long-term strategic management. ISBN 0-915299-55-0 / 208 pages / $19.95 / Order code EVS-BK

# The Profit Management Institute (PMI)

Unless an accounting system shared the values of the new manufacturing strategies, it will not reflect what is really going on within an organization. In a Just-In-Time environment, operating performance can no longer be measured by antiquated notions of labor, machine utilization and overhead absorption, because it results in inconsistent and unreliable data. The "World Class Management Accounting" course presents a simplified accounting system that supports the elimination of waste in all segments of the company. This two-day intense and interactive workshop is a revolutionary new way to approach a business's need for information. You'll acquire new tools that marketing, sales, production, finance, and executive managers can use to make day-to-day decisions. For more information about PMI's course in "World Class Management Accounting," please call 1-800-888-6485.

Productivity Press, Inc., Dept. BK, P.O. Box 3007, Cambridge, MA 02140 1-800-274-9911

# COMPLETE LIST OF TITLES FROM PRODUCTIVITY PRESS

Akao, Yoji (ed.). **Quality Function Deployment: Integrating Customer Requirements into Product Design**
ISBN 0-915299-41-0 / 1990 / 320 pages / $75.00 / order code QFD

Asaka, Tetsuichi and Kazuo Ozeki (eds.). **Handbook of Quality Tools: The Japanese Approach**
ISBN 0-915299-45-3 / 1990 / 336 pages / $59.95 / order code HQT

Belohlav, James A. **Championship Management: An Action Model for High Performance**
ISBN 0-915299-76-3 / 1990 / 272 pages / $29.95 / order code CHAMPS

Christopher, William F. **Productivity Measurement Handbook**
ISBN 0-915299-05-4 / 1985 / 680 pages / $137.95 / order code PMH

D'Egidio, Franco. **The Service Era: Leadership in a Global Environment**
ISBN 0-915299-68-2 / 1990 / 194 pages / $29.95 / order code GSM

Ford, Henry. **Today and Tomorrow**
ISBN 0-915299-36-4 / 1988 / 286 pages / $24.95 / order code FORD

Fukuda, Ryuji. **CEDAC: A Tool for Continuous Systematic Improvement**
ISBN 0-915299-26-7 / 1990 / 144 pages / $49.95 / order code CEDAC

Fukuda, Ryuji. **Managerial Engineering: Techniques for Improving Quality and Productivity in the Workplace** (rev.)
ISBN 0-915299-09-7 / 1986 / 208 pages / $39.95 / order code ME

Hatakeyama, Yoshio. **Manager Revolution! A Guide to Survival in Today's Changing Workplace**
ISBN 0-915299-10-0 / 1986 / 208 pages / $24.95 / order code MREV

Hirano, Hiroyuki. **JIT Factory Revolution: A Pictorial Guide to Factory Design of the Future**
ISBN 0-915299-44-5 / 1989 / 227 pages / $49.95 / order code JITFAC

Hirano, Hiroyuki. **JIT Implementation Manual: The Complete Guide to Just-In-Time Manufacturing**
ISBN 0-915299-66-6 / 1990 / 1000 + pages / $3500.00 / order code HIRJIT

Horovitz, Jacques. **Winning Ways: Achieving Zero Defect Service**
ISBN 0-915299-78-X / 1990 / 176 pages / $24.95 / order code WWAYS

Japan Human Relations Association (ed.). **The Idea Book: Improvement Through TEI (Total Employee Involvement)**
ISBN 0-915299-22-4 / 1988 / 232 pages / $49.95 / order code IDEA

Japan Human Relations Association (ed.). **Quality Service Idea Book: Improvements for the Office and Retail Through TEI**
ISBN 0-915299-65-8 / 1990 / 272 pages / $49.95 / order code SIDEA

Japan Management Association (ed.). **Kanban and Just-In-Time at Toyota: Management Begins at the Workplace** (Revised Ed.), Translated by David J. Lu
ISBN 0-915299-48-8 / 1989 / 224 pages / $36.50 / order code KAN

Japan Management Association and Constance E. Dyer. **The Canon Production System: Creative Involvement of the Total Workforce**
ISBN 0-915299-06-2 / 1987 / 251 pages / $36.95 / order code CAN

Productivity Press, Inc., Dept. BK, P.O. Box 3007, Cambridge, MA 02140 1-800-274-9911

Jones, Karen (ed.). **The Best of TEI:** Current Perspectives on Total Employee Involvement
ISBN 0-915299-63-1 / 1989 / 502 pages / $175.00 / order code TEI

Karatsu, Hajime. **Tough Words For American Industry**
ISBN 0-915299-25-9 / 1988 / 178 pages / $24.95 / order code TOUGH

Karatsu, Hajime. **TQC Wisdom of Japan:** Managing for Total Quality Control, Translated by David J. Lu
ISBN 0-915299-18-6 / 1988 / 136 pages / $34.95 / order code WISD

Kobayashi, Iwao. **20 Keys to Workplace Improvement**
ISBN 0-915299-61-5 / 1990 / 264 pages / $34.95 / order code 20KEYS

Lu, David J. **Inside Corporate Japan:** The Art of Fumble-Free Management
ISBN 0-915299-16-X / 1987 / 278 pages / $24.95 / order code ICJ

Merli, Giorgio. **Total Manufacturing Management:** Production Organization for the 1990s
ISBN 0-915299-58-5 / 1990 / 224 pages / $39.95 / order code TMM

Mizuno, Shigeru (ed.). **Management for Quality Improvement:** The 7 New QC Tools
ISBN 0-915299-29-1 / 1988 / 324 pages / $59.95 / order code 7QC

Monden, Yasuhiro and Michiharu Sakurai (eds.). **Japanese Management Accounting:** A World Class Approach to Profit Management
ISBN 0-915299-50-X / 1989 / 568 pages / $59.95 / order code JMACT

Nachi-Fujikoshi (ed.). **Training for TPM:** A Manufacturing Success Story
ISBN 0-915299-34-8 / 1990 / 320 pages / $59.95 / order code CTPM

Nakajima, Seiichi. **Introduction to TPM:** Total Productive Maintenance
ISBN 0-915299-23-2 / 1988 / 149 pages / $39.95 / order code ITPM

Nakajima, Seiichi. **TPM Development Program:** Implementing Total Productive Maintenance
ISBN 0-915299-37-2 / 1989 / 428 pages / $85.00 / order code DTPM

Nikkan Kogyo Shimbun, Ltd./Factory Magazine (ed.). **Poka-yoke:** Improving Product Quality by Preventing Defects
ISBN 0-915299-31-3 / 1989 / 288 pages / $59.95 / order code IPOKA

Ohno, Taiichi. **Toyota Production System:** Beyond Large-Scale Production
ISBN 0-915299-14-3 / 1988 / 162 pages / $39.95 / order code OTPS

Ohno, Taiichi. **Workplace Management**
ISBN 0-915299-19-4 / 1988 / 165 pages / $34.95 / order code WPM

Ohno, Taiichi and Setsuo Mito. **Just-In-Time for Today and Tomorrow**
ISBN 0-915299-20-8 / 1988 / 208 pages / $34.95 / order code OMJIT

Perigord, Michel. **Achieving Total Quality Management:** A Program for Action
ISBN 0-915299-60-7 / 1990 / 384 pages / $39.95 / order code ACHTQM

Psarouthakis, John. **Better Makes Us Best**
ISBN 0-915299-56-9 / 1989 / 112 pages / $16.95 / order code BMUB

Robson, Ross (ed.). **The Quality and Productivity Equation:** American Corporate Strategies for the 1990s
ISBN 0-915299-71-2 / 1990 / 558 pages / $29.95 / order code QPE

**Productivity Press, Inc., Dept. BK, P.O. Box 3007, Cambridge, MA 02140 1-800-274-9911**

Shetty, Y.K and Vernon M. Buehler (eds.). **Competing Through Productivity and Quality**
ISBN 0-915299-43-7 / 1989 / 576 pages / $39.95 / order code COMP

Shingo, Shigeo. **Non-Stock Production: The Shingo System for Continuous Improvement**
ISBN 0-915299-30-5 / 1988 / 480 pages / $75.00 / order code NON

Shingo, Shigeo. **A Revolution In Manufacturing: The SMED System**, Translated by Andrew P. Dillon
ISBN 0-915299-03-8 / 1985 / 383 pages / $70.00 / order code SMED

Shingo, Shigeo. **The Sayings of Shigeo Shingo: Key Strategies for Plant Improvement**, Translated by Andrew P. Dillon
ISBN 0-915299-15-1 / 1987 / 208 pages / $39.95 / order code SAY

Shingo, Shigeo. **A Study of the Toyota Production System from an Industrial Engineering Viewpoint** (rev.)
ISBN 0-915299-17-8 / 1989 / 293 pages / $39.95 / order code STREV

Shingo, Shigeo. **Zero Quality Control: Source Inspection and the Poka-yoke System**, Translated by Andrew P. Dillon
ISBN 0-915299-07-0 / 1986 / 328 pages / $70.00 / order code ZQC

Shinohara, Isao (ed.). **New Production System: JIT Crossing Industry Boundaries**
ISBN 0-915299-21-6 / 1988 / 224 pages / $34.95 / order code NPS

Sugiyama, Tomo. **The Improvement Book: Creating the Problem-Free Workplace**
ISBN 0-915299-47-X / 1989 / 236 pages / $49.95 / order code IB

Suzue, Toshio and Akira Kohdate. **Variety Reduction Program (VRP): A Production Strategy for Product Diversification**
ISBN 0-915299-32-1 / 1990 / 164 pages / $59.95 / order code VRP

Tateisi, Kazuma. **The Eternal Venture Spirit: An Executive's Practical Philosophy**
ISBN 0-915299-55-0 / 1989 / 208 pages / $19.95 / order code EVS

**Productivity Press, Inc., Dept. BK, P.O. Box 3007, Cambridge, MA 02140 1-800-274-9911**

# AUDIO-VISUAL PROGRAMS

Japan Management Association. **Total Productive Maintenance: Maximizing Productivity and Quality**
ISBN 0-915299-46-1 / 167 slides / 1989 / $749.00 / order code STPM
ISBN 0-915299-49-6 / 2 videos / 1989 / $749.00 / order code VTPM

Shingo, Shigeo. **The SMED System**, Translated by Andrew P. Dillon
ISBN 0-915299-11-9 / 181 slides / 1986 / $749.00 / order code S5
ISBN 0-915299-27-5 / 2 videos / 1987 / $749.00 / order code V5

Shingo, Shigeo. **The Poka-yoke System**, Translated by Andrew P. Dillon
ISBN 0-915299-13-5 / 235 slides / 1987 / $749.00 / order code S6
ISBN 0-915299-28-3 / 2 videos / 1987 / $749.00 / order code V6

**TO ORDER:** Write, phone, or fax Productivity Press, Dept. BK, P.O. Box 3007, Cambridge, MA 02140, phone 1-800-274-9911, fax 617-868-3524. Send check or charge to your credit card (American Express, Visa, MasterCard accepted).

**U.S. ORDERS:** Add $4 shipping for first book, $2 each additional for UPS surface delivery. CT residents add 8% and MA residents 5% sales tax.

**INTERNATIONAL ORDERS:** Write, phone, or fax for quote and indicate shipping method desired. Pre-payment in U.S. dollars must accompany your order (checks must be drawn on U.S. banks). When quote is returned with payment, your order will be shipped promptly by the method requested.

**NOTE:** Prices subject to change without notice.